From India to the Planet Mars

From India to the Planet Mars

A CASE OF MULTIPLE PERSONALITY WITH IMAGINARY LANGUAGES

Théodore Flournoy

With a Foreword by C. G. Jung and Commentary by Mireille Cifali

Edited and Introduced by Sonu Shamdasani

PRINCETON UNIVERSITY PRESS

PRINCETON, NEW JERSEY

Published by Princeton University Press,
41 William Street, Princeton, New Jersey 08540
In the United Kingdom: Princeton University Press, Chichester, West Sussex

Originally published in 1899; English translation
by Daniel B. Vermilye published in 1901

New introduction by Sonu Shamdasani is copyright © 1994
by Princeton University Press

Library of Congress Cataloging In Publication Data

Flournoy, Théodore, 1854–1920.
  [Des Indes à la planète Mars. English]
  From India to the planet Mars : a case of multiple personality with imaginary
languages / by Théodore Flournoy ; with a preface by C. G. Jung and commentary by
Mireille Cifali ; edited and introduced by Sonu Shamdasani.
      p.   cm.
  Originally published: New York : Harper & Bros., 1900.
  Includes bibliographical references.
  ISBN 0-691-03407-9 (CL)—ISBN 0-691-00101-4 (PA)
  1. Smith, Hélène, d. 1929.   2. Mediums—Switzerland—Geneva—Case
studies.   3. Parapsychology—Investigation.   I. Cifali, Mireille.
II. Shamdasani, Sonu, 1962–   .   III. Title.
BF1283.S618F5613   1994
133.8'092—dc20
[B]   93-45446

First Princeton Paperback printing, 1994

Princeton University Press books are printed on acid-free paper and meet the guidelines
for permanence and durability of the Committee on Production Guidelines for Book
Longevity of the Council on Library Resources

10   9   8   7   6   5   4   3   2   1

Printed in the United States of America

Table of Contents

Editorial Note (1994)

THÉODORE FLOURNOY's *Des Indes à la Planète Mars: Etude sur un cas de somnambulisme avec glossolalie* was published at the end of 1899. It was translated into English in the following year by Daniel B. Vermilye, under the title *From India to the Planet Mars: A Study of a Case of Somnambulism with Glossolalia*, (New York, Harper & Brothers). Unfortunately, the latter was, without indication, an abridgement. The 1994 edition reproduces this translation. In addition, Flournoy's preface, which was omitted from it, has been newly translated and restored, together with the bulk of the omitted passages, which have been placed in an appendix. An asterisk in the text (*) indicates that the consecutive passage is in appendix 2. The translator's introduction to the 1900 edition has in turn been omitted.

C. G. Jung's tribute to Flournoy has been included as a preface and is published in English for the first time. This was originally an appendix to the German edition of Jung's *Memories, Dreams, Reflections: Erinerungen, Träume, Gedanken von C. G. Jung*, which was not included in the English edition. It is published with the permission of the Jung estate.

Mireille Cifali's commentary "La Fabrication du Martien: Genèse d'une Langue Imaginaire," originally appeared in *Langages* 91 (1988), and has been translated and included in an appendix.

These changes have occasioned a new subtitle, *A Case of Multiple Personality with Imaginary Languages*, to differentiate this edition from earlier editions, and to indicate the contemporary contexts that the text resituates itself within, which are explored in the introduction and appendix.

Sonu Shamdasani

Foreword

Théodore Flournoy[1]

C. G. Jung

DURING the time of my relationship to Freud I found a fatherly friend in Théodore Flournoy. He was already an old man when I got to know him. Unfortunately he died only a few years later. As I was still a doctor at the Burghölzli when I read his book, *From India to the Planet Mars*, it made a great impression on me. I wrote to Flournoy that I wanted to translate it into German. It was after half a year that I received his reply, in which he apologized for having let my question lie unanswered for so long. To my regret, he had already appointed another translator.[2]

Later I visited him in Geneva, and as I gradually recognized where Freud's limits lay, I went to him from time to time, and I talked with him. It was important to me to hear what he thought of Freud, and he said very intelligent things about him. Most of all, he put his finger on Freud's rationalism, which made much of him understandable, as well as explaining his onesidedness.

In 1912 I induced Flournoy to attend the congress in Munich, at which the break between Freud and myself took place. His presence was an important support for me.

I had the feeling in those years—and especially after the parting of ways with Freud—that I was still too young to be independent. I still needed support, and above all someone with whom I could talk openly. This I found in Flournoy, and therefore he soon represented to me a kind of counterpoise to Freud. With him I could really discuss all the problems that scientifically occupied me—for example, on somnambulism, on parapsychology, and the psychology of religion. I had no one else who shared my interests in these matters. Flournoy's views lay completely in my line and gave me many a suggestion. His concept of the "imagination créatrice," which particularly interested me, was an idea I adopted from him.

I learned a great deal from him—above all, the way and manner to consider a patient, the loving absorption in its history. This was how I borrowed one of his cases, namely that of Miss Miller in *Transformations and Symbols of the Libido* (1912), and subjected it to a careful analysis.

[1] From *Erinnerungen, Träume, Gedanken von C. G. Jung*, Aufgezeichnicht und herausgegeben von Aniela Jaffé, (Olten: Walter-Verlag, 1988), pp. 378–79.

[2] [It was only in 1914 that an anonymous German translation appeared—ED.]

I had long been interested in the connections of the fantasy products of schizophrenics, and Flournoy helped me to understand them better. He saw the problems whole, and above all saw them objectively. To him, the facts were important, what took place. He went at a case with the utmost caution and never lost sight of the whole. My fundamental impression of Flournoy's scientific attitude was that he had a truly "objective" approach, and by comparison with Freud that seemed to me a very great merit. Freud had a dynamic and penetrating way: he expected something from his cases. Flournoy wanted nothing. He saw with detachment, and saw clearly. Under the influence of Freud I acquired knowledge, but nothing became clear. Flournoy taught me to maintain a distance between myself and the object, and supported me in the effort to classify and maintain things in a broad horizon. His method was more descriptive, without letting in suppositions, and in spite of a warm and lively interest in the patient, he always held himself at a considerable distance. Thus he never lost sight of the whole.

Flournoy was a cultivated and distinguished personality, very finely educated, intellectually balanced, and with a differentiated sense of proportion. All this was very beneficial for me. He was a professor of philosophy and psychology. He was strongly influenced by Jamesian pragmatism—a viewpoint that is uncongenial to the German spirit and has therefore not been given the attention it deserves. But pragmatism is especially for psychology not of little importance. What I especially esteemed in Flournoy was his philosophical manner of consideration and above all his critical judgement, which was founded on a comprehensive culture.

Translated by Sonu Shamdasani

Introduction

Encountering Hélène
Théodore Flournoy and the Genesis of Subliminal Psychology

Sonu Shamdasani

ENTER THE MEDIUMS

In the seances at the fin de siècle, women became men and men became women. There was no limit to who one could be or to how many. Terrestrials and extraterrestrials swapped places and exchanged notes on their habitations. Plato and Socrates returned to offer courses in postmortem dialectics. The departed returned to repledge their loves and continue their intrigues. Evidently the spirits had a rather theatrical way about them and a taste for the decidedly camp, not to mention for black comedy. Linguistic and aesthetic forms were broken, which paved the way for the artistic convulsions that were to come. Religious dogmas came crashing down as new creeds were announced. Before telecommunications, the mediums were telepathic transatlantic operators, connecting party lines between the living and the dead. Even then, the switchboards were jammed. Time and space coupled in new, unforeseen combinations. Philosophers wondered about the effects of these rappings on the creaking structures of philosophy. The effects were felt as far away as therapeutic consulting rooms; yet here, if a subject spoke, wrote, or acted, it sought no therapy. There was no desire to end the trance, and for a while psychology itself was entranced.

PSYCHOLOGY AT THE SEANCE

At end of the nineteenth century, many of the leading psychologists—Freud, Jung, Ferenczi, Bleuler, James, Myers, Janet, Bergson, Stanley Hall, Schrenck-Notzing, Moll, Dessoir, Richet, and Flournoy—frequented mediums. It is hard today to imagine that some of the most crucial questions of the "new" psychology were played out in the seance, nor how such men could have been so fascinated by the spirits. What took place in the seances enthralled the leading minds of the time, and had a crucial bearing on many of the most significant aspects of twentieth-century psychology, linguistics, philosophy, psychoanalysis, literature, and painting, not to mention psychical research. For a while crucial issues in these disciplines found themselves played out in the transports of the mediumistic trance. A form of transvaluation took place.

In psychology's encounter with the seance, there is one remarkable text that stands out among them all. At the close of 1899 a book appeared bearing the improbable title *From India to the Planet Mars: A Study of a Case of Somnambulism with Glossolalia*. It staged the improbable encounter between two protagonists and the "subliminal romances" that enveloped them. She was Élise Müller, shop girl, Marie Antoinette, the princess Simandini, and a regular visitor to Mars: under his gaze, she became Hélène Smith, immortalized as a psychological case history of multiple personality. He was Théodore Flournoy, psychologist, professor, and scientist: under her gaze he became her former love, the prince Sivrouka.

There is today no school of Flournoyian psychology, no training institutes that bear his name. Furthermore, he is usually absent from histories of psychology in the English-speaking world, and the term "subliminal psychology" does not even feature in dictionaries. It is startling to realize that a great deal of what was supposedly discovered by Freud and Jung was already present in the work of Flournoy, which, moreover, is extremely pertinent to some of the most vexing issues in psychology today.

BECOMING SIVROUKA[1]

Flournoy was born on August 13, 1854, two years before Freud. Like Janet, he had the benefit of both a medical and a philosophical formation.[2] In 1878 he received his M.D. from the University of Strasbourg. He then went to Leipzig where he studied experimental psychology with Wilhelm Wundt for two years. Fortuitously, this coincided with Wundt's founding of the psychological laboratory at the University of Leipzig. On Flournoy's return, as Henri Ellenberger puts it, he "introduced psychological science into Switzerland."[3]

In 1891 he was appointed professor of psychophysiology at the University of Geneva. At his insistence he was placed in the Faculty of Sciences,

[1] For the best work to date on Flournoy, see Mireille Cifali, "Théodore Flournoy, la découverte de l'inconscient," *Le Bloc-Notes de la psychanalyse* 3 (1983): pp. 111–31, which together with the reissue of the original edition of Flournoy's *Des Indes à la Planète Mars* (Paris: Seuil, 1983), can be said to mark the advent of the new Flournoy scholarship.

[2] The best study of Flournoy's early formation is R. Goldsmith, "The Life and Work of Théodore Flournoy," Ph.D. thesis, Michigan State University, 1979. This study is the most comprehensive work on Flournoy in English to date, and deserves to be better known.

[3] Ellenberger, "The Scope of Swiss Psychiatry" (1957), in *Beyond the Unconscious: Essays of Henri F. Ellenberger in the History of Psychiatry*, ed. Mark S. Micale (Princeton: Princeton University Press, 1993), p. 181.

rather than the Faculty of Philosophy. The following year he founded a psychological laboratory at the University of Geneva. However, it was not as an experimental psychologist that Flournoy was to make his mark. In an almost identical manner as his lifelong friend William James, Flournoy quickly became disaffected by the limitations of laboratory psychology and yearned for a psychology that would embrace the whole personality, including its transcendent dimensions. The issue for Flournoy was how to get there. In 1896, in an article on the psychological laboratory, Flournoy noted:

> an hour passed in the nursery or at a so-called spiritist seance poses many more psychological problems, and more vital ones, which one wouldn't resolve in several years consecrated to specifically *laboratory* work.[4]

PSYCHOLOGY IN NEED OF A SUBJECT

For psychology to establish itself, it required subjects. Applicants for the role of principal subject were duly forthcoming, including the hysteric, the criminal, the genius, the mentally defective, the child, and the medium, not to mention the frog.

It is hard to imagine that the medium played a similar role to that played in psychology today by the child. This was principally due to William James, Frederic Myers, and Théodore Flournoy. How did this take place? What was it about mediums that qualified them to serve as the subject for psychology?

The latter half of the nineteenth century witnessed the emergence of modern spiritualism. Through spiritualism, the cultivation of trances— with the attendant phenomena of trance speech, glossolalia, automatic writing, and crystal vision—became widespread. While for spiritualists interest in the phenomena lay solely in the messages conveyed, rather than in the mode of their conveyance, it was the latter that was to provide psychologists with their subject matter.

Prominent psychiatrists and psychologists condemned the spread of spiritualism as a psychic epidemic, and the spiritualists locked horns with the medical and psychiatric communities. In 1885 Eduard von Hartmann wrote: "Spiritism is at present threatening to become a public calamity, to which every government has to direct its attention."[5] Wilhelm Wundt

---

[4] Flournoy, *Notice sur le laboratoire de psychologie de l'université de Genève* (Geneva: Eggiman, 1896), p. 24, cited in Cifali, "Théodore Flournoy, la découverte de l'inconscient," p. 115, trans. mine. In this article, Cifali traces the mode in which Flournoy moved from introspective, experimental psychology to a dynamic psychology of the subliminal.

[5] Eduard von Hartmann, "Spiritism," *Light*, August 22, 1885, p. 409, (trans. C. C. Massey). On the conflict between the medical and spiritualistic communities, see J. P. Williams,

proclaimed: "No man of science, truly independent and without parti pris, could be interested in occult phenomena."[6]

In 1900, Flournoy stated that it was precisely due to the enormous place of spiritualist, mediumistic, and occult phenomena in the preoccupations of the public at large that psychology should concern itself with such phenomena and subject them to rigorous experimental study.[7]

Through spiritualism a new social role, and indeed a profession, came into being: that of the medium. In the 1850s a book appeared entitled *The Mediums' Book* by Allen Kardec, which had, and indeed continues to have, a tremendous influence. It was a "how to do it" guide to becoming a medium, containing everything from practical suggestions to an all-encompassing worldview of reincarnation. Kardec claimed that "everyone possesses the germ of the qualities necessary for becoming a medium."[8] He defines a medium in the following way: "Every one who is in any degree influenced by spirits is, by that very fact, a medium."[9] The omnipresence of spirit influence leads Kardec to claim that "there are few persons in whom some rudiments of medianimity are not found. We may therefore assume that everyone is a medium."[10] Hence the observation of mediums held center stage, through those who wished to materialize spiritualist hypotheses.

Kardec's theory of mediumship facilitated its subsequent psychological interpretation. For Kardec, mediumship was an exemplary way of understanding the human condition; hence the study of a fully developed medium would provide the best insight into it. He claimed that the phenomena of mediumship were due to the intervention of spirits. Thus, his taxonomy of the forms and grades of mediumship resulted in a pneumatology. In the psychological study of mediums the exemplary status accorded to them was retained, though now their phenomena were no longer primarily disclosive of the actions of the spirits, but of the "subconscious" or "subliminal" imagination. By attempting to find an intrapsy-

---

"Psychical Research and Psychiatry in Late Victorian Britain: Trance as Ecstasy or Trance as Insanity," in *The Anatomy of Madness: Essays in the History of Psychiatry*, ed. W. Bynum, R. Porter, and M. Shephard, vol. 1 (London: Tavistock/Routledge, 1985); E. Brown, "Neurology and Spiritualism in the 1870's," *Bulletin for the History of Medicine* 57 (1983): pp. 563–77; and S. Shortt, "Physicians and Psychics: The Anglo-American Medical Response to Spiritualism, 1870–1890," *Journal of the History of Medicine and Allied Sciences* 39 (1984): pp. 339–55. The debates in the Anglo-American context were broadly similar to the debates in Europe.

[6] Cited by Flournoy, *Spiritism and Psychology*, trans. H. Carrington (New York: Harper Bros., 1911), p. 21.

[7] Flournoy, "Observations psychologiques sur le spiritisme," *IV Congrès International de Psychologie*, ed. P. Janet (Paris: Alcan, 1901), pp. 103–4.

[8] A. Kardec, *The Medium's Book*, trans. Anna Blackwell (São Paulo: Lake, 1975), p. xv.

[9] Ibid., p. 172.

[10] Ibid.

chic source for mediumistic communications, these investigators deci-
sively contributed to the discovery of the unconscious.

GOTHIC PSYCHOLOGY

The pioneer of the psychological study of mediumship was Frederic
Myers. André Breton wrote:

> In spite of the regrettable fact that so many are unacquainted with the work of
> F.W.H. Myers, which anteceded that of Freud, I think we owe more than is
> generally conceded to what William James called the gothic psychology of
> F.W.H. Myers which, in an entirely new and still more exciting world, led us to
> the admirable explorations of Théodore Flournoy.[11]

For Myers, whom Flournoy called the founder of subliminal psychology, psychology itself was merely a vehicle to approach what he claimed
was the only question worth asking: namely, does love survive the grave?
William James claimed that Myers's work would be the most important
psychology in the twentieth century. In a series of brilliant articles in the
1880s, Myers charted out the whole domain of abnormal and supranormal
psychology. For Myers, in contradistinction to his contemporaries such as
Freud and Janet, the unconscious, or as he termed it, the subliminal—
the secondary personalities revealed in trance states, dreaming, crystal
gazing, and automatic writing—potentially possessed a higher intelligence than one's waking or supraliminal personality and often served to
convey messages of guidance.

A critical shift took place through the work of Myers, James and Flournoy. They argued that the crucial issue was no longer the simple question
of whether the alleged spiritualist experiences were valid or not. Either
way, they claimed, such experiences seemed to promise greater insight
into the composition of the subliminal, and hence into human psychology
as a whole.

The investigations of Myers paved the way for Flournoy and provided
him with an initial orientation. Myers ended up embracing the spiritist
hypothesis and attempted to unite science and religion in an overarching
synthesis in his posthumous volume *Human Personality and Its Survival
of Bodily Death*. Flournoy, by contrast, attempted to maintain a purely
psychological viewpoint and stressed that one needed to distinguish between subliminal psychology and Myers's philosophico-religious system.
Flournoy saw himself as continuing the former.

Who were the mediums? Flournoy provides a description of the "current or average type of ordinary medium":

---

[11] Breton, "The Automatic Message," in *What Is Surrealism? Selected Writings* (London:
Pluto, 1989), p. 100. For a reappraisal of Myers, see my "Automatic Writing and the Discovery of the Unconscious," *Spring* 54 (1993): pp. 100–131.

A person, ordinarily of the feminine sex, who has never experienced psychic phenomena (except, perhaps a little somnambulism or day-dreams and some presentiments) experiences a great sorrow, such as the death of a dear one, and soon after attends a seance for the first time. She tries the table or automatic writing. Rapidly she becomes a typtological medium, or automatic writer, and obtains communications which do not surpass, in any way, her own capabilities, but which strike her and enchant her in the beginning by reason of their so-called emanation from the dead. Little by little, however, the monotony of the messages, their intrinsic mediocrity, the rarity or even absence of all proof convincingly supernatural, sometimes the obsessional or lying character of the pretended revelations, deprive her of her first enthusiasm, and at the end of several months, or even years, the medium ceases to practice. Nothing is usually left to her either of good or evil as the result of this "phase" of mediumship except a certain latent predisposition which renders her capable of practicing mediumship with more or less ease whenever she tries; and at the basis of her nature a real inclination for spiritist doctrines, with the desire to see them one day scientifically demonstrated. [12]

For the spiritualists the capacity to receive messages from spirits was the defining characteristic of mediums. While Flournoy rejected this claim, he nevertheless argued that mediums formed a specific psychological type. Flournoy described their distinguishing trait in the following manner:

All the difference between mediums and ordinary people, is that with the latter there is practically a very marked trench between dream and waking. . . . With the mediums on the contrary . . . there is not a stable barrier between sleep and waking. [13]

Flournoy described Myers' notion of the subliminal as follows:

Between our ordinary consciousness [the supraliminal] and our latent consciousness [the subliminal] there are perpetual changes and fluctuations along their border; the level of separation is not constant; the partition is not impervious; the threshold is not fixed between these parts of our being; there occur phenomena of osmosis from one to the other, or mingling, as between liquids or varying density, when the bottle is shaken. . . . constantly, also, messages are sent from our subliminal regions to our personal consciousness, carrying with them, in the most diverse forms (as sensory automatisms) contents of the most varied value—visual hallucinations, auditory hallucinations, submerged ideas, emotions, irrational impulses, etc. [14]

[12] Flournoy, *Spiritism and Psychology*, p. 46.
[13] Flournoy, "Nouvelles Observations sur un cas de somnambulisme avec glossolalia," *Archives de Psychologie* 1 (1902): p. 127, trans. mine.
[14] Flournoy, *Spiritism and Psychology*, pp. 57–58.

Hence for Myers and Flournoy, the medium represented someone in whom the threshold between the supraliminal and the subliminal was particularly permeable, and it was for this reason that mediums became the preeminent subjects of subliminal psychology. They enabled the study of the subconscious imagination with much greater ease than other subjects.

MEDIUM OR HYSTERIC?

In *The Principles of Psychology* William James wrote: "Mediumistic possession in all its grades seems to form a perfectly natural special type of alternate personality."[15] Mediumship was viewed as a special subset of multiple personality. The significant difference was that in cases of mediumship the state of "possession" usually took place only within the seance and seemed compatible with psychological "health." The question of the interpretation of mediumship was a contested and divisive issue. The similarity with cases of hysteria and multiple personality led prominent psychologists such as Charcot, Binet, and Janet to assimilate it under those headings. In *Alterations of the Personality*, while discussing experiments on hysterical subjects, Binet wrote: "There is no essential difference between the experiments which I have now described and the more spontaneous experiments that the spiritists practice upon themselves."[16]

For proponents of the new French psychopathology, the assimilation of the mediumistic trance to the trances observed in hysterics rendered superfluous the specific interpretive paradigms that Myers and Flournoy erected around it. In 1895, Janet argued that the medium was a pathological type and that the phenomena exhibited: "have laws and are explained in the same manner by a serious trouble in the mental operation of perception, which we have described under the name of psychological disaggregation."[17]

The question that remained for Janet was whether or not the medium was always a hysteric. He suggests not. He cites a case he observed while in Charcot's service, with somnambulism and automatic writing, which was clearly not a hysteric. Concerning mediumship, the following questions remained for Janet: "What are these forms? What is their relation with hysteria? How does automatic writing modify itself in these cases?

[15] James, *The Principles of Psychology* (New York: Holt, 1890/London: Macmillan, 1918), p. 393.

[16] Binet, *Alterations of the Personality*, trans. H. G. Baldwin (London: Chapman Hall, 1896), p. 325.

[17] Janet, "Le Spiritisme Contemporain," *Revue Philosophique* 33 (1892): p. 419, trans. mine.

These are the problems that one could resolve by the observation of numerous mediums."[18]

Hence for the psychopathologists the cultivation of dissociation that spiritualism propagated was deplorable, leading them to regard it as a psychic epidemic. In 1899 Flournoy addressed this issue. He stated that it was insufficient to simply refer to the phenomena of hypnotism, hysteria, and dissociation to explain mediumship—though on the surface, such an assimilation was easy to make. Flournoy argues that mediumship could be accompanied by the best of health. Hence the public at large was quite right to resist viewing the phenomena of mediumship as the result of hysteria or autohypnotization. In addition, he notes that there were Anglo-Saxon scientists who, on the contrary, saw hysteria as a pathological degeneration of mediumistic genius. Hence Flournoy argues that mediumship and its distinct manifestations and particular conditions of appearance should be studied in their specificity, without simply being classified in preexisting psychopathological categories.[19]

In Search of a Medium

> I found much that was moving, when I had climbed to
> the top storey of some house in Soho or Holloway, and,
> having paid my shilling, awaited, among servant girls, the
> wisdom of some fat old medium. That is an absorbing
> drama, though if my readers begin to seek it they will
> spoil it, for its gravity and simplicity depend on all, or all
> but all, believing that their dead are near.[20]
>
> William Butler Yeats

> The seeress is now more common in the land. . . . Modern seeresses are of two classes: the Bond street class,
> who divine for the fair sex; and the class who are studied
> by eminent psychologists, like Professor James, Professor
> Richet and Professor Flournoy.[21]
>
> Andrew Lang

From the outset, the task for Flournoy was how to find a medium. Once he had found her, she would so mark his life, that he would have great difficulty forgetting her.

---

[18] Janet, ibid., p. 424, trans. mine.

[19] Flournoy, "Genèse de quelques prètendus messages spirites," *Revue Philosophique* 47 (1899): p. 145.

[20] William Butler Yeats, "Swedenborg, Mediums, and the Desolate Places" (1914) in *Explorations* (London: Macmillan, 1962), pp. 30–31.

[21] Andrew Lang, "Three Seeresses," *Anglo-Saxon Review*, Sept. 1900, p. 63.

In 1892 Flournoy wrote: "We only wait the appearance in our country of a Eusapia [Palladino] or of a willing Mrs. Piper whom we would welcome with open arms."[22] Flournoy's casting call for such a figure is well documented in his letters to William James. On December 18, 1893, Flournoy wrote to James:

I try to penetrate into the spiritualistic world of our city, but it is rather difficult. At present they do not have very outstanding mediums; I should be very content, indeed, if I were only able to observe closely those who experience the phenomena about which I hear, but they surround themselves with solitude and darkness.[23]

After several months without a sign, Flournoy wrote to James on March 18, 1894: "The few mediums and subjects of telepathic hallucinations etc. whom I have been able to reach in the last three months in Geneva have not furnished me with decisive phenomena."[24]

Eighteen months later he had finally found her. On the September 4, 1895, he wrote to James:

I was forgetting to tell you what has interested me most during the last six months: it is a certain medium (nonprofessional, unpaid) of a spiritualist group, into which they have agreed to accept me in spite of my neutral position, I have attended about twenty of the seances . . . psychologically, it is very interesting, because this woman is a veritable museum of all possible phenomena and has a repertoire of illimitable variety: she makes the table talk,—she hears voices, —she has visions, hallucinations, tactile and olfactory,—automatic writing— sometimes complete somnambulism, catalepsy, trances, etc. All the automatism, sensory and motor, of Myers,—all the classical hysterial phenomena— present themselves in turn, in any order and in the most unexpected fashion, varying from one time to another. The contents of these phenomena are always of former events, going back a few or many years, being perfectly correct, generally having to do with the ancestors of the persons present. The good faith of the medium is indisputable, and the strangeness of her revelations are calculated to convince the spiritualists of this group. However, in the 5 or 6 cases which concerned deceased members of my family, I finally had proof that these persons all had, some fifty years ago, personal contact with the parents of the medium; and the most natural supposition is that these revelations, invariably exact and dealing with odd facts, are reminiscences of accounts which the medium had heard from the mouth of her parents in childhood. . . . The great majority of the phenomena were evidently the automatic reproduction of for-

[22] Flournoy, *Notice sur le laboratoire*, p. 17, trans. Goldsmith in "The Life and Work of Théodore Flournoy," p. 148.
[23] *The Letters of William James and Théodore Flournoy*, ed. R. Le Clair (Madison: University of Wisconsin Press, 1966), p. 29.
[24] Ibid., p. 33.

gotten memories—or memories registered unconsciously. There is actually in the nature of this medium a second personality who perceives and recalls instants which escape ordinary awareness. . . . I have the definite impression that the extraordinary revelations obtained in the seances, for the most part . . . are phenomena of "Cryptomnesia."—What is irritating in this kind of observation is the difficulty of making it precise, the medium and the members of the group having a holy terror of everything which resembles an "experiment."[25]

Who did Flournoy encounter? Was it really Élise Müller, a Genevan shop assistant? Or was she someone who at that moment was still malleable, capable of becoming someone, of taking on any role—including that of a subject for a yet to be founded psychological science—of becoming a "veritable museum of all possible phenomena," which had already been taxonomied, classified, "dissociated" through the analytic lenses of the new psychology—for whom his text would be her spectacular genesis?

BECOMING HÉLÈNE

Who was she—who became Hélène Smith? She was born Élise-Catherine Müller on December 9, 1861, in Martigny, Switzerland. At the time that Flournoy encountered her, she worked as a salesperson in a silk shop. He was introduced to her seances by August Lemaître. At that time, there were two main types of mediums: professional mediums, who charged a fee, and amateur mediums, who performed for free. She was of the latter variety, which was to have a marked effect on what ensued. Lemaître was the first to write about her. In 1897 he published an article entitled "Contribution à l'étude des phenomenes psychiques,"[26] in which Élise Müller appeared; intriguingly, Lemaître gave her sex as male. She had not yet become "Hélène Smith." Lemaître stressed the quality of her character: "Our medium is a medium of good faith, a medium who says the truth and in whom I have full confidence."[27] Lemaître seemed to support the spiritist interpretation of her material. His article was critically responded to by M. Lefébure, who deplored the lack of material that Lemaître published:

If, in effect, M. L . . . has kept several phrases or speeches of the mediums, if he will publish them, and if the Indianists would show there, supported by

---

[25] Ibid., pp. 47–48. In a landmark article, "Psychiatry and Its Unknown History," in *Beyond the Unconscious*, Ellenberger depicted a recurrent pattern in which a psychologist encounters a patient, usually female, and develops a long, complex, and ambiguous relation, which forms the basis of his theories, and discusses Flournoy and Hélène Smith as a case in point.

[26] Lemaître, *Annales des Sciences Psychiques* 7 (1897): pp. 65–68.

[27] Ibid., p. 69, trans. mine.

proofs, a real dialect and an appropriate sense, spiritism would certainly have made a great step.[28]

Thus the stage was already set. In a subsequent issue Flournoy wrote to the editor to explicitly distance himself from the viewpoint of Lemaître, who had cited him by name. In doing so, he announced his project by writing that he planned to give "a purely psychological interpretation" of the "so curious" phenomena of the medium "without recourse to spirits, notions of incarnations, anteriorities, etc."[29] Thus Flournoy's reading was already from the outset a revisionist reading.

The question remains as to how she acquired her pseudonym. Olivier Flournoy, Flournoy's grandson, notes that according to the opinion of Denise Werner, Flournoy's granddaughter, Élise Müller probably chose it herself. He notes, significantly enough, that Hélène was the name of one of Flournoy's own daughters, born in 1891, whom Élise would have met.[30]

ENTRANCING PSYCHOLOGY

The question of trance states has been taken up in many discourses, in the course of which countless definitions have been proposed and properties adduced. In *The Principles of Psychology* William James wrote:

> The three states of Charcot, the strange reflexes of Heidenhain, and all the other bodily phenomena which have been called direct consequences of the trance-state itself, are not such. They are products of suggestion, the trance-state having no particular outward symptoms of its own; but without the trance-state there, those particular suggestions could never have been successfully made.[31]

James trenchantly points out the pitfalls that this held for the development of psychology:

> Any sort of personal peculiarity, any trick accidently fallen into in the first instance by some one subject, may, by attracting attention, become stereotyped, serve as a pattern for imitation, and figure as the type of a school. The first

---

[28] Lefébure, "Remarques sur les experiences de M. Lemaître," *Annales des Sciences Psychiques* 7 (1897): p. 180, trans. mine.

[29] Flournoy, *Annales des Sciences Psychiques* 7 (1897): p. 256, trans. mine.

[30] O. Flournoy, *Théodore et Léopold: De Théodore Flournoy à la Psychanalyse. Correspondance et documents de Hélène Smith—Ferdinand de Saussure—August Barth—Charles Michel* (Neuchâtal: A La Bacconière, 1986), p. 35.

[31] James, *Principles of Psychology*, p. 601. On James's dynamic psychology of the subliminal, see Eugene Taylor, *William James on Exceptional Mental States: The 1896 Lowell Lectures* (Amherst: University of Massachusetts Press, 1984).

subject trains the operator trains the succeeding subjects, all of them in perfect good faith conspiring together to evolve a perfectly arbitrary result. With the extraordinary perspicacity and subtlety of perception which subjects often display for all that concerns the operator with whom they are en rapport, it is hard to keep them ignorant of anything he expects. Thus it happens that one easily verifies on new subjects what one has already seen on old ones, or any desired symptom of which one may have heard or read.[32]

Thus for James it was psychology itself that was in a state of "heightened suggestibility," or highly prone to "autosuggestion." James was here backing up Josef Delboeuf's views. In 1886, Delboeuf wrote:

Without any doubt there is an undeniable influence of the hypnotizer on the hypnotized—like master, like disciple. But the subjects themselves, principally the very first one, train the experimenter who directs them, and, without being aware of it, determine his method and his maneuvers. In a way then, turning the proverb around, one could say: like disciple, like master. This action of first disciple on the master is then reported to other disciples who report his procedures, and thus are created the schools that have the monopoly of special phenomena.[33]

For James and Flournoy, the investigation of trance states was a central question if a psychology worthy of the name was to develop.[34] Within this enterprise, the investigations of mediums held pride of place. For Flournoy the crucial issue was the differential interpretation of trance states. Was there a specificity to the mediumistic trance, in revealing capacities that outstripped waking consciousness? The possibility of subliminal psychology rested upon an affirmative answer to this question.

From the time of the Marquis de Puységur, the trance state had been attributed remarkable properties, such as clairvoyance, telepathy, hypermnesia and lucidity. These attributes were further explored in the remarkable case of Justinus Kerner, the "seeress of Prevost," which in many ways forms the main precursor to Flournoy's study. From Puységur through Kerner came the notion of the trance as possessing properties that outstripped one's waking self. This tradition differed markedly from

[32] James, *Principles of Psychology*, p. 601.

[33] J. Delboeuf, "De l'influence de l'education et de l'imitation dans le somnambulisme provoqué," *Revue Philosophique* 22 (1886), quoted in Theta Wolf, *Alfred Binet* (Chicago: University of Chicago Press, 1973), p. 149. For recent elucidations of the significance of Delbouef, see Jacqueline Carroy, *Hypnose, suggestion et psychologie: L'invention de sujets* (Paris: Presses Universitaires de France, 1991); and François Duyckaerts, *Joseph Delboeuf: Philosophe et hypnotiseur* (Paris: Les Empêcheurs de penser en rond, 1992).

[34] On the issue of trance states, see especially Mikkel Borch-Jacobsen, "Mimetic Efficacity," in *The Emotional Tie: Psychoanalysis, Mimesis, Affect* (Stanford: Stanford University Press, 1992).

the view of the trance held by Charcot, for whom the capacity to be hypnotized was a symptom of hysteria, which crucially shaped the views of Freud.

The mediumistic trance is an instance of the cultivation of trance states, which have been crossculturally known. Mikkel Borch-Jacobsen differentiates two main approaches to the therapeutics of the trance, one represented by psychoanalysis, the other by "traditional" therapies. In his reading, the telos of psychoanalysis resides in attempting to put an end to the trance (the dissolution of transference, etc.). Such an approach may be termed "allopathic." In contrast to this lies the "homeopathic" approach of "traditional" therapies, whose strategies do not take the form of a war against the trance, but attempt to achieve an altered relation to it. Borch-Jacobsen writes:

> It is not a question, in the "traditional" therapies on which hypnosis models itself, of suppressing the evil of which the patient suffers (his absence of identity, his mimetic madness), but of attesting to the limit of its spectacular, ritual aggravation. A few examples, forcibly simplified. The Thonga "mad of the gods," once having exorcised the evil spirit that possessed them, became the "mad" of a beneficent spirit.[35] Sister Jeanne of the Angels, at first possessed by the "demon" Urbain Grandier, became a sort of professional mystic.[36] Gilberte Rochette, ex-"neurotic," became the great priestess of the magnetic lodge of Lyon.[37] Bertha von Pappenheim, ex-"case" of double personality, became the pythoness of Breuer. (Must one add: the analysands, at the end of the transferential "pass," become analysts?) Consequently, little matter whether the so-called "symptom" disappeared or not. Above all it is important that it was taken in charge, raised up, "cultivated" by the so-called "therapy."[38]

The latter history of Hélène Smith may be adumbrated to the list above—in her 'second' life, as a religious painter, Hélène Smith finally found her metier. Within subliminal psychology there was a valorization of the trance—if the mediums were not seen as the portal to the beyond, at the very least they were attributed capabilities and powers far exceeding that accorded to "normal" psychology.

Flournoy's study was by no means the first lengthy and detailed study of a medium. The study of Mrs. Piper is usually seen as inaugurating the careful investigation of the mediumistic trance. These previous studies, such as Hodgson's of Mrs. Piper, had been primarily motivated by the wish to find and authenticate genuine proof of the existence of the be-

---

[35] L. de Heutsch, "La folie des dieux," in *Pourquoi l'epouser?* (Paris: Gallimard, 1971).

[36] M. de Certeau, *La Possession de Loudun* (Paris: Juillard, 1970).

[37] F. Rausky, *Mesmer ou la revolution therapeutique* (Paris: Payot, 1977).

[38] Borch-Jacobsen, "Dispute," in *Hypnose et Psychanalyse: Reponses à Mikkel Borch-Jacobsen*, ed. Leon Chertok (Paris: Dunod, 1987), p. 211, trans. mine.

yond, and to obtain veridical communications from the dead. The main alternative paradigms had been fraud or telepathy, neither of which play a prominent role in Flournoy's text. The innovation of *From India to the Planet Mars* was that it was the first major study of what Myers called pseudo-possession, whose main goal was to disprove the supernatural origin of the phenomena and to give an account of their psychogenesis. In such a manner it established a devastating skeptical paradigm in psychical research.

DISCOVERING THE UNCONSCIOUS

Ellenberger notes that by 1900 four different aspects of the unconscious had been demonstrated: its conservative function, the capacity of storing a number of memories and perceptions; its dissolutive function, the tendency for dissociation and automatic actions; its creative function, and its mythopoetic function, the capacity to fabricate mythopoetic subliminal romances.[39] It is significant that Flournoy was a major pioneer in the exploration of all of these aspects.

In *From India to the Planet Mars* Flournoy often refers almost interchangeably to the subliminal and the subconscious. While in the case of the former term his usage denotes a direct continuity with its use by Myers, who coined it, he vastly expands the meaning of the latter term over its use by its coiner, Janet. Claparède gives the following account of the advance of Flournoy's conception over Janet's:

> The discovery and psychological and biological interpretation of this creative activity of the subconscious is that which here seems to me to mark the great progress of the theory of Flournoy over that of Janet. For the French savant . . . it is above all the normal activity of the spirit which is creative. The other activity, that of the second self, is only conservatory. . . . To this totally passive character of the subconscious [Janet's]. . . . Flournoy substitutes a veritable and original creative activity, often much more powerful than that of consciousness.[40]

In 1900 Flournoy noted that while there was much work on the role of unconscious perception and latent memories, the subliminal imagination had not been studied with the care it merited. For Flournoy the sublimi-

---

[39] Ellenberger, *The Discovery of the Unconscious* (New York: Basic Books, 1970), pp. 315–18.

[40] Claparède, "Théodore Flournoy: Sa vie et son oeuvre," *Archives de Psychologie* 17 (1923): p. 58, trans. mine.

nal imagination was the source of the conscious imagination, rather than the other way around. He notes:

> This imaginative process of foreign personification has already unfurled itself in the dream, in hypnotism, and in many pathological obsessions, etc.; but it acquires a wholly particular practical importance in the phenomena called mediumistic.[41]

Because mediumship presented in an exemplary way the workings of the subliminal imagination, Flournoy held that its study of mediumship could in turn illuminate the psychology of dreams, hypnosis, and obsessions.

Flournoy emphasized four main functions of the unconscious: its creative activity, its protective function, its compensatory function, and its play tendency. These four feature prominently in Flournoy's interpretation of Hélène's trances: Léopold, her spirit guide, is seen to represent the protective function or teleological automatism, that intervenes and assists Hélène when she is in difficulty; her anterior and extraterrestrial existences are seen as providing a compensation for the vicissitudes of her circumstances; her creations of the Martian and "Hindu" languages are seen as remarkable acts of creativity. For Flournoy her trances represent a reversion to an earlier developmental stage of childhood that, he argues, following the work of Karl Groos, is characterized by play. As play has a preparatory function, this reversion is compensatory, and enables access to a level of creativity that has been lost. One could say that Hélène's trances were Flournoy's unconscious, which he would never again find so fully revealed.

The material for this subliminal activity was provided by the phenomenon of cryptomnesia.

CRYPTOMNESIA

Since the time of the magnetists, attention has been paid to the hypermnesic properties of the trance. These capacities seem to suggest that there was a great deal of information that, although once perceived, now lay outside of the reach of conscious attention. The unconscious was designated as the location of these hidden memories. It was principally Flournoy who attempted to map the extent of this phenomena and trace the transformations that such memories were subject to while in a latent state.

Cryptomnesia plays a crucial role in Flournoy's analysis as the main alternative paradigm to the spiritualistic hypothesis. The significance of

---

[41] Flournoy, "Observations psychologiques sur le spiritisme," p. 107, trans. mine.

the phenomenon had been noted by Janet, who refers to a piece in the *Revue Spirite* by M. Goupil on automatic writing that presents an example of cryptomnesia. Janet notes that he has seen and described similar facts and can supply an explanation:

> When a certain sensation finds itself bound to subconscious acts, there is, at that moment, a particular and corresponding anesthesia for the ordinary personality. When automatic writing manifests a certain memory with persistence, there is a corresponding amnesia for the normal consciousness.[42]

Janet finds such descriptions valuable and regrets that there are not more like it. It was precisely this lacuna that was filled preeminently by *From India to the Planet Mars*.

Flournoy's account of cryptomnesia presented a model of memory that attempted to account for the interrelation of memory and fantasy. For Flournoy what was presented as a memory—in the case of Hélène, of an anterior existence—in actuality represented a hidden and forgotten memory that had been through a process of subconscious elaboration.[43] Significantly enough, this was presented in the interregnum between Freud's confessional retraction of his seduction theory in private to Fliess and his public retraction several years later.

FLOURNOY'S RECEPTION

On the first of January, 1900, James wrote to Flournoy:

> Upon my word, dear Flournoy, you have done a bigger thing here than you know; and I think that your volume has probably made the decisive step in converting psychical research into a respectable science. The tone and temper are so admirable, the style so rich and human, the intellectual equipment so complete, that it is a performance which must strike every reader, whatever his antecedent presuppositions may have been, as of first-rate quality. . . . The great thing about your writing is your charming style. You and Delboeuf are the only worthy successors to Voltaire. Your book has only one defect and that is that you don't dedicate it to me. . . . As I am passing off the scene . . . it would have been pleasant to have my name preserved for ever in the early pages of your immortal work.[44]

[42] Janet, "Le Spiritisme Contemporain," p. 428, trans. mine.
[43] For a review of the literature on cryptomnesia, see Ian Stevenson, "Crytomnesia and Parapsychology," *Journal of the Society for Psychical Research* 52 (1983): pp. 1–30; for recent experimental work on cryptomnesia, see Alan Brown and Dana Murray, "Cryptomnesia: Delineating Inadvertent Plagiarism," *Journal of Experimental Psychology. Learning, Memory and Cognition* 15 (1989): pp. 432–42. Flournoy's work on cryptomnesia is also shadowed in the current preoccupation with "False Memory Syndrome."
[44] *The Letters of William James and Théodore Flournoy*, pp. 90–91.

Subsequently, in response to Flournoy's follow up study, "Nouvelles Observations," on June 13, 1902, James wrote to Flournoy:

> It completes an invaluable monograph which puts into our possession for all time a term of compassion, which all future discussers of "psychic" individuals will have to take into account of in their conclusions. I need hardly repeat that your conclusions seem to me to be the only legitimate ones to draw. But what a wonderful extension the case gives to our notion of subconscious activities and to cryptomnesic activities. . . . I do wish that someone could continue work with Miss Smith. Some of her phenomena have grazed so closely upon the supernormal that one would like to see whether she ever does pass the barrier, as I believe it can be passed. . . . All that you say about method, etc. is simply splendid, classic, masterly.[45]

Flournoy's book received a glowing notice in the *Bibliothèque Universelle*: "There has been a long time since a new work has produced in our French Switzerland as great a sensation as the book recently published by Théodore Flournoy."[46] Claparède notes that due to its success, Flournoy acquired a vast popularity. After only three months the book went into its third edition. *The Figaro* noted: "The world of psychologists has been overturned by the appearance of a book by M. Théodore Flournoy. It is the history of a case probably unique in science."[47] Flournoy's successful combination of a literary and "scientific" style led to extremely laudatory reviews in both the popular press and in psychological journals. It was read both as a treatise in psychology and as a novel.

The following notices give further indication of its reception. *The Dial* stated: "To all who can take a serious interest in its subject matter Professor Flournoy's book will doubtless appear as important as interesting."[48] *The Popular Science Monthly* observed:

> M. Flournoy has been unusually successful in revealing the starting points of the several automatisms and of connecting them with intelligible developments of the medium's mental life. . . . This case has many analogies with other cases that have been recorded, but goes beyond most of them in the complexity and bizarre character of the unconscious elaborations and feats of memory and creative imagination which it entails. . . . The special value of this account thus lies in the accuracy of the description and the success with which the account has been made thoroughly intelligible and significant.[49]

---

[45] *The Letters of William James and Théodore Flournoy*, pp. 127–28.
[46] April, 1900, p. 197, trans. mine.
[47] March 7, 1900. Cited by Claparède, "Théodore Flournoy," p. 47, trans. mine.
[48] September 16, 1900, p. 180.
[49] October, 1900, pp. 662–63.

The Nation noted:

> A very few years ago the production of this remarkable book would have been impossible. Its heroine . . . would have excited only scientific aversion or contempt; and, the superstitious interpretation of the curious phenomena she exhibits being left unopposed, her case would have served only to confirm the religious dogmas of spiritualism, or would perhaps have started a new sect whose faith would have baffled any attempt to ascertain the actual facts. As it is, the case has had the good fortune to fall into the hands of a singularly competent, unprejudiced, and tactful investigator in M. Flournoy.[50]

The book was favorably reviewed in the *American Journal of Psychology* by G. W. Patrick, who noted:

> As an example of method this book is to be highly commended, and method is what is needed now in the study of automatism. Any one who should complain that the case of Mlle. Smith is not sufficiently "remarkable" to merit 420 pages of minute description fails to understand the importance of the study of secondary personality. The author's intimations of the infantile and reversionary character of the secondary personality are of interest in the light of recent theories.[51]

Several months later a second review of the book appeared in the *American Journal of Psychology*, this time by E. B. Titchener. He commented that as the book was attracting so much attention on the part of psychologists as well as the general public, he would take the opportunity of the publication of the English translation to discuss it further. Titchener wrote that Flournoy:

> had done his work with extreme acumen. Indeed, when one remembers the almost infinite possibilities of suggestion to which "Mdlle. Smith" has been exposed in the confines of her trances [a point sufficiently stressed by the author], one marvels at the high measure of success in explanation that M. Flournoy has attained. Few psychologists will dispute his conclusion that the "secondary personalities" "do not have their existence outside of Mdlle. Smith," but have their genesis within her mental life. And even those who, like the present writer, have no great affection for the "subliminal self" . . . even they will readily admit that M. Flournoy's methodical study proves the high value of subconscious imagination as a working hypothesis.[52]

[50] June 14, 1900, p. 462.
[51] April 1900, p. 430.
[52] January 1901, p. 267.

In the *Psychological Review*, Joseph Jastrow praised the book, writing:

> We have a truly classical instance of the psychological comprehensiveness of the automatic self in exceptional cases. M. Flournoy has thus accomplished a valuable task and has presented his material with unusual skill.[53]

Jastrow welcomed the skepticism of the book and looked forward to the day when the phenomena of mediumship would be completely explained through psychological means alone. He was critical of Flournoy's acceptance of the reality of telepathy and telekinesis, which he felt was out of harmony with the rest of Flournoy's skeptical analysis.

Extraterrestrial voyages were all the rage. In the *Revue Philosophique*, Albert de Rochas noted:

> Today, with the great interest that there has been among the spiritists for the writings of Flammarion on the planet Mars and the revelations of the theosophists on the Hindu Masters, it's Mars and the Orient which are fashionable. For two years I too have studied a distinguished lady who likewise makes her way in an etheric body on the planet Mars. She moreover describes it totally differently than Mlle. Smith. . . . This lady had also been an arab princess of great beauty, engaged to a sheik, of whom I was then the brother. One sees that apart from the language, we find here the same psychological details as in the case of Mlle. Smith.[54]

Spiritualists were up in arms about the book, for understandable reasons. They published a whole brochure against Flournoy: *Autour "Des Indes à la Planète Mars."*[55] In "Nouvelles Observations," Flournoy trenchantly replied at length to their critiques. Yet not all spiritualists criticized the book. It received a lengthy positive review in *Light*. The reviewer welcomed it as a "most valuable contribution," noting:

> It is worthy of consideration by the Spiritualists of England and America, especially with regard to the fact that it shows how large a part of the phenomena usually attributed to "control" may be referred to involuntary emergings from the sub-conscious of the medium. Supposing even that some readers may differ from the author's conclusions in this respect, yet this book unquestioningly demonstrates to what a large extent the telepathic transmission is conditioned and controlled by the medium's subconsciousness.[56]

Flournoy's study was used to illuminate similar cases in history. Andrew Lang, in "Three Seeresses" boldly undertook a comparative historical

---

[53] 1900, p. 491.
[54] 49 (1900), pt. 1, p. 652, trans. mine.
[55] *Société d'Etudes Psychiques de Genève* (Geneva: Georg & Cie, 1901).
[56] June 2, 1900, p. 255.

study of Joan of Arc, Mrs. Piper, and Hélène Smith. He argued that the psychological study of these later cases enables us to understand their illustrious predecessor, and to see her apparitions—analogous to Hélène's Léopold, or Mrs. Piper's Phinuit, as her dream-selves.

In *Mind*, F.C.S. Schiller hailed the book as a classic. He wrote: "Prof. Flournoy's medium well deserved the study he has bestowed upon her . . . her case has greatly extended our knowledge of the nature and capacities of the subliminal consciousness."[57]

However, Schiller found Flournoy's explanations unsatisfactory. He wrote:

> They neither account for the persistence with which such cases assume a spiritistic form, nor do they supply a principle to account for the selection of recondite and pseudo-evidential memories in lieu of those which ordinary paths of association would normally reproduce.[58]

Reviewers highlighted the discrepancy between Flournoy's interpretation of Hélène's material and her value system. In his review of "Nouvelles Observations," Schiller noted:

> To reduce the ex-Ranee Simandini of Chandraghiri, the ex-Queen of France, the protégée of discarnate Cagliostro, the recipient of telepathic communication from trusty correspondents throughout the solar system, to a mere dreamer of dreams constructed by an ill-regulated sub-consciousness must be painful to the least sensitive vanity.[59]

For some commentators, the powers that Flournoy was claiming for the subliminal creative imagination seemed to require no less of a leap of faith than the spiritualist hypothesis. Schiller takes issue with Flournoy's recourse to the subliminal consciousness to explain her material, and writes: "I cannot feel there is so much to choose between it and Spiritism."[60]

Myers's response took the form of a characteristically nuanced article entitled "Pseudo-Possession." Describing Flournoy's book as brilliant, he writes: "Few writers on matter of difficult controversy have ever produced so delightful an impression of absolute, instinctive candour as Professor Flournoy."[61] Myers opens his discussion by noting:

> Professor Flournoy's book indicates in a remarkable way how things have moved in the psychology of the last twenty years. The book,—a model of fairness throughout,—is indeed, for the most part, critically destructive in its treatment

[57] 1900, p. 549.
[58] Ibid.
[59] Schiller, *Proceedings of the Society for Psychical Research* (1903), p. 246.
[60] Ibid., p. 248.
[61] Myers, *Proceedings of the Society for Psychical Research* (1901), p. 385.

of the quasi-supernormal phenomena with which it deals. But what a mass of conceptions a competent psychologist now takes for granted in this realm, which the official science of twenty years ago would scarcely stomach hinting at![62]

The spectrum of laudatory response is impressive. Historians have been much taken with the contemporary response (or lack of response) to Freud's *Interpretation of Dreams*. Initially at least, it was quite eclipsed by Flournoy's exploration of Hélène's subliminal dreams.

MULTIPLE PERSONALITY I

At the end of the nineteenth century, there was an epidemic of multiple personality. In a pivotal study, Ian Hacking studied the history of Multiple Personality Disorder, focusing on the various hosts that facilitated it.[63] Hacking argues that at the end of the nineteenth century spiritualism was one of the main hosts for multiple personality, due to the possibility that one of the secondary personalities was in actuality a discarnate entity, or, in other terms, the dead. This transition from spiritualism to multiple personality is very clearly depicted in *From India to the Planet Mars*. While Flournoy rejects the extrapsychic existence of the figures in Hélène's trances, and regards them as intrapsychic, he still regards them as personalities. In this way, the psychologization of mediumship leads to a multiple personality model.[64]

From India to the Planet Mars was the first psychological study of multiple personality that became a best-seller, which played a key role in its dissemination. Further, its dramatic novelistic style presented the prototype for Morton Prince's classic study of multiple personality, *The Dissociation of a Personality*.[65] In this regard, Flournoy's book was stylistically innovative, as it established the genre of the novelistic book-length treat-

---

[62] Ibid, p. 396.

[63] Hacking, "Multiple Personality Disorder and Its Many Hosts," *History of the Human Sciences* 5 (1992): pp. 3–31.

[64] The transition from spiritualism to multiple personality in the American context is well depicted by Michael Kenny in *The Passion of Ansel Bourne: Multiple Personality in American Culture* (Washington: Smithsonian Institution Press, 1986), which, however, omits to take account of the significance of *From India to the Planet Mars*, which provides the crucial link between the spiritualistically inspired investigations of Mrs. Piper and Morton Prince's purely psychological study of Miss Beauchamp.

[65] See especially Ruth Leys, "The Real Miss Beauchamp: Gender and the Subject of Imitation" in *Feminists Theorize the Political*, ed. J. Butler and J. Scott (New York, Routledge, 1992). Leys's analysis of interplay between Prince and Miss Beauchamp, particularly the manner in which she depicts Prince's relegation and objectification of mimesis, in modeling the psychological subject, is very pertinent in relation to the interplay between Flournoy and Hélène Smith.

ment of multiple personality, which has continued to play a crucial role in its cultural dissemination to this day.

THE BRIDE STRIPPED BARE, BY HER BACHELORS EVEN

In "Nouvelles Observations," Flournoy gave a lengthy supplementary account of the subsequent development of her mediumship. He wrote: "It seemed to me certain on the whole that the close reading of *From India* by Hélène influenced the subsequent development of her mediumship."[66] Her Martian and ultra-Martian cycles were followed by Uranian and Lunar cycles, that broadly speaking, had the same structure.

The clamorous reception of the book was not without effects on its heroine. She felt betrayed by Flournoy and particularly incensed at the mockery that she was subject to in some of the press notices.[67] She barred Flournoy from attending her seances. The aftermath of the book led to a bitter and prolonged dispute between Flournoy and Hélène, which ended in a complete rupture. The overriding reason for this was Flournoy's completely counterposed interpretation of her mediumship. In their correspondence, Flournoy addressed his letters to Élise Müller. She usually replied as Hélène Smith. She demanded the royalties for the book. Flournoy eventually gave her half the royalties and donated the other half to the *Archives de Psychologie*, which he founded. Flournoy protested that she was having all the benefits of being both a fee-paying and a nonfee-paying medium.[68]

Her instant celebrity, however, was not without its benefits. Hélène Smith attracted the attention of a wealthy American benefactress whose patronage enabled her to leave her job and devote herself to her calling. For a while she continued to give seances, but she eventually ceased to do them altogether, and increasingly she developed a new orientation and devoted herself to religious paintings. In 1907, Lemaître wrote a study of this new turn, in which he claimed:

> In its essential lines, the current artistic phase of Hélène remains sufficiently comprehensible to our eyes and does not differ appreciably from her other somnambulic productions. . . . This automatic activity is set up by the same process.[69]

[66] Flournoy, "Nouvelles Observations," p. 105, trans. mine.

[67] See Hélène Smith's letter in the *Gazette de Lausanne*, January 8, 1902, in reply to a review, in O. Flournoy, *Théodore et Léopold*, pp. 134–35.

[68] Flournoy to Charles Pospech, March 29, 1902, in O. Flournoy, *Théodore et Léopold*, p. 152.

[69] Lemaître, "Un Nouvelle Cycle Somnambulique de Mlle Smith: Ses peintures religieuses," *Archives de Psychologie* 7 (1907): pp. 66–67, trans. mine.

After her death on June 29, 1929 in Geneva, her paintings were exhibited in Geneva and Paris, and were the subject of a lengthy volume by Walter Deonna, *De la Planète Mars en Terre Sainte: Art et Subconscient. Un médium peintre: Hélène Smith*, which also chronicles the subsequent events in her life. Deonna notes that she dreamed of writing a second volume of *From India to the Planet Mars*, which she would publish herself, written in a wholly other spirit. He claims that the rupture with Flournoy was one of the causes of her new mystical orientation, as she sought to add another coloration to her fantasies to evade his critique. Hélène herself wrote in 1912:

> This man constantly tormented and agitated me. He brought troubling waves in my life. . . . The work of the tableaux would never have been executed if I had remained in Flournoy's entourage, I am persuaded of it. God delivered, precipitating events, opening a new way for me.[70]

Claparède contested Deonna's view of her new turn, stating on the contrary that she always had a penchant for painting, which she was able to pursue due to her newfound financial freedom.[71]

In the aftermath of their involvement, she felt persecuted by Flournoy. After being observed by him for years, she felt that he was spying on her. In 1909, she wrote: "M.F. . . . continues to send me spies. To what end, I don't know. Perhaps he wants to make an article concerning me."[72] Her experiences with Flournoy clearly left a mark. She refused to exhibit, sell, or even let her paintings be photographed, though she did eventually donate them to a museum in Geneva. Her work continued to attract the interest of psychologists and the popular press. In 1927 she wrote:

> I am not someone who loves to exhibit herself. I do not wish at any price to be a subject. I have . . . suffered too much, been too maltreated because of this gift of mediumship, which I did not seek out.[73]

Hélène claimed that she had no need of the control of men, which would be like a profanation, and that in her religious mission she felt only the need of the control of God.

Deonna notes that while she renounced her belief in the reality of her Hindu and Martian existences, she remained convinced that she had been Marie Antoinette, and she remained an adept of spiritualism. She remained unmarried, never meeting the "dreamed of being, the fiancé

---

[70] *De la Planète Mars en Terre Sainte: Art et subconscient. Un médium peintre: Hélène Smith* (Paris: De Boccard, 1932), p. 54, trans. mine.

[71] Claparède, review of *De la Planète Mars en Terre sainte*, *Archives de Psychologie* 23 (1932): p. 376.

[72] *De la Planète Mars en Terre Sainte*, p. 52, trans. mine.

[73] Ibid., p. 56, trans. mine.

of the soul," whom she awaited. Deonna noted that friends and visitors
saw her as a "priestess of the beyond," and that entering her apartment on
the rue Liotard felt like entering a chapel. In 1927, to the great loss of
posterity, she declined the invitation of Charles Richet to write her
memoirs.[74]

DREAMING OF HÉLÈNE

After the publication of *From India to the Planet Mars*, Hélène claimed
that she was the cause of Flournoy's notoriety[75] and the "modest instrument" of his glory.[76] If Flournoy had "made" Hélène Smith, she, nevertheless, would claim that she had made him. Flournoy, no less than
Hélène, was irrevocably marked by their encounter. For Hélène this took
the form of a turning away from anything that resembled her time in
"Flournoy's entourage." On his part, Flournoy never ceased to search,
unsuccessfully, for another Hélène. This very search seemed to suggest
that he was attempting to decipher something about their encounter that
he had missed at the time. He ended "Nouvelles Observations" on a less
than sanguine note. His reflections highlight a phenomena for which Martin Orne would later coin the term "demand characteristics":

> It is not good that a medium be studied for too long by the same investigator,
> because the latter, despite his precautions, inevitably ends by shaping the so
> suggestible subconscious of his subject. . . . In other terms, a sort of ossification
> menaces the medium who knows—or believes—herself to be an object of con-
> tinual surveillance from near and far, puts her little by little in a quasi-
> impossibility to furnish other categories of phenomena than that which she sub-
> consciously imagines to be waited for by him.[77]

From India to the Planet Mars was Flournoy's masterpiece. Never again
would he find such a subject, though he went to great lengths attempting
to do just that.

In 1911, not long after he had finally come to a settlement with Hélène,
Flournoy published his last major work on mediums, which can in part be
read as his response to their embroilment, and as an autocritique.

In March 1898 Flournoy had sent out a questionnaire on mediumship
to the members of the Société d'Etudes Psychiques de Genève, and received seventy-two replies. Ten years later he did a follow-up study.
Flournoy's survey was one of the most detailed qualitative surveys that

[74] Cited in ibid., p. 4.
[75] Hélène Smith, letter to the editor, *Gazette de Lausanne*, January 7, 1902, in O. Flournoy, *Théodore et Léopold*, p. 135.
[76] Hélène Smith to Flournoy, March 4, 1901, ibid., p. 121.
[77] Flournoy, "Nouvelles Observations," p. 116, trans. mine.

had been conducted up till then in psychology. However, he did not get the results he hoped for:

> This was hardly the mine of exceptional cases and marvellous phenomena which I had dreamed of. . . . nothing for example that approaches the beautiful subliminal imagination, creator of languages and myths, which at the same time I saw unfold in the somnambulisms of Mlle Smith.[78]

Flournoy found the replies "perfectly indigestible." However, he found himself morally obliged to his respondents to publish the material. He was faced with the ethical dilemma of how to maintain his critical freedom and respect the rights of the respondents, who were deprived of replying in the volume. As a solution he published the book in two parts: the first containing the verbatim replies, and the second his general reflections. While Flournoy had obtained the permission from each individual to publish their replies, he notes that the practical impossibility of maintaining the anonymity of subjects will continue to be the great obstacle to publications of mediumistic phenomena. These questions still vex psychologists and clinicians today. Flournoy's discussion and attempt to resolve them remains one of the most sophisticated.

Flournoy's survey shows his sensitivity to the problem of using a single case as a paradigm, in marked contrast to Freud and Jung. His scrupulous documenting of a failed experiment that undercuts his thesis shows his integrity. The survey suggested that Hélène Smith was an atypical case and it questioned the theories he had developed from her case. Flournoy had hoped that his study of the development of her mediumship would in turn shed light on psychological development in general: such was the dream of subliminal psychology.

The singularity of the encounter was missed by Flournoy, yet it continued to haunt him. The threat was posed—could his psychology itself be a subconscious subliminal romance, one which equally had to dissimulate its origins? Was his "science" the mirror image of her subliminal romances?

The Unconscious: Structured like Martian?

A dramatic moment ensued, when, faced with the "Hindu" language of Hélène, Flournoy called upon the services of his friend the linguist Ferdinand de Saussure. The linguist Roman Jakobsen was later to describe their collaboration as:

> a beautiful example of collaboration between psychologists and linguists that

---

[78] Flournoy, *Espirits et Médiums: Mélanges de Métapsychique et de psychologie* (Geneva: Kündig, 1911), p. 2, trans. mine.

should be imitated and inspire new researches in the topic of the structural analysis of the delirious, individual manifestations of glossolalia.[79]

Her Martian language attracted the attention of another linguist, Victor Henry, who devoted a whole book to it.[80] In his review of Henry's book, Flournoy noted: "It is very poignant to see a professional linguist consecrate a volume to the analysis of an idiom that does not exist, or at least only exists in the subconscious imagination of a somnambulist."[81]

In his book, Henry argued that the processes that underlay the creation of Martian were the same processes that underlay natural languages. Hence the study of Martian provided the unique opportunity for catching a glimpse into the genesis of languages.

Hélène's linguistic practices continue to attract the attention of linguists today and feature at the forefront of debate in part, but not only on account of the role of Saussure. Marina Yaguello notes that at the turn of the century there was massive outbreak of speaking in tongues, or glossolalia. This has a contemporary parallel in the emergence of the Pentecostalist church, with currently around eight million members, mostly in the United States, which serves as the contemporary host for glossolalia and xenoglossia (speaking in unknown languages). Yaguello notes the significance of Hélène Smith for linguistics as follows:

> Her case is exemplary for two reasons. In the first place, there is the quality of the phenomenon observed. The languages devised by the medium, especially Martian, reach a level of sophistication, consistency and permanence which gives them, in spite of their infantile character, a sufficiently convincing pseudo-linguistic character to have caught the attention of linguists as distinguished as Saussure and V. Henry. This formal perfection is rarely attained by other subjects recorded in history. The second reason has to do with the observer and the quality of his observations. If cases of pathological glossolalia have benefited from the attention of psychiatrists, those involving mediums or members of religious sects have for the most part only been described by believers. It is only recently that scholars with a neutral stance towards the phenomena have begun to study it using the methods of experimental psychology. . . . Flournoy's study, in spite or rather because of the ambiguity of the author's relationship to the medium, remains a model of its kind.[82]

---

[79] Cited by Jean-Jacques Courtine, "Pour Introduire aux glossolalies: Un hommage à Michel de Certeau," *Langages* 91 (1988): p. 5, trans. mine. This special issue shows the paradigmatic role that is still played by Hélène Smith in the study of glossolalia.

[80] Henry, *Le Langage Martien* (Paris: J. Maisonneuve, 1901). For a commentary on Henry's text, see Marina Yaguello, *Lunatic Lovers of Language: Imaginary Languages and Their Inventors*, trans. C. Slater (London: Athlone, 1991).

[81] Flournoy, *Archives de Psychologie* 1 (1901): p. 99, trans. mine.

[82] Yaguello, *Lunatic Lovers of Language*, p. 88. Yaguello presents a detailed discussion of Hélène's Martian, locating it in the context of the invention of imaginary languages. See also

Yaguello notes that crucial linguistic questions arise from Hélène's languages: first, are they, properly speaking, languages, and if so, do they point to a universal linguistic competence, such as Noam Chomsky might claim? She answers the first question, like Flournoy and Henry before her, in the affirmative:

> However poor it is both in structure and vocabulary, Martian does seem to fulfil the double function of language postulated by Benveniste: 1) semiotic: it is a system with identifiable signs; 2) semantic: these signs can be combined in utterances in such a way to produce meanings.[83]

The significance of Saussure's reading of Hélène's "Hindu" is taken up by Tzetan Todorov. He seizes upon Saussure's comments on the genesis of her languages, seeing them as a window onto the genesis of Saussure's own linguistics. Saussure is struck by the remarkable fact that one feature of her "Hindu" language, its absence of the letter "f," exactly duplicates the structure of Sanskrit. Todorov focuses on this episode of the missing f. He writes that Saussure (who for Hélène was the reincarnation of the Hindu "Miousa") is more prepared "to acknowledge the supernatural (transmigration of Mlle. Smith's soul) than to modify his method of investigation—which here touches upon the principle of symbolic functioning."[84]

Todorov claims that Saussure fails to admit the existence of a "logic of symbolism other than that of language." Todorov argues that it is here that Henry's interpretation of the missing "f," surpasses Saussure's. For Henry, her Martian and Sanskritoid productions are subconsciously governed by an injunction to entirely avoid French. Hence as the word "French" begins with the letter "f," she avoids this as much as possible. For Todorov, the significance of this episode lies in the fact that:

> it prefigures in a remarkable way Saussure's relations with symbolic phenomena to the very end of his career . . . his impasses have exemplary value: they anticipate those of a large sector of modern linguistics.[85]

One reviewer of Henry's book put forward a more prosaic alternative interpretation for the missing "f": "I should rather ascribe it to a peculiar paralysis of certain muscles of the lips which may beset her in her abnormal states of consciousness."[86]

Hélène's languages feature prominently in Michel de Certeau's work

---

her appendix "Psychanalyse et linguiste: première rencontre" in the 1983 edition of *Des Indes à la planète Mars.*

[83] Yaguello, *Lunatic Lovers of Language*, p. 95.

[84] Todorov, "Saussure's Semiotics," in *Theories of the Symbol* (London: Blackwell, 1982), p. 259.

[85] Ibid., p. 265.

[86] Fred Corybeare, review of *Le Langage Martien, Hibbert Journal*, July 1903, p. 54.

on glossolalia, for whom she again takes on the role of a paradigm case. For de Certeau, "What utopia is to social space, glossolalia is to oral communication."[87] He notes:

> This fiction of language never ceases to be taken for a language and treated as such. It never ceases to be *compelled* to mean something. It excites an impulse to decrypt and decipher which never wearies and which always supposes the organization of meaning lurking behind the series of sounds.[88]

De Certeau argues that glossolalia has continually been interpreted "as if one must write in the place where it speaks."[89] For de Certeau, such interpretations are marked by a "hermeneutic morality," in which the privileged terms of sense, reality, and work replace those of masks, fiction, play, atopia. He notes however, that there exists a troubling equivocation between glossolalia and its interpretation:

> But the explication, a stranger to the glossolalic saying, is at the same time necessary: a stranger, because in absenting itself of all effective language, this saying abandons to the commentary all the burden of meaning. . . . It implicates already the exteriority of a commentary, strangeness necessary to its proper autonomization.[90]

De Certeau's analysis has been taken up and critically extended recently by Dan Rosenberg, who challenges de Certeau's reading, arguing:

> It is outstandingly clear that the desire operative here was not de Certeau's unfettered desire to speak but rather a desire to (linguistic) structure. . . . The transgressiveness of Smith's seances lay not, as de Certeau contends, in their trajectory out of language and toward pure vocalization but in their repeated competence at producing convincing simulacra of language outside of the legitimating places where language ought to have been.[91]

The issues raised in these linguistic discussions by implication concern not only the interpretation of Hélène's linguistic productions, but also of all her material. As such they pose questions concerning the status of psychology itself and the equivocal interrelation between Hélène's material and Flournoy's psychology—the one designated as fantastic, the other

[87] Michel de Certeau, "Utopies Vocales: Glossolalies," *Traverses* 20 (1980): p. 28, trans. mine.

[88] De Certeau, "Utopies Vocales," p. 30., trans. Dan Rosenberg, in "Linguistic Utopias: Michel de Certeau, Glossolalia and the Martian Language," paper presented to the Theory, Culture and Society Tenth Anniversary Meeting, August 18, 1992.

[89] De Certeau, "Utopies Vocales," p. 30, trans. mine.

[90] Ibid., p. 32., trans. mine. For a study of Hélène Smith's glossolalia in the context of its scene of enunciation, see Mireille Cifali, "Une glossolale et ses savants: Élise Müller alias Hélène Smith," in *La Linguistique Fantastique*, ed. J. Clims (Paris: De Noël, 1985).

[91] Rosenberg, "Linguistic Utopias," p. 6.

sanctioned as "science." The subsequent dispute between Flournoy and Hélène over copyright, authorship, and property, staged this issue in a spectacular fashion.

In his reading of Hélène's languages, Courtine writes:

> To the simple interrogation: "who speaks and to whom?", the glossolalist replies, "It is an Other than me who speaks; and this other is again she/he to whom my speak addresses itself, since it is his/hers."[92]

The mode in which this question of "who speaks" is played out in glossolalia is taken up by Marina Yaguello. She writes:

> What distinguishes the glossolalist from someone speaking an ordinary language is that he or she isn't the person speaking. The relationship of person is missing, there is no I standing at the source of the utterance at the centre of the discourse, no I taking responsibility for the act of utterance and involved by virtue of this in a spatio-temporal continuity. Hélène Smith speaks at the dictation of spirits and extra-terrestrial beings. . . . And yet in glossolalia there certainly is an ego at the centre, but it is a non-linguistic ego, which unlike the I of a language system, the I acting as a "shifter" pronoun in speech, cannot pass from one individual to another. It is outside the social system, and belongs to the speaker, who takes possession of language by this means.[93]

The temptation would clearly be felt to assign another subject to the site of enunciation, to put an end to this troubling equivocation—hence the nomination of multiple personality—which is Flournoy's move. This other speech becomes a site around which another scene becomes nominated, organized and cartographized—the unconscious. However, this annexation restores this speech to the type of intelligibility that it would exceed. Here, the possibility of a psychology that exceeded classical introspective psychology, with its self-transparent locutor at the center, was glimpsed, only for it to be subsumed by the interpretive strategies that would install another subject as the source of this other speech.

In respect to this endless game of commentary on Hélène Smith, Rosenberg aptly comments:

> The example of Hélène Smith indicates that the compulsion to mean, to signify, does not only elide the desire to speak, to vocalize, to articulate. It also elides the desire to language, desire to structure, to invention . . . we thus need to examine our own tendency to put back up the boundaries that Hélène Smith did us the service of breaking down.[94]

[92] J-J. Courtine, "Les Silences de la Voix," *Langages* 91 (1988): p. 9, trans. mine.
[93] Yaguello, *Lunatic Lovers of Language*, p. 96.
[94] Rosenberg, "Linguistic Utopias," p. 7.

LIFE AFTER MARS: FLOURNOY'S DECLINE

In the first two decades of the twentieth century, psychological interest in mediums waned dramatically. While the public interest in mediums was safeguarded by the perennial nature of the question of life after death, the interest of psychologists was not.

The mode in which the psychological study of mediums contributed to its own decline is apparent in Stanley Hall's 1918 article, "A Medium in the Bud."[95] Hall narrates how he was consulted by a young woman of twenty, in an "incipient stage" of mediumship, which included an account of life on Mars. Following Flournoy, he saw her fantasies as an outcome of adolescent developmental processes, a compensation for what was lacking in her environment. In addition, Hall puts forward the following motive for the cultivation of such states. Hall highlights the:

> love of the utter abandon involved in this state. Inhibitions are thrown to the wind. While the normal ego is controlled, the control can let itself go and express the very deepest and most secret things in the soul, often with a frankness that ordinary social conventions would make impossible. Thus there is a sudden freedom from responsibility and sensitive, shrinking, repressed natures, who would above all things dread to shock or violate convention in phrase or manner, are freed from the necessity of even being agreeable or primly proper, which must often become irksome, hedged about as they are by so many senseless taboos. In the trancoidal state these are all removed, for the nonce, from one level of her soul, and she can blurt out things which ordinarily maidenly modesty would never permit her to say or hear. Such tender and delicate girls often feel themselves possessed by some rugged, potent and uncouth male spirit, and delight to swagger in diction and manner, to be blunt, slangy, to uncork and vent elements of conduct for which nothing in normal experience gives such opportunity or such incentive. The girl is thus using new powers and some sense may be the better for it.[96]

Hall's interpretation significantly valorizes the freedom from social constraints and taboos occasioned by the trance, in offering young women opportunity to circumvent traditional gender stereotypes. Hall's essay provided one of the swan songs of the psychological study of mediums. For once the productions of the mediumistic trance are seen as simply the manifest level of latent, repressed sexuality, the specific interest occasioned by them is lost. The study of mediums would then have little specific to recommend it, nor would it shed light in turn on the general patterns of development, as Flournoy dreamed. In 1909, in his "The Con-

[95] Hall, *American Journal of Psychology* 29 (1918): pp. 144–58.
[96] Ibid., p. 154.

fidences of a 'Psychical Researcher'," while expounding the unexplained residuum of metaphysics, James concludes:

> Vast, indeed, and difficult is the inquirer's prospect here, and the most significant data for his purpose will probably be just these dingy little mediumistic facts which the Huxleyan minds of our time find so unworthy of their attention.[97]

However, James's prospectus was not to be, and it was his rival Stanley Hall who provided what could be taken as the epitaph for this epoch in psychology:

> The next generation will be hardly able to believe that prominent men in this way wasted their energies in chasing such a will-of-the-wisp as the veracity of messages or the reality of a post-mortem existence, which they no more prove than dreams of levitation prove that man can hover in the air at will.[98]

The 1909 Congress of Experimental Psychology in Geneva, over which Flournoy presided, was the last at which mediumship featured on the agenda. A whole section was devoted to mediumistic phenomena. Flournoy opened the section by defending its inclusion, which some suspected was a dangerous intrusion of occultism and spiritualism into the discussion. Flournoy claimed that it was no longer possible for scientific psychology to be disinterested in the material phenomena of mediums, such as Eusapia Palladino. Five persons were invited, but only one accepted.[99] From 1900 to 1909, the tide had clearly turned. The mediums were the exemplar of subliminal psychology. With the decline of psychological interest in mediums, subliminal psychology found itself without a subject.

Within psychical research, the paradigm shifted away from the detailed investigation of mediums, with their lack of replicability, to the controlled experimental studies in telepathy under laboratory conditions, predominantly associated with J. B. Rhine.[100]

Geographically speaking, Vienna and Zurich prevailed over Geneva as the leading capitals for the exploration of the unconscious. The ascen-

---

[97] James, "The Confidences of a 'Psychical Researcher,'" in *William James on Psychical Research*, ed. Gardner Murphy and Robert Ballou (London: Chatto and Windus, 1961), p. 325.

[98] Hall, "A Medium in the Bud," p. 154.

[99] *Compte-Rendu du Sixième Congrès internationale de psychologie*, ed. Edouard Claparède (Geneva: Kündig, 1909), p. 827.

[100] The shift in psychical research from the in-depth study of mediums to the laboratory-controlled experiments with card-guessing games, which dominated modern parapsychology, and which ironically reversed Flournoy's intellectual trajectory, is well depicted in S. Mauskopf and M. McVaugh, *The Elusive Science: Origins of Experimental Psychical Research* (Baltimore: Johns Hopkins University Press, 1980).

dance of psychoanalysis has in several respects been seen as responsible for Flournoy's decline. Initially, the paradigm of the hysteric and more critically its particular interpretative school—psychoanalysis—took over. It was claimed that Flournoy failed to comprehend the role of the transference and sexuality, nowhere more so than in his analysis of Hélène Smith. Olivier Flournoy suggests that compared to psychoanalysis, Flournoy's weakness was a reticence toward sexuality.[101] In sum, the psychoanalytic critique was that *From India to the Planet Mars* was not Freud's "Fragment of an Analysis of a Case of Hysteria." Claparède countered this charge by claiming that Flournoy, in seeing Léopold as a "hypnoid formation of essentially psycho-sexual origin" grasped the role of sexuality in hysterical accidents, but dealt with the issue discretely out of a sense of delicacy for Hélène.[102]

At a professional level, Flournoy worked within preexisting institutional structures. His institutional achievements, such as the *Archives de Psychologie* and the psychological laboratory at the University of Geneva, were marked by the open and pluralistic way in which they encompassed and encouraged psychological research, rather than forming his own tightly perimetered school of psychology, in sharp contrast to Freud and Jung.[103] Flournoy's work was marked by an excessive modesty; rather than introduce new and distinctive terminology, Flournoy preferred to use existing terms and simply add a new inflection.

Mireille Cifali states that Freud triumphed over Flournoy because he offered a therapeutic practice.[104] Clearly, not the least of the attractions of psychoanalysis was its provision of a new professional identity and means of acquiring an income. Flournoy, together with Myers and James, felt that a purely clinical approach was an inadequate basis from which to develop a psychology of the personality. Flournoy attempted to establish a comparative psychology based on the in-depth study of lives, rather than a psychotherapy. This agenda was eclipsed in psychology until it was revived by Gordon Allport and, in particular, by Henry Murray, who can be seen as implicitly arguing for a return to Flournoy's agenda.[105]

[101] O. Flournoy, *Théodore et Léopold*, p. 18.

[102] Claparède, "Théodore Flournoy. Sa vie et son oeuvre," p. 63.

[103] On the Freud-Flournoy relation, see Mireille Cifali, "Les chiffres de l'intime," in the 1983 edition of *Des Indes à la planète Mars*; on Flournoy's pivotal role in the Freud-Jung break, see Mireille Cifali, "Le fameux couteau de Lichtenberg," *Le Bloc-Notes de la psychanalyse* 4 (1984): pp. 171–88. Flournoy's influence on Jung was greater and more lasting than Freud's. On their relation, see James Witzing, "Théodore Flournoy: A Friend Indeed," *Journal of Analytical Psychology* 27 (1982): pp. 131–48; and my "A Woman Called Frank," *Spring* 50 (1990): pp. 26–56, which reconstructs the biography of Frank Miller, Flournoy's student who became Jung's key paradigm case.

[104] Cifali, "Théodore Flournoy, la découverte de l'inconscient," p. 127.

[105] Gordon Allport, *The Use of Personal Documents in Psychological Science* (New York:

In the *Archives de Psychologie*, one can graphically see another reason for Flournoy's decline, as the figure of the medium becomes increasingly replaced by that of the child, notably through the early publications of Jean Piaget.[106]

For Flournoy the preeminent tool for psychological exploration was hypnosis, and in *From India to the Planet Mars* he presented one of the most detailed investigations into trance states. After the turn of the century, interest in hypnosis greatly declined. While hypnosis was rehabilitated through the behaviorist methodology of Clark Hull, it was not until the work of Charles Tart and others on "altered states of consciousness,"[107] that the creative potentiality of trance states that so interested Flournoy returned to the psychological agenda, though without reference to his work. Likewise while Flournoy's "play theory" of mediumship antedates the now-fashionable interpretations of hypnotic phenomena in terms of role playing, with Flournoy this led to a dynamic psychology of the subliminal, rather than to a sociobehavioral perspective.

From India to the Planet Mars was one of the classic paradigm cases of multiple personality. In the first two decades of the twentieth century, the reported incidence of multiple personality, together with the interest in dissociative phenomena in general, dramatically declined. The recent revival of Multiple Personality Disorder looks to Janet, rather than Flournoy, as its patron, in line with its psychopathological cast.

HÉLÈNE SMITH: THE PATRON SAINT OF SURREALISM

While Flournoy and Hélène were largely forgotten by psychology, they were regarded as patrons by surrealism. Breton notes, commenting on the heroine of his novel *Nadja*:

> The magic Nadja surrounded herself with was the mind's compensation for the heart's defeat. We see something similar in the case of the celebrated medium Hélène Smith, whose marvellous peregrinations from planet to planet . . . seemed to be aimed mainly at capturing the attentions of Théodore Flournoy, who was caring for her, and whose love she had not managed to win.[108]

Social Science Research Council, 1942); Henry Murray et al., *Explorations in Personality* (New York: Oxford University Press, 1938).

[106] On Flournoy's influence on Piaget through his psychology of religion, see Fernando Vidal, "Jean Piaget and the Liberal Protestant Tradition," in *Psychology in Twentieth-Century Thought and Society*, ed. M. Ash and W. Woodward (Cambridge: Cambridge University Press, 1987).

[107] See Charles Tart, ed., *Altered States of Consciousness*, rev. ed. (New York: Harper-Collins, 1990).

[108] Breton, *Conversations: The Autobiography of Surrealism*, trans. M. Polizzotti (New York: Paragon House, 1993), p. 108.

Throughout *From India to the Planet Mars*, Flournoy never ceases to marvel at the artistic and dramatic powers of Hélène's subconscious creative imagination. On one reading what is left of her romances when shorn of their spiritualistic garb is precisely art. Flournoy was indeed extremely interested in the artistic capabilities that could be released through trance states and he pursued these questions in his report on Magdeleine G., and her somnambulist choreographies.[109] While hypnotized, the untrained Magdeleine performed exquisite dance settings to musical accompaniments, such as by Chopin. The interest that Magdeleine held for Flournoy resided in the fact that the artistic potentiality revealed seemed to transcend her normal capabilities. His descriptions suggest that he was enchanted by her choreographies. Flournoy was interested in the question of whether this hidden creative self might exist in everyone. He argues that hypnosis removed the conscious inhibitions, which enabled the latent creative capacity to emerge. In "The Automatic Message," Breton explicitly acknowledges the debt of surrealism to the explorations of Myers and Flournoy, and credits subliminal psychology as providing one of the conditions of possibility of surrealism. Breton states that Surrealism highlighted "what remained of mediumistic communication once we had freed it from the insane metaphysical implications it otherwise entailed."[110] It was clearly Flournoy who paved the way for this liberation. In "The Automatic Message," Breton clearly states the indebtedness of modern art to mediumship, asking, for instance, "What is Art Nouveau if not an attempt to generalize and adapt mediumistic drawing, painting and sculpture to the art of furniture and decoration?"[111] At a stylistic level, mediums could flagrantly transgress artistic and linguistic conventions, since their productions usually were not presented as artworks. More significant was the utilization of automatic writing and drawing as a means of production.[112] From this perspective, Breton described "the prodigious" Hélène Smith quite simply as "the richest case of all."[113]

Feminists Reclaim the Mediums

Recent feminist historiography has done a great service in opening up a reappraisal of the social and psychological construction of mediumship. Their work has done a great deal in recovering from oblivion many lost heroines. They have depicted the service rendered to the struggle for

---

[109] Flournoy, "Chorégraphie somnambulique; le cas de Magdeleine G.," *Archives de Psychologie* 3 (1904): pp. 357–74.

[110] Breton, *Conversations*, p. 64.

[111] Breton, "The Automatic Message," p. 104.

[112] On this issue, see my "Automatic Writing and the Discovery of the Unconscious."

[113] Breton, "The Automatic Message," p. 102.

women's rights by the spiritualist movement. Alex Owen argues that "Victorian spiritualism was another of the hidden or forgotten factors in women's long struggle for increased effectiveness, status and autonomy."[114] Through these readings a new consensual view of the role of mediumship has recently developed. Ann Braude argues that "Spiritualism's greatest contribution to the crusade for women's rights probably lay in the new role of spirit medium."[115] The accessibility of this new role lay in the congruence between Victorian ideals of "true womanhood" and the qualities required for mediumship. Vieda Skultans claims that:

> Victorian stereotypes of femininity bear a remarkable resemblance to the ideal medium. The following adjectives can equally well describe the ideal woman as the ideal medium: unsophisticated, innocent, passive, young, tender, feeling, intuitive and so on.[116]

Ann Braude argues:

> The very qualities that rendered women incompetent when judged against norms for masculine behaviour rendered them capable of mediumship. Mediumship allowed women to discard limitations on women's roles without questioning accepted ideas about women's nature.[117]

Similarly, Judith Walkowitz suggests that the value of the seance was that it allowed women "to engage in a subtle subversion—but not repudiation —of the 'separate sphere' construction of true womanhood."[118] The value of mediumship is seen here in its provision of a specific social setting, the seance, that permitted transgressive behaviors. Alex Owen claims that:

> within the seance, and in the name of spirit possession, women openly and flagrantly transgressed gender norms. Female mediums, with the approval of those present, often assumed a male persona which was at total odds with the Victorian Idea of respectable womanhood. Whilst male mediums were also known to assume a female spirit voice or personality, their seances did not involve the dramatic and theatrical representations for which the women became famous.[119]

[114] Alex Owen, *The Darkened Room: Women, Power and Spiritualism in Late Victorian England* (London: Virago, 1989), introduction.

[115] Ann Braude, *Radical Spirits: Spiritualism and Women's Rights in Nineteenth-Century America* (Boston: Beacon Press, 1989), p. 82.

[116] Vieda Skultans, "Mediums, Controls and Eminent Men" in *Women's Religious Experience*, ed. Pat Holden (London: Croom Helm, 1983), p. 23.

[117] Braude, *Radical Spirits*, p. 83.

[118] Judith Walkowitz, "Science and Seance: Transgressions of Gender and Genre in Late Victorian London," *Representations* 22 (1988): p. 9.

[119] Owen, *The Darkened Room*, p. 11.

This emphasis on the transgression of gender roles leads to a highlighting of the role of sexuality in the seances. Janet Oppenheim writes:

> There may also have been a potent element of sensual enjoyment, possibly subconscious, that enhances the seances. Without exaggerating the extent of sexual repression in Victorian society, one can surmise that the holding of hands and the caressing of spirit forms might have been stimulating not only to the sitters, but also to the young women whose emerging sexuality was denied natural means of expression.[120]

An implicit Freudian teleology organizes such readings: beneath the manifest level of a concern with the other world lies the latent level of repressed sexuality, which psychoanalysis would eventually unmask. This narrative provides an account for the demise of mediumship: clearly, when sexuality comes out of the darkened room the subterfuge of invoking departed spirits in order to hold hands is no longer required. However, there is a problem in this approach: at times it fails to adequately take into account the specificity of the practices involved, in particular the phenomena of trance states. Significantly, the feminists have concentrated upon the role of mediums in the spiritualist movement, and so far not dealt at length with such cases as that of Hélène Smith, where the study of mediumship itself gave rise to a psychology. For something different begins to emerge when the mediums are turned to not only to mediate the dead, but to mediate a new psychology. The trance takes on another form. Janet perceptively notes that the psychological study of mediums itself had a profound effect on the spiritualists. He notes: "Despite their affected indifference, the spiritists have submitted to the influence of the psychological researches and have been profoundly changed."[121] More critically, such "historical" readings, which present a silent recapitulation of Stanley Hall's reading of the social significance of mediumship, fail to see that they themselves arose at a particular historical juncture, at the close of psychology's fascination with the mediums.

Multiple Personality, Channeling and Past Lives: Three Cases of Déjà Vu

While Flournoy's work became completely forgotten after his death, psychology today ironically finds itself grappling with many of the issues that were Flournoy's prime concerns. This is nowhere more apparent than in three contemporary movements: multiple personality disorder, channel-

---

[120] Janet Oppenheim, *The Other World. Spiritualism and Psychical Research in England, 1850–1914* (Cambridge: Cambridge University Press, 1988), p. 21.

[121] Janet, "Le Spiritisme Contemporain," p. 427, trans. mine.

ing and past-life regression therapy. Significantly, we find Hélène Smith's cycles forming the ghostly template of these movements.

Multiple Personality II

Recent years have seen the rise of a massive epidemic of Multiple Personality Disorder, largely in North America. This has taken place on a far larger scale than its nineteenth-century predecessor, with advocates claiming that up to one in ten of the population is in fact a "multiple." This clinician-launched epidemic provides a capital lesson in how not to read history, as syndromes are selectively revived and the same errors amnesiacally repeated, but this time on a far larger scale. As Ian Hacking puts it, in the late twentieth century child abuse came to play the role of the host for multiple personality, and it was this that led to its current epidemic explosion.[122] As two recent advocates of MPD, as it is called, put it:

> The new paradigm of MPD states that it is a complex, chronic form of developmental posttraumatic dissociative disorder, primarily related to severe, repetitive childhood abuse or trauma, usually beginning before the age of five. In MPD, it is thought that dissociative defenses are used to protect the child from the full psychological impact of severe trauma, usually extreme repetitive child abuse. Under the pressure of developmental factors, secondary structuring and personification by the child of the traumatically induced dissociated states of consciousness leads to development of multiple "personalities."[123]

Aspects of Flournoy's work have been (cryptomnesically?) rediscovered —such as the "protector personalities" and the "inner self helpers"— which mirror Flournoy's descriptions of teleological automatisms.[124]

A critical new development took place when MPD began increasingly to be seen as resulting from Satanic Ritual Abuse. The "memories" recovered, usually under hypnosis, of Satanic Ritual Abuse led therapists to believe in the veracity of the accounts and to argue that such cults truly exist.[125] At the same time, one finds a rash of accounts of UFO abductions, again usually solicited under hypnosis. For Flournoy no doubt the

[122] Hacking, "Multiple Personality Disorder and Its Many Hosts." On the current multiple personality epidemic, see especially Mikkel Borch-Jacobsen, "Pour introduire la personnalite multiple," in *Importance de l'hypnose*, ed. Isabelle Stengers (Paris: Les Empêcheurs de penser en rond, 1993).

[123] R. Loewenstein and D. Ross, "Multiple Personality and Psychoanalysis: An Introduction," *Psychoanalytic Inquiry* 12 (1992): p. 7.

[124] See Frank Putnam, *Diagnosis and Treatment of Multiple Personality Disorder* (New York: Guildford Press, 1989), pp. 109–10.

[125] See especially Sherrill Mulhern, "Satanism and Psychotherapy: A Rumour in Search of an Inquisition," in Richardson, Best, and Bromley ed., *The Satanism Scare* (New York: Social Institutions and Social Change Series, 1991).

Satanic rumor and its extraterrestrial counterpart would be seem akin to Hélène's romances—the subliminal elaboration of cryptomnesias.

Channeling: Léopold's Revenge?

In the twentieth century, psychology and the mediums largely went their separate ways. The spiritualist churches continued to be the host for traditional mediumship, and those that sought to contact the dead. However, recent times have seen a remarkable return of mediums, now rebaptized as "channelers." The host responsible for this has been the New Age movement. The mode in which the messages are conveyed remains remarkably the same as in nineteenth-century mediumship—automatic writing, trance speech, inner dictation, etc. A critical shift in emphasis has taken place, however, concerning the nature of the disembodied entities. Now the entities that communicate are usually taken as spiritual beings, as opposed to the deceased. A fair sprinkling of extraterrestrials completes the population clamoring to get their messages across. Thus, while in the context of nineteenth-century mediumship Hélène Smith was somewhat atypical—as Flournoy found out through his survey—her case takes on a surprising exemplarity when set against the exploits of contemporary channelers.

Now, as then, trance states played a crucial role. Jane Roberts, the channeler for the bestselling *Seth* books, describes "becoming Seth" in a manner that evokes Hélène "becoming Léopold":

> Each time Seth spoke, I was in trance, and it was Seth who smiled out at students through my opened eyes. . . . I "turned into Seth" time and time again, taking off my mental clothes and exchanging them for psychological Olympian garb; Olympian only in that Seth displays a superabundance of energy, compassion, wisdom, and exuberance.[126]

In the channelled literature, the entities are invariably wise figures who have come to aid struggling humans. The descriptions of the channeled entities bear a close resemblance to Flournoy's description of the teleological automatism: the helpful, protective, and guiding figure who is the personification of wisdom and knowledge. From Flournoy's perspective, one could typify channeling as the cultivation of teleological automatisms. Flournoy's text still forms the most devastating skeptical psychological paradigm against the insistence of the channelers that their messages stem from outside their psyches. After Hélène, Flournoy was

---

[126] Jane Roberts, *Conversations with Seth*, vol. 1, ed. Susan Watkins (Englewood Cliffs, N.J.: Prentice-Hall, 1980), p. 1

disappointed not to find similar phenomena evinced by other mediums. Perhaps late twentieth-century California would have been a better stomping ground for him.

How does one account for the different profiles of late nineteenth-century mediumship and late twentieth-century channeling? Nineteenth-century spiritualism arose out of the erosion of Christianity through the rise of secularization and the concomitant concern for personal immortality and the postmortem survival of the soul.[127] In the current new age, by contrast, personal survival is less of an issue; it has been replaced by the quest for the transcendence of Western culture, and the search for spiritual guidance through alternate philosophies and cultures.[128] The different nature of these respective hosts in part elucidates the different configurations of the trance.

The concurrent reemergence of multiple personality and mediumship under the guise of channeling presents us with a recapitulation of precisely the issue of the differential interpretation of trance states that preoccupied Flournoy. The differential traits of channeling and MPD broadly replicate those of their nineteenth-century precursors.[129]

In channeling, the trance states are deliberately cultivated. Hence while MPD has been an epidemic launched by clinicians, channeling has been launched by the channelers themselves. Channelers tend to access their "sources" in prescribed sessions, without the fugue states and amnesias that are taken to characterize MPD. Channelers insist on what Breton termed the "exogeneity of the dictating principle." Most critically, while MPD is regarded as a pathology, channeling, in its circles, is a socially sanctioned activity that is taken as promoting spiritual well-being. Dureen Hughes notes that: "Trance-channeling is best described as a personal-growth or developmental activity," which she argues can be seen as representing the quest for a personalized, revealed religion.[130]

---

[127] See especially J. P. Williams, "The Making of Victorian Psychical Research: An Intellectual Elite's Approach to the Spiritual World," Ph.D thesis, Cambridge University, 1984. See also John Cerullo, *The Secularization of the Soul: Psychical Research in Modern Britain* (Philadelphia: Institute for the Study of Human Issues, 1982); and Oppenheim, *The Other World*.

[128] For a characterization of the current new age that establishes its linkage with the new age at the end of the nineteenth century, see Martin Green, *Prophets of a New Age: The Politics of Hope in 1800, 1900 and 2000* (New York: Scribner, 1992).

[129] See Dureen Hughes, "Differences between Trance Channeling and Multiple Personality Disorder," *Journal of Transpersonal Psychology* 24 (1992): pp. 181–92.

[130] Hughes, "Blending with an Other: An Analysis of Trance-Channeling in the United States," *Ethos* 19 (1991): pp. 161–84. See also Jon Klimo, *Channeling: Investigations on Receiving Information from Paranormal Sources* (Los Angeles: Tarcher, 1987).

Marie Antionettes, or Past-Life Regression Therapy

Recent years have also seen an astonishing rise in past-life regression therapy, which in most instances resembles a curious grafting of the notion of metempsychosis onto an early Breuer-Freud model of trauma and catharsis. The personalities that emerge, often under the influence of hypnosis, are claimed to stem from previous incarnations of the subject. Roger Woolger, a contemporary champion of past-life regression therapy, notes that Flournoy:

> established a skeptical paradigm, namely cryptoamnesia [*sic*], which remains to this day one of the positivist's most devastating weapons in dismissing the claim that past life memories are in fact derived from historical events unknown to the subject.[131]

It is strange to hear Flournoy described as a positivist! Woolger notes that he "naturally" entertains the notion of cryptomnesia on those "rare" occasions when someone presents a past life as a well-known historical personage. Even in these cases, Woolger notes that he makes no attempt to discount it via research, as the therapeutic value of such "reminiscences" are what is claimed to be important. Clearly, Flournoy's attempt to provide a dynamic explanation of such fantasies—in terms of their compensatory value, etc.—is not taken into account.

REDISCOVERING THE UNCONSCIOUS

The subliminal psychology that Flournoy established fell into oblivion in the early decades of the twentieth century, and the subjects that he had fought so hard to place on the mainstream psychological agenda returned to the fringe. Is it going too far to say, that with the rise of these epidemic movements, we see some of the unfortunate consequences of this?

If this is indeed the case, then the study of the history of psychology—the questioning of the standards of legitimation by which particular psychologies became regnant, rescripting history in the process, while others are relegated to psychology's "unconscious"—the depiction of how psychology constructs its fabulous genesis, its subliminal romances—is of critical importance to today's psychological agenda.

It was Ellenberger who initially rescued Flournoy from oblivion in *The Discovery of the Unconscious*. It is appropriate to leave the final words to him:

> Flournoy was a great explorer of the mythopoetic unconscious, particularly in his book *From India to the Planet Mars*. . . . Today, we seldom hear of the

---

[131] Woolger, *Other Lives, Other Selves: A Jungian Psychotherapist Discovers Past Lives* (New York: Doubleday/Wellingborough, U.K.: Crucible, 1987), p. 64.

mythopoetic unconscious. What psychoanalysts call fantasies represent a minute part of mythopoetic manifestations. We have lost sight of the importance of this terrible power—a power that fathered epidemics of demonism, collective psychoses among witches, revelations of spiritualists, the so-called reincarnations of mediums, automatic writing, the mirages that lured generations of hypnotists, and the profuse literature of the subliminal imagination. . . . unfortunately neither Freud nor Jung became aware of the role of the mythopoetic unconscious. [132]

[132] "Freud in Perspective: A Conversation with Henri F. Ellenberger," *Psychology Today*, March 1973, p. 56. For an account of Ellenberger's work and the current historical research in this vein, see Mark Micale, "Henri F. Ellenberger and the Origins of European Psychiatric Historiography," and his bibliographic essay in *Beyond the Unconscious*.

From India to the Planet Mars

Preface

THE DOUBLE TITLE of this work indicates its mixed and deficient nature. At the outset, it should have been a *Study of a Case of Somnambulism*, which is to say, a short monograph aiming solely at accuracy and limited to some natural occurrences of interest to psychologists or physiologists. But circumstances have caused it to be otherwise. Certain local disputes, the evident impossibility of confining to specialists alone the knowledge of a case to which the curiosity of a more extended public already pertained, and even further considerations have made me stray from my purely scientific objective so as to aim my study at popularization. If I had only opted candidly for that and immediately renounced all rigor of method! If I had made it my task to extract from a complex case, passing without stopping *From India to the Planet Mars* and to other matters just as unforeseen, all that it contained of anecdotal interest, of moral considerations, of historical comparisons, and of literary possibilities! But I would not have known how to do it. Divided and undecided, I have remained the slave of opposing directions between which it was necessary to choose. I have tried to keep two pots on the boil, and one knows what comes from that!

Such is the origin of this book, of a length disproportionate to the importance of its contents. Too bristling with technical terms and crude interpretations meaning nothing to ordinary people, too filled with elementary and banal explanations to deserve the attention of professionals, it neither has the form required by the former, nor the grounding which the latter are in their right to demand. Nevertheless, I publish it—as an example not to be followed—so as not to have to think about it any longer and consoling myself with the fact that afterwards no one shall be compelled to buy it or to read it.

This being said to ease my conscience as an author, the much sweeter duty remains for me of expressing my acknowledgment of those who have helped me with my task.

I must mention first and foremost my excellent colleague, Professor Auguste Lemaître, whose name I am almost obliged to cite next to my own at the head of this study, so much is it in various ways a product of our mutual collaboration. M. Lemaître, who has made me come to know the remarkable medium whose phenomena fill the following pages, has observed and followed her for nearly six years, with an attentiveness equal to my own. He has let me profit without restriction, not only from his notes and papers, but, and this is something more precious still, from his personal impressions as a sagacious observer and penetrating psychologist.[1] He also offered to read the majority of the proofs for this book; however, my sluggishness or my stubbornness having not always heeded his corrections, one must in no way hold him responsible for errors of orthography or style that still impair my prose. As regards ideas, however, despite a frequent exchange of points of view, we have not ended up agreeing on all points of detail (which is in no way surprising in these matters) though we hardly differ, I should think, on the general way in which to understand and interpret the present case. So it is good to say it once and for all, for the benefit of the circle or *spiritist* friends of the medium, in the allusions I have managed to make here and there, that M. Lemaître is completely exonerated.

M. E. Demole, Doctor of Science, the numismatic scholar and editor of the *Revue suisse de Photographie* who attended many of our seances, has had the kindness to take a significant number of photographs of poses and of somnambulistic scenes which the person in question unfortunately has not allowed to be published due to questions of reservation and modesty, and to which we could only bow. M. C. Roch has agreed to be in charge of keeping the records at most of our meetings. I owe to the extreme kindness of Prof. Cuendet, Vice President of the Société d'Etudes Psychiques de Genève, the communication of several documents and observations showing the sign of perfect common sense. Despite the inevitable difference of our points of view, the relations I have had with him have always been marked by the most candid cordiality. My brother M. E. Flournoy has done me great service by his wide-ranging bibliographical research. Numerous other people, I regret I cannot name them all here, have given me useful information about the events to which I could not personally be a witness.

In the study of the Arab and Hindu data which come into question in chapter 8, I have had recourse to the illumination of several orientalists in our country. These are: M. Léop. Favre and Prof. Luc. Gautier of Geneva, M. A. Glardon, a former missionary in India and honorary member of the Society for Psychical Research in London, at Tour-de-Peilz (Vaud); and my distinguished colleagues at the University of Geneva, MM. E. Montet, Professor of Arabic, P. Oltramare, Professor of History

---

[1] M. Lemaître has published on this case in the *Annales des Sciences psychiques* of Dr. Dariex (vol. 7 [1897], pp. 65, 181), two articles to which I often find occasion to direct the reader. These articles by M. Lemaître constitute, along with my paper on the Martian language for the Société de Physique et d'Histoire naturelle de Genève (6 April 1899; *Archives des Sciences Physiques et Naturelles* 8, p. 90), all that has been published up to now on the present case.

of Religions, and F. de Saussure, Professor of Sanskrit. Through the agency of these gentlemen, I have also obtained the opinions of two eminent foreign Indianists, MM. A. Barth in Paris and C. Michel in Liege. Would that all these scholars will accept this expression of gratitude and pardon me that I have taken the liberty of quoting various passages from their letters that seemed to me to throw an instructive light on disputed points. In particular I must dearly thank M. de Saussure for the patience and the inextinguishable kindness he has brought to the examination of our "Hindu" texts.

It is finally and above all to the medium herself, to Mlle. Hélène Smith, the heroine of this book, that I most heartily need to express my acknowledgment—and that of the reader—for the permission to print which she has granted to this volume. For it is not superfluous to attach importance to the fact that I here find myself in the presence of a delicate problem of professional deontology. Medical doctors find no hesitation in publishing in their specialist journals, apart from proper names, the interesting cases that they encounter in the course of their hospital practice or through their private clientele; it is an accepted fact that this right of scientific propriety belongs to them in addition to (and sometimes instead of) their honorarium, and the general public is not disturbed by it. Likewise, scientists who work with *paid* subjects take themselves to be the sole proprietors of the data which they are able to collect, and every scope is provided for them to publish without regard to the preferences of the individuals from whom the data originate. But this is not at all the case for a poor psychologist working with people who are not ill, who present their strange phenomena out of pure good will, and of whom the said phenomena are so striking, so admired by a large audience, that it would only be a question of publishing the smallest fragment before it was quickly known and the subject described easily recognized by many of the readers. How to act in such a case? Does one have the right, vis-à-vis science and truth, to be completely disinterested in the instructive matters to which one bears witness, and to lock oneself up in prudent silence about the facts, whereas curious onlookers have no scruples about having and transmitting opinions that are much more crude and therefore ill-informed? Does one have the right, vis-à-vis individuals, to hand over to the general public, and in a light which is inevitably not that to which they were accustomed, facts hitherto confined to a limited circle of friends and acquaintances? These are most embarassing questions. So, awaiting that common practice should come to follow exact rules on this point, I have stayed with the simplest option, which consists in subjecting my manuscript or my proofs to the medium herself and only to print with her consent.

It is obvious that I would not have dreamt of such a project with just anybody. For, on the one hand, it would be out of the question for me to give up any of my freedom insofar as thinking and writing in accordance with my ideas; but how far are there, on the other hand, mediums who would accept to see their phenomena put on display and explained in a fairly scientific manner, that is to say very differently from the way that generally prevails in the spiritist settings where their capabilities are developed? In this particular case, fortunately, the difficulty seems smaller to me thanks to the elevated and distinguished character of the medium with which I was dealing. Mlle Smith, in fact, seemed to me to be a remarkably intelligent person and highly gifted, far above ordinary prejudices, very broad-minded, independent in thought, and consequently able to consent, through the simple love of truth and scientific progress, to the fact that a psychological study was made of her capacity as a medium with the risk of reaching results being in little conformity with her personal impressions and the opinion of her milieu.

My hopes have not been disappointed. Indeed, Mlle. Smith did express, on more than one occasion, a certain astonishment at my way of interpreting the most remarkable phenomena of her capacity as a medium; she is far from being in agreement with my conclusions; she even severely attacks my methods of analysis, and she reckons that I often "pervert" the facts due to my desire to bring them into line with my basic explanations as a prosaic psychologist; in brief, her judgments are on the whole and on crucial points in striking opposition to mine. That was to be expected. But, and this is the fact that I want to stress, she in no way took advantage of these inevitable differences of appreciation in order to impede in the slightest way my study and try to restrain my liberty. Even in the cases where our disagreements became most sensitive to her, she testified to a scientific tolerance, an elevation of point of view, and I would say a self-sacrifice, which I certainly do not often encounter. She has thus made this work not only possible but relatively easy, for which I must express to her my most sincere and heartfelt thanks.

A further word on my rare citation of authors. The considerable literature concerning hypnotism and psychopathology, not to speak of ordinary psychology or the history of spiritism or occult sciences, would easily have supplied me with numerous comparisons regarding a case touching on all these areas, and I could have accumulated at the bottom of these pages, without going beyond my subject, references to several hundred different works or articles. I preferred to deprive myself of this pleasure—or save myself this trouble!—so as not to make a volume already too large even heavier; and so I have limited myself to some bibliographical pointers that occured to me of their own accord through memory. There are, however, some theories pertaining to other partly coinciding areas, which I must recall. For without perhaps always citing them explicitly, I have constantly borrowed their forms of expression, their views, and their metaphors which, by the way, have now entered more or less into the public domain to the point where it would be difficult to manage practically without them. I particularly want to mention *mental disaggregation* of M. P. Janet, the *double-ego* of M. Dessoir, the *hypnoid states* of MM. Breuer and Freud, and above all the *subliminal consciousness* of M. Myers.[2] I could in no way present these theories here nor discuss them in their context and with regard to their respective value; the last in particular, that of M. Myers, so much surpasses the level of ordinary scientific conceptions by flying high and at a pace which at times reaches the mysticism of true metaphysics (which I far from blame him), that one cannot dream of appreciating it on the basis of an individual case, something which I would moreover be most embarrassed to do. But I will at least name these theories in this preface, in recognition of all that I owe them in terms of valuable suggestions and convenient formulations.

Florissant, near Geneva, November 1899

P.S. Although I attach little importance to nominal definitions—too little no doubt, for I think I have often lacked consistency and fixity in my vocabulary—it does not seem pointless for me to provide the nonspecialist reader with brief indications concerning some terms which frequently recur under my pen.

The word *medium* is applied in the spiritist milieu to any individual supposed to be able to serve as an intermediary between the living and spirits of the dead or others. Since it is an inconvenience in an exposition of scientific facts to employ a terminology implying disputable doctrinal affirmation, English and American psychologists, being practical, liberally substitute for the word *medium* that of *automatist*, which does not prejudge anything and simply designates individuals presenting the phenomena of automatism—that is to say which are involuntary and often unknown to the subject, though marked by intelligence—whereas the spiritists see an interference by disincarnate spirits (significant dreams, veridical hallucinations, mechanical writing, dictation through the table, etc.). Awaiting that *automatist* becomes acceptable in French, I have retained the term *medium*, but abstracting it from its etymological sense and any spiritist hypothesis, as a convenient word to designate individuals presenting the said phenomena whatever else be the true explanation of these latter.

---

[2] P. Janet, *L'Automatisme psychologique* (Paris, 1889). *Etat mental des hystériques*, etc. M. Dessoir, *Das Doppel-Ich* (Berlin, 1890). Breuer und Freud, *Studien uber Hysterie* (Vienna, 1895). F.W.H. Myers, "The Subliminal Consciousness," *Proceedings of the Society for Psychical Research* 7, p. 298, and the following volumes.

To the word *medium* is linked *medianimistic* (*médianimique*), *medi-animism* (*médianimisme*), which suggest even more strongly this idea of intermediary souls (*media anima*) having the capacity for entering into a rapport with inhabitants of another world; and *mediumnity* (*médiumnité*), *mediumnism* (*médiumnisme*), etc., which conserve precisely through their *n* an etymological vestige of this very doctrine. It seemed preferable to me, since I took the word *medium* stripping it of its dogmatic sense, to form directly (which is to say without the introduction of this awkward *n* with spiritist undertones) the derivatives *mediumist* (*médiumique*), *mediumity* (*médiumité*), etc., following the example of the Germans who already use *Mediumität*. This does not exclude elsewhere the occasional use of *medianimistic*, *mediumnity*, etc., when one has to evoke particularly the memory of the spiritist theories.

The words *subliminal* (*sub limen*; *under der Schwelle*; under the threshold), and *subconscious* or *unconscious* are practically synonymous and designate phenomena and processes that one has some reason to believe are conscious even though they are unknown to the subject, since they take place so to speak below the level of its ordinary consciousness. The question, of course, remains open to knowledge, if and up to what point, in each particular case, these hidden processes are really accompanied by consciousness, or whether they go back to the pure mechanism of "unconscious cerebration," in which case the expression "subliminal consciousness" can no longer be applied but metaphorically, which is, however, no reason to banish it.

The adjective *oneiric* (from the Greek *oneiron*, dream) is actually acceptable in French; perhaps it is regrettable that the word "dreamy," being less scholarly but clearer and which has been used at times in the past, did not prevail.

Finally, by *cryptomnesia* I understand the fact that certain forgotten memories reappear without being recognized by the subject, who believes to see in them something new. In the communications or messages supplied by the mediums, the first question (but not the only one) that always crops up is knowing if, at the point where the spirits make the disincarnate or some other supernatural cause interfere, one is not simply dealing with cryptomnesia, with latent memories of the medium that resurface, in an at times very disfigured form through the work of subliminal imagination or reasoning, such as it happens so often in our ordinary dreams.

The square brackets [ ] enclose my personal interspersed remarks within other citations or contexts.

Translated by Michael Münchow

CHAPTER ONE

Introduction

IN THE MONTH of December, 1894, I was invited by M. Aug. Lemaître, Professor of the College of Geneva, to attend some seances of a non-professional medium, receiving no compensation for her services, and of whose extraordinary gifts and apparently supernormal faculties I had frequently heard.

Having gladly accepted the invitation of my worthy colleague, I found the medium in question, whom I shall call Mlle. Hélène Smith, to be a beautiful woman about thirty years of age, tall, vigorous, of a fresh, healthy complexion, with hair and eyes almost black, of an open and intelligent countenance, which at once invoked sympathy. She evinced nothing of the emaciated or tragic aspect which one habitually ascribes to the sibyls of tradition, but wore an air of health, of physical and mental vigor, very pleasant to behold, and which, by-the-way, is not often encountered in those who are good mediums.

The number of those invited to take part in the seance being complete, we seated ourselves in a circle, with our hands resting upon the traditional round table of spiritistic circles. Mlle. Smith—who possesses a triple mediumship: visual, auditive, and typtological[1]—began, in the most natural manner, to describe the various apparitions which passed before her eyes in the partially darkened room. Suddenly she stops and listens; she hears a name spoken in her ear, which she repeats to us with astonishment; then brief sentences, the words of which are spelled out by raps on the table, explain the meaning of the vision. Speaking for myself alone (there were three of us to divide the honor of the seance), I was greatly surprised to recognize in scenes which passed before my eyes events which had transpired in my own family prior to my birth. Whence could the medium, whom I had never met before, have derived the knowledge of events belonging to a remote past, of a private nature, and utterly unknown to any living person?

The astounding powers of Mrs. Piper, the famous Boston medium, whose wonderful intuition reads the latent memories of her visitors like an open book, recurred to my mind, and I went out from that seance with renewed hope of finding myself some day face to face with the "supernormal"—a true and genuine supernormal—telepathy, clairvoy-

[1] *I.e.*, Spirit-rapping—the faculty of obtaining responses by means of raps upon a table.

ance, spiritistic manifestations, it matters not by what name it be called, provided only that it be wholly out of the ordinary, and that it succeed in utterly demolishing the entire framework of established present-day science.

I was able at this time to obtain general information only concerning the past of Mlle. Smith, but it was all of a character favorable to her, and has since been fully confirmed.

Of modest bearing and an irreproachable moral character, she has for years earned an honorable living as an employee of a commercial house, in which her industry, her perseverance, and her high character have combined to secure her a very responsible and important position.

Some three years prior to the date of my introduction to her she had been initiated into a spiritistic group, where her remarkable psychic powers almost immediately manifested themselves; and she then became a member of various other spiritistic circles. From its commencement her mediumship manifested the complex type to which I have already alluded, and from which it has never deviated. Visions in a waking state, accompanied by typtological dictation and auditive hallucinations, alternately appeared. From the point of view of their content these messages had generally a bearing on past events usually unknown to the persons present, but which were always verified by referring to biographical dictionaries or to the traditions of the families interested. To these phenomena of retrocognition or of hypermnesia were joined occasionally, according to the environment, moral exhortations, communicated through the table, more frequently in poetry than in prose, addressed to the sitters; medical consultations, accompanied by prescriptions generally appropriate; communications from parents or friends recently deceased; or, finally, revelations as piquant as they were unverifiable concening the *antériorités* (that is, the previous existences) of the sitters, almost all of whom, being profound believers in spiritism, would not have been at all surprised to learn that they were the reincarnations respectively of Coligny, of Vergniaud, of the Princess Lamballe, or of other notable personages. It is necessary, finally, to add that all these messages seemed to be more or less bound up with the mysterious presence of a "spirit" answering to the name of Léopold, who assumed to be the guide and protector of the medium.

I at once undertook to improve my acquaintance with Hélène Smith. She freely consented to give seances for my benefit, alternating with a series which she was giving M. Lemaître, and another for the benefit of Prof. Cuendet, vice-president of the Geneva Society (spiritistic) for Psychic Studies, all of which I was permitted to attend. In this way I have been able to be present at the greater part of Hélène's seances during the past five years. The personal observations that I have thus been able to make, reinforced by notes on sittings which I was unable to attend, kindly furnished me by MM. Lemaître and Cuendet, form the basis of the study which follows; to which must be added, however, certain letters of Mlle. Smith, as well as the numerous and very interesting conversations I have held with her either immediately preceding or following her seances, or at her home, where I also have had the advantage of being able to talk with her mother. Finally, various documents and accessory information, which will be cited in their respective time and place, have also been of assistance in enabling me partially to elucidate certain obscure points. Notwithstanding all these sources of information, however, I am still very far from being able to disentangle and satisfactorily explain the complex phenomena which constitute Hélène's mediumship.

Dating from the period at which I made the acquaintance of Mlle. Smith (*i.e.*, from the winter of 1894–95), while most of her spiritistic communications have continued to present the same character as to form and content as before, a double and very important modification in her mediumship has been observed.

1. As to their psychological form.—While up to that time Hélène had experienced partial and limited automatisms only—visual, auditive, typtomotor hallucinations—compatible with the preservation to a certain extent of the waking state, and not involving noticeable loss of memory, from that time and with increasing frequency she has been subject to an entire loss of consciousness and a failure to retain, on returning to her normal state, any recollection of what has transpired during the seance. In physiological terms, the hemisomnambulism without amnesia, which had been her stopping-point up to that time, and which the sitters mistook for the ordinary waking state, was now transformed into total somnambulism with consecutive amnesia.

In spiritistic parlance, Mlle. Smith now became completely entranced, and having formerly been an ordinary visual and auditive medium, she now advanced to the higher plane of an "incarnating medium."

I fear that this change must in a great measure be attributed to my influence, since it followed almost immediately upon my introduction to Hélène's seances. Or, even if the total somnambulism would have inevitably been eventually developed by virtue of an organic predisposition and of a tendency favorable to hypnoid states, it is nevertheless probable that I aided in hastening its appearance by my presence as well as by a few experiments which I permitted myself to make upon Hélène.

As is well known, mediums are usually surrounded by a halo of veneration, which prevents any one from touching them during their trances The idea would never occur to any ordinary frequenter of spiritistic circles to endeavor to ascertain the condition of the medium's sensory and motor functions by feeling her hands, pinching the flesh, or pricking the skin with a pin. Silence and immobility are the strict rule, in order not to hinder the spontaneous production of the phenomena, and a few questions or brief observations on the receipt of a message is all that is permissible by way of conversation, and no one therefore would, under ordinary circumstances, dare to attempt any manipulation of the medium. Mlle. Smith had always been surrounded by this respectful consideration, and during the first three seances I conformed myself strictly to the passive and purely contemplative attitude of the other sitters. But at the fourth sitting my discretion vanished. I could not resist a strong desire to ascertain the physiological condition of the charming seeress, and I made some vigorous elementary experiments upon her hands, which lay temptingly spread out opposite me on the table. These experiments, which I renewed and followed up at the succeeding seance (February 3, 1895), demonstrated that there is present in Mlle. Smith, *during her visions*, a large and varied assortment of sensory and motor disturbances which had hitherto escaped the notice of the sitters, and which are thoroughly identical with those that may be observed in cases of hysteria (where they are more permanent), and those that may be momentarily produced in hypnotic subjects by suggestion. This was not at all astonishing, and was to have been expected. But one consequence, which I had not foreseen, did occur when, four days after my second experimental seance, Mlle. Smith fell completely asleep for the first time* at a sitting with M. Cuendet (February 7th), at which I was not present. The sitters were somewhat frightened, and, in trying to awaken her, discovered the rigidity of her arms, which were considerably contractured. Léopold however, communicating by means of the table upon which she was leaning, fully reassured them, and gave them to understand that such sleep was not at all prejudicial to the medium. After assuming various attitudes and indulging in some amusing mimicry, Mlle. Smith awoke in excellent spirits, retaining as a last recollection of her dream that of a kiss which Léopold had imprinted upon her forehead.

From that day on somnambulisms were the rule with Hélène, and the seances at which she did not fall completely asleep for at least a few moments formed rare exceptions to the course of events during the next four years. It is a great deprivation for Mlle. Smith that these slumbers ordinarily leave her no memory upon her awakening of what has transpired in her trance, and she longs for the seances of former times when the visions unfolded themselves before her eyes, furnishing her with a pleasing spectacle which was always unexpected, and which, continually being renewed, caused the seances to be to her a source of great delight. For the sitters, on the other hand, these scenes of somnambulism and incarnation, together with the various physiological phenomena of catalepsy, lethargy, contractures, etc., which accompanied them, added great variety and additional interest to Hélène Smith's remarkable and instructive triple mediumship.

The greater sometimes implies the less: simultaneously with the access of complete somnambulism came new forms and innumerable shades of hemisomnambulism. The triple form of automatism which distinguished the first years of Mlle. Smith's spiritistic experiences has been wonderfully developed since 1895, and it would now be difficult to name any principal forms of psychic mediumship of which she has not furnished curious specimens. I shall have occasion to cite several of them in the course of this work. Hélène constitutes the most remarkable medium I have ever met, and very nearly approaches the ideal of what might be called the polymorphous, or multiform, medium, in contradistinction to the uniform mediums, whose faculties only concern themselves with one kind of automatism.

2. A modification analogous to that which took place in the psychologic form of the messages consisting of a marked improvement in their depth and importance, was noticeable simultaneously in their content.

Alongside of the unimportant communications, complete at one sitting and independent one of another, which filled up a large part of each of Hélène's seances and in no wise differentiated her faculties from those of the majority of mediums, she manifested from the beginning a marked tendency to a superior systematization and a more lofty chain of visions; communications were often continued through several seances, and reached their conclusion only at the end of several weeks. But from the period at which I made the acquaintance of Mlle. Smith this tendency towards unity began to assert itself still more strongly. Several long somnambulistic dreams began to appear and to develop, the events of which continued to be unfolded through months, even years, and indeed still continue; a species of romance of the subliminal imagination analogous to those "continued stories"* which so many of our race tell themselves in their moments of *far niente*, or at times when their routine occupations offer only slight obstacles to day-dreaming, and of which they themselves are generally the heroes.

Mlle. Smith has no fewer than three distinct somnambulistic romances, and if to these is added the existence of that secondary personality to which I have already alluded, and which reveals itself under the name of Léopold, we find ourselves in the presence of four subconscious creations of vast extent, which have been evolved on parallel lines for several years, and which manifest themselves in irregular alternation during the course of different seances, or often even in the same seance.

All of these have undoubtedly a common origin in Hélène's subliminal consciousness; but in practice, at least, and to all appearance, these imaginative constructions present a relative independence and a diversity of content sufficiently great to render it necessary to study them separately. I shall confine myself at present to a general view of them.

Two of these romances are connected with the spiritistic idea of previous existences. It has, indeed been revealed that Hélène Smith has already lived twice before on this globe. Five hundred years ago she was the daughter of an Arab sheik, and became, under the name of Simandini, the favorite wife of a Hindoo prince named Sivrouka Nayaka, who reigned over Kanara, and built in the year 1401 the fortress of Tchandraguiri. In the last century she reappeared in the person of the illustrious and unfortunate Marie Antoinette. Again reincarnated, as a punishment for her sins and the perfecting of her character, in the humble circumstances of Hélène Smith, she in certain somnambulistic states recovers the memory of her glorious avatars of old, and becomes again for the moment Hindoo princess or queen of France.

I will designate under the names of "Hindoo" or "Oriental" cycle and "Royal" cycle the whole of the automatic manifestations relative to these two previous existences. I shall call the third romance the "Martian" cycle, in which Mlle. Smith, by virtue of the mediumistic faculties, which are the appanage and the consolation of her present life, has been able to enter into relation with the people and affairs of the planet Mars, and to unveil their mysteries to us. It is in this astronomical somnambulism that the phenomenon of glossolalia[2] appears, which consists of the fabrication and the use of an unknown language, and which is one of the principal objects of this study, we shall see, however, that analogous facts are likewise presented in the Hindoo cycle.

The personality of Léopold maintains very complex relations with the preceding creations. On the one hand, it is very closely connected with the Royal cycle, owing to the fact that the name of Léopold is only a pseudonym under which is concealed the illustrious Cagliostro, who, it appears, was madly infatuated with Queen Marie Antoinette, and who now, discarnate and floating in space, has constituted himself the guardian angel in some respects of Mlle. Smith, in whom after a long search he has again found the august object of his unhappy passion of a century ago.

On the other hand, this rôle of protector and spiritual guide which he assumes towards Hélène confers upon him a privileged place in her somnambulisms. He is more or less mixed up in the greater part of them; assists at them, watches over them, and perhaps in a measure directs them. He also occasionally appears in the midst of a Hindoo or a Martian scene, delivering his message by certain characteristic movements of the hand.

---

[2] Glossolalia signifies the "gift of tongues," or the ability to speak foreign languages without having consciously acquired them.

To sum up: sometimes revealing himself by raps upon the table, the taps of a finger, or by automatic writing; sometimes incarnating himself completely and speaking by the mouth of Mlle. Smith while entranced— Léopold fulfils in these seances the multiple and varied functions of spirit-guide, giving good advice relative to the manner of acting towards the medium; of stage-manager hidden behind the scenes watching the performance and ready at any time to intervene; of benevolently disposed interpreter willing to furnish explanations of all that is obscure; of censor of morals sharply reprimanding the sitters when he deems it necessary; of sympathetic physician prompt at diagnosis and well versed in the pharmacopaeia, etc. He also appears under his own name of Cagliostro to the somnambulistic gaze of the resuscitated Marie Antoinette and answers her questions by means of auditive hallucinations. Nor is this all: to make our summary complete, it is necessary also to investigate the personal connection of Mlle. Smith with her invisible protector. She often invokes and questions Léopold at her own convenience, and while he remains sometimes for weeks without giving any sign of life, he at other times readily responds to her by means of voices or visions which surprise her while fully awake in the course of her daily duties, and in which he lavishes upon her in turn material or moral advice, useful information, or the encouragement and consolation of which she has need.

Although I have accused myself of perhaps having had much to do with the transformation of Hélène's hemisomnambulism into complete trances, I believe myself, however, altogether innocent of the origin, and therefore of the subsequent development, of the great subliminal creations of which I have spoken. The first, that of Léopold, is of very early date, even going back probably, as we shall see, prior to Mlle. Smith's initiation into spiritism. As to the three cycles, they did not, it is true, commence to display their full amplitude until after I had made Hélène's acquaintance; and since they start from the time when she first became subject to veritable trances, it would seem as though that supreme form of automatism is the only one capable of allowing the full expansion of productions so complex, and the only psychological *container* appropriate and adequate to such a *content*. But the first appearance of all three was clearly prior to my presence at the seances. The Hindoo dream, where I shall be found playing a rôle which I did not seek, evidently began (October 16, 1894) eight weeks before my admission to Mlle. Smith's seances. The Martian romance, which dates from the same period, is closely connected, as I shall also show, with an involuntary suggestion of M. Lemaître, who made the acquaintance of Hélène in the spring of 1894, nine months before my introduction to her. The Royal cycle, finally, had been roughly outlined at seances held at the home of M. Cuendet, in December, 1893. Nevertheless, I repeat, only since 1895 have the exuberant growth and magnificent flowering of that subliminal vegetation taken place under the stimulating and provocative influence, albeit wholly unintentional and altogether unsuspected at the time, of the varied environments of Mlle. Smith's seances.

As far as the indiscreet revelations in regard to my own family, which so much astonished me at my first meeting with Mlle. Smith, are concerned, as well as the innumerable extraordinary facts of the same kind with which her mediumship abounds, and to which she owes her immense reputation in spiritistic circles, it will suffice to return in the closing chapters of this book.

CHAPTER TWO

Childhood and Youth of Mlle. Smith

THE PSYCHOLOGICAL history of Mlle. Smith and her automatisms is naturally divided into two separate periods by the important fact of her initiation into spiritism at the beginning of 1892. Before that time, not suspecting the possibility of voluntary communication with the world of disincarnate spirits, she naturally manifested nothing more than a few spontaneous phenomena, the first flutterings of her mediumistic faculties which still lay dormant, the exact nature and progress of which it would be interesting to know in detail; unfortunately, in the absence of written documents concerning that pre-spiritistic period, we are confined to the statements of Hélène and her parents in regard to it, and the untrustworthiness of the memory in connection with events of a remote past is only too well known.

The spiritistic period, on the contrary, extending over the last seven years, and infinitely more fertile in artificially promoted (e.g., the seances) as well as in spontaneous manifestations, is much better known to us; but in order to comprehend it intelligently, it is necessary first to pass in review the few facts which we have been able to gather relating to the pre-spiritistic period—that is to say, the childhood and youth of Mlle. Smith. That will be the subject of this chapter.

Mlle. Smith has lived in Geneva since her infancy. After attending school, she entered as an apprentice, at the age of fifteen, a large commercial house, where, as I have already stated, she still remains, and where, little by little, she has risen to a very responsible position. Her father, a merchant, was a Hungarian, and possessed a remarkable facility for languages, which is of interest to us in presence of the phenomena of glossolalia, a subject which will be discussed hereafter. Her mother is a Genevese. Both enjoyed excellent health and attained a venerable old age. Hélène had a younger sister who died in early childhood, and two brothers older than herself, who are now fathers of families and established abroad, where they have had successful business careers.

I am not aware that M. Smith, who was a man of positive character, ever displayed any phenomena of automatisms. Mme. Smith, however, as well as her grandmother, has experienced several thoroughly characteristic phenomena of that kind, and one, at least, of Hélène's brothers, it appears, could easily have become a good medium. This is another instance of the distinctly hereditary tendency of mediumistic faculties.

M. Smith, a man of active and enterprising character, died quite suddenly, probably of an embolism, at the age of seventy-five years. He had left Hungary in his youth, and finally established himself at Geneva, after having travelled extensively in Italy and Algiers, where he remained for several years. He spoke fluently Hungarian, German, French, Italian, and Spanish, understood English fairly well, and also knew Latin and a little Greek. It would seem that his daughter has inherited these linguistic aptitudes, but only in a latent and subliminal manner, for she has always detested the study of languages, and rebelled against learning German, in which she took lessons for three years.

Mme. Smith, who is a kind-hearted woman, with much good, practical sense, is sixty-seven years of age. Neither she nor her husband was ever a nervous or psychopathic subject, but both showed a marked tendency to broncho-pulmonary affections of a somewhat alarming type. Mme. Smith has, besides, suffered frequently from rheumatism. Hélène does not appear to have inherited these tendencies; she has always enjoyed robust health, and has not even had the slight diseases usually incidental to childhood.

Although both M. and Mme. Smith were Protestants, through a chain of peculiar circumstances their daughter was baptized a Catholic shortly after her birth, her name being inscribed some months later on the register of the Protestant church of Geneva. The memory of this unusual baptism has certainly not been lost by Hélène's subliminal imagination, and has duly contributed to the hypothesis of a mysterious origin. Of the years of childhood I know nothing specially interesting. At the intermediate school, at which she passed only a year, and where I have consulted the records of her class, she was not distinguished either for good or ill from the point of view of deportment, but she certainly did not reveal the full measure of her intelligence, since she failed to pass the examinations at the end of the year, a fact which decided her entrance upon an apprenticeship. On the other hand, the worthy pastor who gave her religious instruction somewhat later, and who has never lost sight of her since, has furnished me with most eulogistic testimonials as to her character; he remembers her as a young girl of serious disposition, intelligent, thoughtful, faithful in the discharge of her duties, and devoted to her family.

M. Smith never showed the least trace of mediumistic phenomena; from having been very indifferent, or even hostile, to spiritism until his daughter began to interest herself in it, he finally succumbed to her influence and became a believer in that doctrine towards the close of his life. Mme. Smith, on the contrary, has always been predisposed to it, and has experienced several phenomena of that nature in the course of her life. At the period of the epidemic of "table-tipping" which raged in our country about the middle of this century, she too experimented quite successfully for a while upon the table with her friends and acquaintances. Later, she had some sporadic visions. The following is one of the most typical. While her little daughter three years old was ill, Mme. Smith awoke in the middle of the night and saw an angel, of dazzling brightness, standing by the side of the little bed with its hands stretched out above the child; after some moments the apparition gradually dissolved. Mme. Smith awakened her husband and told him of the fatal significance which she attached to the vision, but he, unable to see anything, ridiculed her superstitious fears. As a matter of fact, the child died on the following day, to the great surprise of the physician attending her. This is a fine example of true maternal presentiment, subconsciously felt and transferring itself into the normal consciousness by a visual hallucination which borrowed for its symbolic content an appropriate popular image.

Mme. Smith never knew her mother, who died shortly after her birth; but she recalls and has related to me some characteristic visions of her grandmother, who brought her up; various phenomena connected with one of Hélène's brothers (hearing of steps in the night, etc.) have proved to her that one of her sons, at least, is a medium.

Hélène Smith was certainly predisposed, both by heredity and temperament, to become a medium, as soon as the outward opportunity—that is, the suggestions of spiritism—should present itself.

It is evident, indeed, from her recital of events, that she was more or less visionary from her infancy. It does not appear, however, that she ever manifested phenomena capable in themselves of attracting the attention of her family. I have not been able to discover any indication whatever of crises or attacks of an abnormal nature, not even of sleep-walking. Her automatisms have been always almost entirely confined to the sensory or mental sphere, and it is only from her own narratives that other people have any knowledge of them. They assume the double form of reveries more or less conscious, and of hallucinations properly so called.

1. *Reveries.*—The habit of falling into reverie, of building castles in the air, of transporting one's self into other conditions of existence, or of telling one's self stories in which one plays the chief rôle, is more frequent among women than among men, and in childhood and youth than in mature years.* This propensity seems to have always been extremely marked in the case of Mlle. Smith, since from her school-girl days she has shown herself to be of a sedentary and domestic temperament, preferring the quiet companionship of her mother to the games of her comrades, and her needle-work to out-door recreations. The fragments which have survived in Hélène's conscious memory are all that is known to us of the content of these reveries, but it suffices, nevertheless, to reveal to us the general tone of her fictions, and to show us that the images suddenly surging up before her mental vision had a peculiar, often very fantastic, character,

and which enables us to see in them the beginnings of her later great somnambulistic romances. It is to be noticed also that the designs, embroideries, varied artistic works, which were always the favorite occupations of her moments of leisure and in which she excels, were almost always, from her infancy, not copies of exterior models, but the products of her own invention, marked with the bizarre and original stamp of her internal images. Moreover, these pieces of work grew under her fingers with an ease and rapidity that astonished herself. They made themselves, as it were.

She was always fond of indulging in day-dreams, and recalls many a half-hour passed motionless in an easy-chair, on which occasions she was accustomed to see all kinds of strange things, but, being of a very reticent nature, she seldom mentioned them to her parents for fear of not being understood. She used to see highly colored landscapes, a lion of stone with a mutilated head, fanciful objects on pedestals, etc. She does not remember the details, but does clearly recollect that they all bore a close resemblance to her Hindoo and Martian visions of later years.

These phantasmagoria also appeared to her in the night. She remembers, among other things, to have seen, when about fourteen or fifteen years old, a bright light thrown against the wall of her room, which then seemed to be filled with strange and unknown beings. She had the impression of being fully awake, but it suddenly occurred to her that she must have been dreaming, and it was only then that she comprehended that it was really a "vision" which she had experienced.

2. *Hallucinations.*—In the foregoing examples it would be difficult to say to exactly which category the psychologic facts belong, especially the nocturnal phenomena, and one may hesitate whether to regard them as simple dreams of a very vivid character, hypnagogic or hypnopompic[1] visions, or as veritable hallucinations. On the other hand, we undoubtedly have the right to give the latter designation to the numerous apparitions which Mlle. Smith has when in full possession of her senses in the daytime.

One day, for example, as she was playing out-of-doors with a friend, she saw some one following her, and mentioned the fact to her companion, who could not see any one. The imaginary individual, after having followed her around a tree for a moment, disappeared, and she was unable to find him again.

Of an entirely different order are the strange characters which she remembers having sometimes involuntarily substituted for French letters

---

[1] This term is used to designate the visions which manifest themselves at the moment of awakening from sleep immediately prior to complete awakening, and which form a pendant to the well-known, much more frequent hypnagogic hallucinations, arising in the intermediate state between sleep and waking.

when writing to her friends, which must be regarded as graphomotor hallucinations. These were undoubtedly the same characters which at other times appeared to her in visual images.

This was the prelude to the phenomenon so frequently experienced by her in the last few years, and of which we shall hereafter see many examples—namely, automatic writing, mingling with her ordinary chirography in her waking state.

Alongside of hallucinations like these, which do not show any intentional or useful character and are only a capricious and fortuitous irruption into the normal consciousness, mere dreams or fancies filling up the subconscious strata, there are also manifested in Hélène's case some hallucinations of a manifest utility, which have in consequence the sense of messages addressed by the subliminal consciousness of the subject to her normal consciousness, by way of warning and protection. It is to be noted that these hallucinations, which might be called teleological, have lately been claimed by Léopold, although he has no recollection of, and does not assert himself to be the author of, the earlier ones.

The following is a curious example: At about the age of seventeen or eighteen, Hélène was returning from the country one evening, carrying a fine bouquet of flowers. During the last minutes of the journey she heard behind her a peculiar cry of a bird, which seemed to her to warn her against some danger, and she hastened her steps without looking behind. On her arrival at home the cry followed her into her room without her having been able to see the creature from which it emanated. She went tired to bed, and in the middle of the night awoke in great pain, but was unable to cry out. At that moment she felt herself gently lifted, together with the pillow on which she lay, as if by two friendly hands, which enabled her to recover her voice and call her mother, who hastened to comfort her, and carried the flowers, which were too odorous, out of the room. Léopold, on being interrogated recently during a somnambulism of Hélène as to this incident, coming up again after so many years, has a very clear recollection of it and gives the following explanation.

It was not really the cry of a bird, but it was he, Léopold, who caused Hélène to hear a sort of whistle, hoping thereby to attract her attention to the danger lurking in the bouquet of flowers, in which was a great deal of garden-mint of powerful odor. Unfortunately Hélène did not understand, and retained the bouquet in her room. He adds that his failure to give a more clear and intelligible warning was due to the fact that it was at that time impossible for him to do so. The whistle which Hélène took for the cry of a bird was all that it was in his power to utter. It was again he who intervened at the moment of her nocturnal illness by raising her head in order to enable her to call for help.

I have no reason to doubt the substantial accuracy either of the account given by Hélène and her mother, or of the explanation recently furnished by Léopold. The incident belongs to the category of well-known cases where a danger of some sort not suspected by the normal personality, but which is subconsciously known or recognized, is warded off by a preservative hallucination, either sensory (as here—the cry of the bird) or motor (as in the lifting of the body). The subliminal consciousness is not always able to give a clear message; in the present case, the auditive automatism remained in a state of elementary hallucination, a simple whistle, without being able to elevate it to a distinct verbal hallucination. Its general warning sense, however, was understood by Hélène, thanks to the confused feeling of danger that she felt at the same time. Moreover, this confused feeling, which caused her to quicken her steps, it seems to me, ought not to be considered as the consequence of the whistle she heard, but rather as a parallel phenomenon; the appearance or the odor of the mint she was carrying, while not attracting her conscious attention, nevertheless dimly roused in her an idea of the danger lurking in the flowers, and that idea in turn affected her clear consciousness under the double form of a vague emotion of danger and a verboauditive translation which did not go so far as to formulate itself explicitly.

Under circumstances of a nature calculated to cause a strong emotional shock, and especially when the psychic sphere which involves the sentiment of modesty is strongly acted upon, Hélène has a visual hallucination of a man clothed in a long, brown robe, with a white cross on his breast, like a monk, who comes to her aid, and accompanies her in silence as long as the necessity for his presence continues. This unknown protector, always silent, each time appearing and disappearing in a sudden and mysterious manner, is no other than Léopold himself, according to the recent affirmations of the latter.

We should naturally expect that Hélène would have had in her youth many striking experiences of prevision, marvellous intuition, divination, etc., which are among the most diffuse forms of teleological automatism. Such, however, does not seem to have been the fact; neither she nor her mother has recounted to me anything remarkable of this nature, and they confine themselves to a general affirmation of frequent presentiments, which were subsequently justified as to the persons and events with which they were connected.

All the examples which I have above cited concur in bringing to light the strong penchant of Mlle. Smith towards automatism. But from the point of view of their meaning there is a notable difference between the teleological phenomena, presentiments or hallucinations of a manifest utility, and those which have none—mere reveries and other perturbations, which are altogether superfluous, if not actually detrimental, to Hélène's normal personality.

There are dreams and other automatisms absolutely useless which have insinuated themselves without rhyme or reason into Hélène's normal life. One does not know how or in what manner to interpret these phenomena, capricious and fortuitous as they seem to be, and they remain isolated, inconsiderable facts, without bearing and without interest, since they cannot be attached to any central principle, to one mother-idea or fundamental emotion.

We are, therefore, reduced to certain conjectures, the most reasonable of which is that these diverse fragments make part of some vast subconscious creation, in which all the being of Mlle. Smith, crushed and bruised by the conditions which the realities of life have imposed upon her, as is more or less the case with each one of us, gave free wing to the deep aspirations of its nature and expanded into the fiction of an existence more brilliant than her own. All that we know of Hélène's character, both as a child and as a young girl, shows us that her dominant emotional note was a sort of instinctive inward revolt against the modest environment in which it was her lot to be born, a profound feeling of dread and opposition, of inexplicable *malaise*, of bitter antagonism against the whole of her material and intellectual environment. While showing herself always very devoted to her parents and brothers, she had only feeble natural affinities for them. She felt like a stranger in her family and as one away from home. She had a feeling of isolation, of abandonment, of exile, which created a sort of gulf between her and her family. So strong were these feelings that she actually one day seriously asked her parents if it was absolutely certain that she was their daughter, or whether it was not possible that the nurse might some day by mistake have brought home another child from the daily walk.

This want of adaptation to her environment, this sort of mysterious homesickness for an unknown country, shows itself in a characteristic manner in the following fragment of narrative, in which Hélène, who has always attributed great importance to dreams, tells of one in which an isolated house figured.

To me this retired mansion, in which I lived alone, isolated, represents my life, which from my infancy has been neither happy nor gay. Even while very young I do not remember to have shared any of the tastes or any of the ideas of the members of my family. Thus during the whole of my childhood I was left in what I call a profound isolation of heart. And in spite of all, in spite of this complete want of sympathy, I could not make up my mind to marry, although I had several opportunities. A voice was always saying, "Do not hurry: the time has not arrived; this is not the destiny for which you are reserved." And I have listened to that voice, which has absolutely nothing to do with conscience, and I do not regret it, for since I have engaged in spiritism I have found myself so surrounded with sympathy and friendships that I have somewhat forgotten my sad lot.

This quotation speaks volumes in regard to the turn of mind and the emotional disposition which ruled Hélène as a little girl. It is surely, so to speak, the vulgar story and the common lot of all; many a child, many a youth, many an unrecognized genius, feel themselves suffocating in their too narrow environment when the latent energies of life begin to ferment. But there are differences in kind and in degree. With Mlle. Hélène Smith the sentiment of not having been made for her environment, and of belonging by nature to a higher sphere, was intense and lasting. Her mother always had the impression that Hélène was not happy, and wondered that she was so serious, so absorbed, so wanting in the exuberance of spirits natural to her age. Her father and her brothers, not comprehending the real reasons for this absence of gayety, taxed her very unjustly with pride and hauteur, and accused her sometimes of despising her humble surroundings. There are shades of feeling which can only be understood when they have been experienced. Hélène well knew that she really had no contempt for her material and social environment, which, on the contrary, inspired her with respect, but which simply was not congenial to her nature and temperament.

To this fundamental feeling of imprisonment in a too paltry sphere was joined, in Hélène's case, a timid disposition. Darkness, the least noise, the creaking of the furniture, made her tremble; by day, a person walking behind her, an unexpected movement, the ringing of the door-bell, gave her the impression that some one wishing to harm her had come to seize her and carry her off. On the whole, Hélène's tendency to be startled by everything and nothing constituted with her a grievous panophobia, a state of fear and insecurity which greatly strengthened her impression of want of union—of *mésalliance*—with an environment to which she was decidedly superior.

It is easy now to see the connection between that depressing emotionalism which was the attribute of Hélène's childhood and the slightly megalomaniac tone of her later subliminal romances. The idea intrudes itself that, in spite of—or by reason of—their apparent contrast, these two traits are not independent of each other, but bound by the tie of cause and effect. But this causal connection is in great danger of being interpreted in a precisely inverse sense by the empirical psychologist and the metaphysical occultist. The latter will explain Mlle. Smith's curious impression of strangeness and superiority to the base conditions of her actual existence, by her illustrious previous incarnations; the psychologist, on the contrary, will see in that same impression the wholly natural origin of her grandiose somnambulistic personifications. In default of a complete understanding, always dubious, between these so different points of view, of which we shall speak later, it will be advisable to adopt at least a provisional *modus vivendi*, based on the party-wall of the native constitution or individual character of Mlle. Smith. On the farther side of that wall, *in eternity,* so to speak, *a parte ante* which precedes the arrival of Hélène into this life, the occultist will have full latitude to imagine such a succession of existences as it shall please him in order to explain the character she has had from her infancy. But on this side of the wall—that is to say, within the limits of her present life—the psychologist will have the right to ignore all these prenatal metempsychoses, and taking for his point of departure the innate constitution of Hélène, without troubling himself about anything she may have received by the accidents of heredity or preserved from her royal pre-existences, he will endeavor to explain by that same constitution, as it reveals itself in her daily life, the genesis of her subliminal creations under the action of occasional exterior influences. The occultist, then, can have the pleasure of regarding Mlle. Smith's characteristic trait as a child, that impression of solitude and wandering about in a world for which she was not made, as *the effect* of her real past greatnesses, while the psychologist will be permitted to see in it *the cause* of her future dreams of grandeur.

The emotional disposition which I have depicted, and which is one of the forms under which the maladaptation of the organism, physical and mental, to the hard conditions of the environment, betrays itself, seems therefore to me to have been the source and starting-point for all the dreamings of Hélène in her childhood. Thence came these visions, always warm, luminous, highly colored, exotic, bizarre; and these brilliant apparitions, superbly dressed, in which her antipathy for her insipid and unpleasant surroundings betrays itself, her weariness of ordinary, commonplace people, her disgust for prosaic occupations, for vulgar and disagreeable things, for the narrow house, the dirty streets, the cold winters, and the gray sky. Whether these images, very diverse, but of the same brilliant quality, were already existent in Hélène's subconscious thought while still a child or a young girl, we are unable to say. It is, however, probable that their systematization was far from attaining to such a degree of perfection as they have presented during the past few years under the influence of spiritism.

All the facts of automatism to which Hélène can assign a vaguely approximate date group themselves around her fifteenth year, and are all included between the limits of her ninth and twentieth years.

This evident connection with a phase of development of major importance has been confirmed to me by Léopold on various occasions, who says that he appeared to Hélène for the first time in her tenth year, on an exceptional occasion of extreme fright, but after that, not until about four

years later, because the "physiological conditions" necessary to his apparition were not yet realized. The moment they were realized, he says, he
began to manifest himself, and it is at the same period, according to him,
that Hélène commenced to recover memories of her Hindoo existence,
under the form of strange visions of which she comprehended neither the
nature nor the origin.

After the age of about twenty years, without affirming or believing that
her visions and apparitions ceased altogether, Mlle. Smith has no striking
recollections of any, and she has not told me of any psychic phenomenon
experienced by her in the series of years immediately preceding her entrance into spiritism. We may infer from this, with some reason, that the
ebullitions of the imaginative subconscious life gradually became calm
after the explosion of the period we have mentioned. They had been ap-
peased. The conflict between Hélène's inner nature and the environment
in which she was forced to live became less fierce. A certain equilibrium
was established between the necessities of practical life and her inward
aspirations. On the one hand, she resigned herself to the necessities of
reality; and if her native pride could not yield to the point of condescending to a marriage, honorable undoubtedly, but for which she felt she was
not intended, we must nevertheless pay homage to the perseverance, the
fidelity, the devotion which she always brought to the fulfilment of her
family and business duties. On the other hand, she did not permit the
flame of the ideal to be extinguished in her, and it reacted upon her environment as strongly as possible, making its imprint upon her personality
well marked.

She introduced a certain stamp of elegance into the modest home of her
parents. She arranged for herself a small *salon,* coquettish and comfortable in its simplicity. She took lessons in music, and bought herself a
piano. She hung some old engravings on her walls, secured some Japanese vases, a jardinière filled with plants, cut flowers in pretty vases, a
hanging lamp with a beautiful shade of her own make, a table-cover which
she had put together and embroidered herself, some photographs curiously framed according to her own design; and out of this harmonious
whole, always beautifully kept, she evolved something original, bizarre,
and delightful, conforming well to the general character of her fantastic
subconsciousness.

At the same time that Mlle. Smith succeeded in accommodating herself
to the conditions of her existence, the state of latent timidity in which she
lived gradually diminished. She is still occasionally overcome by fear, but
much less frequently than formerly, and never without a legitimate exterior cause.

Indeed, judging her by these latter years, I do not recognize in her the
child or young girl of former days, always timid, trembling, and fright-

ened, taciturn and morose, who has been depicted to me by herself and her mother.

It seems to me, then, that the wildness of the dreams and automatisms, which were symptoms of a tendency to mental disintegration, which marked the years of puberty, was succeeded by a progressive diminution of these troubles and a gradual gaining of wisdom on the part of the subliminal strata. We may presume that this harmonization, this reciprocal adaptation of the internal to the external, would in time have perfected itself, and that the whole personality of Mlle. Smith would have continued to consolidate and unify itself, if spiritism had not come all of a sudden to rekindle the fire which still slumbered under the ashes and to give a new start to the subliminal mechanism which was beginning to grow rusty.

The suppressed fictions aroused themselves, the reveries of former years resumed their sway, and the images of subliminal phantasy began to be more prolific than ever under the fertile suggestions of occult philosophy, rallying-points or centres of crystallization—such as the idea of former existences and reincarnations—around which they had only to group and organize themselves in order to give birth to the vast somnambulistic constructions the development of which we shall be obliged to follow.

CHAPTER THREE

Mlle. Smith Since Her Initiation into Spiritism

HAVING ENDEAVORED in the preceding chapter to reconstruct in its chief characteristics the history of Mlle. Smith up to the time when spiritism begins to be mixed up with it, I would have preferred in the present chapter to make a detailed study of her psychological life during these last years, without however, as yet, touching upon the content, properly so called, of her automatisms. Not having been able to accomplish this design to my satisfaction, for want of time and patience, I shall endeavor at least to systematize my notes somewhat by grouping them under four heads. I shall trace the birth of Hélène's mediumship as far as it is possible for me to do so from the meagre accounts I have been able to procure concerning a time at which I was not acquainted with her. Then, passing to facts with which I am more familiar, I will describe rapidly her normal state as I have been able to see it for the last five years. This would have been the place for a study of individual psychology, but I have been compelled to abandon the idea on account of multiple difficulties. Finally, I will offer a few remarks on the abnormal side of her existence, which it is convenient to divide into two groups, namely, *the spontaneous*—that is to say, springing up of themselves in the course of her ordinary life; or those *provoked* by the voluntary seeking for favorable circumstances, and which constitute the seances properly so called.

I. THE MEDIUMISTIC BEGINNINGS OF MLLE. SMITH

In the winter of 1891–92 Mlle. Smith heard spiritism spoken of by one of her acquaintances, Mme. Y., who lent her Denis's book, *Après la Mort*. The perusal of this work having vividly excited Hélène's curiosity, Mme. Y. agreed to accompany her to her friend, Mlle. Z., who was interested in the same questions, and who produced automatic writing. They then decided to form a circle for regular experimentation. I take from the notes which Mlle. Z. has had the kindness to furnish me, the account, unfortunately very brief, of the seances at which Hélène's mediumistic faculties first made their appearance.

It was on the 20th of February, 1892, that I made the acquaintance of Mlle. Smith. She was introduced to me by Mme. Y., for the purpose of endeavoring to form a spiritistic group. She was then altogether a novice in spiritism, never having attempted anything, and did not suspect the faculties that have since developed themselves in her.

February 20.—First reunion: We seat ourselves at the table; we succeed in making it oscillate. We regard Mme. Y. as the medium upon whom we can reckon. We try for writing. We receive through me encouragements to proceed.

February 26.—Progress; the table moves itself considerably, salutes one by one all the members of the group, and gives us certain names, of which only one is recognized . . . Writing: Mlle. Smith, who tries for the first time, writes mechanically, her eyes closed, some phrases, of which we can decipher some words.

March 11.—Nothing at this seance, except a communication written by myself.

March 18.—Progress; clear communication by the table. Attempt to experiment in the darkness (which was not absolute, the hall outside having some incandescent lights which diffused a feeble light; we could distinguish each other with difficulty). Mlle. Smith sees a balloon, now luminous, now becoming dark: she has seen nothing up to this time. Writing: Mlle. Smith writes mechanically a quite long communication from the father of M. K. [a Bulgarian student present at the seance]; advice to him.

At this point the sitters became so numerous that they broke up into two groups, of which the one continuing to meet with Mlle. Z. does not concern us. Mlle. Smith became a member of the other, which met at the house of a lady named N., where weekly seances were held for a year and a half (up to the end of June, 1893). The records of these meetings, kept by Mme. N., are unfortunately very brief and obscure on many points of interest to the psychologist. Those of the first months are in the handwriting of Mlle. Smith, who acted as secretary of the group for thirty seances. As she only took down at the time the headings of the communications of the spirits and wrote out the remainder on the following day, we cannot rely very strongly on the objective accuracy of these accounts, which, however, have the advantage of presenting to us the mediumship of Hélène, as related by herself. She speaks of herself in the third person.

The following is a summary of the two first seances held in this new environment:

March 25, 1892.—Eleven persons around a large and heavy dining-table of oak with two leaves. The table is set in motion, and several spirits come and give their names (by raps), and testify to the pleasure it gives them to find themselves among us. It is at this seance that Mlle. Smith begins to distinguish vague gleams with long white streamers moving from the floor to the ceiling, and then a magnificent star, which in the darkness appears to her alone throughout the whole of the seance. We augur from this that she will end by seeing things more distinctly and will possess the gift of clairvoyance.

April 1.—Violent movements of the table, due to a spirit who calls himself David and announces himself as the spiritual guide of the group. Then he gives way to another spirit who says he is Victor Hugo, and the guide and protector of Mlle. Smith, who is very much surprised to be assisted by a person of such importance. He soon disappears. Mlle. Smith is very much agitated; she has fits of shivering, is very cold. She is very restless, and sees suddenly, balancing itself above the table, a grinning, very ill-favored face, with long red hair. She is so frightened that she demands that the lights be lit. She is calmed and reassured. The figure disappears. Afterwards she sees a magnificent bouquet of roses of different hues being placed on the table before one of the sitters, M. P. All at once she sees a small snake come out from underneath the bouquet, which, crawling quickly, perceives the flowers, looks at them, tries to reach the hand of M. P., withdraws for an instant, comes back slowly, and disappears in the interior of the bouquet. Then all is dissolved and three raps are given on the table, terminating the seance. [M. P. interprets the meaning of the vision of the bouquet and the serpent as a symbolic translation of an emotional impression experienced by Mlle. Smith].

Such was the birth of Hélène's mediumship. Scarcely anything happened on the 20th of February, when the movements of the table were not attributed to her (although in all probability she caused them); in the following seances she appeared in two attempts at automatic writing (unfortunately lost) in imitation of the writing medium with whom she was sitting. The outcome of this second attempt leads us to suppose that Hélène's faculties would have developed rapidly in that direction if she had not abandoned it and changed her environment.

Her visual faculty, suggested by the experiments at obscure seances, shows itself on the 18th and 25th of March in the form of elementary hallucinations or vague figures having their point of departure probably in the simple entoptical phenomena, the retina's own light, consecutive images, etc. Then, encouraged by the predictions of the sitters, she attained on the 1st of April to visions properly so called, having a varied content and a real or symbolic signification. At the same time her typtological automatism was perfecting itself. We recognize it in the name of Victor Hugo, coming especially for Mlle. Smith, and suspect it to have been a name already given at the second seance.

Auditive hallucinations follow closely upon the visual, but it is impossible to know at just what date, as the records do not clearly indicate whether the messages recorded had that origin or were rapped out on the table. To these known forms of automatism must be added the frequent phenomena of emotion, shiverings, sadness, restlessness, fear, etc., which are experienced by Hélène without knowing why, and are afterwards found to be in perfect conformity to, and in evident connection with, the content of those emotional phenomena which they generally precede by a few moments.

Thus, in a half-dozen weekly seances, the mediumship of Mlle. Smith was invested with a complex psychological aspect, which from that time it preserved intact for three years, and of which I was a witness after I made her acquaintance. This rapidity of development is not at all unusual; but there is this peculiarity about Hélène, that her mediumistic faculties, after their first appearance, remained for a long time stationary, and then underwent all at once, in the spring of 1895, the enormous transformation and tremendous expansion which I have described in the first chapter, and to which I will not again refer.

II. Mlle. Smith in Her Normal State

I was about to say that in her normal state Mlle. Smith is normal. Certain scruples restrain me, and I correct myself by saying that in her ordinary state she seems just like anybody else. By this I mean that outside of the gaps which the seances and the spontaneous eruptions of automatism make in her life, no one would suspect, observing her performance of her various duties, or in talking with her on all sorts of subjects, all that she is capable of in her abnormal states, or the curious treasures which are concealed in her subliminal strata.

With a healthy and ruddy complexion, of good height, well proportioned, of regular and harmonious features, she breathes health in everything. She presents no visible stigmata of degeneration. As to psychic defects or anomalies, with the exception of her mediumship itself, I know of none, the timidity of her youth having entirely disappeared. Her physical strength is marvellous, as shown by the fact that she bears up under the strain of a business which demands nearly eleven hours of her time each day, nearly all of which she is compelled to stand on her feet,* and from which she takes only one week's vacation in summer. Besides this confining work away from home, she assists her mother about the house, morning and evening, in the housekeeping duties, and finds time besides to read a little, to practise at her piano, and to make the lovely handiwork, which she designs and executes herself with remarkable originality and good taste. To a life so full must be added, besides, the spiritistic seances which she is generally willing to give on Sunday, and sometimes on a weekday evening, very disinterestedly, to persons who are interested in psychic questions or who desire to consult Léopold on important subjects.

While hesitating to affirm that a person presenting phenomena so extraordinary as those of mediumship is perfectly normal in other respects, I am pleased to discover that as far as Mlle. Smith is concerned, through my conversations with her and as the result of my investigations concerning her, she does not present a single abnormality, physical, intellectual, or moral, between the periods of the irruptions of her automatisms. Her field of vision, which she has permitted me to measure with a Landolt perimeter, is normal for white as well as for colors, for which latter she has a very delicate perception. There is no trace of tactile anaesthesia in her hands. There is no known motor trouble. The tremor of the index-finger gives a line, of four oscillations per second on an average, differing not at all from the lines obtained from persons perfectly normal (see Fig. 2).

It cannot be expected that I should paint a full moral and intellectual portrait of Mlle. Smith, as I should be in danger of hurting her feelings in case my attempt should come to her notice. I can only touch on a few points. One of the most striking is her great native dignity; her bearing, her manners, her language are always perfect, and have a certain quality of *noblesse* and pride which accords well with her somnambulistic rôles. On occasion she shows a stately and regal hauteur. She is very impressionable, and feels little things very keenly. Her antipathies as well as her sympathies are quick, lively, and tenacious. She is energetic and persevering. She knows very well what she wants, and nothing passes her by unperceived, nor does she forget anything in the conduct of others towards her. "I see everything, nothing escapes me, and I forgive but never forget," she has often said to me. Perhaps a severe moralist would find in her a certain exaggeration of personal sensibility, but that sort of self-love is a very common characteristic of human nature, and is very natural in mediums who are continually exposed to public criticism.

She is very intelligent and highly gifted. In conversation she shows herself vivacious, sprightly, and sometimes sarcastic. Psychic problems, and all questions connected with mediumistic phenomena, of which she is herself so striking an example, occupy her mind a great deal and form the principal subject of her private thoughts and of her conversations with people in whom she is interested.

Her philosophical views are not wanting in originality or breadth. She does not believe in spiritism, in the generally accepted sense of the term, and has never consented, in spite of the advances which have been made to her, to become a member of the Geneva Society (spiritistic) for Psychic Studies, because, as she says, she has no fixed ideas on subjects so obscure, does not care for theories, and "does not work in the interest of any party." She investigates, she observes she reflects and discusses, having adopted for her motto, "The truth in all things, for all things, and always."

There are two points in regard to which she is uncompromising—namely, the objective reality of Léopold, and the supernormal content of her automatisms. No one dares tell her that her great invisible protector is only an illusory apparition, another part of herself, a product of her sub-conscious imagination; nor that the strange peculiarities of her medium-istic communications—the Sanscrit, the recognizable signatures of de-ceased persons, the thousand correct revelations of facts unknown to her—are but old forgotten memories of things which she saw or heard in her childhood. Such suppositions being contrary to her inmost beliefs, and seemingly false in fact, easily irritate her, as being in defiance of good sense and an outrage on truth. But outside of these two subjects she will examine and discuss coolly any hypothesis one chooses. The idea that she should be the reincarnation of a Hindoo princess or of Marie Antoinette, that Léopold is really Cagliostro, that the visions called Martian are really from the planet Mars, etc., all seem to her to conform fully to the facts; but these beliefs are not indispensable to her, and she is ready, should they prove to be false, to change to other theories—as, for example, te-lepathy, a mixture of occult influences, a mysterious meeting in her of intuitions coming from some higher sphere, etc.

Undoubtedly the supposition of her pre-existences in India and on the throne of France seems to her to explain in a plausible manner the feel-ing, which has followed her from childhood, of belonging to a world higher than that in which the chance of birth has imprisoned her for this life; but she does not affirm a positive belief in that brilliant past, is not wholly convinced of it, and remains in a sensible state of expectancy of the true explanation of these ultimate mysteries of her life.

There is another subject, also, which is close to her heart. She has heard it said that in the eyes of scientists and physicians mediums are considered to be fools, hysterical subjects, or insane, or, in any event, abnormal, in the bad sense of the word. But in the light of the experience of every day of her life, she protests vigorously against this odious insinua-tion. She declares emphatically that she is "perfectly sane in body and mind, not in the least unbalanced," and repels with indignation the idea there can be any serious abnormality or the least danger in mediumship such as she practises. "I am far from being abnormal," she wrote me re-cently, "and I have never been so clear of vision, so lucid, and so apt to judge correctly as since I have begun to develop as a medium."

Léopold, too, speaking through her voice during her trances, has more than once solemnly testified as to her perfect health. He has also returned to the subject by letter; we shall find farther on a very interesting certifi-cate of mental equilibrium dictated by him and written by him with her hand, as if to give more weight to his declarations (see Fig. 8, p. 84).

It is incontestable that Hélène has a very well-organized brain, as is evidenced by the admirable manner in which she manages the important and complicated department which is under her direction in the commer-cial establishment in which she is employed. To accuse her of being insane, simply because she is a medium, as some charitable souls (the world is full of them) do not hesitate to do sometimes, is, to say the least, a most inadmissible *petitio principii*.

The opinion which Mlle. Smith holds in her normal state concerning her automatic faculties is altogether optimistic; and there is nothing to prove her in the wrong. She regards her mediumship as a rare and precious privilege, with which nothing in the world would induce her to part. True, she also sees in it the reason for the malevolent and unjust judgments, the jealousies, the base suspicions, to which the ignorant multitude have in all ages subjected those who have succeeded in elevating themselves above it through the possession of faculties of this kind. But, on the whole, the disadvantages are more than counterbalanced by gains of a high order, and the inward satisfaction attached to such a gift.* And here I desire to emphasize the statement, once for all, that Hélène does not belong to the class of professional mediums, nor to those who use their mediumship for the purpose of coining money. Mlle. Smith, who earns her living in the position which her intelligence and fitness have secured for her, and through which her family enjoys a modest ease, never accepts any pecuniary compensation for her seances or consultations. Such a traffic in faculties which have a sort of religious signification in her eyes would be absolutely repugnant to her feelings.

Hélène's spontaneous automatisms have often aided her in, without ever having interfered with, her daily occupations. There is, happily for her, a great difference in intensity between the phenomena of her seances and those which break in upon her habitual existence, the latter never having caused such disturbance of her personality as the former.

In her daily life she has only passing hallucinations limited to one or two of the senses, superficial hemisomnambulisms, compatible with a certain amount of self-possession—in short, ephemeral perturbations of no importance from a practical point of view. Taken as a whole, the interventions of the subliminal in her ordinary existence are more beneficial to her than otherwise, since they often bear the stamp of utility and appropriateness, which make them very serviceable.

Phenomena of hypermnesia, divination, lost objects mysteriously recovered, happy inspirations, true presentiments, correct intuitions—in a word, teleological automatisms of every sort—she possesses in so high a degree that this small coin of genius is more than sufficient to compensate for the inconveniences resulting from the distraction and momentary absence of mind with which the vision is accompanied.

In the seances, on the contrary, she presents the most grave functional alterations that one can imagine, and passes through accesses of lethargy, catalepsy, somnambulism, total change of personality, etc., the least of which would be a very disagreeable adventure for her if it should happen to occur in the street or at her office.

But here I am obliged to leave Hélène's ordinary state to enter upon the study of her automatisms.

III. Spontaneous Automatic Phenomena

The automatisms which occur outside the seances in Mlle. Smith's every-day life, those, at least, which she is able to recall and narrate, are of a frequency very variable and utterly independent of any known circumstances; sometimes presenting themselves two or three times in the same day; at others, two or three weeks will elapse without a single one. Extremely diverse in their form and content, these phenomena may be divided into three categories, based upon their origin. The first proceed from impressions received by Hélène in moments of special suggestibility; the second are the fortuitous apparitions above the ordinary level of her consciousness, the romances in process of elaboration to which we are coming; the last, which differ from the two preceding species (which are always useless, if not detrimental) by their beneficial character and their adaptation to the needs of the moment, are roused by those teleological automatisms to which I have already called attention as having occurred in her childhood, and which have shared in the general recrudescence of her subconscious life under the lash of the spiritistic experiences.

Let us pass these different cases rapidly in review.

1. Permanence of Exterior Suggestions

The spiritistic reunions are naturally their principal source. I do not mean that she has there been subjected to experiments in post-hypnotic suggestion. Justice to all those who have attended the seances compels the statement that they have never abused the suggestibility which she shows on such occasions, by suggesting ideas of such a nature as to cause her annoyance on the following days. The most that has been attempted has been the suggestion of some small matters by way of harmless experiment, to be executed by her a few moments after awaking from her trance. There is no need of intentional suggestions to influence her in a lasting manner; therefore we have avoided as far as possible everything that might leave disagreeable traces behind, and have suggested to her before the end of the seance that she have on the morrow no headache, fatigue, etc.; but it sometimes happens that certain incidents, often absolutely insignificant, are engraved on her memory in a most unlooked-for manner and assail her as inexplicable obsessions during the ensuing week. The following are some specimens of involuntary suggestion, which generally linger for three or four days, but may occasionally continue for twelve or fifteen.

Hélène told me one Sunday that she had been possessed several times during the day by the hallucinatory image of a straw hat, the inside of which was turned towards her, and which remained vertically in the air about three or four feet in front of her, without being held by any one. She had the feeling that this hat belonged to me, and I happened finally to recollect that at the seance of the preceding Sunday I happened to fan myself with this very hat during her final trance, the image of which had been engraved on her mind in one of the flashes in which she opened her eyes and closed them again instantly before her final awaking. This obsession, said she, was very strong on Monday and the following day or two, but lessened somewhat towards the end of the week.

At another time she preserved during a whole week the sensation of the pressure of my thumb on her left eyebrow. (Compression of the external frontal and suborbital nerves is a means I often employ to hasten her awaking, after a hint given by Léopold.)

There happened to her also twice in the same day an auditive and visual hallucination of an aged person whom she did not recognize, but the extremely characteristic description of whom corresponds so well with that of a gentleman of Geneva who had been mentioned to her a few days previously, immediately before the commencement of a seance (when she was probably already in her state of suggestibility), that there is scarcely any doubt but that these apparitions were the consequence of that conversation.

Following another seance where she had, at the beginning of a Hindoo scene, made vain efforts to detach a bracelet from her left wrist, she preserved for three days the feeling of something grasping that wrist, without understanding what it could be.

In the same way, various feelings of sadness, anger, a desire to laugh or to weep, etc., the cause of which she was unable to explain, have often followed her for a considerable length of time after the seances of which these feelings were the manifest emotional echo. This is often the effect of our dreams on our waking state: we forget the dreams, but their influence remains, and is often more marked in the dreams of a hypnotized person or a somnambulist than in those of ordinary sleep.

The seances are not the exclusive source of the involuntary suggestions which trouble Mlle. Smith in her daily life without any benefit to herself. It is evident that on every occasion when she finds herself in that particular condition of least resistance which we, in our ignorance of its intrinsic nature, designate by the convenient name of "suggestibility," she is exposed to impressions capable of returning to assail her in the course of her daily occupations. Fortunately this condition of suggestibility does not seem to develop itself readily in her outside of the spiritistic reunions.

2. Irruptions of Subliminal Reveries

I shall have too many occasions to cite concrete examples of visions, voices, and other spontaneous outpourings of the work of imagination, which are continually going on under the ordinary consciousness of Mlle. Smith, to dwell long on this point. Some general remarks will suffice.

The connection which the unforeseen phenomena maintain with those of the seances themselves is very varied. Sometimes we are able to recognize them as reproductions, more or less incomplete, of episodes which occurred at the preceding seances, and consider them simple echoes or post-hypnotic repetitions of these last. Sometimes, on the contrary, it appears that we have to deal with preparatory rehearsals of scenes which will unfold themselves at length and will be continued at some later seance. Finally, sometimes it is a question of tableaux, having no connection with those which fill up the seances; they are like leaves, flying away never to return, romances which are continually being fabricated in the deep subliminal strata of Mlle. Smith's consciousness.

Hélène, in fact, does not long remember, nor in much detail, with a few exceptions, those visions which take place in her ordinary state, and which occur most frequently early in the morning, while she is still in bed, or just after she has arisen and while working by the light of her lamp; sometimes in the evening, or during the brief moments of rest in the middle of the day, and, much more rarely, while in the full activity of waking hours she is at her desk. If she had not long since, at my request, and with great good will, acquired the habit of noting in pencil the essential content of these apparitions, either during the apparition itself (which she is not always able to do) or else immediately afterwards, we should have still more deficiencies in the plot of her romances to deplore. Hélène's psychological state, during her spontaneous visions, is known to me only by her own descriptions. She is fortunately a very intelligent observer and a good psychologist.

Her narratives show that her visions are accompanied by a certain degree of obnubilation. For a few moments, for instance, the room, the light of the lamp, disappear from before her eyes; the noise of the wheels in the street ceases to be heard; she feels herself becoming inert and passive, while a feeling of bliss and ecstatic well-being permeates her entire individuality in the presence of the spectacle which appears to her; then the vision, to her great regret, slowly fades from her view, the lamp and the furniture reappear, the outside noises again make themselves heard, and she is astonished that the idea did not occur to her to put down in pencil the strange words she has heard, or that she did not touch or caress, for example, the beautiful birds of many-colored plumage flying and singing around her. Sometimes she has maintained sufficient presence of mind to scribble from dictation the words striking her ear; but the wretched handwriting proves that her attention, all absorbed by the apparition, could not follow the pencil, and that the hand directed it badly. At other times the reverse is the fact. It appears in the course of the vision as though some one took hold of her arm and guided it in spite of herself; the result is splendid calligraphies, wholly different from her own handwriting, executed without her knowledge, and during the execution of which her mind was wholly absent, if we can judge from the surprise she shows on awaking when she finds before her these strange writings, and from analogous scenes which transpire at the seances.

The preceding is applicable especially to the more frequent cases—that is, to the morning or evening visions which happen to her at home, in that intermediate condition between sleep and waking, always so favorable, as we know, to the development of unconscious cerebration. But there are innumerable shades and gradations between this middle type, so to speak, and its opposite extremes; on the one hand is the fortunately very exceptional case where she is seized with ecstasy while at her place of business; and, on the other hand, that in which the automatism limits itself to inscribing some unknown characters or words in another hand than her own in her correspondence and writings—peculiar *lapsus calami*, which she is not slow to perceive on coming to herself.

The following is an example of a case of ecstasy:

Having ascended one day to an upper story, to look for something in a dark store-room, she had an apparition of a man in a turban and large white cloak, whom she had the impression of recognizing,[1] and whose presence filled her with a delightful calm and profound happiness. She could not recall the conversation which passed between them, which, though in an unknown language, she nevertheless had the feeling of having perfectly comprehended. On the departure of the mysterious visitor she was astonished to find herself brought back to sombre reality, and stupefied on noting by her watch that the interview had lasted much longer than it had seemed to do. She preserved all that day a delicious feeling of well-being as the effect of the strange apparition.

The phenomenon of mingling strange writing with her own is of relatively frequent occurrence, and we shall see divers specimens of it in the following chapters, apropos of the romances to which it especially be-

---

[1] Vision relating to the Oriental cycle; the man was the Arab sheik, the father of Simandini.

longs. I will give here only one complex example, which will serve at the same time as an illustration of a special kind of automatism, very harmless, to which Helane is also subject, and which consists in making verses, not without knowing, but at least without intending to do so, and in connection with the most trifling matters.

There are times when, in spite of herself, she feels compelled to speak in distinct rhymes of eight feet, which she does not prepare, and does not perceive until the moment she has finished uttering them.[2] In this particular case it is by a quatrain (a very unusual occurrence) that she replies to some one who had consulted her in regard to some blue ribbon. But this quatrain, by its style, by the vision of the blond head of a child which accompanies it, and by the manner also in which she writes it, causes us to hazard the conjecture that it is an inspiration depending on the underlying Royal cycle; while in the following letter, in which she narrates the affair to M. Lemaître, her pen inscribes, all unknown to her, strange characters evidently due to the cropping out of the Martian cycle, of which she speaks in the letter (see Fig. 1, a passage of that letter making a Martian M and V in the words *vers* and *rimait*):

> I have heard some Martian words this afternoon, but have not been able to retain them in my mind. I send you those heard a few days ago, when I had the vision of which I am about to make you the design (Martian lamp). Yesterday morning I for the first time spoke in verse, without being aware of it; it was only on finishing the sentence that I perceived that it rhymed, and I reconstructed it to assure myself of the fact. A little later, on examining some ribbons, I began anew to speak in verse, and I send those also: they will amuse you. It is a curious thing that I had at that same moment the vision of the blond curly head of a child bound with a blue ribbon. The vision lasted more than a minute. What is still more curious, I do not at all recollect having worn ribbons of that shade as a child: I remember some rose-colored, some red, but I have no recollection whatever of any blue ribbons. I really do not know why I spoke these words; it is

[2] The following are some of these impromptu rhymes, surely up to the level of the circumstances which inspired them, but by which we ought not to judge the *conscious* poetic faculties of Mlle. Smith:

To a little girl proud of her new shoes:
> "Marcelle est là, venez la voir,
> Elle a ses petits souliers noirs."

In a "culinary" discussion:
> "Vous détestez les omelettes,
> Autant que moi les côtelettes."

To a person slightly vain:
> "Vos richesses, ma chère amie,
> Ne me font point du tout envie!"

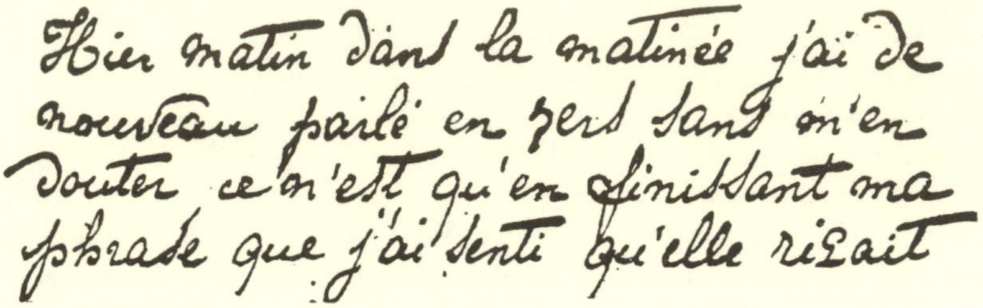
Hier matin dans la matinée j'ai de
nouveau parlé en vers sans m'en
douter ce n'est qu'en finissant ma
phrase que j'ai senti qu'elle rimait

Fig. 1. Fragment of a letter (normal handwriting) of Mlle. Smith, containing two Martian letters. (Collection of M. Lemaître.)

the more amusing. I was obliged to speak them, I assure you, in spite of myself. I was eager to put them on paper, and I noticed in writing them down that, for a moment, the handwriting was not regular, that is, it was slightly different from mine.

Here is the quatrain, the pencil impression of which is too faint to enable a fac-simile to be reproduced here, and in it I have indicated by italics the words and syllables the calligraphy or orthography of which differs from that of Hélène and becomes the style of autornatic handwriting called that of Marie Antoinette:

> Les nuances de ces rubans
> *Me* rappelent *mes* jeunes ans;
> Ce bleu *ver*di je m'en sou*vien*,
> Sans mes cheveux *alloit* si bien!

The head of curly blond hair, ornamented with blue ribbons, also figures in the visions of the Royal cycle, and appears to belong, as is here the case, sometimes to Marie Antoinette herself, sometimes to one or other of her children, especially the Dauphin.

While it is generally easy to connect these eruptions of the subliminal volcano with the various dreams from which they emanate, such is not always the case, and there are visions the origin of which is doubtful and ambiguous. We must not forget that, alongside of the grand cycles of Hélène which are better known, there also float in her latent imagination innumerable small accessory systems, more or less independent, which supply a large part of the seances, such as revelations of former events connected with the families of the sitters, etc.; it is not always possible to identify the fragments coming from these isolated dreams.

3. Teleological Automatisms

The spontaneous phenomena of this category, possessing as a common characteristic a practical utility for Hélène more or less marked, can be subdivided into two classes, according to their direct attachment to the personality of Léopold, or their not belonging to any distinct personality, and which only express in a vivid manner the result of the normal working, although more or less unconscious, of the faculties of memory and of reason. I confine myself now to citing one case of each of these classes, of which we shall see other examples in the chapters relating to Léopold and to supernormal appearances.

One day Mlle. Smith, wishing to take down a large and heavy object from a high shelf, was prevented from so doing by the fact that her uplifted arms seemed as though petrified and incapable of being moved for some seconds; she saw in this a warning and gave up her intention. In a later seance Léopold said that it was he himself who had caused Hélène's arms to become rigid, in order to prevent her from attempting to lift the object which was too heavy for her and would have caused some accident to befall her.

On another occasion a clerk who sought vainly for a certain pattern asked Hélène if she knew what had become of it. Hélène replied mechanically and without reflection, "Yes, it was sent to Mr. J." (a customer of the firm); at the same time there appeared before her in large black figures about eight or ten inches in height the number 18, and she added, instinctively, "It was eighteen days ago." This statement caused the clerk to smile, because of its improbability, the rule of the house being that customers to whom patterns were lent for examination must return them inside of three days or a messenger would be sent for them. Hélène, struck by this objection, and having no conscious recollection of the affair, replied, "Really, perhaps I am wrong." Meanwhile, an investigation of the date indicated in the records of the house showed that she was perfectly correct. It was through various negligences, with which she had nothing at all to do, that the pattern had not been sent for or recovered. Léopold, on being asked, has no recollection of this circumstance, and does not appear to have been the author of this automatism of cryptomnesia, nor of many other analogous phenomena through which Hélène's subconscious memory renders her signal services and has gained for her a well-merited and highly valued reputation.

Thus we see that if the spontaneous automatisms of Mlle. Smith are often the vexatious result of her moments of suggestibility, or the tempestuous irruption of her subliminal reveries, they also often assume the form of useful messages. Such compensation is not to be despised.

IV. The Seances

Mlle. Smith has never been hypnotized. In her instinctive aversion, which she shares with the majority of mediums, to anything that seems like an attempt to experiment upon her, she has always refused to allow herself to be put to sleep. She does not realize that in avoiding the idea she has actually accepted the reality, since her spiritistic experiences in reality constitute for her an auto-hypnotization, which inevitably degenerates into a hetero-hypnotization, as she is brought under the influence of one or other of the persons present at the seance.

All her seances have somewhat of the same psychologic form, the same method of development running through their immense diversity of content. She places herself at the table with the idea and the intention of bringing into play her mediumistic faculties. After an interval, varying from a few seconds to a quarter of an hour, generally in a shorter time if the room is well darkened and the sitters are perfectly silent, she begins to have visions, preceded and accompanied by very varied sensory and motor disturbances, after which she passes into a complete trance. In that state, it rarely happens, and then only for a few moments, that she is entirely unconscious of the persons present, and, as it were, shut up within her personal dream and plunged into profound lethargy (hypnotic syncope) Ordinarily she remains in communication, more or less close, with one of the sitters, who thus finds himself in the same relation towards her as a hypnotizer towards his subject, and able to take advantage of that *rapport*, by giving her any immediate or future suggestions that he may desire. When the seance consists only of waking visions, it lasts generally only a short time—an hour to an hour and a half—and is ended quickly by three sharp raps upon the table, after which Mlle. Smith returns to her normal state, which she scarcely seems to have left. If the somnambulism has been complete, the seance is prolonged to double that length of time, and often longer, and the return to the normal state comes slowly through phases of deep sleep, alternating with relapses into somnambulistic gestures and attitudes, moments of catalepsy, etc. The final awakening is always preceded by several brief awakenings, followed by relapses into sleep.

Each of these preliminary awakenings, as well as the final one, is accompanied by the same characteristic movements of the features. The eyes, which have been for a long time closed, open wide, stupidly staring into vacancy, or fix themselves slowly on the objects and the sitters within their range of vision, the dilated pupils do not react, the face is an impassive and rigid mask, devoid of expression. Hélène seems altogether absent. All at once, with a slight heaving of the breast and raising of the head, and a quick breath, a gleam of intelligence illumines her countenance, the mouth is gracefully opened, the eyes become brilliant, the entire countenance lights up with a pleasant smile and gives evidence of her recognition of the world and of her return to herself. But with the same suddenness with which it appeared, that appearance of life lasts but a second or two, the physiognomy resumes its lifeless mask, the eyes becoming haggard and fixed close again, and the head falls on the back of the chair. This return of sleep will be followed by another sudden awaking, then perhaps by several more, until the final awaking, always distinguished, after the smile at the beginning, by the stereotyped question, "What time is it?" And by a movement of surprise on learning that it is so late. There is no memory of what has transpired during the seance.

A complete description of the psychological and physiological phenomena which present themselves, or which might be obtained in the course of the seances, would detain me too long, since there is absolutely nothing constant either in the nature or in the succession of the phenomena, and no two seances are evolved exactly in the same manner. I must confine myself to some striking characteristics.

Three principal symptoms, almost contemporaneous generally, announce that Mlle. Smith is beginning to enter into her trance.

There are on the one side emotional or coenaesthetic modifications, the cause of which is revealed a little later in the subsequent messages. Hélène is, for instance, seized by an invincible desire to laugh, which she cannot or will not explain; or she complains of sadness, fear, of different unpleasant sensations, of heat or of cold, of nausea, etc., according to the nature of the communications which are approaching and of which these emotional states are the forerunners.

There are, on the other hand, phenomena of systematic anaesthesia (negative hallucinations), limited to those sitters whom the coming messages concern. Hélène ceases to see them, while continuing to hear their voices and feel their touch; or, on the contrary, she is astonished to no longer hear them, though she sees their lips moving, etc.; or, finally, she does not perceive them in any manner, and demands to know why they are leaving when the seance is hardly begun. In its details this systematic anaesthesia varies infinitely, and extends sometimes to but one part of the person concerned, to his hand, to a portion of his face, etc., without it always being possible to explain these capricious details by the content of the following visions; it would seem that the incoherence of the dream presides over this preliminary work of disintegration, and that the normal perceptions are absorbed by the subconscious personality eager for material for the building up of the hallucinations which it is preparing.

Systematic anaesthesia is often complicated with positive hallucinations, and Hélène will manifest her surprise at seeing, for example, a strange costume or an unusual coiffure. This, in reality, is the vision which is already being installed.

The third symptom, which does not manifest itself clearly in her, but the presence of which can be often established before all the others by investigation, is a complete allochiria,[3] ordinarily accompanied by various other sensory and motor disturbances. If, at the beginning of the seance, Hélène is asked, for example, to raise her right hand, to move the left index-finger, or to close one eye, she begins straightway to carry into effect these different acts; then all at once, without knowing why and without hesitation, she deceives herself in regard to the side, and raises her left hand, moves her right index-finger, closes the other eye, etc. This indicates that she is no longer in her normal state, though still appearing to retain her ordinary consciousness, and with the liveliness of a normal person discusses the question of her having mistaken her right hand or eye for her left, and vice versa. It is to be noted that Léopold, on such occasions of pronounced allochiria, does not share this error in regard to the side. I have assisted at some curious discussions between him and Hélène, she insisting that such a hand was her right, or that the Isle Rousseau is on the left as one passes the bridge of Mont Blanc or coming from the railway station, and Léopold all the while, by means of raps upon the table, giving her clearly to understand she was wrong.[4]

A little after the allochiria, and sometimes simultaneously with it, are to be found various other phenomena, extremely variable, of which I here cite only a few. One of her arms is contractured as it rests upon the table, and resists the efforts of the sitters to lift it up, as though it were a bar of iron.* Sometimes this contracture does not exist before, but establishes itself at the same instant that some one touches the forearm, and increases in proportion to the efforts which are made to overcome it. There is no regularity in the distribution of the anaesthesia (changing from one instant to another), the contractures, or convulsions which the hands and arms of Hélène exhibit. It all seems due to pure caprice, or to depend only on underlying dreams, of which little is known.*

If Hélène is experimented upon and questioned too long, the development of the original visions is obstructed, and she easily reaches a degree of sensibility where she falls into the standard class of public representations of hypnotism—a charmed and fascinated state in which she remains riveted before some brilliant object, as, for example, the ring, trinkets, or cuff-button of one of the sitters; then precipitates herself in a frenzy upon the object, and tries to secure it; or assumes emotional attitudes and poses

---

[3] The confusion of sensations in the two sides of the body, as when a person locates in the right leg a touch upon the left leg.

[4] See, on allochiria, P. Janet, *Stigmates mentaux des hystériques,* pp. 60–71; and *Névroses et idées fixes,* vol. i. p. 234.

under the influence of joyous airs upon the piano; experiences suggested hallucinations of all kinds, sees terrible serpents, which she pursues with a pair of pincers; beautiful flowers, which she smells with deep respirations and distributes to the sitters; or, again, bleeding wounds which have been made on her hand, and which cause her to shed tears. The commonplace character of these phenomena causes their long continuance to be deprecated, and the ingenuity of all is exercised in endeavoring by different means, none of which is very efficacious or very rapid, to plunge her into profound and tranquil sleep, from which she is not long in passing of her own accord into complete somnambulism and in taking up the thread of her personal imaginations.

If all these disturbing investigations have been successfully avoided, the spontaneous development of the automatisms is effected with greater rapidity and fulness. It is possible then to behold, in the same seance, a very varied spectacle, and to listen, besides, to certain special communications made in a semi-waking state to one or other of the sitters: then, in complete somnambulism, a Hindoo vision is presented, followed by a Martian dream, with an incarnation of Léopold in the middle, and a scene of Marie Antoinette to wind up with. Ordinarily two of these last creations will suffice to fill up a seance. One such representation is not performed without the loss of considerable strength by the medium, which shows itself by the final sleep being prolonged sometimes for an hour, interrupted, as I have said, by repetitions of the preceding somnambulistic scenes, easily recognizable by certain gestures or the murmuring of characteristic words. Passing through these diverse oscillations and the ephemeral awaking, of which I have spoken above, Hélène finishes by returning to her normal state; but the seances which have been too long continued or too full of movement leave her very much fatigued for the rest of the day. It has also sometimes happened to her to re-enter the somnambulism (from which she had probably not completely emerged) during the course of the evening or on returning home, and only to succeed in recovering her perfectly normal state through the assistance of a night's sleep.

As to the real nature of Hélène's slumbers at the end of the seances, and her states of consciousness when she awakes, it is difficult for me to pronounce, having only been able to observe them under unfavorable conditions—that is, in the presence of sitters more or less numerous and restless. The greater part certainly consist of somnambulisms, in which she hears all that passes around her, since although she seems profoundly asleep and absent, the suggestions then given her to be carried out after awaking are registered and performed wonderfully—at least when Léopold, who is almost always on hand and answers by movements of one finger or another to questions put to him, does not make any opposition or declare that the suggestion shall not be carried out! There are also brief moments when Hélène seems to be in a profound state of coma and kind of syncope without trace of psychic life; her pulse and respiration continue to be regular, but she does not react to any excitation, her arms, if raised, fall heavily, no sign of Léopold can be obtained, and suggestions made at that instant will not be acted upon.

These lethargic phases, during which all consciousness seems to be abolished, are generally followed by cataleptic phases in which the hands and arms preserve every position in which they may be placed, and continue the movements of rotation or of oscillation which may be forced upon them, but never for more than one or two minutes.

In default of more complete experiments, I submit the following comparison of Hélène's muscular force and of her sensibility to pain before and after a seance lasting nearly three hours, the second half being in full somnambulism. At 4.50 o'clock, on sitting down at the table three dynamometric tests with her right hand gave kilos. 27.5, 27, 25—average, 26.5. The sensibility to pain measured on the back of the median phalanx of the index-finger with the algesiometer of Griesbach, gave for the right, grs. 35, 40, 20, 20—average, 29; for the left, 35, 20, 20, 15—average, 22.5 grs. (Sensibility slightly more delicate than that of another lady present at the seance, not a medium and in perfect health.)

At 7.45 o'clock, some minutes after the final awaking: dynamometer, right hand, 8, 4.5, 4.5—average, 5.7; algesiometer, complete analgesia both as to right and left, on the whole of the back of the index as well as the rest of the hand and wrist, the maximum of the instrument (100 grs.) was attained and passed without arousing any painful sensation but only an impression of contact.

One hour later, after dinner: dynamometer 22, 22, 19—average, 21; algesiometer, 20, 18 for the right: 15, 20 for the left. It is possible, then, to say that her muscular force and sensibility to pain, both normal immediately before her entrance upon the seance, are still abolished in the first fifteen minutes after awaking, but are found to be restored in about an hour. Perception of colors, on the contrary, appeared to be as perfect immediately after awaking as before the seance. The tremor of the index-finger, normal before the seance, is very much exaggerated in its amplitude for a certain time after awaking and reflects sometimes the respiratory movements, as can be seen by the curves of Fig. 2. This denotes a great diminution of kinesthetic sensibility and of voluntary control over the immobility of the hand.

The state in which Mlle. Smith carries out the post-hypnotic suggestions made to her in the course of her somnambulisms, when they do not come into collision with either the pronounced opposition of Léopold or the states of lethargy of which I have spoken, is interesting on account of

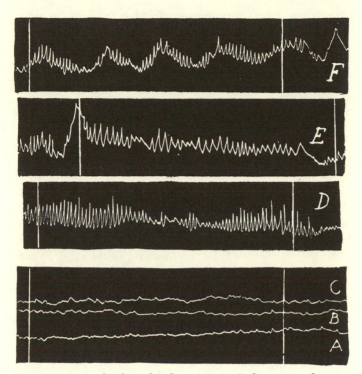

Fig. 2. Tremor of right index-finger. A, B, C, fragments of curves taken in the normal state before the seance (A and C with closed eyes; B with open eyes looking at the index-finger); D, E, F, fragments of curves received in succession a quarter of an hour after the seance. The curve F reflects the respiratory oscillations. The curves go from right to left, and the interval between the two vertical lines is ten seconds.

its varied character, which seems to depend upon the greater or less ease with which the hallucination or the act suggested can be reconciled with Hélène's normal personality. Their execution in the full waking state seems to be confined to suggestions of simple acts, free from absurdity, the idea of which would be easily accepted and carried out by the normal self when the desired moment arrived. If, on the contrary, it is a question of more complicated and difficult things, compatible, however, with the rational points of view of the normal waking state, Hélène falls momentarily into somnambulism for the execution of the order given, unless she has permanently remained in that state, in spite of her apparent awaking, in order not to re-enter definitely and completely upon her ordinary state until after the execution of the order, of which there then remains to her no recollection whatever.

From the foregoing facts we may conclude that little or nothing of that which goes on around her escapes her subconscious intelligence, and it is from this source that her somnambulistic romances are nourished afresh.

A word more as to the preparation for the seances. I do not refer to a conscious preparation, but to a subliminal incubation or elaboration, unknown by her, showing itself on the level of her ordinary personality in the form of fugitive gleams and fragmentary images during her sleep at night or the moments of awaking in the morning. Mlle. Smith, in reality, has no hold, possesses no influence, upon the nature of her visions and somnambulisms. She is able, undoubtedly, up to a certain point, to aid their appearance in a general way, by cultivating tranquillity of mind, securing darkness and silence in the room, and by abandoning herself to a passive attitude of mind; or to hinder it, on the other hand, by movement, or distraction of attention; but with the fixed and concrete content itself of her automatisms she has nothing to do and no share in the responsibility for it. So far as her great cycles or her detached messages are concerned, they are fabricated in her in spite of herself, and without her having a word to say about their production, any more than one has in the formation of his dreams. When it is recollected, on the other hand, that the phenomena of incubation, of subliminal preparation, or unconscious cerebration, are universal facts, playing their rôle in the psychology of every human being, we can rely upon finding them also among the mediums, and upon their holding a place with them much more important than with others, owing to the fact that their subconscious life is so much more fully developed.

With each one of us the expectation or the simple perspective of any event—a departure, a visit, an errand, or undertaking to do anything, a letter to write, in short, all the more insignificant incidents of daily existence, when they are not absolutely unforeseen—promote a psychological adaptation more or less extended and profound.

Alongside of and underneath the conscious expectancy, certain physical or mental attitudes, voluntarily assumed in view of the event, always effect an underlying preparation of an inward kind, a change which we may regard, according to the side from which we consider the individual, as a peculiar psychical orientation or cerebral adjustment, a modification in the association of ideas or in the dynamics of the cortical nerves. But everything points to the fact that in persons gifted with mediumship this underlying preparation is capable of assuming on occasion a greater importance than is the case with ordinary mortals, a much more complete independence of the ordinary consciousness.

To return to Mlle. Smith, when she knows some time in advance who will be present at her next seance, and what people she will almost surely meet there, it would be altogether natural that such previous knowledge of the environment and of the sitters would influence her subliminal thoughts and in some degree direct the course of the latent incubation. It may well be asked, therefore, whether the varied spectacle which the seances furnish is really always impromptu and has its birth on the spur of the moment like ordinary dreams, or whether it has been subconsciously thought out, the seance being only the performance of an arrested programme, the representation *coram populo* of scenes already ripened in the deep subliminal strata of the medium.

Neither of these two hypotheses, held to exclude the other, answers to the facts, but there is some truth in both of them.

The *menu* of the seances—if the expression is permissible—is always composed of one or two *plats de résistance,* carefully prepared in advance in the subliminal laboratories, and of various *hors d'oeuvres* left to the inspiration of the moment. To speak more exactly, the general plot, the chief lines and more striking points of the scenes which unfold themselves are fixed according to a previous arrangement, but the details of execution and accessory embellishments are entirely dependent upon chance circumstances. The proof of this is found, on the one hand, in the suppleness, the perfect ease, the appropriateness with which Hélène's automatisms—if we can still apply the word automatism to those cases in which spontaneity, self-possession, free use of all the faculties constitute the dominant characteristics—often adapt themselves to unexpected situations in the environment or capricious interruptions on the part of the sitters; on the other hand, in the fact that Léopold, interrogated at the beginning of the seance, ordinarily knows very well and announces the principal vision or incarnations which are about to make their appearance, provided, at least, the spectators do not hinder their unfolding by their tempestuous clamor for something else.

The animated conversations, sometimes full of spirited repartee, between Léopold or Marie Antoinette and the sitters, could not have been prepared in advance, and are altogether opposed to the stereotyped repetition which is generally expected of automatic phenomena. But, on the other hand, such repetition, almost entirely mechanical and devoid of sense, presents itself on frequent occasions. I have, for instance, seen somnambulistic scenes presented which were entirely misplaced, and constituted at the time veritable anachronisms, which would have perfectly fitted the situation eight days previously in another environment, and for which the aforesaid scenes had been evidently intended; but, having been withheld until the last moment by unforeseen circumstances, the following seance gets the benefit of these postponed messages.

Here is proof that Hélène's subliminal imagination prepares up to a certain point her principal productions, in view of the conditions and surroundings under which the seance will probably take place, and also that these products, once elaborated, must be eliminated and poured forth with a sort of blind necessity, at the right or the wrong time, whenever the entrance of Hélène into a favorable hypnoid state furnishes them an opportunity so to do. It follows also that her normal personality has nothing whatever to do with the preparation of the seances, since she can neither suppress nor change scenes badly adapted to the actual environment, the appearance of which sometimes greatly annoys Mlle. Smith when they are recounted to her after the seance; nor can she provoke the messages, the production of which she desires and vainly hopes for—as, for example, a medical consultation with Léopold, the incarnation of a deceased parent, or a scene from one cycle rather than from the others, for the benefit of a sitter who particularly desires it, and whom she is very desirous to please.

Much more could be said concerning the psychological side of the seances of Mlle. Smith, but I must limit myself. It will be possible to gain a more complete idea of this subject by studying the illustrations in the following chapters on the chief cycles of her brilliant subliminal fantasy.

CHAPTER FOUR

The Personality of Léopold

Is LÉOPOLD really Joseph Balsamo, as he pretends? Or, since he has nothing in common with the famous thaumaturgist of the last century, save a certain superficial resemblance, is he, at any rate, a real being, separate from, and independent of Mlle. Smith? Or, finally, is he only a pseudo-reality, a kind of allotropic modification of Hélène herself, a product of her subliminal imagination, just like our dream creations and the rôles suggested to a hypnotic subject?

Of these three suppositions it is the last which to my mind is undoubtedly the true one, while in Mlle. Smith's eyes it is as certainly the false view. It would be hard to imagine a more profound difference of opinion than that which exists between Mlle. Smith and myself on this subject. It is I always, who get the worst of a discussion with her concerning it. I yield for two reasons. First, out of politeness; and, secondly, because I understand Hélène perfectly, and, putting myself in her place, realize that I should think exactly as she does about the matter.

Given her surroundings and personal experiences, it is impossible for her to do otherwise than believe in the objective distinct existence of that mysterious being who constantly enters into her life in a sensible and quasi-material way, leaving her no room to doubt. He presents himself before her endowed with corporeality like that of other people, and hides objects which are behind him exactly as an ordinary individual of flesh and bone would do. He talks into her ears, generally into the left, in a characteristic voice, which appears to come from a variable distance, sometimes about six feet off, sometimes much farther. He jars the table on which she has placed her immobile arms, takes hold of her wrist and writes with her hand, holding the pen in a manner unlike her, and with a handwriting wholly different from hers. He puts her to sleep without her knowledge, and she is astonished to learn upon awaking that he has gesticulated with her arms and spoken through her mouth in the deep bass voice of a man, with an Italian accent, which has nothing in common with the clear and heautiful quality of her feminine voice.

Moreover, he is not always on hand. He by no means answers Hélène's appeals on all occasions; is not at her mercy; far from it. His conduct, his manifestations, his comings and goings cannot be predicted with any certainty, and testify to an autonomous being, endowed with free-will, often otherwise occupied or absent on his own affairs, which do not permit of his holding himself constantly at the disposal of Mlle. Smith. Sometimes he remains for weeks without revealing himself, in spite of her wishing for him and calling upon him. Then, all at once, he makes his appearance when she least expects him. He speaks for her in a way she would have no idea of doing, he dictates to her poems of which she would be incapable. He replies to her oral or mental questions, converses with her, and discusses various questions. Like a wise friend, a rational mentor, and as one seeing things from a higher plane, he gives her advice, counsel, orders even sometimes directly opposite to her wishes and against which she rebels. He consoles her, exhorts her, soothes, encourages, and reprimands her; he undertakes against her the defence of persons she does not like, and pleads the cause of those who are antipathetic to her. In a word, it would be impossible to imagine a being more independent or more different from Mlle. Smith herself, having a more personal character, an individuality more marked, or a more certain actual existence.

Hélène is also fortified in this conviction by the belief not only of members of her own family, but by that of other cultivated people who, having attended many of her seances, have no doubt whatever of Léopold's objective and separate existence. There are those who believe so firmly in the reality of this superior being, invisible to them, that they are in the habit of calling upon him during the absence of Mlle. Smith. Naturally they obtain responses, through the table or otherwise, and that causes unforeseen complications sometimes when she comes to learn of it. For while she admits theoretically—and Léopold himself has often declared the same thing—that he extends his surveillance and protection from afar over other spiritistic groups, and especially over all Hélène's friends and acquaintances, in practice and in fact, however, it happens that neither he nor she will willingly admit the authenticity of those pretended communications from Léopold obtained in the absence of the medium of his predilection. It is generally some deceiving spirit who has manifested in his place on these occasions. These denials, however, do not prevent those who have become believers from continuing to believe in the omnipresence of this good genius, or from teaching their children to revere him, to make vows and address prayers to him. It must not be forgotten that spiritism is a religion. This also explains the great respect shown to mediums, which is like that accorded to priests.

It follows that, without in the least refraining from speaking ill of them whenever they think they have a grievance against them, on the other hand they bestow on them the same marks of respect as are only accorded to the most sublime product of the human race.

I have known a *salon* where, on the centre table, in full view and in the place of honor, were two photographs in beautiful frames: on the one side the head of Christ, on the other the portrait of—Mlle. Hélène Smith.

Among other believers, with less ideal but more practical aspirations, no business matter of importance is closed, no serious decision made, until Léopold has been consulted through Hélène as an intermediary, and the cases are too numerous to mention in which he has furnished important information, prevented a heavy precuniary loss, given an efficacious medical prescription, etc.

It is easily seen how all the successes obtained by Léopold, and the mystical veneration which many very estimable persons accord him, must contribute to strengthen the faith of Hélène in her all-powerful protector. It is in vain that, against this absolute assurance, one seeks to avail one's self of the arguments of contemporary psychology. The example of the fictions of the dream, the analogies taken from hypnotism and from psychopathology, considerations of mental disintegration, the division of the consciousness and the formation of second personalities, all these refined subtleties of our modern scientists break in pieces like glass against immovable rock. I shall not undertake to combat a proposition which, for her, has incontestably so much evidence in its favor, and which resolves all difficulties in the most felicitous manner and in conformity to good common-sense.

Nevertheless, since each individual has a right to his own opinion in the world, I beg leave to assume, for the time being, that Léopold does not exist outside of Mlle. Smith, and to try to discover his possible genesis in the mental life of the latter—solely by hypothesis and by means of psychological experiment. Therefore, readers who have little taste for this kind of academic composition had better skip this chapter.

I. Psychogenesis of Léopold

A description of the development of Léopold is not easy, since he has a double origin, apparent and real, like the cranial nerves which give so much trouble to the students of anatomy.

His apparent origin, or, I should say, the moment when he is outwardly separated from the personality of Hélène, and manifests as an independent "spirit," is relatively clear and well marked; but his actual origin, profoundly enfolded in the most inward strata of Hélène's personality and inextricably mixed up with them presents great obscurities and can only be determined in a very conjectural manner. Let us begin with the apparent origin, or the first appearance of Léopold at the seances.

It is easy to understand that, once initiated into spiritism and plunged into a current of ideas where the comforting doctrine of spirit-guides and protectors holds an important place, Mlle. Smith did not delay in coming into possession of, like all good mediums, a disincarnate spirit specially attached to her person. She even had two in succession, Victor Hugo and

Cagliostro. It is not a question of a simple change of name of the guide of Hélène, who presented himself first under the aspect and the name of the great poet and then afterwards adopted that of the renowned thaumaturgist, but there were, at least at the beginning, two different personalities, apparently hostile to each other, one of whom by degrees supplanted the other, after a struggle, a trace of which is found in the very incomplete reports of the seances of that period. Three phases can also be distinguished in the psychogenesis of Mlle. Smith's guide: an initial phase of five months, during which Victor Hugo reigns alone; a phase of transition of about a year, when the protection of Victor Hugo is seen to be powerless to protect Hélène and her spiritistic group against the invasion of an intruder called Léopold, who claims and manifests an increasing authority over the medium by virtue of mysterious relations in the course of a previous existence; finally, the present period, which has lasted for six years past, in which Victor Hugo no longer figures, and which may be dated approximately from the moment when it was revealed that Léopold is only an assumed name, under which he hides in reality the great personality of Joseph Balsamo.

I do not find any fact worthy of mention in the first phase, in which Victor Hugo, who seems to have appeared as the guide of Mlle. Smith about the 1st of April, 1892 (see above, p. 33), played a rôle of no importance. In the second phase, however, it is necessary to cite some extracts from the reports of the seances of the N. group, in order to throw light upon the singular character which Léopold manifested there from the beginning.

August 26, 1892.—"A spirit announces himself under the name of Léopold. He comes for Mlle. Smith, and seems to wish to have a great authority over her. She sees him for some moments, he appears to be about thirty-five years of age, and is clothed altogether in black. The expression of his countenance is rather pleasing, and through answers to some questions which we put to him we are given to understand that he knew her in another existence, and that he does not wish her to give her heart to any one here below. . . . Mlle. Smith recognizes her guide, Victor Hugo. She is made happy by his arrival, and asks his protection against the obsession of this new spirit. He answers that she has nothing to fear, that he will always be present. She is joyful at being guarded and protected by him, and feels that she has nothing to fear."

September 2.— . . ."Léopold comes also, but Mlle. Smith fears nothing, since her guide (Victor Hugo) is there to protect her."

September 23.— . . ."An unpleasant evening. A spirit announces himself. It is Léopold. He speaks to us at once: 'I am here. I wish to be master of this sitting.' We are very much disappointed, and do not expect any good of him. He tries, as he had already done once before, to put Mlle.

Smith to sleep, who has great difficulty in struggling against this sleep. She rises from the table, hoping by this means to rid herself of him, and that he will give up his place to others. She returns in about ten minutes, but he is still there, and apparently has no intention of abandoning his place. We summon our friends (spiritual) to our aid. . . . They take Léopold's place momentarily, but very soon Léopold returns; we struggle with him, we desire him to go away, but neither soft nor hard words have any effect; before that dogged determination we realize that all our efforts will be useless, and we decide to close the seance."

October 3.—"[Manifestation by the favorite spirits of the group, who declare] that they have not been able to come, as they would have liked to do; that they were prevented by the spirit of Léopold, who is trying to introduce himself to us; that we should repulse him as much as possible, persuaded that he does not come for any good end. I do not know whether we shall be able to rid ourselves of him, but we greatly fear that he will injure us and retard our advancement."

October 7.— . . ."Léopold announces himself. We try to reason with him; we do not wish to forbid his coming, but we ask of him that he shall come as a friend to all, and not in the rôle of master. He is not satisfied; appears to bear much malice. We trust he will come to have better feelings. He shows himself, walks around the table, bows to us, and salutes each one with his hand, and retires again, leaving his place to others."

October 14.—"[After a quarter of an hour of motionless and silent waiting in darkness around the table Mlle. Smith is questioned, and she is shaken in vain.] She is asleep. By the advice of persons present we allow her to remain asleep, when, at the end of five minutes, the table raises itself, a spirit announces himself. It is Victor Hugo; we ask if he has anything to say; he answers yes, and spells out: *Wake her; do not allow her ever to sleep.* We try to do so. We are nervous about that sleep; we have great difficulty in awakening her."

January 6, 1893.—"After twenty minutes of waiting, Léopold arrives, and, as is his habit, puts the medium to sleep for some minutes; he torments us, and prevents our friends (disincarnate) from coming to the table. He vexes us in every way, and goes contrary to all our wishes. In presence of that rancor the sitters regret the indications of ill-humor they have shown towards him, and deplore having to pay so dear for them. It is with difficulty that the medium can be awakened."

February, 1893.—"In one of the seances of this month a remarkable thing happened: the spirit of Léopold, who was very much irritated on that day, twice in succession took away her chair from our medium and carried it to the farther end of the room, while Mlle. Smith fell heavily to the floor. Not expending this wretched farce, Mlle. Smith struck her knee so hard that for several days she suffered pain in walking. We were obliged to terminate the seance; we were not comfortable. Why this animosity?"

This word *animosity* describes very well the conduct and the feelings that Léopold seemed to have towards the N. group and against his placid rival, Victor Hugo. The personal recollections of the sitters whom I have been able to interrogate confirm the substantial physiognomy of the two figures.* That of Hugo is, in effect, effaced and altogether eclipsed by the totally opposite character of the arrogant Léopold, who takes a peculiar pleasure in the rôle of vindictive and jealous mischief-maker, obstructing the appearance of the "spirits" desired by the group, putting the medium to sleep, or causing her to fall on the floor, forbidding her to give her heart to another, and breaking up the seances as far as he is able. It seems to have finally resulted in the meetings of the N. group coming to an end at the beginning of the summer; then comes a break of six months, after which I find Mlle. Smith on the 12th of December inaugurating a new series of seances, with an entirely different spiritistic group organized by Prof. Cuendet. Here Victor Hugo very rarely appears, and never in the rôle of guide, which rôle is freely accorded, without objection, to Léopold, whose real identity (Cagliostro) was no secret to any one in the new environment. It was, therefore, in the course of the year 1893, at a period which cannot be precisely determined from the records, that the rivalry of these two personalities was terminated by the complete triumph of the second.

It follows from the preceding recital that the appearance of Léopold in seances of the N. group was a phenomenon of manifest contrast, of hostility, and of antagonism towards that group.

It is a difficult and delicate task to pronounce upon the complex spirit of an environment of which one was not a part, and in regard to which one possesses only a few and not very concordant incidents. The following, however, seem to be the facts:

The N. group, much more numerous than is convenient in seances of that kind, was composed of very varied elements. Alongside of serious believers were ordinarily some students who boarded with one of the ladies of the group, and who do not appear to have felt the seriousness of spiritistic reunions.

That age has no mercy, and the profound signification of the seances often escaped their superficial and frivolous intelligence. Under such conditions Mlle. Smith was inevitably compelled to experience two contrary impressions. On the one hand, she perceived herself admired, made much of, feted, as the unrivalled medium, which she really was, and upon whom the group depended for its existence; on the other hand, her secret instincts and high personal dignity could not but be offended by the familiarities to which she was exposed in this mixed environment.

I regard the two rival and successive guides of Hélène as the expression of this double sentiment. If she had been brought up like an American woman, or if her nature had been a degree less fine, the frivolity of the seances would undoubtedly have only given more warmth and brilliancy to Victor Hugo; instead of which, the victorious colors of Léopold are raised over a nature of great native pride, extremely sensitive on the point of feminine dignity, and whose severe and rigid education had already exalted her sense of self-respect. After a struggle of a year between these two personifications of opposite emotional tendencies, the second, as we have seen, finally triumphs; and Mlle. Smith withdraws from the N. group, which at the same time breaks up.

The idea I have formed of Léopold is now apparent. He represents, to my mind, in Mlle. Smith, the synthesis, the quintessence—and the expansion, too—of the most hidden springs of the psychological organism. He gushes forth from that deep and mysterious sphere into which the deepest roots of our individual existence are plunged, which bind us to the species itself, and perhaps to the Absolute, and whence confusedly spring our instincts of physical and moral self-preservation, our sexual feelings. When Hélène found herself in an environment not exactly dangerous, but where she simply ran the risk, as in the N. group, of yielding to some inclination contrary to her fundamental aspirations, it is then that Léopold suddenly springs up, speaking as the master, taking possession of the medium for himself, and indicating his unwillingness that she should attach herself to any one here below. We here recognize the same principle of self-protection and self-preservation which was already active in her as a young girl in the teleological automatisms arising on the occasion of certain emotional shocks, of which I have spoken on p. 22.

But, by these considerations, we have travelled very far from the original appearance of Léopold in the seance of the 26th of August, 1892, towards his actual, more ancient origin. This seems to date from a great fright which Hélène had in the course of her tenth year. As she was walking along the street, on her way home from school, she was attacked by a big dog. The terror of the poor child can well be imagined, and from which she was happily delivered by a personage clothed in a long brown robe with flowing sleeves and with a white cross on the breast, who, appearing to her suddenly and as by a miracle, chased the dog away, and disappeared before she had time to thank him. But, according to Léopold, this personage was no other than himself, who on this occasion for the first time appeared to Hélène, and saved her by driving away the dog.

This explanation was given by Léopold on the 6th of October, 1895, in a seance in which Hélène experienced, in a somnambulistic state, a repetition of that scene of fright, with heart-rending cries, gestures of struggle and defence, attempts at flight, etc. In the waking state she very well recalls this episode of her childhood, but cannot accept Léopold as the person who came to her rescue, but believes it to have been a priest or member of some religious order who rushed to her assistance and drove the animal away. Her parents also recollected the incident, which she told them one day on returning from school in a very excited state, and after which she could not for a long time encounter a dog in the street without hiding herself in the folds of her mother's dress. She has since always preserved an instinctive aversion towards dogs.

We have seen (p. 25) that after this first incident, matters remained *in statu quo* for four years, up to the time when the age of puberty began to favor the development of the Oriental visions. Here, Léopold, to whom we owe this information, does not altogether agree with himself, for at one time he says that it was he himself who furnished Mlle. Smith with her visions of India, at another time he says that they are reminiscences of one of her former existences.

Alongside of these varied visions, Léopold has clearly appeared under the form of the protector in the dark robe in a number of cases. I will only cite two examples, one very remote, the other quite recent.

One day Hélène went to consult her family physician for some trifling ailment, who, having known her for a long time and being an old friend of her family, presumed to give her an innocent kiss. He was quite unprepared for the explosion of wrath which this familiarity provoked, and hastened to make his apologies: but what is of interest to us in this connection is the fact that under the shock of this emotion her defender of the brown robe appeared before her in the corner of the room, and did not leave her side until she had reached home.

A short time ago this same protector, always in the same costume, accompanied her several days in succession while she was traversing a little-frequented part of the route towards her place of business. One evening, also, he appeared to her at the entrance to the street leading to the locality in question, in the attitude of barring the way, and obliged her to make a detour to regain her house.

Mlle. Smith has the impression—and several indications go to show that she is not deceived—that it is with the purpose of sparing her some unpleasant sight or a dangerous encounter that Léopold, in the brown robe, appears to her under perfectly well-known conditions. He rises before her always at a distance of about ten yards, walks, or rather glides, along in silence, at the same rate as she advances towards him, attracting and fascinating her gaze in such a manner as to prevent her turning her eyes away from him either to the right or the left, until she has passed the place of danger. It is to be noted that whereas Léopold, under other circumstances—for instance, at the seances—shows himself to her in the most varied costumes and speaks on all subjects, it is always under his hieratic aspect, silent, and clothed in his long dark robe, that he appears to her on those occasions of real life in which she is exposed to feelings of fright peculiar to her sex, as he appeared to her on that first occasion in her tenth year.

The hints I have given sufficiently justify, I think, my opinion that the real and primordial origin of Léopold is to be found in that deep and delicate sphere in which we so often encounter the roots of hypnoid phenomena, and to which the most illustrious visionaries, such as Swedenborg,[1] seem to owe a great part not only of the intellectual content but of the imaginative form, the hallucinatory wrapping, of their genius. There is a double problem to be solved in Mlle. Smith's case. Why have these instinctive feelings and emotional tendencies which are common to the entire human race succeeded in developing in her a product so complex and highly organized as is the personality of Léopold? and why, in the second place, does that personality believe itself to be Joseph Balsamo?

I instantly reply that these two results are, to my mind, entirely the effect of autosuggestion. To explain the first, the simple fact of her being occupied with spiritism and engaged in mediumistic experiments, is sufficient. Take any individual having in her subconsciousness memories, scruples, emotional tendencies, put into her head spiritistic leanings, then seat her at a table, or put a pencil in her hand: even though she may not be of a very impressionable or suggestible temperament, or inclined to the mental disintegration which the general public calls the mediumistic faculty, nevertheless, it will not be long before her subliminal elements group themselves and arrange themselves according to the "personal" form to which all consciousness tends,[2] and which discloses itself outwardly by communications which have the appearance of coming directly from disincarnate spirits.

In the case of Mlle. Smith, Léopold did not exist under the title of a distinct secondary personality before Hélène began to be occupied with spiritism. It was at the seances of the N. group, by an emotional reaction against certain influences, as we have seen, that he began, little by little, to take shape, aided by memories of the same general tone, until he finally grew into an apparently independent being, revealing himself through the table, manifesting a will and a mind of his own, recalling analogous former incidents of Hélène's life, and claiming for himself the merit of having intervened in it in the rôle of her protector.

Once established, this secondary self could not do otherwise than to grow, and to develop and strengthen itself in all directions, assimilating to itself a host of new data favoring the state of suggestibility which ac-

[1] See Lehmann's *Auberglaube und Zauberei*, p. 217 *et seq*. Stuttgart, 1898.

[2] W. James, "Thought Tends to Personal Form." *Principles of Psychology*, vol. i. p. 225 *et seq*. New York, 1890.

companies the exercise of mediumship. Without the spiritism and the autohypnotization of the seances, Léopold could never have been truly developed into a personality, but would have continued to remain in the nebulous, incoherent state of vague subliminal reveries and of occasional automatic phenomena.

The second problem, that of explaining why this secondary personality, once established, believes itself to be Cagliostro rather than any other celebrated personage, or of remaining simply the anonymous guardian angel of Mlle. Smith, would demand a very complete knowledge of the thousand outside influences which have surrounded Hélène since the beginning of her mediumship, and which may have involuntarily influenced her.

But on this point I have only succeeded in collecting a very few incidents, which leave much still to be desired, and are of such a character that it is entirely permissible for any one to claim that the purely psychological origin of that personality is not clearly established, and to prefer, if he chooses, the actual intervention of the disincarnate Joseph Balsamo to my hypothesis of autosuggestion.

The following, however, are the facts advanced by me in support of the latter:

The authoritative and jealous spirit, the evident enemy of the N. group, who manifested himself on the 26th of August, 1892, under the name of Léopold,* did not reveal his identity as that of Cagliostro until some time afterwards, under the following circumstances:

One of the most regular attendants at the reunions of the N. group was a Mme. B., who had long been an adherent of spiritism, and who had previously attended numerous seances at the house of M. and Mme. Badel, a thoroughly convinced couple of amateurs, now deceased, whose *salon* and round table have held a very honorable place in the history of Genevese occultism. But I learned from Mme. B. that one of the disincarnate spirits who manifested himself oftenest at the seances of M. and Mme. Badel was this very Joseph Balsamo. There is, indeed, no figure in history which accords better with the idea of a posthumous return to the mysteries of the round table than that of the enigmatic Sicilian, especially since Alexandre Dumas, *père*, has surrounded him with an additional halo of romance.

Not content with the public reunions of the N. group, Mme. B. often invited Hélène to her house for private seances, of which no record was made. At one of these, Hélène having had a vision of Léopold, who pointed out to her with a wand a decanter, Mme. B. suddenly thought of a celebrated episode in the life of Cagliostro, and after the seance she proceeded to take from a drawer and show to Hélène an engraving taken from an illustrated edition of Dumas, representing the famous scene of the decanter between Balsamo and the Dauphin at the chateau of Taverney. At the same time she gave utterance to the idea that the spirit who manifested himself at the table by means of Hélène's hands was certainly Joseph Balsamo; and she expressed her astonishment that Hélène had given him the name of Léopold, to which Hélène replied that it was he himself who had given that name. Mme. B., continuing her deductions, told Mlle. Smith that perhaps she had formerly been the medium of the great magician, and consequently had been Lorenza Feliciani in a former life. Hélène at once accepted the idea, and for several weeks considered herself to be the reincarnation of Lorenza, until one day a lady of her acquaintance remarked that it was impossible, Lorenza Feliciani having never existed save in the imagination and the romances of Alexandre Dumas, *père*.[3]

Thus dispossessed of her supposed former existence, Hélène was not long in declaring through the table that she was Marie Antoinette. As to Léopold, a short time after Mme. B. had hypothetically identified him with Cagliostro, he himself confirmed that hypothesis at a seance of the N. group, dictating to the table that his real name was Joseph Balsamo.*

One fact, however, is certain, namely, that save for the vague affirmation that he had known Hélène in a previous existence,* Léopold had never pretended to be Cagliostro, or given any reason for being thought so, before the reunion where Mme. B., who had been for some time accustomed to manifestations of that personage, announced the supposition and showed Mlle. Smith immediately after the seance (at a moment when she was probably still in a very suggestible state) an engraving from Dumas' works representing Balsamo and the Dauphin. From that day Léopold, on his part, never failed to claim that personality, and progressively to realize the character of the rôle in a very remarkable manner, as we shall see.

II. Personification of Balsamo by Léopold

There is no need, I think, to remind the reader of the well-known fact—so often described under the names of objectivity of types,* personification, change of personality, etc.—that a hypnotized subject can be transformed by word into such other living being as may be desired, according to the measure in which his suggestibility on the one hand and the vividness of his imagination and the fulness of his stored-up knowledge or memories on the other enables him to fulfil the rôle which is imposed upon him. Without investigating here to what extent mediums may be likened to hypnotized subjects, it is undeniable that an analogous phe-

---

[3] Alexandre Dumas, *père*, *Memoirs of a Physician*, chap. xv.

nomenon takes place in them; but the process is more gradual, and may extend itself over several years. In place of the immediate metamorphosis which modifies at one stroke and instantly, conformably to a prescribed type, the attitude, the physiognomy, the gestures, the words, the intonations of voice, the style, the handwriting, and other functions besides, we are, in the case of the medium, in the presence of a development formed by successive stages arranged according to grades, with intervals of different lengths, which finally succeed in creating a complete personality, all the more astonishing, at first sight, because the involuntary suggestions have not been noticed, the accumulations of which have little by little caused its birth. This process of development is present in a high degree in the case of Mlle. Smith, in the elaboration of her secondary personality, Léopold-Cagliostro.

In the beginning, in 1892 and 1893, this "spirit" only manifested himself by the brief periods of sleep which he induced in Hélène at certain seances, by raps struck upon the table, by visions in which he showed himself clothed in black and of youthful appearance, and, more rarely, by auditive hallucinations. His character and the content of his messages were summed up in imperious, authoritative, domineering manners, with the pretension of claiming Mlle. Smith all for himself, of defending her against the influences of the N. group, and, finally, of detaching her from that environment.

There was nothing, however, in this general character of monopoly and of protection which specially recalled the Balsamo of history or of romance. The personification of complete objectivity of this established type really began only in 1894, when Léopold had no longer to struggle with an environment foreign to his nature. The subconscious psychological task of realization of the proposed model could then be followed by him more freely; in spiritistic terms, Joseph Balsamo was able to manifest himself and make himself known in a manner more complete through Hélène as an intermediary, while continuing to follow and protect her as the reincarnation of the royal object of his passion.

At the seances held with M. Cuendet, Léopold frequently showed himself to Hélène clothed after the fashion of the last century and with a face like that of Louis XVI., under the different phases of his multiplex genius. He also showed himself to her in his laboratory, surrounded by utensils and instruments appropriate to the sorcerer and alchemist that he was; or, again, as the physician and possessor of secret elixirs, the knowledge of which is productive of consultations or remedies for the use of sitters who need them; or, again, as the illumined theosophist, the verbose prophet of the brotherhood of man, who diffuses limping Alexandrine verses— which seem to have been inherited from his predecessor, Victor Hugo— containing exhortations a little weak at times, but always stamped with a pure moral tone, elevated and noble sentiments, and a very touching religious spirit—in short, a fine example of that "Athico-deific verbiage" (if I may be allowed the expression, which is an Americanism), which, both in prose and in verse, is one of the most frequent and estimable products of mediumship.*

But it was not until 1895 that Léopold, benefiting by the progress made by the automatic phenomena in Hélène, multiplied and perfected his processes of communication. The first step consisted in substituting, in his dictations by spelling, the movements of the hand or of a single finger for those of the whole table. This was the immediate result of a suggestion of mine.

The second step in advance was the handwriting, which shows two stages. In the first, Léopold gave Hélène the impression of a phrase (verbo-visual hallucination), which she copied in pencil on a sheet of paper, in her own handwriting. The second, which was only accomplished five months later, and which consisted in writing directly with Hélène's hand, permitted the immediate establishment of three curious facts. One is, that Léopold holds his pen in the usual manner, the handle resting between the thumb and the index-finger, while Hélène, in writing, always holds her pen-handle or pencil between the index and middle fingers, a very rare habit with us. The next is that Léopold has an entirely different handwriting from that of Hélène, a calligraphy more regular, larger, more painstaking, and with marked differences in the formation of the letters (see Figs. 3 and 4). The third is that he uses the style of handwriting of the last century, and puts an *o* instead of an *a* in the tenses of the verbs, *j'amois*, for *j'amais*, etc. These three characteristics he has never departed from during all the four years that I have been accumulating specimens of his handwriting.

The following is a résumé of the seances at which these two innovations took place.

April 21, 1895.—As I had just asked Léopold a question which he did not like, Hélène, being in a state of hemisomnambulism, with a pencil and some sheets of paper placed before her, in the hope of obtaining some communication (not from Léopold), seemed about to plunge into a very interesting perusal of one of the blank sheets; then, at my request, which she with difficulty comprehended, she commenced to write rapidly and nervously on another sheet, in her usual handwriting, a copy of the imaginary text which Léopold was showing her ("in fluid letters," as he said afterwards at the seance) as follows: "*My thoughts are not thy thoughts, and thy wishes are not mine, friend Flournoy—Léopold.*" At the final awakening Hélène recognized perfectly her own handwriting in his phrase, but had no recollection of the occurrence.

September 22, 1895.—After different visions and some stanzas of Vic-

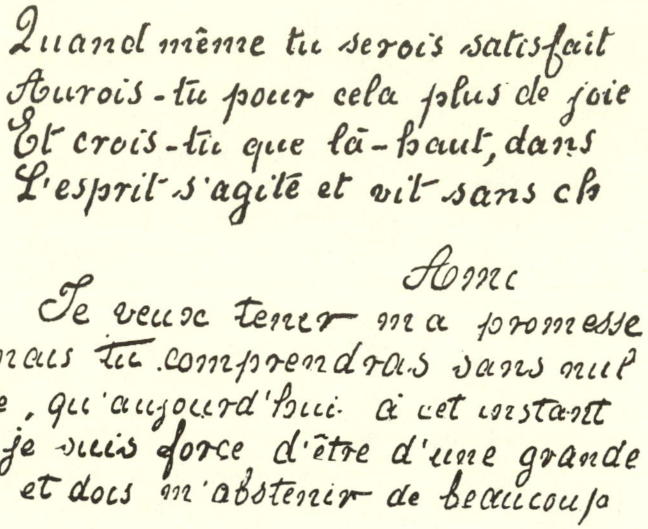

> Quand même tu serois satisfait
> Aurois-tu pour cela plus de joie
> Et crois-tu que là-haut, dans
> L'esprit s'agite et vit sans ch
>
> Aime
> Je veux tenir ma promesse
> mais tu comprendras sans nul
> te, qu'aujourd'hui à cet instant
> je suis force d'être d'une grande
> et dois m'abstenir de beaucoup

Fig. 3. Handwriting of Léopold. Fragments of two letters, one in Alexandrine verse, the other in prose, entirely in the hand of Léopold, automatically written by Mlle. Smith in spontaneous hemisomnambulism.

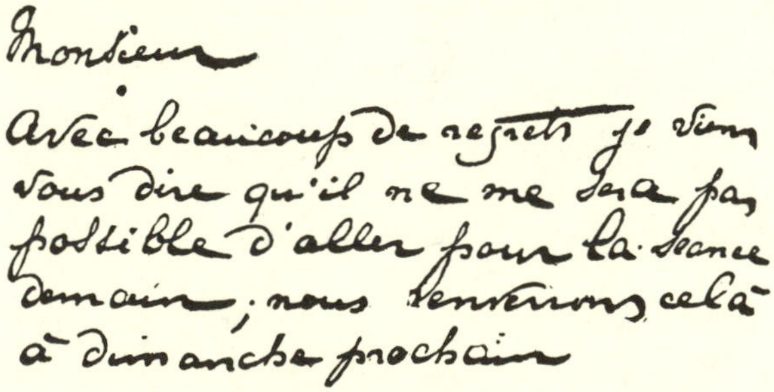

> Monsieur
> Avec beaucoup de regrets je viens
> vous dire qu'il ne me sera pas
> possible d'aller pour la France
> demain; nous renverrons cela
> à dimanche prochain

Fig. 4. Normal handwriting of Mlle. Smith.

tor Hugo, dictated by the table, Hélène appeared to suffer considerably in her right arm, which she was holding at the wrist with her left hand, when the table at which she was seated gave out the following, dictated by Léopold: "I shall hold her hand," meaning that it was he, Léopold, who was causing Mlle. Smith to suffer pain by seizing her right hand. As she seemed to feel very badly and began to weep, Léopold was asked to desist; but he refused, and, still speaking through the table, said, "Give her some paper," then, "More light." Writing material was furnished her and the lamp brought in, which Hélène gazed at fixedly, while Léopold continued to dictate (this time with the little finger of her left hand), "Let her gaze on the lamp until she forgets the pain in her arm." She then seemed, in fact, to forget her pain, and to find satisfaction in looking at the lamp; then she fastened her eyes on the paper, and seemed to read something there which she endeavored to copy in pencil. But here the right hand began a curious alternation of contrary motions, expressing in a very clear manner a contest with Léopold, who was trying to compel her to hold the pencil in a certain way, which Hélène refused to do, with a great pretence of anger. She persisted in holding it between the index and middle fingers, as was her wont, while Léopold wanted her to hold it in the usual way, between the thumb and the index-finger, and said: "I do not wish her to . . . she is holding the pencil very badly." The right index-finger then went through a very comical gymnastic performance, being seized with a tremor, which caused her to place it on one side or the other of the pencil, according to whether it was Léopold or Hélène who was victorious; during this time she frequently raised her eyes, with a look sometimes reproachful, sometimes supplicating, as if to gaze at Léopold standing by her side endeavoring to force her to hold the pencil in the manner he preferred. After a contest of nearly twenty minutes, Hélène, vanquished and completely subdued by Léopold, seemed to be absent, while her hand, holding the pencil in the manner she did not like, wrote slowly the two following lines, followed by a rapid and feverish signature of Léopold:

> "Mes vers sont si mauvais que pour toi j'aurois dû
> Laisser à tout jamais le poète têtu.—LÉOPOLD."

An allusion, which was of no importance, to a remark made by me at the commencement of the seance on the verses of Victor Hugo and those of Léopold frequently dictated by the table. The seance lasted some time longer; on awakening, Hélène vaguely remembered having seen Léopold, but knew nothing more concerning the handwriting scene.

It is a fact that while her other incarnations are always accomplished passively and without any struggle, that of Léopold has the peculiarity of regularly provoking more or less resistance on the part of Hélène. "I do not make of her all that I wish . . . she is headstrong. . . . I do not know whether I shall succeed. . . . I do not believe I can master her to-day. . . ." replies he often when asked to incarnate himself or write with her hand, and, indeed, his efforts often fail. There exists between Hélène and her guide a curious phenomenon of contrast and opposition, which only breaks out in the higher and more recent forms of motor automatism, the handwriting, the speech, or the complete incarnation, but from which the sensory messages and simple raps on the table or of the finger are free. It is very possible that the idea, very antipathetic to Hélène, of the hypnotizer mastering his subjects in spite of themselves—of the disincarnated Cagliostro using his medium as a simple tool—has been subconsciously the origin of this constant note of revolt against the total domination of Léopold, and of the intense suffering which accompanied his first incarnations, and which has slowly diminished through her becoming accustomed to the process, though it has never been completely banished.

After the handwriting, in its turn came speech, which also was attained by means of two stages. In a first attempt Léopold only succeeded in giving Hélène his intonation and pronunciation after a seance in which she suffered acutely in her mouth and in her neck, as though her vocal organs were being manipulated or removed; she began to talk in a natural tone, and was apparently wide awake and feeling well, but spoke with a deep bass voice, and a strong, easily recognizable Italian accent. It was not until a year later that Léopold was finally able to speak himself by the mouth of Mlle. Smith, while she was completely entranced, and who did not retain on awakening any memory of this strange occurrence. Since then the complete control of the medium by her guide is a frequent occurrence at the seances, and affords a tableau very characteristic and always impressive.

Léopold succeeds in incarnating himself only by slow degrees and progressive stages. Hélène then feels as though her arms had been seized, or as if they were absent altogether; then she complains of disagreeable sensations, which were formerly painful, in her throat, the nape of her neck, and in her head; her eyelids droop; her expression changes; her throat swells into a sort of double chin, which gives her a likeness of some sort to the well-known figure of Cagliostro. All at once she rises, then, turning slowly towards the sitter whom Léopold is about to address, draws herself up proudly, turns her back quickly, sometimes with her arms crossed on her breast with a magisterial air, sometimes with one of them hanging down while the other is pointed solemnly towards heaven, and with her fingers makes a sort of masonic sign, which never varies. Soon after a series of hiccoughs, sighs, and various noises indicate the difficulty Léopold is experiencing in taking hold of the vocal apparatus; the words come forth slowly but strong; the deep bass voice of a man, slightly confused, with a pronunciation and accent markedly foreign, certainly more like Italian than anything else. Léopold is not always easily understood, especially when his voice swells and thunders out a reply to some indiscreet question or to the disrespectful remarks of some skeptical sitter. He speaks thickly, pronounces g like j, and all his u's like ou, accents the final syllables, embellishes his vocabulary with obsolete words, or words which do not fit the circumstances, such as *fiole* for *bouteille*, *omnibus* for *tramways*, etc. He is pompous, grandiloquent, unctuous, sometimes severe and terrible, sometimes also sentimental. He says "thee" and "thou" to everybody, and appears to believe that he is still grand-master of the secret societies, from the emphatic and sonorous manner in which he pronounces the words "Brother" or "And thou, my sister," by which he addresses the sitters. Although he generally addresses himself to one of them in particular, and holds very little collective discourse, he is in touch with every one, listens to everything that is said, and each one may have his turn in conversation with him. Ordinarily he keeps his eyelids closed: he has, nevertheless, been persuaded to open his eyes in order to permit the taking of a photograph by a flash light. I regret that Mlle. Smith would not consent to the publication of her photographs, either in her normal state or in that of Léopold, in connection with the reproduction of a portrait of Cagliostro.[4] The reader may assure himself that when she incarnates her guide she really assumes a certain resemblance of features to him, and there is something in her attitude which is sometimes somewhat theatrical, but sometimes really majestic, which corresponds well to the generally received idea of this personage, whether he is regarded as a clever impostor or as a wonderful genius.

Speech is the apogee of the incarnations of Léopold; often interrupted by fits of hiccoughs and spasms it seems to be injurious to Hélène's organism, and there are some seances at which attempts to produce it fail to succeed. Léopold, on these occasions, indicates his impotence and the fatigue of the medium by his gestures, and is then reduced to the necessity of expressing himself by digital dictations or handwriting, or else to giving Hélène verbo-auditive hallucinations, the content of which she repeats in her natural voice.

From the point of view of ease and mobility of the entire organism, there is a notable difference between Léopold and the other incarnations of Hélène: these last seem to be effected with much more facility than in the case of that of her guide par excellence. In the case of the Hindoo princess and that of Marie Antoinette, the perfection of the play, the suppleness and freedom of movement, are always admirable. It is true there is no question here, according to the spiritistic doctrine and the subconscious ideas of Mlle. Smith, of incarnations properly so called, since it is she herself who simply returns to that which she formerly was, by a sort of reversion or prenatal ecmnesia; she does not undergo, in consequence, any foreign possession, and can in these rôles preserve her natural identity and the entire disposition of her faculties. But still the occasional incarnation of different personalities, such as those of deceased parents or

---

[4] The one which is found, for example, at the beginning of the *Vie de Joseph Balsamo*, etc., translated from the Italian (3d edition, Paris, 1791), and which has been several times reproduced. Mlle. Smith has hanging over her fireplace a fine copy of this portrait.

friends of the spectators, are often more easily and quickly effected than that of Léopold. Hélène moves in these cases with more vivacity and changes of attitude. In the rôle of Cagliostro, on the other hand, with the exception of the grandiose and not very frequent movements of the arms, once standing, she remains motionless, or only with difficulty advancing a little way towards the person to whom she addresses her discourse.

The content of the oral conversations of Léopold, as well as of his other messages by the various sensory and motor processes, is too varied for me to describe here: the numerous examples scattered through this work only can give an idea of it.

III. Léopold and the True Joseph Balsamo

It would naturally be supposed that Léopold would have given us, by means of the psychological perfection of his partial or total incarnations and by the content of his messages, such a living likeness of Cagliostro that there would have been occasion to ask whether it is not really the latter who actually "returns," in the same way that Dr. Hodgson and his colleagues ask themselves whether it is not actually George Pelham who manifests himself through Mrs. Piper. Let us suppose, for example, that Léopold possessed a handwriting, an orthography, a style identical with that which is found here and there in the manuscripts of Joseph Balsamo; that he spoke French, Italian, or German, as that cosmopolitan adventurer did, and with all the same peculiarities; that his conversations and messages were full of precise allusions to actual events in his life, and also of unpublished but verifiable facts, etc. In that case the difficult and delicate task of proving that Mlle. Smith had no knowledge through normal methods of these thousand exact features would still remain, and we should not be forced to ask whether this *soi-disant* authentic revenant is simply a very well-gotten-up simulacrum, an admirable reconstruction, a marvellous imitation, such as the subliminal faculties are only too glad to produce for the diversion of psychologists and the mystification of the simple.

This problem is not given to us. I regret it, but it is true, nevertheless—to my mind, at least, for in these matters it is prudent to speak only for one's self—that there is no reason to suspect the real presence of Joseph Balsamo behind the automatisms of Mlle. Smith.

That there are very curious analogies between what is known to us of Cagliostro and certain characteristic traits of Léopold, I do not deny, but they are precisely such as accord very well with the supposition of the subliminal medley.

Let us consider first the handwriting. To facilitate the comparison, I have reproduced here (see pp. 70, 72, and 73) some fragments of letters of

Cagliostro and of Léopold and of Hélène. Let us suppose—which is, perhaps, open to discussion—that the handwriting of Léopold, by its regularity, its firmness, resembles that of Balsamo more than that of Mlle. Smith; the degree of resemblance does not, I think, go beyond that which might be expected considering the notorious fact that handwriting reflects the psychological temperament and modifies itself in accordance with the state of the personality.[5]

It is well known how the calligraphy of a hypnotized subject varies according to the suggestion that he shall personate Napoleon, Harpagon, a little girl, or an old man; there is nothing surprising in the fact that the hypnoid secondary personality of Hélène, which imagines itself to be the powerful and manly Count of Cagliostro, should be accompanied by muscular tensions communicating to the handwriting itself a little of that solidity and breadth which are found in the autograph of Balsamo. To this, however, the analogy is limited. The dissimilarities in the detail and the formation of the letters are such that the only conclusion which they warrant is that Mlle. Smith, or her subconsciousness, has never laid eyes on the manuscripts of Cagliostro. They are, indeed, rare, but the facilities she might have had, of which she has not thought of taking advantage, for consulting in the Geneva public library the same volume from which I took Fig. 5, would prove, at least, her good faith and her honesty, if it were in the least necessary. The extravagant signature of Léopold with which all his messages are subscribed (see Fig. 7) recalls in no wise that of Alessandro di Cagliostro at the bottom of Fig. 5.

The archaic forms of orthography, *j'aurois* for *j'aurais*, etc., which appear above the first autograph of Léopold (see p. 65), and which occur again in the messages of Marie Antoinette, constitute a very pretty hit, of which the ordinary self would probably never dream by way of voluntary imitation, but by which the subconscious imagination has seen fit to profit. It is undoubtedly a matter for wonderment that Mlle. Smith, who has not gone very deep into literary studies, should, nevertheless, have retained these orthographic peculiarities of the eighteenth century; but we must not overlook the fineness of choice, the refined sensibility, the consummate, albeit instinctive, art which presides over the sorting and storing away of the subconscious memories. By some natural affinity, the idea of a personage of a certain epoch attracts and gathers into its net everything that the subject can possibly learn or hear spoken concerning the fashion of writing, of speaking, or acting, peculiar to that epoch. I do not know whether Balsamo ever used the French language and the orthography that Léopold employs. Even if he did, it would not weaken the

---

[5] See, *e.g.*, Ferrari, Hericourt, and Richet, "Personality and Handwriting," *Revue philosophique*, vol. xxi, p. 414.

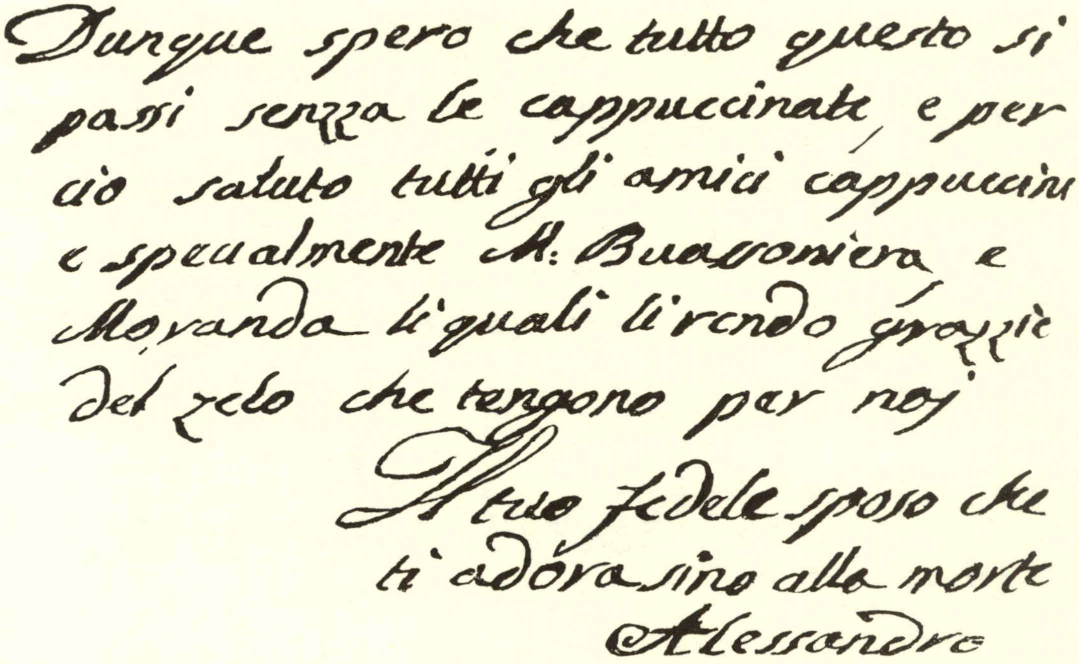

Dunque spero che tutto questo si
passi senzza le cappuccinate, e per
cio saluto tutti gli amici cappuccini
e specialmente M: Buasconiera e
Moranda li quali li rendo grazzie
del zelo che tengono per noi

Il tuo fedele sposo che
ti adora sino alla morte
Alessandro

Fig. 5. Handwriting of Joseph Balsamo. Fragment of a letter to his wife, reproduced in *L'Isographie des Hommes célèbres*.

hypothesis of the subliminal imitation, but if, on the other hand, it should be ascertained that he did not, the hypothesis would be greatly strengthened thereby.

As for the speech, I am ignorant as to how, with what accent and what peculiarities of pronunciation, Balsamo spoke the French tongue, and to what degree, in consequence, his reconstruction by Hélène's subliminal fantasy correctly hits it. If this point could be cleared up, it would probably be found to be just like that of the handwriting. Nothing could be more natural than to ascribe to the *chevalier d'industrie* of Palermo a very masculine, deep-bass voice, and, it goes without saying, as Italian as possible. It must be noted, too, that Mlle. Smith often heard her father speak that language, which he knew very well, with several of his friends; but that, on the other hand, she does not speak it, and has never learned it. Léopold, however, does not know Italian, and turns a deaf ear when any one addresses him in that language.* The intonation, the attitude, the whole physiognomy, in short, accord with these remarks.* As to the extremely varied content of the conversations and messages of Léopold, we are not obliged to consider Balsamo as their necessary author. When everything relating to Mlle. Smith and the sitters, but which has nothing to do with the last century, has been swept aside, together with the spiritistic dissertations in regard to the "fluid" manner in which Léopold exists, perceives, and moves, the three subjects or categories of communications still remain, which merit a rapid examination.

In the first place, there are the answers of Léopold to the questions put to him concerning his terrestrial life. These answers are remarkably evasive or vague. Not a name, not a date, not a precise fact does he furnish. We only learn that he has travelled extensively, suffered greatly, studied deeply, done much good, and healed a great many sick folk; but now he sees things too lofty to think any more about historic details of the past, and it is with unconcealed disgust or direct words of reproach for the idle curiosity of his carnal questioners that he hastens to turn the conversation, like Socrates, to moral subjects and those of a lofty philosophy, where he feels evidently more at ease. When he is further pressed he becomes angry sometimes, and sometimes ingenuously avows his ignorance, enveloping it meanwhile in an air of profound mystery. "They are asking the secret of my life, of my acts, of my thoughts. I cannot answer." This does not facilitate investigation of the question of identity.

In the second place come the consultations and medical prescriptions. Léopold affects a lofty disdain for modern medicine and phenic acid. He is as archaic in his therapeutics as in his orthography, and treats all maladies after the ancient mode. Baths of pressed grape-skins for rheumatism, an infusion of coltsfoot and juniper-berry in white wine for inflammations of the chest, the bark of the horsechestnut in red wine and

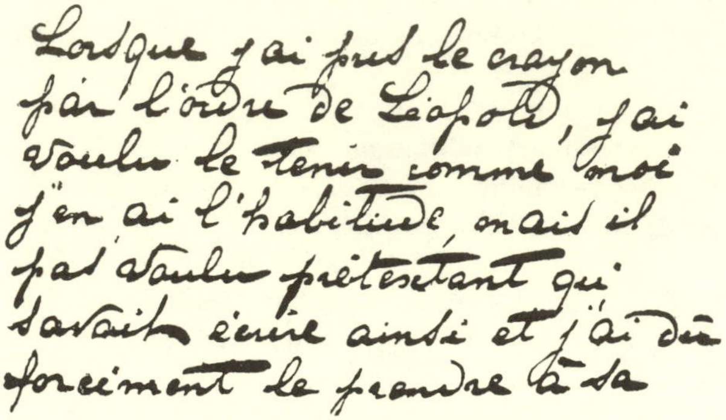
Lorsque j'ai pris le crayon
par l'ordre de Léopold, j'ai
voulu le tenir comme moi
j'en ai l'habitude, mais il
pas voulu prétextant qui
savait écrire ainsi et j'ai dû
forcément le prendre à sa

Fig. 6. Normal handwriting of Mlle. Smith.

douches of salt water as tonics, tisanes of hops and other flowers, camomile, oil of lavender, the leaves of the ash, etc.; all these do not accord badly with what Balsamo might have prescribed a century or more ago. The misfortune, from the evidential point of view, is that Mlle. Smith's mother is extremely well versed in all the resources of popular medicine where old recipes are perpetuated. She has had occasion to nurse many sick people in her life, knows the virtues of different medicinal plants, and constantly employs, with a sagacity which I have often admired, a number of those remedies spoken of as "old-women's," which make the young doctors fresh from the clinic smile, but to which they will more than once resort in secret after a few years of medical experience.*

Finally, there still remain the sentiments of Léopold for Hélène, which he claims are only the continuation of those of Cagliostro for Marie Antoinette. My ignorance of history does not permit me to pronounce categorically on this point. That the Queen of France did have some secret interviews with the famous "gold-maker," due to simple curiosity or to questions of material interest, there is no doubt, I believe; but that his feelings for his sovereign were a curious combination of the despairing passion of Cardinal Rohan for the queen, with the absolute respect which Alexandre Dumas, *père,* ascribes to Joseph Balsamo towards Lorenza Feliciani, appears to me less evident.

In short, if the revelations of Léopold have truly unveiled to us shades of feeling of Count Cagliostro hitherto unsuspected, and of which later documentary researches shall confirm the historic correctness—why, so much the better, for that will finally establish a trace of the supernormal in the mediumship of Hélène!*

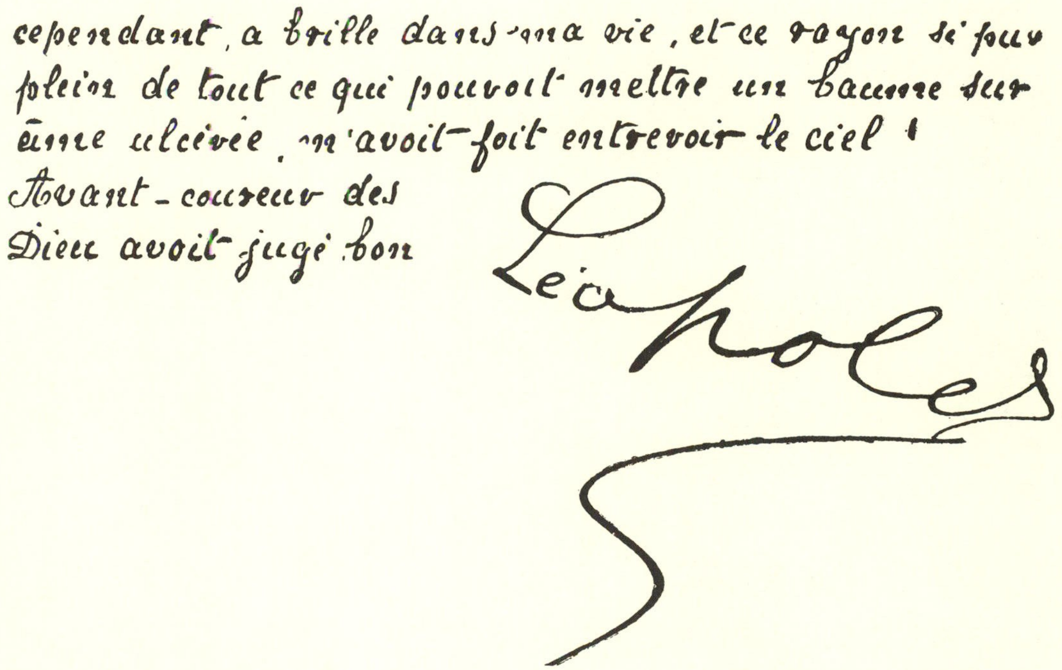

Fig. 7. Handwriting of Léopold. Fragment and signature of one of his letters, written by Mlle. Smith, in spontaneous hemisomnambulism.

IV. Léopold and Mlle. Smith

The connection between these two personalities is too complex for a precise description. There is neither a mutual exclusion, as between Mrs. Piper and Phinuit, who appear reciprocally to be ignorant of each other and to be separated by the tightest of partitions; nor a simple jointing, as in the case of Felida X.,* whose secondary state envelops and overflows the whole primary state. This is more of a crossing of lines, but of which the limits are vague and with difficulty assignable. Léopold knows, foresees, and recalls very many things of which the normal personality of Mlle. Smith knows absolutely nothing, not only of those which she may simply have forgotten, but of those of which she never had any consciousness. On the other hand, he is far from possessing all the memories of Hélène; he is ignorant of a very great part of her daily life; even some very notable incidents escape him entirely which explains his way of saying that, to his great regret, he cannot remain constantly by her, being obliged to occupy himself with other missions (concerning which he has never enlightened us) which oblige him often to leave her for a time.

These two personalities are, therefore, not co-extensive; each one passes beyond the other at certain points, without its being possible for us to say which is, on the whole, the more extended. As to their common domain, if it cannot be defined by one word with entire certainty, it appears, nevertheless, to be chiefly constituted by its connection with the innermost ranges of the being, both physiological and psychological, as might be suspected from what I remarked above concerning the real origin of Léopold. Physician of the soul and of the body, director of conscience, and at the same time hygienic counsellor, he does not always manifest himself immediately, but he is always present when Hélène's vital interests are involved. This will be made clearer by two or three concrete examples, which will at the same time illustrate some of the psychological processes by which Léopold manifests himself to Hélène.*

It must be admitted that there is a disagreement and opposition as complete as possible (but how far does this "possible" go?) when Hélène, in at least an apparently waking state, converses with her guide, manifestly by a partial sensory or motor automatism; for example, in the case cited on page 44, where Léopold, not sharing the allochiria of Hélène, declared by the table that she was wrong, so emphatically that she protested and became angry; also, when in verbo-auditive hallucinations, or by automatic handwriting, he enters into discussion with her, and she holds her own with him; or, again, when the organism seems to be divided up between two different persons, Léopold speaking by Hélène's mouth, with his accent, and uttering his own ideas to her, and she complaining, in writing, of pains in her head and throat, without understanding their cause. Nevertheless, in these cases of division of the consciousness, which appear to amount to its cutting in two, it is doubtful whether this plurality is more than apparent. I am not positive of having ever established with Hélène a veritable simultaneity of different consciousnesses. At the very moment at which Léopold writes by her hand, speaks by her mouth, dictates to the table, upon observing her attentively I have always found her absorbed, preoccupied, as though absent; but she instantaneously recovers her presence of mind and the use of her waking faculties at the end of the motor automatism. In short, that which from the outside is taken for the coexistence of distinct simultaneous personalities seems to me to be only an alternation, a rapid succession between the state of Hélène-consciousness and the state of Léopold-consciousness; and, in the case where the body seems to be jointly occupied by two independent beings—the right side, for instance, being occupied by Léopold, and the left by Hélène, or the Hindoo princess—the psychical division has never seemed to me to be radical, but many indications have combined to make me of the opinion that behind all was an individuality perfectly self-conscious, and enjoying thoroughly, along with the spectators, the comedy of the plural existences.

A single fundamental personality, putting the questions and giving the answers, quarrelling with itself in its own interior—in a word, enacting all the various roles of Mlle. Smith—is a fitting interpretation, which accords very well with the facts as I have observed them in Hélène, and very much better than the theory of a plurality of separate consciousnesses, of a psychological polyzoism, so to speak. This last theory is doubtless more convenient for a clear and superficial description of the facts, but I am not at all convinced that it conforms to the actual condition of affairs.*

It is a state of consciousness *sui generis*, which it is impossible adequately to describe, and which can only be represented by the analogy of those curious states, exceptional in the normal waking life, but less rare in dreams, when one seems to change his identity and become some one else.

Hélène has more than once told me of having had the impression of *becoming* or *being* momentarily Léopold. This happens most frequently at night, or upon awakening in the morning. She has first a fugitive vision of her protector; then it seems that little by little he is submerged in her; she feels him overcoming and penetrating her entire organism, as if he really became her or she him.* These mixed states are extremely interesting to the psychologist; unhappily, because they generally take place in a condition of consecutive amnesia, or because the mediums do not know how, or do not wish, to give a complete account of them, it is very rare that detailed descriptions are obtained.*

Between the two extremes of complete duality and complete unity numerous intermediate states are to be observed; or, at least, since the consciousness of another cannot be directly penetrated, these mixed states may be inferred from the consequences which spring from them.

It has happened, for example, that, believing they were dealing with Léopold alone, thoroughly incarnated and duly substituted for the personality of Mlle. Smith, the sitters have allowed to escape them on that account some ill-timed pleasantry, some indiscreet question or too free criticisms, all innocent enough and without evil intention, but still of a nature to wound Hélène if she had heard them, and from which the authors would certainly have abstained in her presence in a waking state.

Léopold has not stood upon ceremony in putting down these imprudent babblers, and the incident, generally, has had no further consequences. But sometimes the words and bearing of Mlle. Smith for days or weeks afterwards show that she was aware of the imprudent remarks, which proves that the consciousness of Léopold and her own are not separated by an impenetrable barrier, but that osmotic changes are effected from the one to the other. It is ordinarily pointed and irritating remarks which cause the trouble, which goes to prove that it is the feelings of self-love or personal susceptibility that form in each one of us the inmost fortifications of the social self, and are the last to be destroyed by somnambulism, or that they constitute the fundamental substratum, the common base by which Léopold and Mlle. Smith form a whole and mingle themselves in the same individuality.

The psychological process of this transmission is varied from another cause. Sometimes it appears that the consecutive amnesia of the trance has been broken as to the most piquant details, and that Hélène clearly remembers that which has been said, in the presence of Léopold, disagreeable to herself. Some times it is Léopold himself who repeats to her the unpleasant expressions which have been used, with commentaries calculated to lessen their effect and to excuse the culprits: for it is an interesting trait of his character that he undertakes with Hélène the defence of those same persons whom he reprimands and blames, a contradiction not at all surprising when it is psychologically interpreted, considering the habitual conflict of emotional motives or tendencies, the warfare which opposite points of view is incessantly carrying on in our inmost being. Sometimes, again, it is in a dream that the junction is effected between the somnambulistic consciousness of Léopold and the normal consciousness of Hélène.

Apropos of the last case, here is an example containing nothing disagreeable, in which Hélène remembered in her waking state a nocturnal dream, which was itself a repetition or echo, in natural sleep, of a somnambulistic scene of the previous evening.

In a seance at which I assisted, shortly after my recovery from an attack of congestion of the lungs, Hélène, completely entranced, has a vision of Léopold-Cagliostro, who, in the role of sympathetic physician, comes to hold a consultation with me. After some preliminaries she kneels down by my chair, and, looking alternately at my chest and at the fictitious doctor standing between us, she holds a long conversation with him, in which she explains the condition of my lungs, which she sees in imagination, and the treatment which Léopold prescribes, somewhat as follows:

It is the lungs . . . it is darker . . . it is one side which has been affected . . . You say that it is a severe inflammation—and can that be healed? . . . Tell me, what must be done . . . Oh, where have I seen any of these plants? . . . I don't know what they are called . . . those . . . I don't understand very well . . . those synantherous? . . . Oh, what a queer name . . . Where are they to be found? . . . You say it belongs to the family of . . . then it has another name? Tell me what it is . . . some *tissulages* [sic] . . . Then you think this plant is good for him? . . . Ah! but explain this to me . . . the fresh leaves or the dried flowers? Three times a day, a large handful in a pint . . . and then honey and milk. . . . I will tell him that he must drink three cups a day.

Then followed very detailed directions as to treatment, various infusions, blisters, etc. The whole scene lasted more than an hour, followed by complete amnesia, and nothing was said to Hélène about it, as it was half-past six in the evening, and she was in haste to return home. The next day she wrote me a seven-page letter in which she described a very striking dream she had had during the night.

I fell asleep about two o'clock in the morning and awaked at about five. Was it a vision? Was it a dream I had? I don't really know what to consider it and dare not say; but this I do know, I saw my dear friend Léopold, who spoke to me a long time about you, and I think I saw you also. I asked him what he thought of your state of health. . . . He replied that in his opinion it was far from re-established. That the pain you feel in the right side came from an inflammation of the lung which has been seriously affected . . . You will doubtless laugh when I tell you that he also described the remedies you ought to take. . . . One of them is a simple plant, which is called, as nearly as I can remember, Tissulage or Tussilache, but has also another name, which I cannot recollect, but the first name will doubtless suffice, since he says you are familiar with the plant.*

What I have said concerning Léopold is also applicable to the other personifications of Mlle. Smith. The normal consciousness of Hélène mingles and fuses itself in every way with the somnambulistic consciousness of Simandini, of Marie Antoinette, or some other incarnation, as we shall soon see. I pass now to the examination of some detailed examples, destined to throw light upon the role which Léopold plays in Hélène's existence.

Let us begin by listening to Léopold himself. Among his numerous messages, the following letter, written in his fine handwriting by the hand of Mlle. Smith—in response to a note in which I had begged him (as a spiritual being and distinct from her) to aid me in my "psychic researches" —contains information for which I had not asked, but which was none the less interesting. It must not be forgotten that it is the disincarnate adorer of Marie Antoinette who is writing:

> FRIEND,—I am pleased and touched by the mark of confidence you have deigned to accord me. The spiritual guide of Mademoiselle [Smith], whom the Supreme Being in his infinite goodness has permitted me to find again with ease, I do all I can to appear to her on every occasion when I deem it necessary; but my body, or, if you prefer, the matter of little solidity of which I am composed, does not always afford me the facility of showing myself to her in a positive human manner. [He, in fact, appeared to her often under the form of elementary visual hallucinations, a luminous trail, whitish column, vaporous streamer, etc.]
>
> That which I seek above all to inculcate in her is a consoling and true philosophy, which is necessary to her by reason of the profound, unhappy impressions, which even now still remain to her, of the whole drama of her past life. I have often sown bitterness in her heart [when she was Marie Antoinette], desiring only her welfare. Also, laying aside everything superfluous, I penetrate into the most hidden recesses of her soul, and with an extreme care and incessant activity I seek to implant there those truths which I trust will aid her in attaining the lofty summit of the ladder of perfection.
>
> Abandoned by my parents from my cradle, I have, indeed, known sorrow early in life. Like all, I have had many weaknesses, which I have expiated, and God knows that I bow to His will!
>
> Moral suffering has been my principal lot. I have been full of bitterness, of envy, of hatred, of jealousy. Jealousy, my brother! what a poison, what a corruption of the soul!
>
> Nevertheless, one ray has shone brightly into my life, and that ray so pure, so full of everything that might pour balm on my wounded soul, has given me a glimpse of Heaven!
>
> Herald of eternal felicity! ray without spot! God deemed best to take it before me! May his holy name be blessed!
>
> Friend, in what manner shall I reply to you? I am ignorant myself, not knowing what it will please God to reveal to you, but through her whom you call Mademoiselle [Smith], God willing, perhaps we shall be able to satisfy you.
>
> Thy friend,
>
> LÉOPOLD.

We can see, under the flowing details of the spiritistic ideas and his role as the repentant Cagliostro, that the dominant characteristic of Léopold is his deep platonic attachment for Mlle. Smith, and an ardent moral solicitude for her and her advance toward perfection. This corresponds perfectly with the character of the numerous mesages which he addresses to her in the course of her daily existence, as may be seen from the following specimen. He is referring to a case where, after having warned her on two occasions during the day by auditive hallucinations that he would manifest himself in the evening, he gives her, in fact, by automatic writing in his own hand, the encouragement she was actually in need of under the circumstances in which she found herself.

One morning, at her desk, Hélène heard an unknown voice, stronger and nearer to her than is usual with Léopold, say to her: *"Until this evening"*; a little later the same voice, which she now recognized as that of Léopold, but of a quality rougher and nearer to her than was his habit, said to her: *"You understand me well, until this evening."* In the evening, having returned home, she was excited at supper, left the table in haste towards the end of the meal, and shut herself up in her room with the idea that she would learn something; but, presently, the instinctive agitation of her hand indicated to her that she should take her pencil, and having done so, she obtained in the beautiful calligraphy of Léopold the following epistle. (She says that she remained wide awake and self-conscious while writing it, and it is the only occasion of a similar character when she had knowledge of the content.)

MY BELOVED FRIEND,—Why do you vex yourself, torment yourself so? Why are you indignant, because, as you advance in life, you are obliged to acknowledge that all things are not as you had wished and hoped they might be? Is not the route we follow on this earth always and for all of us strewn with rocks? is it not an endless chain of deceptions, of miseries? Do me the kindness, my dear sister, I beg of you, to tell me that from this time forth you will cease from endeavoring to probe too deeply the human heart. In what will such discoveries aid you? What remains to you of these things, except tears and regrets? And then this God of love, of justice, and of life—is not He the one to read our hearts? It is for Him, not for thee, to see into them.

Would you change the hearts? Would you give them that which they have not, a live, ardent soul, never departing from what is right, just, and true? Be calm, then, in the face of all these little troubles. Be worthy, and, above all, always good! In thee I have found again that heart and that soul, both of which will always be for me all my life, all my joy, and my only dream here below.

Believe me: be calm: reflect: that is my wish.

Thy friend,

LÉOPOLD.

I have chosen this example for the sake of its brevity. Hélène has received a number of communications of the same kind, sometimes in

verse, in which the moral and religious note is often still more accentuated. In the greater part we meet with, as in the next to the last phrase of
the foregoing letter, an allusion to the presumed affection of Cagliostro for
Marie Antoinette. It is to be noticed that there is nothing in these excellent admonitions that a high and serious soul like that of Mlle. Smith
could not have drawn from its own depths in a moment of contemplation
and meditation.*

Is it a benefit or an injury to the moral and truly religious life to formulate itself thus clearly in verbal hallucinations rather than to remain in the
confused but more personal state of experienced aspirations and strongly
expressed emotions? Do these inspirations gain or lose in inward authority and subjective power by assuming this exterior garb and this aspect of
objectivity? This is a delicate question, probably not susceptible of a uniform solution.*

In the following incident, which I relate as an example among many
other similar ones, it is no longer, properly speaking, the moral and religious sentiments personified in Léopold, but rather the instinct of reserve
and of defence peculiar to the weaker sex, the sense of the proprieties,
the self-respect, tinctured with a shade of exaggeration almost amounting
to prudery.

In a visit to Mlle. Smith, during which I inquired whether she had
received any recent communications from Léopold, she told me she had
only seen him two or three times in the last few days, and had been struck
by his "restless and unhappy" air, instead of the air "so pleasant, so sweet,
so admirable," which he generally has. As she did not know to what to
attribute this change of countenance, I advised her to take her pencil and
to wrap herself in meditation, with the hope of obtaining some automatic
message.

In about a minute her expression indicated that she was being taken
possession of; her eyes were fixed on the paper, upon which her left hand
rested, the thumb and little finger being agitated and continually tapping
(about once a second), the right hand having tried to take the pencil between the index and middle finger (the manner of Hélène), ended by
seizing it between the thumb and the index finger, and traced slowly in
the handwriting of Léopold:

> Yes, I am restless | pained, even in anguish. | Believest thou, friend, that it is
> with satisfaction | that I see you every day accepting the attentions, the flat-
> teries; | I do not call them insincere, but of little worth, and little praiseworthy |
> on the part of those from whom they come.|

This text was written at six separate times (marked by the vertical bars),
separated by brief moments of full wakefulness, when the tappings of the
left hand ceased, and when Hélène, repeating in a loud voice what she

was about to write, is very much astonished, does not know to what Léopold alludes, then at my request takes her pencil to obtain an explanation, and falls asleep again during the following fragment. At the end of this bit, as she persists in saying that she is ignorant of what he refers to, I proceed to question Léopold, who replies that for several days Hélène has permitted herself to be courted by a M. V. (perfectly honorably), who often found himself on the same street-car with her, had made a place for her beside him the last few mornings, and had paid her some compliments on her appearance.

These revelations excited the laughter and protestations of Hélène, who commenced to deny that it could have come from Léopold, and accused me of having suggested it to her little finger; but the right hand took the pencil and traced these words in the handwriting and with the signature of Léopold: "I only say what I think, and I desire that you refuse henceforth all the flowers that he may offer you.— Léopold." This time Hélène remembered the incident, and recollected that yesterday morning he had offered her a rose which he was wearing as a boutonnière.

Eight days later I paid another visit to Hélène, and after an effort to secure some handwriting, which was not successful, but resulted in a Martian vision (see Martian text No. 14), she had a visual hallucination of Léopold, and losing consciousness of the actual environment and of my presence also, as well as that of her mother, she flung herself into a running conversation with him in regard to the incident of eight days previously:

> Léopold . . . Léopold . . . don't come near me [repulsing him]. You are too severe, Léopold! . . . Will you come on Sunday? I am going to be at M. Flournoy's next Sunday. You will be there . . . but take good care that you do not . . . No, it is not kind of you always to disclose secrets. . . . What must he have thought? . . . You seem to make a mountain out of a mole-hill. . . . And who would think of refusing a flower? You don't understand at all. . . . Why, then? It was a very simple thing to accept it, a matter of no importance whatever . . . to refuse it would have been impolite. . . . You pretend to read the heart. . . . Why give importance to a thing that amounts to nothing? . . . It is only a simple act of friendship, a little token of sympathy . . . to make me write such things on paper before everybody! not nice of you!

In this somnambulistic dialogue, in which we can divine Léopold's replies, Hélène took for the moment the accent of Marie Antoinette (see below, in the "Royal cycle"). To awaken her, Léopold, who had possession of Hélène's arms, made some passes over her forehead, then pressed the frontal and suborbital nerves of the left side, and made me a sign to do the same with those of the right. The seance of the next day but one, at my house, passed without any allusion by Léopold to the incident of the street-car, evidently on account of the presence of certain sitters to whom he did not wish to reveal Hélène's secrets. But, three days after, in a new visit, during which she told me of having had a waking discussion concerning the future life (without telling me with whom), she again wrote, in the hand of Léopold: "It is not in such society as this that you ought so seriously to discuss the immortality of the soul." She then confessed that it was again on the street-car, and with M. V., that she had held that conversation while a funeral procession was passing. There was never anything that might have been of a compromising character in the exchange of courtesies and the occasional conversations of Mlle. Smith with her neighbor of the street-car. The trouble that it caused poor Léopold was very characteristic of him, and well indicated the severe and jealous censor who formerly had worried the N. group; there can be heard again the echo of that voice, "which has absolutely nothing to do with the conscience" (see pp. 23 and 57), and which has hitherto prevented Hélène from accepting any of the suitors whom she has encountered in the course of her journey through life. This austere and rigorous mentor, always wide awake, and taking offence at the least freedom which Mlle. Smith allows herself in the exchange of trifling courtesies, represents, in fact, a very common psychological attribute; it is not every well-bred feminine soul that carries stored in one of its recesses, where it manifests its presence by scruples more or less vaguely felt, certain hesitations or apprehensions, inhibiting feelings or tendencies of a shade of intensity varying according to the age and the temperament.

It is not my part to describe this delicate phenomenon. It suffices me to remark that here, as in the ethico-religious messages, the personality of Léopold has in no way aided the essential content of those inward experiences of which Mlle. Smith is perfectly capable by herself; the form only of their manifestation has gained in picturesque and dramatic expression in the *mise-en-scène* of the automatic handwritings and of the somnambulistic dialogue. It seems as though the suggestive approach of my presence and my questions had been necessary to excite these phenomena; it is, however, very probable to judge from other examples, that my influence only hastened the explosion of Léopold in formulated reproaches, and that his latent discontent, hitherto noticed in the "restless and suffering air" of his fugitive visual apparitions, would have terminated, after a period of incubation more or less prolonged, in breaking out into spontaneous admonitions, auditive or written.

It can be divined that in this role of vigilant guardian, of an almost excessive zealousness for the honor or the dignity of Mlle. Smith, Léopold is again, to my mind, only a product of psychological duplication. He represents a certain grouping of inward desires and secret instincts, which the hypnoid predisposition encouraged by spiritism, has brought into a peculiar prominence and given an aspect of foreign personality; in the same way, in the phantasmagoria of the dream, certain after-thoughts, almost unperceived while awake, rise to the first plane and become transformed into contradictory fictitious personages, whose cutting reproaches astonish us sometimes on awakening by their disturbing truthfulness.

A final example will show us Léopold, in his role of watcher over the health of Mlle. Smith and adviser of precautions which she ought to take. He is not troubled about her general health; when she had *la grippe*, for instance, or when she is simply worn out with fatigue, he scarcely shows himself. His attention is concentrated upon certain special physiological functions, of the normal exercise of which he takes care to be assured. He does not otherwise seem to exercise a positive action upon them, and cannot modify them in any way; his office seems to be confined to knowing beforehand their exact course, and to see that Hélène is not guilty of any imprudence which may impede them.

Léopold here shows a knowledge and prevision of the most intimate phenomena of the organism which has been observed in the case of secondary personalities, and which confers upon them, in that respect at least, an unquestionable advantage over the ordinary personality. In the case of Mlle. Smith, the indications of her guide are always of a prohibitive nature, calculated to prevent her from taking part in spiritistic reunions at a time at which she believes herself able to do so with impunity, but which he, endowed with a more refined coenaesthetic sensibility, thinks she ought not to undertake. He has for several years formally laid his ban upon every kind of mediumistic exercises at certain very regular periods.

He has also on numerous occasions compelled her by various messages, categorical auditive hallucinations, diverse impulses, contractures of the arms, forcing her to write, etc., to modify her plans and to abandon seances already arranged. This is a very clear form of teleological automatism.

As a specimen of this spontaneous and hygienic intervention of Léopold in the life of Hélène, I have selected the letter given below, because it combines several interesting traits. It well depicts the energy with which Mlle. Smith is compelled to obey her guide.

The passage from the auditive to the graphic form of automatism is also to be noticed in it. Apropos of this, in the page of this letter reproduced in Fig. 8 (see p. 84), it is made clear that the transition of the hand of Hélène to that of Léopold is accomplished brusquely and in a decided manner. The handwriting is not metamorphosed gradually, slowly, but continues to be that of Mlle. Smith, becoming more and more agitated, it

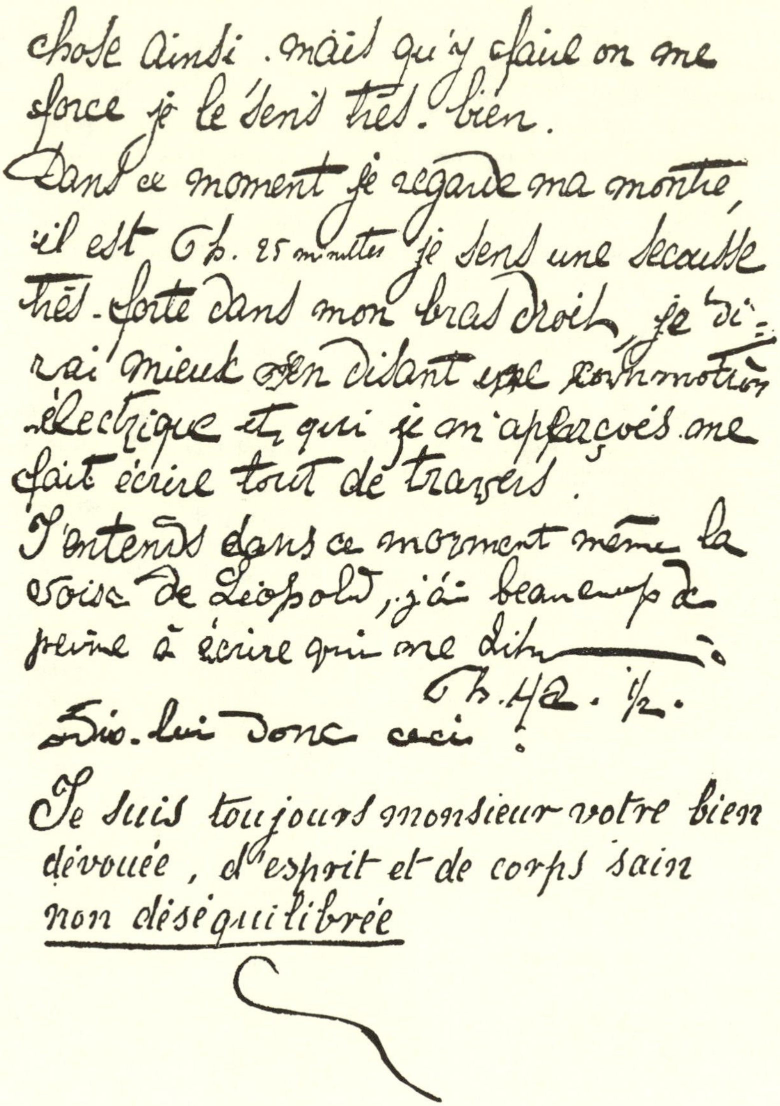

chose ainsi . mais qu'y faire on me
force je le sens très. bien.
Dans ce moment je regarde ma montre,
il est 6 h. 25 minutes je sens une secousse
très. forte dans mon bras droit, je di-
rai mieux en disant une commotion
électrique et qui je m'aperçois me
fait écrire tout de travers.
J'entends dans ce moment même la
voix de Léopold, j'ai beaucoup de
peine à écrire qui me dit ———— :
6 h. 42 . 1/2 .
Dis. lui Donc ceci !

Je suis toujours monsieur votre bien
dévouée, d'esprit et de corps sain
non déséquilibrée

Fig. 8. A page from a letter of Mlle. Smith, showing the spontaneous irruption of the personality and the handwriting of Léopold during the waking
state of Hélène.

is true, and rendered almost illegible by the shocks to the arm of which Léopold takes hold up to the moment when, suddenly and by a bound, it becomes the well-formed calligraphy of Cagliostro.

January 29, 6.15 A.M.

MONSIEUR,—I awoke about ten minutes ago, and heard the voice of Léopold telling me in a very imperious manner, "Get up out of your bed, and quickly, very quickly, write to your dear friend, M. Flournoy, that you will not hold a seance to-morrow, and that you will not be able to go to his house for two weeks, and that you will not hold any seance within that period." I have executed his order, having felt myself forced, compelled in spite of myself, to obey. I was so comfortable in bed and so vexed at being obliged to write you such a message; but I feel myself forced to do what he bids me.

At this moment I am looking at my watch; it is 6.25 o'clock. I feel a very strong shock in my right arm—I might better speak of it as an electric disturbance—and which I perceive has made me write crooked. I hear also at this instant the voice of Léopold. I have much difficulty in writing what he tells me: "6.42½. Say to him this: *I am, sir, always your very devoted servant, in body and mind, healthy and not unbalanced.*"

I stopped for some moments after writing these words, which I saw very well, after having written them, were in the handwriting of Léopold. Immediately afterwards, a second disturbance, similar to the first, gave me a fresh shock, this time from my feet to my head. It all passed so quickly that I am disturbed and confused by it. It is true that I am not yet quite well. Is this the reason why Léopold prevents my going to Florissant to-morrow? I do not know, but, nevertheless, am anxious to follow his advice.

Mlle. Smith always submits obediently to the commands of her guide, since, whenever she has transgressed them, through forgetfulness or neglect, she has had cause to repent it.

It is clear that in this role of special physician of Mlle. Smith, always *au courant* of her state of health, Léopold could easily be interpreted as personifying those vague impressions which spring forth continually from the depths of our physical being, informing us as to what is passing there.

A neuralgic toothache is felt in a dream hours before it makes itself felt in our waking consciousness, while some maladies are often thus foreshadowed several days before they actually declare themselves. All literature is full of anecdotes of this kind; and the psychiatrists have observed that in the form of circular alienation, where phases of melancholic depression and maniacal excitation alternately succeed one another more or less regularly with intervals of normal equilibrum, it is frequently in sleep that the first symptoms of the change of humor can be detected which has already begun in the depths of the individuality, but will only break forth on the outside a little later. But all the hypnoid states are connected, and it is not at all surprising that, in the case of a subject inclined to automatism, these confused presentiments should arise with the appearance of a foreign personality which is only a degree higher than the process of dramatization already so brilliantly at work in our ordinary dreams.

It will be useless to lengthen or further multiply examples of the intervention of Léopold in the life of Mlle. Smith. Those which I have given show him under his essential aspects, and suffice to justify Hélène's confidence in a guide who has never deceived her, who has always given her the best counsel, delivered discourses of the highest ethical tone, and manifested the most touching solicitude for her physical and moral health. It is easy to understand that nothing can shake her faith in the real, objective existence of this precious counsellor.

It is really vexatious that the phenomena of dreams should be so little observed or so badly understood (I do not say by psychologists, but by the general public, which prides itself on its psychology), since the dream is the prototype of spiritistic messages, and holds the key to the explanation of mediumistic phenomena. If it is regrettable to see such noble, sympathetic, pure, and in all respects remarkable personalities as Léopold reduced to the rank of a dream creation, it must be remembered, however, that dreams are not always, as idle folk think, things to be despised or of no value in themselves: the majority are insignificant and deserve only the oblivion to which they are promptly consigned. A very large number are bad and sometimes even worse than reality; but there are others of a better sort, and "dream" is often a synonym for "ideal."

To sum up, Léopold certainly expresses in his central nucleus a very honorable and attractive side of the character of Mlle. Smith, and in taking him as her "guide" she only follows inspirations which are probably among the best of her nature.

CHAPTER FIVE

The Martian Cycle

THE TITLE of this book would naturally commit me to a review of the
Hindoo romance before investigating the Martian cycle. Considerations
of method have caused me to reverse this order. It is better to advance
from the simple to the complex, and while we certainly know less concerning the planet Mars than of India, the romance which it has inspired
in the subliminal genius of Mlle. Smith is relatively less difficult to explain
than the Oriental cycle. In fact, the former seems to spring from pure
imagination, while in the latter we meet with certain actual historical elements, and whence Hélène's memory and intelligence have gained a
knowledge of them is an extremely difficult problem for us to solve. There
is, then, only *one* faculty at work in the Martian romance, as a professional
psychologist would say, while the Oriental cycle calls several into play,
making it necessary to treat of it later, on account of its greater psychological complexity.

While the unknown language which forms the vehicle of many of the
Martian messages cannot naturally be dissociated from the rest of the
cycle, it merits, nevertheless, a special consideration, and the following
chapter will be entirely devoted to it. It does not figure in the present
chapter, in which I shall treat of the origin and the content only of the
Martian romance.

I. ORIGIN AND BIRTH OF THE MARTIAN CYCLE

"We dare to hope," says M. Camille Flammarion, at the beginning of his
excellent work on the planet Mars, "that the day will come when scientific
methods yet unknown to us will give us direct evidences of the existence
of the inhabitants of other worlds, and at the same time, also, will put us
in communication with our brothers in space."[1] And on the last page of his
book he recurs to the same idea, and says: "What marvels does not the
science of the future reserve for our successors, and who would dare to say
that Martian humanity and terrestrial humanity will not some day enter
into communication with each other?"

This splendid prospect seems still far off, along with that of wireless
telegraphy, and almost an Utopian dream, so long as one holds strictly to

---

[1] C. Flammarion, *La Planète Mars et ses conditions d'habitabilité*, p. 3. Paris, 1892.

the current conceptions of our positive sciences. But break these narrow limits; fly, for example, towards the illimitable horizon which spiritism opens up to its happy followers, and as soon as this vague hope takes shape, nothing seems to prevent its immediate realization: and the only cause for wonder is found in the fact that no privileged medium has yet arisen to have the glory, unique in the world, of being the first intermediary between ourselves and the human inhabitants of other planets; for spiritism takes no more account of the barrier of space than of time. The "gates of distance" are wide open before it. With it the question of means is a secondary matter; one has only the embarrassment of making a choice. It matters not whether it be by intuition, by clairvoyance, by telepathy, or by double personality that the soul is permitted to leave momentarily its terrestrial prison and make the voyage between this world and others in an instant of time, or whether the feat is accomplished by means of the astral body, by the reincarnation of disincarnate omnisciences, by "fluid beings," or, in a word, by any other process whatever. The essential point is, according to spiritism, that no serious objection would be offered to the possibility of such communication. The only difficulty would be to find a mediumistic subject possessing sufficient psychical faculties. It is a simple question of fact; if such a one has not yet been found, it is apparently only because the time is not yet ripe. But now that astronomers themselves appeal to those "unknown methods of actual science" to put us *en rapport* with other worlds, no doubt spiritism—which is the science of to-morrow, as definite as absolute religion—will soon respond to these legitimate aspirations. We may, therefore, expect at any moment the revelation so impatiently looked for, and every good medium has the right to ask herself whether she is not the being predestined to accomplish this unrivalled mission.

These are the considerations which, to my mind, in their essential content inspired in the subliminal part of Mlle. Smith the first idea of her Martian romance. I would not assert that the passages from M. Flammarion which I have quoted came directly to the notice of Hélène, but they express and recapitulate wonderfully well one of the elements of the atmosphere in which she found herself at the beginning of her mediumship. For if there are no certain indications of her ever having read any work on the "heavenly worlds" and their inhabitants, either that of M. Flammarion or of any other author, she has, nevertheless, heard such subjects discussed. She is perfectly familiar with the name of the celebrated astronomical writer Juvisy, and knows something of his philosophical ideas, which, by-the-way, is not at all surprising when we consider the popularity he enjoys among spiritists, who find in him a very strong scientific support for their doctrine of reincarnation on other planets.

I also have evidence that in the circle of Mme. N., of which Hélène was a member in 1892, the conversation more than once turned in the direction of the habitability of Mars, to which the discovery of the famous "canals" has for some years specially directed the attention of the general public.* This circumstance appears to me to explain sufficiently the fact that Hélène's subliminal astronomy should be concerned with this planet. It is, moreover, quite possible that the first germs of the Martian romance date still further back than the beginning of Hélène's mediumship. The Oriental role shows indications of concerning itself with that planet, and the very clear impression which she has of having in her childhood and youth experienced many visions of a similar kind "without her noticing them particularly," gives rise to the supposition that the ingredients of which this cycle is composed date from many years back. Possibly they may have one and the same primitive source in the exotic memories, descriptions, or pictures of tropical countries which later branched out under the vigorous impulsion of spiritistic ideas in two distinct currents, the Hindoo romance on the one side and the Martian on the other, whose waters are mingled on more than one occasion afterwards.

While, on the whole, therefore, it is probable that its roots extend back as far as the childhood of Mlle. Smith, it is nevertheless with the Martian romance, as well as with the others, not a mere question of the simple cryptomnesiac return of facts of a remote past, or of an exhumation of fossil residue brought to light again by the aid of somnambulism. It is a very active process, and one in full course of evolution, nourished, undoubtedly by elements belonging to the past, but which have been recombined and moulded in a very original fashion, until it amounts finally, among other things, to the creation of an unknown language. It will be interesting to follow step by step the phases of this elaboration: but since it always, unfortunately, hides itself in the obscurity of the subconsciousness, we are only cognizant of it by its occasional appearances, and all the rest of that subterranean work must be inferred, in a manner somewhat hypothetical, from those supraliminal eruptions and the scanty data which we have concerning the outward influences which have exerted a stimulating influence upon the subliminal part of Hélène. It was in 1892, then, that the conversations took place which were to prepare the soil for this work of lofty subliminal fantasy, and planted in Hélène's mind the double idea, of enormous scientific interest, that she could enter into direct relation with the inhabitants of Mars, and of the possibility, unsuspected by scientists, but which spiritism furnishes us, of reaching there by a mediumistic route. I doubt, however, whether that vague suggestion on the part of the environment would have sufficed to engender the Martian dream—since for more than two years no sign of its eruption mainfested itself—without the intervention of some fillip more concrete, capable of giving a start to the whole movement. It is not easy, unfortunately, for want of records of the facts, to assign with precision the circumstances under which and the moment when Hélène's subconscious imagination received that effective impulsion, but an unequivocal trace is discovered, as I am about to show in the contemporaneous report of the proceedings of the first distinctly Martian seance of Mlle. Smith.

In March, 1894, Hélène made the acquaintance of M. Lemaître, who, being exceedingly interested in the phenomena of abnormal psychology, was present with others at some of her seances, and finally begged her to hold some at his house. At the first of these (October 28, 1894), Hélène met a lady, a widow, who was greatly to be pitied. Besides suffering from a very serious affection of the eyes, Mme. Mirbel had been terribly afflicted by the loss of her only son, Alexis, seventeen years old, and a pupil of M. Lemaître. While not yet fully convinced of the truth of spiritism, it is easy to understand that Mme. Mirbel was very anxious to believe in that consolatory doctrine, and ready to accept it, if only some proofs could be furnished her; and what more convincing testimony could she ask or receive than that of a message from her beloved child? Moreover, it was probably not without a secret hope of procuring a communication of this nature that she accepted the invitation which M. Lemaître had sent her with the idea of procuring some moments of distraction for the unhappy mother. As happens frequently in Hélène's case, this first seance fully satisfied the desires of the sitters and surpassed their expectations. Speaking only of that which concerns Mme. Mirbel, Hélène had the vision, first, of a young man, in the very detailed description of whom there was no difficulty inrecognizing the deceased Alexis Mirbel; then of an old man whom the table called Raspail, brought by the young man that he might treat his mother's eyes, who thus had the double privilege of receiving through the table words of tenderness from her son, and from Raspail directions for the treatment of the affection of her eyes. Nothing in that seance recalled in any way the planet Mars, and it could not be foreseen from anything that occurred there that Alexis Mirbel, disincarnated, would return later under the name of Esenale as official interpreter of the Martian language.

It was altogether different a month later (November 25), at the second reunion at M. Lemaître's, at which Mme. Mirbel was again present. On this occasion the astronomical dream appeared at once and dominated the entire seance.

From the beginning, says the report of the seance, Mlle. Smith perceived, in the distance and at a great height, a bright light. Then she felt a tremor which almost caused her heart to cease beating, after which it seemed to her as though her head were empty and as if she were no longer in the body. She found herself in a dense fog, which changed successively from blue to a vivid rose color, to gray, and then to black: she is floating, she says; and the table, supporting itself on one leg, seemed to express a very curious floating movement. Then she sees a star, growing larger, always larger, and becomes, finally, "as large as our house." Hélène feels that she is ascending; then the table gives, by raps: "Lemaître, that which you have so long desired!" Mlle. Smith, who had been ill at ease, finds herself feeling better; she distinguishes three enormous globes, one of them very beautiful. "On what am I walking?" she asks. And the table replies: "On a world—Mars." Hélène then began a description of all the strange things which presented themselves to her view, and caused her as much surprise as amusement. Carriages without horses or wheels, emitting sparks as they glided by; houses with fountains on the roof; a cradle having for curtains an angel made of iron with outstretched wings, etc. What seemed less strange, were people exactly like the inhabitants of our earth, save that both sexes wore the same costume, formed of trousers very ample, and a long blouse, drawn tight about the waist and decorated with various designs. The child in the cradle was exactly like our children, according to the sketch which Hélène made from memory after the seance.

Finally, she saw upon Mars a sort of vast assembly hall, in which was Professor Raspail, having in the first row of his hearers the young Alexis Mirbel, who, by a typtological dictation, reproached his mother for not having followed the medical prescription which he gave her a month previously: "Dear mamma, have you, then, so little confidence in us? You have no idea how much pain you have caused me!" Then followed a conversation of a private nature between Mme. Mirbel and her son, the latter replying by means of the table; then everything becomes quiet, the vision of Mars effaces itself little by little; the table takes the same rotary movement on one foot which it had at the commencement of the seance; Mlle. Smith finds herself again in the fogs and goes through the same process as before in an inverse order. Then she exclaims: "Ah! here I am back again!" and several loud raps on the table mark the end of the seance.

I have related in its principal elements this first Martian seance, for the sake of its importance in different respects.

The initial series of coenaesthetic hallucinations, corresponding to a voyage from the earth to Mars, reflects well the childish character of an imagination which scientific problems or the exigences of logic trouble very little. Without doubt spiritism can explain how the material difficulties of an interplanetary journey may be avoided in a purely mediumistic, fluid connection; but why, then, this persistence of physical sensations, trouble with the heart tremor, floating sensation, etc.? However it may be, this series of sensations is from this time on the customary prelude, and, as it were, the premonitory *aura* of the Martian dream, with certain modifications, throughout all the seances; sometimes it is complicated with auditive hallucinations (rumbling, noise of rushing water, etc.), or sometimes olfactory (disagreeable odors of burning, of sulphur, of a coming storm), oftener it tends to shorten and simplify itself, until it is either reduced to a brief feeling of *malaise*, or to the initial visual hallu- cination of the light, generally very brilliant and red in which the Martian visions usually appear.

But the point to which I wish to call special attention is that singular speech of the table, on the instant at which Mlle. Smith arrives on the distant star, and before it is known what star is concerned: "Lemaître, that which you have so much wished for!" This declaration, which may be considered as a dedication, so to speak, inscribed on the frontispiece of the Martian romance, authorizes us in my opinion, in considering it and interpreting it in its origin, as a direct answer to a wish of M. Lemaître, a desire which came at a recent period to Hélène's knowledge, and which has enacted with her the initiatory role of her astronomical dream.

It is true that M. Lemaître himself did not understand at the moment to what this preliminary warning referred, but the note which he inserted at the end of his report of that seance is instructive in this regard: "I do not know how to explain the first words dictated by the table: 'Lemaître, that which you have so much wished for!' M. S. reminds me that in a conversa- tion which I had with him last summer I said to him: 'It would be very interesting to know what is happening upon other planets.' If this is an answer to the wish of last year, very well."

It must be added that M. S., who had been sufficiently struck by this wish of M. Lemaître to remember it for several months, was, during all of the time referred to, one of the most regular attendants upon the seances of Mlle. Smith; and, to one who knows by experience all that happens at the spiritistic reunions, before, after, and during the seance itself, there could hardly be any doubt but that it was through M. S., as intermediary, that Mlle. Smith had heard mentioned M. Lemaître's regret at our rela- tive ignorance of the inhabitants of other planets. This idea, probably caught on the wing during the state of suggestibility which accompanies the seances, returned with renewed force when Hélène was invited to hold a seance at the house of M. Lemaître, and made more vivid also by the desire, which is always latent in her, of making the visions as interest- ing as possible to the persons among whom she finds herself. Such is, in my opinion, the seed which, falling into the ground and fertilized by for- mer conversations concerning the inhabitants of Mars and the possibility of spiritistic relations with them, has served as the germ of the romance, the further development of which it remains for me to trace.

One point which still remains to be cleared up in the seance, as I come to sum up, is the singularly artificial character and the slight connection between the Martian vision, properly so called, and the reappearance of

Raspail and Alexis Mirbel. We do not altogether understand what these personages have to do with it. What need is there of their being to-day found on the planet Mars simply for the purpose of continuing their interview with Mme. Mirbel, begun at a previous seance, without the intervention of any planet? The assembly-hall at which they are found, while it is located on Mars, is a bond of union all the more artificial between them and that planet in that there is nothing specifically Martian in its description and appears to have been borrowed from our globe. This incident is at bottom a matter out of the regular course, full of interest undoubtedly for Mme. Mirbel, whom it directly concerns, but without intimate connection with the Martian world. It was evidently the astronomical revelation, intended for M. Lemaître, and ripened by a period of incubation, which should have furnished the material for this seance; but the presence of Mme. Mirbel awoke anew the memory of her son and of Raspail, which had occupied the preceding seance, and these memories, interfering with the Martian vision, become, for good or ill, incorporated as a strange episode in it without having any direct connection with it. The work of unification, of dramatization, by which these two unequal chains of ideas are harmonized and fused the one with the other through the intermediation of an assembly-hall, is no more or no less extraordinary than that which displays itself in all our nocturnal phantasmagoria, where certain absolutely heterogeneous memories often ally themselves after an unexpected fashion, and afford opportunity for confusions of the most bizarre character.

But mediumistic communications differ from ordinary dreams in this—namely, the incoherence of the latter does not cause them to have any consequences. We are astonished and diverted for a moment as we reflect upon a dream. Sometimes a dream holds a little longer the attention of the psychologist, who endeavors to unravel the intricate plot of his dreams and to discover, amid the caprices of association or the events of the waking state, the origin of their tangled threads. But, on the whole, this incoherence has no influence on the ultimate course of our thoughts, because we see in our dreams only the results of chance, without value in themselves and without objective signification.

It is otherwise with spiritistic communications, by reason of the importance and the credit accorded them.

The medium who partially recollects her automatisms, or to whom the sitters have detailed them after the close of the seance, adding also their comments, becomes preoccupied with these mysterious revelations; like the paranoiac, who perceives hidden meanings or a profound significance in the most trifling coincidences, she seeks to fathom the content of her strange visions, reflects on them, examines them in the light of spiritistic notions; if she encounters difficulties in them, or contradictions, her con-

scious or unconscious thought (the two are not always in accord) will undertake the task of removing them, and solving as well as possible the
problems which these dream-creations, considered as realities, impose
upon her, and the later somnambulisms will bear the imprint of this labor
of interpretation or correction.

It is to this point we have come at the commencement of the astronomical romance of Mlle. Smith. The purely accidental and fortuitous conjunction of the planet Mars and Alexis Mirbel in the seance of the 25th of
November determined their definitive welding together. Association by
fortuitous contiguity is transformed into a logical connection.*

II. LATER DEVELOPMENT OF THE MARTIAN CYCLE

This development was not effected in a regular manner; but for the most
part by leaps and bounds, separating stoppages more or less prolonged.
After its inauguration in the seance of November 25, 1894, it suffered a
first eclipse of nearly fifteen months, attributable to new preoccupations
which had installed themselves on the highest plane of Mlle. Smith's subconsciousness and held that position throughout the whole of the year
1895.*

Compared with the seance of November, 1894, that of February, 1896
(of which a resume follows), shows interesting innovations. Raspail does
not figure in it and henceforth does not appear again, which was probably
due to the fact that Mme. Mirbel had failed to make use of the method of
treatment which he had prescribed for her eyes. Young Mirbel, on the
contrary, sole object of the desires and longings of his poor mother, occupies the highest plane, and is the central figure of the vision. He now
speaks Martian and no longer understands French, which complicates the
conversation somewhat. Further, not possessing the power of moving tables upon our globe, it is through the intervention of the medium, by
incarnating himself momentarily in Mlle. Smith, that he henceforth com-
municates with his mother. These two latter points in their turn cause
certain difficulties to arise, which, acting as a ferment or a suggestion will
later usher in a new step in the progress of the romance: Alexis Mirbel
cannot return to incarnate himself in a terrestrial medium if he is imprisoned in his Martian existence; he must first terminate that and return
to the condition in which he again floats in interplanetary space; which
"fluid" or wandering state permits him at the same time to give us the
French translation of the Martian tongue; since, according to spiritism, a
complete memory of previous existences, and consequently of the various
languages pertaining to them, is temporarily recovered during the phases
of disincarnation.

These anticipatory hints will assist the reader in following more easily the thread of the somnambulistic romance in the resume of its principal stages.

February 2, 1896.—I sum up, by enumerating them, the principal somnambulistic phases of this seance, which lasted more than two hours and a half, and at which Mme. Mirbel assisted.

1. Increasing hemisomnambulism, with gradual loss of consciousness of the real environment—at the beginning the table bows several times to Mme. Mirbel, announcing that the coming scene is intended for her. After a series of elementary visual hallucinations (rainbow colors, etc.), meaning for Mme. Mirbel that she would finally become blind, Hélène arose, left the table, and held a long conversation with an imaginary woman who wished her to enter a curious little car without wheels or horses. She became impatient towards this woman, who, after having at first spoken to her in French, now persisted in speaking in an unintelligible tongue, like Chinese. Léopold revealed to us by the little finger that it was the language of the planet Mars, that this woman is the mother of Alexis Mirbel, reincarnated on that planet, and that Hélène herself will speak Martian. Presently Hélène begins to recite with increasing volubility an incomprehensible jargon, the beginning of which is as follows (according to notes taken by M. Lemaître at the time, as accurately as possible): "**Mitchma mitchmon mimini tchouainem mimatchineg masichinof mézavi patelki abrésinad navette naven navette mitchichénid naken chinoutoufiche**" . . . From this point the rapidity prevented the recognition of anything else, except such scraps as "**téké . . . katéchivist . . . meguetch,**" . . . or "**méketch . . . kété . . . chiméké.**" After a few minutes, Hélène interrupts herself, crying out, "Oh, I have had enough of it; you say such words to me I will never be able to repeat them." Then, with some reluctance, she consents to follow her interlocutrix into the car which was to carry her to Mars.

2. The trance is now complete. Hélène thereupon mimics the voyage to Mars in three phases, the meaning of which is indicated by Léopold: a regular rocking motion of the upper part of the body (passing through the terrestrial atmosphere), absolute immobility and rigidity (interplanetary space), again oscillations of the shoulders and the bust (atmosphere of Mars). Arrived upon Mars, she descends from the car, and performs a complicated pantomime expressing the manners of Martian politeness: uncouth gestures with the hands and fingers, slapping of the hands, taps of the fingers upon the nose, the lips, the chin, etc., twisted courtesies, glidings, and rotation on the floor, etc. It seems that is the way people approach and salute each other up there.

3. This sort of dance having suggested to one of the sitters the idea of performing upon the piano, Hélène suddenly fell upon the floor in an evidently hypnotic state, which had no longer a Martian character. At the

cessation of the music she entered into a mixed state, in which the memory of the Martian visions continually mingle themselves with some idea of her terrestrial existence. She talks to herself. "Those dreams are droll, all the same. . . . I must tell that to M. Lemaître. When he [the Martian Alexis Mirbel] said 'Good-day' to me, he tapped himself upon the nose. . . . He spoke to me in a queer language, but I understood it perfectly, all the same," etc. Seated on the ground, leaning against a piece of furniture, she continues, soliloquizing in French, in a low voice, to review the dream, mingling with it some wandering reflections. She finds, for example, that the young Martian (Alexis) was a remarkably big boy for one only five or six years old, as he claimed to be, and that the woman seemed very young to be his mother.

4. After a transitory phase of sighs and hiccoughs, followed by profound sleep with muscular relaxation, she enters into Martian somnambulism and murmurs some confused words: "**Késin ouitidjé**" . . . etc. I command her to speak French to me; she seems to understand, and replies in Martian, with an irritated and imperious tone, I ask her to tell me her name; she replies, "**Vasimini Météche.**" With the idea that, perhaps, she "is incarnating" the young Alexis, of whom she has spoken so much in the preceding phase, I urge Mme. Mirbel to approach her, and thereupon begins a scene of incarnation really very affecting; Mme. Mirbel is on her knees, sobbing bitterly, in the presence of her recovered son, who shows her marks of the most profound affection and caresses her hands "exactly as he was accustomed to do during his last illness," all the time carrying on a discourse in Martian (**tin is toutch**), which the poor mother cannot understand, but to which an accent of extreme sweetness and a tender intonation impart an evident meaning of words of consolation and filial tenderness. This pathetic duet lasted about ten minutes, and was brought to an end by a return to lethargic sleep, from which Hélène awakened at the end of a quarter of an hour, pronouncing a short Martian word, after which she instantly recovered the use of her French and her normal waking state.

5. Questioned as to what had passed, Hélène, while drinking tea, narrates the dream which she has had. She has a sufficiently clear memory of her journey and of what she has seen on Mars, with the exception of the young man, of whom she has retained only a recollection of the scene of incarnation.

But suddenly, in the midst of the conversation, she begins to speak in Martian, without appearing to be aware of it, and while continuing to chat with us in the most natural manner; she appeared to understand all our words, and answered in her strange idiom, in the most normal tone, and seemed very much astonished when we told her that we did not understand her language; she evidently believes she is speaking French.* By questioning her concerning a visit which she had made a few days before to M. C., and asking her the number and the names of the persons whom she met there, we succeed in identifying the four following Martian words: **Métiche S.**, *Monsieur S.;* **Médache C.**, *Madame C.;* **Métaganiche Smith**, *Mademoiselle Smith;* **kin't'che**, *four.* After which she resumes definitively her French. Interrogated as to the incident which has transpired, she is astounded, has only a hesitating and confused memory of her having spoken at all this evening of her visit to M. C., and does not recognize nor understand the four Martian words given above when they are repeated to her. On several occasions during this seance I had made the suggestion to Hélène that at a given signal, after her awaking, she would recover the memory of the Martian words pronounced by her and of their meaning. But Léopold, who was present, declared that this command would not be obeyed, and that a translation could not be obtained this evening. The signal, though often repeated, was, in fact, without result.

It has seemed to me necessary to describe with some detail this seance, at which the Martian language made its first appearance, in order to place before the reader all the fragments which we have been able to gather, without, of course, any guarantee of absolute accuracy, since every one knows how difficult it is to note the sounds of unknown words. A curious difference is to be noticed between the words picked up in the course of the seance and the four words several times repeated by Hélène, the meaning and pronunciation of which have been determined with complete accuracy in the posthypnotic return of the somnambulistic dream. Judged by these latter, the Martian language is only a puerile counterfeit of French, of which she preserves in each word a number of syllables and certain conspicuous letters. In the other phrases, on the contrary, also making use of later texts which have been translated, as we shall see hereafter, it cannot be discovered what it is. We are constrained to believe that these first outbreaks of Martian, characterized by a volubility which we have rarely met with since then, was only a pseudo-Martian, a continuation of sounds uttered at random and without any real meaning, analogous to the gibberish which children use sometimes in their games of "pretending" to speak Chinese or Indian, and that the real Martian was only created by an unskilful distortion of French, in a posthypnotic access of hemisomnambulism, in order to respond to the manifest desire of the sitters to obtain the precise significance of some isolated Martian words.

The impossibility, announced by Léopold, of procuring a translation that same evening of the pretended Martian spoken for the first time during that seance, and the fact that it could not again be obtained, give some support to the preceding theory.

The circumstance that Hélène, in remembering her dream in phase

No. 3, had the sentiment of having *well understood* this unknown jargon, is not an objection, since the children who amuse themselves by simulating an uncouth idiom—to recur to that example—do not retain the least consciousness of the ideas which their gibberish is assumed to express. It seems, in short, that if this new language was already really established at that time in Hélène's subliminal consciousness to the point of sustaining fluently discourses of several minutes' duration, some phrases at least would not have failed to gush forth, spontaneously sometimes, in the course of ordinary life, and in order to throw light upon visions of Martian people or landscapes. More than seven months had to elapse before that phenomenon, which was so frequent afterwards, began to appear.

May we not see in this half-year a period of incubation, employed in the subliminal fabrication of a language, properly so called—that is to say, formed of precise words and with a definite signification, in imitation of the four terms just referred to—to replace the disordered nonsense of the beginning?

However it may be, and to return to our story, one can imagine the interest which that sudden and unexpected apparition of mysterious speech aroused, and which the authority of Léopold would not allow to be taken for anything other than the language of Mars. The natural curiosity of Hélène herself, as well as that of her friends, to know more about our neighbors of other worlds and their way of expressing themselves should naturally have contributed to the development of the subliminal dream. The following seance, unhappily, did not justify the promise with which it began.

February 16, 1896.—At the beginning of this seance, Hélène has a vision of Alexis Mirbel, who announces, by means of the table, that he has not forgotten his French, and that he will give a translation of the Martian words another day. But this prediction is not fulfilled. Whether Hélène, for the reason that she is not feeling well to-day, or that the presence of some one antipathetic to her has hindered the production of the phenomena, the Martian somnambulism, which seemed on the point of breaking forth, did not make its appearance. Hélène remains in a crepuscular state, in which the feeling of present reality and the Martian ideas on the level of consciousness interfere with and mutually obscure each other. She speaks in French with the sitters, but mingling with it here and there a strange word (such as **méche, chinit, chéque**, which, according to the context, seem to signify *pencil, ring, paper*), and appears far away from her actual surroundings. She is astonished, in particular, at the sight of M. R. occupied in taking notes by the *procès verbal*, and seems to find that manner of writing with a pen or pencil strange and absurd, but without explaining clearly how it was to be otherwise accomplished. The importance of this seance is in the fact that the idea stands out clearly (which was not to be realized until a year and a half later) of a mode of handwriting peculiar to the planet Mars.

This seance, which was almost a failure, was the last of that period. Hélène's health, which became more and more impaired by standing too long on her feet and overwork at her desk, necessitated her taking a complete rest. I have mentioned the fact that during these six months, without any regular seances, she was subject to a superabundance of spontaneous visions and somnambulisms; but these automatisms belonged to the Hindoo or other cycles, and I do not believe that she experienced during that time any phenomena which were clearly related to the Martian romance. On the other hand, as soon as she was re-established in and had returned to her normal mode of life, the latter appeared again with all the more intensity, dating from the following nocturnal vision. (See Fig. 9.)

September 5, 1896.—Hélène narrates that having arisen at a quarter-past three in the morning to take in some flowers that stood upon the window-sill and were threatened by the wind, instead of going back to bed immediately she sat down upon her bed and saw before her a landscape and some peculiar people. She was on the border of a beautiful blue-pink lake, with a bridge the sides of which were transparent and formed of yellow tubes like the pipes of an organ, of which one end seemed to be plunged into the water. The earth was peach-colored; some of the trees had trunks widening as they ascended, while those of others were twisted. Later a crowd approached the bridge, in which one woman was especially prominent. The women wore hats which were flat, like plates. Hélène does not know who these people are, but has the feeling of having conversed with them. On the bridge there was a man of dark complexion (Astané), carrying in his hands an instrument somewhat resembling a carriage-lantern in appearance, which, being pressed, emitted flames, and which seemed to be a flying-machine. By means of this instrument the man left the bridge, touched the surface of the water, and returned again to the bridge. This tableau lasted twenty-five minutes, since Hélène, upon returning to consciousness, observed that her candle was still burning and ascertained that it was then 3.40 o'clock. She is convinced that she did not fall asleep, but was wide awake during all of this vision. (See Figs. 10 and 11.)

From that time the spontaneous Martian visions are repeated and multiplied. Mlle. Smith experiences them usually in the morning, after awaking and before rising from her bed: sometimes in the evening, or occasionally at other times during the day. It is in the course of these visual hallucinations that the Martian language appears again under an auditive form.

September 22, 1896.—During these last days Hélène has seen again on different occasions the Martian man, with or without his flying-machine; for example, he appeared to her while she was taking a bath, at the edge of the bath-tub. She has had several times visions of a strange house the picture of which followed her with so much persistency that she finally painted it (see Fig. 12). At the same time she heard on three different occasions a sentence the meaning of which she does not know, but which she was able to take down with her pencil as follows: "**Dodé né ci haudan té méche métiche Astané ké dé mé véche.**" (As was ascertained six weeks after, by the translation given in the seance of the 2d of November, this phrase indicates that the strange house is that of the Martian man, who is called Astané.)

This phrase was undoubtedly Martian, but what was the meaning of it? After having hoped in vain for nearly a month that the meaning would be revealed in some way or other, I decided to try a disguised suggestion. I wrote to Léopold himself a letter, in which I appealed to his omniscience as well as to his kindness to give me some enlightenment in regard to the strange language which piqued our curiosity, and, in particular, as to the meaning of the phrase Hélène had heard. I asked him to answer me in writing, by means of Hélène's hand. We did not have to wait long for a reply. Hélène received my letter the 20th of October, and on the evening of the 22d, seized with a vague desire to write, she took a pencil, which placed itself in the regular position, between the thumb and the index-finger (whereas she always held her pen between the middle and index-finger), and traced rapidly, in the characteristic handwriting of Léopold and with his signature, a beautiful epistle of eighteen Alexandrine lines addressed to me, of which the ten last are as follows, being an answer to my request that the secrets of Martian be revealed to me:

> Ne crois pas qu'en t'aimant comme un bien tendre frère
> Je te diroi des cieux tout le profond mystère;
> Je t'aideroi beaucoup, je t'ouvriroi la voie,
> Mais à toi de saisir et chercher avec joie;
> Et quand tu la verras d'ici-bas détachée,
> Quand son âme mobile aura pris la volée
> Et planera sur Mars aux superbes couleurs;
> Si tu veux obtenir d'elle quelques lueurs,
> Pose bien doucement, ta main sur son front pâle
> Et prononce bien bas le doux nom d'Esenale![2]

---

[2] Do not think that in loving you as a tender brother
I shall tell you all the profound mysteries of heaven;
I shall help you much, I shall open for you the way,
But it is for you to seize and seek with joy;
And when you shall see her released from here below,
When her mobile soul shall have taken flight
And shall soar over Mars with its brilliant tints;
If you would obtain from her some light,
Place your hand very gently on her pale forehead
And pronounce very softly the sweet name of Esenale!

Fig. 9. Martian landscape. Pink bridge, with yellow railings plunging down into a pale-blue and purple-tinted lake. The shores and hills of a red color, no green being visible. All the trees are of a brick-red, purple, or violet tint. (From the collection of M. Lemaître.)

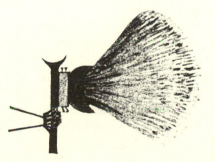

Fig. 10. Flying-machine held by Astané, emitting yellow and red flames. (From the collection of M. Lemaître.)

Fig. 11. Astané. Yellow complexion, brown hair; brown sandals; roll of white paper in his hand; variegated costume, or red and white; brick-red belt and border.

Fig. 12. House of Astané. Blue sky; soil, mountains, and walls of a red color. The two plants, with twisted trunks, have purple leaves; the others have long green lower leaves and small purple higher leaves. The frame-work of the doors, windows, and decorations are in the shape of trumpets, and are of a brownish-red color. White glass (?) and curtains or shades of a turquoise-blue. The railings of the roof are yellow, with blue tips.

Fig. 13. Martian landscape. Greenish-yellow sky. A man with a yellow complexion dressed in white, in a boat of brown, yellow, black, and red colors on a blue-green lake; rose-tinted rock, with white and yellow spots; dark green vegetation; buildings of brown, red, and rose-lilac tints, with white window-panes and curtains of bright blue.

Fig. 14. Martian landscape. Sky of yellow; green lake; gray shores bordered by a brown fence; bell-towers on the shore, in yellow-brown tones, with corners and pinnacles ornamented with pink and blue balls; hills of red rocks; with vegetation of a rather dark green interspersed with rose, purple, and white spots (flowers); buildings at the base constructed of brick-red lattice-work; edges and corners terminating in brown-red trumpets; immense white window panes, with turquoise-blue curtains; roofs furnished with yellow-brown bell-turrets, brick-red battlements, or with green and red plants (like those of Astané's house, Fig. 12). Persons with large white head-dresses and red or brown robes.

Fig. 15. Light-brown and yellow trunk and leaves; double-lobed flowers of a vivid red, out of which proceed yellow stamens like black threads. Fig. 16. Large leaves, light yellowish brown; flowers with purple petals with black stamens and black stems covered with little purple leaves like petals. Fig. 17. Large violet fruit with black spots, surmounted by a yellow and violet plume. The trunk of brown color with black veins, with six branches of the same character ending in a yellow hook. Red-brick soil.

Fig. 18. Astané's ugly beast. The body and tail are rose-colored; the eye is green with a black centre; the head is blackish; the lateral appendices are brownish-yellow, covered, like the whole body, with pink hair.

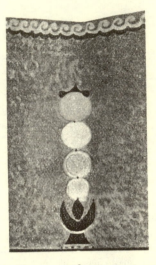

Fig. 19. Martian lamp, standing against a rose and blue-colored tapestry.

Fig. 20. Plant of Martian design. Fire-red flowers; violet-gray leaves.

I have been very sensible to the pledges of fraternal affection that
Léopold has accorded me, but this time I was especially moved, and although the very uncommon name of Esenale meant absolutely nothing to
me, I took care not to forget the singular rule which had been furnished
me. At the following seance an opportunity for using it presented itself,
and Léopold went so far as to direct himself the application of his method
by giving us his instructions, sometimes with one finger, sometimes with
another, during Hélène's Martian trance.

Monday, November 2, 1896.—After various characteristic symptoms of
the departure for Mars (vertigo, affection of the heart, etc.), Hélène went
in a deep sleep. I had recourse to the prescribed method, but Léopold, by
the fingers of the right hand, indicated that the proper moment had not
yet arrived, and said: "When the soul shall again have regained possession
of itself thou shalt execute my order; she will then describe to you, while
still asleep, that which she shall have seen on Mars." Shortly after he
adds, "Make her sit down in an easy-chair" (instead of the uncomfortable
one which she had taken, as was her wont); then, as her peaceful sleep
still continued, he informs us again that she is *en route* towards Mars; that
once arrived up there she understands the Martian spoken around her,
although she has never learned it; that it is not he, Léopold, who will
translate the Martian for us—not because he does not wish to do so, but
because he cannot; that this translation is the performance of Esenale,
who is actually disincarnate in space, but who has recently lived upon
Mars, and also upon the earth, which permits him to act as interpreter,
etc.

After half an hour of waiting, Hélène's calm sleep gave way to agitation,
and she passed into another form of somnambulism, with sighs, rhythmic
movements of the head and hands, then grotesque Martian gestures and
French words murmured softly to the hearing of Léopold, who seems to
accompany her on Mars, and to whom she confides some of her impressions in regard to that which she perceives. In the midst of this soliloquy a
vertical movement of the arm, peculiar to Léopold, indicates that the
moment has arrived for carrying out his directions. I place my hand on
Hélène's forehead, and utter the name of Esenale, to which Hélène replies in a soft, feeble, somewhat melancholy, voice:

Esenale has gone away . . . he has left me alone . . . but he will return, . . . he
will soon return. . . . He has taken me by the hand and made me enter the
house [that which she saw in her vision, and of which she made the drawing a
month ago—see Fig. 12]. . . . I do not know where Esenale is leading me, but
he has said to me, '**Dodé né ci haudan té méche métiche Astané ké dé mé
véche**,' but I did not understand; . . . **dodé**, *this;* **né**, *is;* **ci**, *the;* **haudan**, *house;*
té, *of the;* **méche**, *great;* **métiche**, *man;* **Astané**, *Astané;* **ké**, *whom;* **dé**, *thou;*

mé, *hast;* **véche,** *seen.* . . . This is the house of the great man Astané, whom
thou hast seen. . . . Esenale has told me that. . . . Esenale has gone away. . . .
He will return . . . he will soon return . . . he will teach me to speak . . . and
Astané will teach me to write.

I have abridged this long monologue, constantly interrupted by silences, and the continuation of which I only obtained by having constant
recourse to the name of Esenale as the magic word, alone capable of
extracting each time a few words from Hélène's confused brain. After the
last sentence or phrase, in which one can see a categorical prediction of
the Martian writing, her weak, slow voice was finally hushed, and
Léopold directs by means of his left middle finger the removal of the hand
from the forehead. Then follow the customary alternations of lethargic
sleep, sighs, catalepsy, momentary relapses into somnambulism, etc.
Then she opens her eyes permanently, very much surprised to find herself in the easy-chair. Her brain is greatly confused. "It seems to me as
though I had a great many things on my mind, but I cannot fix upon
anything." By degrees she regains a clear consciousness, but of the entire
seance, which has lasted an hour and a half, there only remain some fragments of Martian visions and no recollection whatever of the scene with
Esenale and that of the translation.

This process of translation, the first application of which is here presented, becomes from this time the standard method.

For more than two years and a half, the imposition of the hand upon
Hélène's forehead and the uttering of the name of Esenale at the proper
moment during the trance constitute the "open sesame" of the Martian-
French dictionary buried in the subliminal strata of Hélène's consciousness. The idea of this ceremonial is evidently to awaken by suggestion—
in a certain favorable somnambulistic phase, which Léopold recognizes
and himself announces by a gesture of the arm—the secondary personality which has amused itself by composing the phrases of this extraterrestrial language.

In spiritistic terms, it amounts to invoking the disincarnate Esenale,
otherwise called Alexis Mirbel, who, having lived on both planets, can
easily devote himself to the functions of an interpreter.

The only difference between this scene of translation and other seances
is in the ease and rapidity with which it is performed. Esenale seems
sometimes to be thoroughly asleep and difficult to awaken; Hélène persists in replying by the stereotyped refrain, and incessantly repeats, in
her soft and melancholy voice, "Esenale has gone away—he will soon
return—he has gone away—he will soon return." Then some more energetic passes or friction on the forehead are necessary, instead of the

simple pressure of the hand, in order to break up this mechanical repetition, which threatens to go on forever, and in order to obtain, finally, the repetition and translation, word by word, of the Martian texts.* Otherwise the voice continues identical with that of the refrain, soft and feeble, and one can never know whether it is Esenale himself who is making use of Hélène's phonetic apparatus without modifying it, or whether it is she herself, repeating in her sleep what Esenale has told her; the categorical distinctness and absence of all hesitation in pronunciation of the Martian are in favor of the former supposition, which is also corroborated by the fact that it was also in this same voice that Alexis Mirbel (Esenale) spoke to his mother in the scenes of incarnation. (See Fig. 13.)

It would be wearisome to recount in detail all the further manifestations of the Martian cycle, which occur frequently in numerous seances and also under the form of spontaneous visions in the daily life of Mlle. Smith. The reader can gain an idea of them both from the remarks of the following paragraph, as well as from the explanatory resumes added to the Martian texts, which will be collected in the following chapter. It merely remains for me to say a word here as to the manner in which the pictures of Hélène relative to Mars, and reproduced in autotype in the Figs. 9 to 20, have been made.

None of these pictures has been executed in complete somnambulism, and they have not, consequently, like the drawings of certain mediums, the interest of a graphic product, absolutely automatic, engendered outside of and unknown to the ordinary consciousness. They are nothing more than simple compositions of the normal consciousness of Mlle. Smith. They represent a type of intermediary activity, and correspond to a state of hemisomnambulism. We have seen above (p. 20) that already in her childhood Hélène seems to have executed various pieces of work in a semi-automatic manner. The same performance is often reproduced on the occasion of the Martian visions, which sometimes pursue her so persistently that she decides to execute them with pencil and brush; work which, in anticipation, often frightens her by its difficulty, but which, when the time comes, accomplishes itself, to her great astonishment, with an ease and perfection almost mechanical. Here is an example:

One Tuesday evening, having already retired, Hélène saw on her bed some magnificent flowers, very different from ours, but without perfume, and which she did not touch, for during her visions she has no idea of moving, and remains inert and passive. The afternoon of the following day, at her desk, she found herself enveloped in a red light, and at the same time felt an indefinable but violent affection of the heart (*aura* of the voyage to Mars). "The red light continues about me, and I find myself surrounded by extraordinary flowers of the kind which I saw on my bed, but they had no perfume. I will bring you some sketches of them on Sunday." She sent them to me, in fact, on Monday, with the following note:

> I am very well satisfied with my plants. They are the exact reproduction of those which it afforded me so much pleasure to behold [No. 3, in Fig. 16, which, beforehand, Hélène despaired of being able to render well], which appeared to me on the latter occasion, and I greatly regret that you were not here to see me execute the drawing: the pencil glided so quickly that I did not have time to notice what contours it was making. I can assert without any exaggeration that it was not my hand alone that made the drawing, but that truly an invisible force guided the pencil in spite of me. The various tints appeared to me upon the paper, and my brush was directed in spite of me towards the color which I ought to use. This seems incredible, but it is, notwithstanding, the exact truth. The whole was done so quickly that I marvelled at it.

The house of Astané (Fig. 12), and the extensive landscapes of Figs. 13 and 14, are also the products of a quasi-automatic activity, which always gives great satisfaction to Mlle. Smith. It is, in a way, her subliminal self which holds the brush and executes, at its pleasure, its own tableaux, which also have the value of veritable originals. Other drawings, on the contrary (for example, the portrait of Astané, Fig. 11), which have given Hélène much trouble without having satisfied her very well, should be regarded as simple copies from memory, by the ordinary personality, of past visions, the memory of which is graven upon her mind in a manner sufficiently persistent to serve as a model several days afterwards. In both cases, but especially in the first, Hélène's paintings may be considered as faithful reproductions of the tableaux which unfold themselves before her, and consequently give us better than most verbal descriptions an idea of the general character of her Martian visions.

Let us see now what kind of information the messages and somnambulisms of Hélène furnish us in regard to the brilliant planet whose complicated revolutions formerly revealed to a Kepler the fundamental secrets of modern astronomy.

III. THE PERSONAGES OF THE MARTIAN ROMANCE

In using the word "romance" to designate the Martian communications, taken as a whole, I wish to state that they are, to my mind, a work of pure imagination, but not that there are to be found in them characteristics of unity and of internal co-ordination, of sustained action, of increasing interest to the final dénouement. The Martian romance is only a succession of detached scenes and tableaux, without order or intimate connection, and showing no other common traits beyond the unknown language spoken in it, the quite frequent presence of the same personages, and a certain fashion of originality, a color or quality badly defined as "exotic" or "bizarre" in the landscapes, the edifices, the costumes, etc.

Of a consecutive plot or intrigue, properly so called, there is no trace.*

Without determining the question, I am inclined, nevertheless, to accord to the Martian romance, in some profound stratum of Hélène's being, a much greater continuity and extent than would appear from judging it solely by the fragments known to us. We have only, in my opinion, a few pages, taken at hazard from different chapters; the bulk of the volume is wanting, and the little we possess does not enable us to reconstruct it in a satisfactory manner. We must, therefore, be content with sorting this debris of unequal importance, according to their content, independently of their chronological order, and grouping them around the principal personages which figure in them.

The anonymous and mixed crowd which forms the base of some of the Martian visions only differs from that of our own country by the large robe common to both sexes, the flat hats, and the sandals bound to the feet by straps. The interest is confined to a small number of more distinct personages having each his own name, always terminating in an *e* with the men and in an *i* with the women, except only in the case of Esenale,* who occupies, however, a place by himself in his quality of disincarnated Martian, fulfilling the function of interpreter. Let us begin by saying a few words about him.

Esenale

We have seen (p. 100) that this name was hinted at by Le Martian words. Then at the first recurrence to this talisman (November 2nd, see p. 107) we learn only that he was a deceased inhabitant of Mars, whose acquaintance Léopold had recently made in interplanetary space. It was only at the following seance (November 8th), where we find Mme. Mirbel, that, after an incarnation of her son Alexis, followed by the scene of translation (see text 3) and in response to questions of the sitters—which answered very well the purpose of suggestion—Léopold affirmed by the left index-finger that Esenale was Alexis Mirbel. It cannot be determined whether that identification constituted a primitive fact which it pleased Léopold to keep secret, only revealing it at the end of a seance at which Mme. Mirbel was present, or whether, as I am inclined to regard it, it was only established at that same seance, under the domination of the circumstances of the moment. As a translator of Martian, Esenale did not show great talent. He had to be entreated, and it was necessary often to repeat his name while pressing or rubbing Hélène's forehead, in order to obtain the exact meaning of the last texts which had been given. He possessed, it is true, an excellent memory, and faithfully reproduced, before giving it word by word, the French for the Martian phrases which Hélène had heard several weeks before and only seen again five or six months afterwards (text 24), and of which there had been no previous opportunity to obtain a translation. But it was to these latter texts, not yet interpreted, that he confined his willingness; on two occasions only did he add, of his own accord, some words of no importance (texts 15 and 36). Text No. 19, for instance, has always remained untranslated, and my later efforts (June 4, 1899) to obtain the meaning of the unknown words **milé piri** have been in vain; moreover, Esenale has not been able to fill up the gaps in text No. 24.*

Alexis Mirbel, after the two first Martian seances, reported on pp. 91 and 96, called Esenale, often accorded his mother, in scenes of incarnation, somewhat pathetic, touching messages of filial tenderness and consolation (texts 3, 4, 11, 15, and 18). It is to be noted that, although opportunities for continuing this role were not wanting, he appears to have completely abandoned it for the last two years. His last message of this kind (October 10, 1897, text 18) followed a month after a curious seance in which Léopold sought to explain to us spontaneously— no one had mentioned the subject—certain flagrant contradictions in the first manifestations of Alexis-Esenale. Here is a résumé of that scene, with the text of Léopold's communication:

September 12, 1897.—After sundry waking visions, Mlle. Smith hears Léopold speaking; her eyes are closed, and, appearing to be asleep, she repeats, mechanically and in a slow and feeble voice, the following words, which her guide addresses to her:

Thou art going to pay close attention. Tell them now [the sitters] to keep as quiet as possible, that is what often mars the phenomena, the comings and goings, and the idle chatter of which you are never weary. You recollect there was, several months ago, a young man, that young man Alexis Mirbel, who came to give counsel to his mother at a reunion you held with M. (I do not understand the name he gave) . . . at Carouge[3] . . . Well, at that moment he happened—that is to say, two days before—to die on . . . (I could not understand the name) . . . where he had been . . . or he had regained life.[4] This is why I have come to tell you to-day he was in that phase of separation of the material part from the soul which permitted him to recollect his previous existence—that is to say, his life here below in this state; he not only recollects his first mother, but can speak once more the language he used to speak with her. Some time after, when the soul was finally at rest, he no longer recollected that first language; he returns, he hovers about (his mother), sees her with joy,

---

[3] Allusion to the seance of November 25, 1894, at M. Lemaître's. See p. 146.
[4] That is to say, he died on Mars, where he had been reincarnated.

but is incapable of speaking to her in your language.[5] Whether it will return to him I do not know and cannot say, but I believe that it will. And now listen.

Here Mlle. Smith seems to awake, opens her eyes, and has a long Martian vision, which she describes in detail. She now sees a little girl in a yellow robe, whose name she hears as **Anini Nikaïné**, occupied with various childish games—*e.g.*, with a small wand she makes a number of grotesque little figures dance in a white tub, large and shallow, full of sky-blue water. Then come other persons, and, finally, Astané, who has a pen in his fingers, and, little by little, takes hold of Hélène's arm and throws her into a deep trance for the purpose of causing her to write text No. 17.

These spontaneous explanations of Léopold are interesting in that they betray clearly the subliminal desire to introduce some order and logic into the incoherences of the mediumistic reveries. It is a form of the process of justification and retrospective interpretation intended to make the incidents of the past accord with the dominant ideas of the present (see p. 94). In appearance, the theory upon which Léopold rested, after having doubtless meditated long, is quite awkward; but perhaps it was difficult for him to do better, since no one can accomplish the impossible.*

Astané

"The great man Astané" is the reincarnation on Mars of the Hindoo fakir Kanga, who was a devoted companion and friend of Simandini. He has preserved in his new existence the special character of savant or of sorcerer, which he formerly possessed in India, and he has equally retained all his affection for his princess of old, who has been restored to him in Mlle. Smith; he frequently utilizes his magic powers to evoke her—that is to say, to re-enter into spiritual communication with her, notwithstanding the distances between their actual places of habitation. The ways and means of that evocation remain, however, enveloped in mystery. We cannot say whether it was Hélène that rejoined Astané on Mars during her somnambulism, or whether it was he who descended "fluidly" towards her and brought to her the odors of the far-distant planet.

When Astané says to Hélène, during a seance: "Come to me an instant. Come and admire these flowers," etc. (text 8), or shows her the curiosities of his Martian abode, it seems as though he had really called her to him through space; but when he appears to her, while awake, at the edge of her bathtub, and expresses his chagrin at finding her still on this miserable earth (text 7), it must be admitted that it is he who has descended to her and inspires her with these visions of an upper world. It is of no importance, on the whole. It is here to be noted that, in these evocations,

[5] Allusion to seance of February 2, 1896. See p. 154

Astané only manifests himself in visual and auditive hallucinations, never in tactile impressions or those of general sensibility; in the sphere of emotion his presence is accompanied by a great calm on the part of Hélène, a profound bliss, and an ecstatic disposition, which is the correlative and pendant of the happiness experienced by Astané himself (texts 10, 17, etc.) at finding himself in the presence of his idol of the past. The social state of Astané—I should rather say his name, his quality of sorcerer, and his previous terrestrial existence in the body of Kanga—was not immediately revealed.

Nevertheless, at his first apparition (September 5, 1896, see p. 99), he rises superior to the crowd, inasmuch as he alone possesses a flying-machine incomprehensible to us. In the following weeks Mlle. Smith hears his name, and sees him again on many occasions, as well as his house (Fig. 12), but it is only at the end of two months and a half that his identity and his "evocative" powers become known, at a seance at which I was not present, and during which Hélène did not, contrary to her usual custom, fall completely asleep. The following is a résumé of the notes, which I owe to the kindness of M. Cuendet:

November 19, 1896.—Contrary to the experience of the preceding seances, Mlle. Smith remained constantly awake, her arms free on the table, conversing and even laughing all the while with the sitters. The messages were obtained by means of visions and typtological dictations. Hélène having asked Léopold how it happens that she had been able to communicate with a being living on Mars, she has a vision in which Astané appears to her in a costume more Oriental than Martian. "Where have I seen that costume?" asks she; and the table replies, *"In India,"* which indicates that Astané is an ex-Hindoo reincarnated on Mars. At the same time Hélène has a vision of an Oriental landscape which she believes she has already seen before, but without knowing where. She sees Astané there, carrying under his arm rolls of paper of a dirty white color, and bowing in Oriental fashion before a woman, also clothed in Oriental garments, whom she also believes she has seen before. These personages appear to her to be "inanimate, like statues."* The sitters ask whether the vision was not a simple tableau (of the past) presented by Léopold; the table replies in the affirmative, then inclines itself significantly towards Mlle. Smith, when some one asked who that Oriental woman might be, and the idea is put forth that possibly she represents Simandini. Finally, to further questions of the sitters, the table (Léopold) dictates again that Astané in his Hindoo existence was called *Kanga*, who was a *"sorcerer of the period"*; then that *"Astané on the planet Mars possesses the same faculty of evocation which he had possessed in India."* Léopold is then asked if the power of Astané is greater than his. *"A different power, of equal strength,"* replies the table. Finally, Hélène desiring to know whether

Astané when he evokes her sees her in her real character or that of her Hindoo incarnation, the table affirms that he sees her in her Hindoo character, and adds: *"and, in consequence, under those characteristics which she [Hélène] possesses to-day and which are in such striking harmony with those of SimaNdini,"* insisting on the N in the middle of the name.

It is to be remarked that at this sitting it was Léopold who gave all the information in regard to the past of Astané, and that he recognizes in him a power over Hélène almost equal to his own. It is strange that the accredited guide of Mlle. Smith, ordinarily so jealous of his rights over her and ready to take offence at all rival pretensions, so freely accords such prerogatives to Astané. This unexpected mildness is still more surprising when the singular similarity of position of these two personages in regard to Hélène is considered. Kanga, the Hindoo fakir, holds in the life of Simandini exactly the same place as Cagliostro in the life of Marie Antoinette, the place of a sorcerer giving beneficial counsel, and at the same time of a platonic adorer, and both of them in their actual roles of Astané and of Léopold preserve for Mlle. Smith the respectful attachment which they had for her illustrious former existences. How is it these two extraterrestrial pretenders do not hate each other the more cordially since their rival claims upon Hélène have identical foundations? But, far from in the least disputing her possession, they assist each other in the most touching fashion. When Astané writes in Martian by Mlle. Smith's right hand that the noise of the sitters threatens to make him insane (see text 20) it is Léopold who comes to his rescue in making them keep silent by his gestures with the left arm. When Léopold indicates to me that the moment for pressing Hélène's forehead has arrived, it is Astané who lends him his pencil in order that the message may be written (see below, seance of September 12, 1897, and Fig. 23), and the exchange of powers takes place between them without the medium experiencing the least shock, and without its betraying itself outwardly otherwise than by the difference of their handwriting. It is true that Léopold's apparitions to Hélène are infinitely more frequent and his incarnations much more complete than those of Astané, who shows himself to her at increasing intervals, and has never attained to speaking by her mouth. It makes no difference: these two personages resemble each other too much for mutual toleration—if they are really two.

My conclusion presses. Astané is, at bottom, only a copy, a double, a transposition in the Hindoo-Martian manner of Léopold. They are two variations of one primitive theme. In regarding these two beings, as I do, in the absence of proof to the contrary, not as real and objective individualities, but as pseudo-personalities, dream fictions, fantastic subdivisions of the hypnoid consciousness of Mlle. Smith, it may be said that it is the same fundamental emotion which has inspired these twin roles, the details of which have been adapted by the subliminal imagination to correspond to the diversity of the circumstances. The contradiction painfully felt between the proud aspirations of the *grande dame* and the vexing ironies of reality has caused the two tragic previous existences to gush forth—intrinsically identical, in spite of the differences of place and epoch—of the noble girl of Arabia, having become Hindoo princess, burned alive on the tomb of her despot of a husband, and of her Austrian highness, having become Queen of France and sharing the martyrdom of her spouse.

On parallel lines, in these two dreams issuing from the same emotional source, it is the universal and constant taste of the human imagination for the marvellous, allied to the very feminine need of a respectful and slightly idolatrous protector, which on the one side has created out of whole cloth the personage of Kanga-Astané, and on the other hand has absorbed, without being careful in modifying authentic history, that of Cagliostro-Léopold. Both are idealistic sorcerers, of profound sagacity, tender-hearted, who have placed their great wisdom at the service of the unfortunate sovereign and made for her, of their devotion, amounting almost to adoration, a tower of strength, a supreme consolation in the midst of all the bitternesses of real life. And as Léopold acts as guide for Hélène Smith in the general course of her actual earthly existence, so Astané seemingly plays the same role in the moments of that life in which Hélène leaves our sublunar world to fly away to the orb of Mars.

If, then, Astané is only a reflection, a projection of Léopold in the Martian sphere, he has there assumed a special coloring, and has outwardly harmonized himself with this new situation.

He is clothed in a voluminous, embroidered robe; he has long hair, no beard, a yellow complexion, and carries in his hand a white roll, on which he writes with a point fastened to the end of the index-finger.

His house (Fig. 12) is quadrangular, with gates and windows, and reminds one by its exterior aspect of some Oriental structure, with a flat roof embellished with plants.

The inside is also appropriate. The furniture recalls ours by force of contrast. We have few details; with the exception of a musical instrument with vertical cylinders, closely related to our organs, upon which Hélène sometimes sees and hears Astané playing, seated on a stool with one foot, resembling a milking-stool.

When we pass to the garden the same amalgam of analogies and unlikenesses to our flora are discovered. We have seen that Hélène has been often haunted in the waking state by visions of Martian plants and flowers, which she finally draws or paints with a facility approaching automatism; these specimens, as also the trees scattered over the landscapes, show that Martian vegetation does not differ essentially from ours. Of the animals we do not know much. Astané has often with him an ugly beast, which caused Hélène much fright on account of its grotesque form— about two feet long, with a flat tail; it has the "head of a cabbage," with a big green eye in the middle (like the eye of a peacock feather), and five or six pairs of paws, or ears all about (see Fig. 18). This animal unites the intelligence of the dog with the stupidity of the parrot, since on the one hand it obeys Astané and fetches objects at his command (we do not know how), while, on the other hand, it knows how to write, but in a manner purely mechanical. (We have never had a specimen of this handwriting). (See Fig. 18.)

In fact, as to other animals, beyond the little black bird cited, without description (text 20), and a species of female deer for the purpose of nursing infants (text 36), Hélène saw only horrid aquatic beasts like big snails, which Astané caught by means of iron nets stretched over the surface of the water.

Astané's property is enclosed by large red stones, on the border of the water, where Hélène loves to retire with her guide to converse in peace and to recall to mind with him the ancient and melancholy memories of their Hindoo existence; the general tone of these conversations is entirely the same as that of her conversations with Léopold.

There is a mountain also of red rocks, where Astané possesses some excavated dwelling-places, a kind of grotto appropriate to the sorcerer-savant which he is.

The corpse of Esenale, admirably preserved, is also to be seen there, among other things, about which the disincarnate Esenale sometimes floats in "fluid" form, and which Hélène still finds soft to the touch, when, after much hesitation, and not without fright, she gained courage to touch it with the end of her finger, at the invitation of Astané. It is also in this house, excavated in the rock, that Astané has his observatory, a pit traversing the mountain, by means of which he contemplates the heavens (text 9), our earth included, by means of a telescope, which the beast with the head of a cabbage brings him.

To these qualities of savant Astané joins those of wise counsellor and of patriarchal governor. We also see a young girl named Matêmi coming to consult him frequently (texts 22 and 28), perhaps on matrimonial affairs, since Matêmi reappears on several occasions with her lover or her fiancé, Siké, and, among others, at a great family fête, presided over by Astané. (See Fig. 19.)

The following are some details concerning that vision, which occupied the greater part of a seance (November 28, 1897). Hélène sees, in a vast, red, initial light, a Martian street appear, lighted neither by lamps nor electricity, but by lights shining through small windows in the walls of the houses. The interior of one of these houses becomes visible to her: a superb, square hall, lighted at each angle by a kind of lamp, formed of four superposed globes,—two blue and two white—not of glass (Fig. 19); under each lamp a small basin, over which was a kind of cornucopia pouring forth water. There were many ornamental plants. In the middle of the hall, a grove, around which are placed a number of small tables with a polished surface like nickel. There are young people in Martian robes; young girls with long hair hanging down their backs, and wearing at the back of the head a head-dress of roses; colored blue or green butterflies attached to the neck.

There were at least thirty speaking Martian (but Hélène did not hear them distinctly). Astané appeared "in a very ugly robe to-day," and showed himself full of friendly gallantry towards the young girls. He seats himself alone at one of the tables while the young people take their places at others, two couples at each. These tables are adorned with flowers different from ours: some blue, with leaves in the shape of almonds; others starry, and as white as milk, scented like musk; others, again, the most beautiful, have the form of trumpets, either blue or fire colored, with large rounded leaves, with black figures. (See Fig. 20.)

Hélène hears Astané pronounce the name "Pouzé." Then come two men in long white trousers with a black sash; one wears a coat of rose color, the other a white one. They carry ornamented trays, and, passing in front of each table, they place square plates upon them, with forks without handles, formed of three teeth an inch in length: for glasses they had goblets like tea-cups, bordered with a silver thread. Then they brought in a kind of basin a cooked animal resembling a cat, which is placed before Astané, who twists it and cuts it rapidly with his fingers, tipped with sharp silver tips; square pieces are distributed, among the guests, on square plates with furrows around the edges for the juice. Every one is filled with a wild gayety. Astané sits at each table in succession, and the girls pass their hands through his hair. New plates are brought, and pink, white, and blue basins tipped with flowers. These basins melt, and are eaten like the flowers. Then the guests wash their hands at little fountains in the corners of the room.

Now one of the walls is raised, like the curtain of a theatre, and Hélène sees a magnificent hall adorned with luminous globes, flowers, and plants, with the ceiling painted, in pink clouds on a pink sky, with couches and pillows suspended along the walls. Then an orchestra of ten musicians arrive, carrying a kind of gilded funnel about five feet in height, with a round cover to the large opening, and at the neck a kind of rake, on which they placed their fingers. Hélène hears music like that made by flutes and sees every one moving; they arrange themselves by fours, make passes and gestures, then reunite in groups of eight. They glide about gently, for it could not be called dancing. They do not clasp each other's waists, but place their hands on each other's shoulders, standing some distance apart. It is terribly warm. It is "boiling hot." They stop, walk, talk, and it is then that Hélène hears a tall young brunette (Matêmi) and a short young man (Siké) exchange the first words of text No. 20. Then they depart in the direction of a large bush with red flowers (*tamiche*) and are soon followed by Ramié and his companion.

At this moment the vision, which has lasted an hour and a quarter, passes away. Hélène, who had remained standing during the whole description, now enters into complete somnambulism, and Astané causes her to write Martian phrases which she had heard and repeated a short time before. During the entire vision Léopold occupied her left hand, which was hanging anaesthetically down her body, and replied by his index-finger to the questions which I asked in a low voice. I thus learned that this Martian scene was not a wedding, or any special ceremony, but a simple family *fète*; that it was no recollection or product of Hélène's imagination but a reality actually passing on Mars: that it was not Léopold but Astané who furnished this vision and caused her to hear the music: that Léopold himself neither saw nor heard anything of it all, yet knows all that Mlle. Smith sees and hears, etc.

This résumé of a family *fète*, presided over by Astané, gives the measure of the originality of the people of Mars. The visions relating to other incidents are of the same order: read the description of the Martian nursery (text 36), of the voyage in a *miza* a sort of automobile, the mechanism of which is entirely unknown to us (text 23), of the operation of chirurgery (text 29), of the games of the little Anini (p. 113, etc.). We see always the same general mixture of imitation of things which transpire among us, and of infantile modifications of them in the minute details.

Pouzé Ramié—Various Personages

Of the other personages who traverse the Martian visions we know too little to waste much time upon them. The name of the one who appears most frequently is Pouzé. He is present at the banquet, and we meet him also in the company of a poor little withered old man with a trembling voice, in connection with whom he occupies himself with gardening or botany, in an evening promenade by the shore of the lake (text 14). He also figures again by the side of an unknown person named Paininé, and he has a son, Saïne, who had met with some accident to his head and had been cured of it, to the great joy of his parents (texts 23 and 24).

Finally, we must devote a few words to Ramié, who manifests himself for the first time in October, 1898, as the revealer of the ultra-Martian world, of which we shall soon take cognizance.* Ramié seems to be a relative of Astané, an astronomer, not so brilliant as Astané, but possessing the same privilege, which the ordinary Martians do not seem to enjoy, of being able to take hold of Hélène's arm, and of writing with her hand.* There is, to my mind, no fundamental difference between Léopold, Astané, and Ramié, in their relation to Hélène; they are only a reproduction in triplicate of one identical emotional relation, and I do not think I am mistaken in regarding these three figures as three very transparent disguises of the same fundamental personality, which is only a hypnoid subdivision of the real being of Mlle. Smith.*

It is much wiser to leave to the future—if the Martian and ultra-Martian romances continue to develop—the task of enlightening ourselves more completely as to the true character of Ramié. Possibly some day we shall also know more concerning the couple called Matêmi and Siké, as well as many others, such as Sazéni, Paininé, the little Bullié, Romé, Fedié, etc., of whom we now know scarcely more than their names, and understand nothing in regard to their possible relationships to the central figures of Astané and Esenale.

IV. Concerning the Author of the Martian Romance

The general ideas which the Martian cycle suggests will most assuredly differ, according to whether it is considered as an authentic revelation of affairs on the planet Mars, or only as a simple fantasy of the imagination of the medium;* and meanwhile, holding myself to the second supposition, I demand from the Martian romance information in regard to its author rather than its subject-matter.

There are two or three points concerning this unknown author which strike me forcibly:

First: He shows a singular indifference—possibly it may be due to ignorance—in regard to all those questions which are most prominent at the present time, I will not say among astronomers, but among people of the world somewhat fond of popular science and curious concerning the mysteries of our universe. The canals of Mars, in the first place—those famous canals with reduplication—temporarily more enigmatical than those of the Ego of the mediums; then the strips of supposed cultivation along their borders, the mass of snow around the poles, the nature of the soil, and the conditions of life on those worlds, in turn inundated and burning, the thousand and one questions of hydrography, of geology, of biology, which the amateur naturalist inevitably asks himself on the subject of the planet nearest to us—of all this the author of the Martian romance knows nothing and cares nothing.* Questions of sociology do not trouble him to a much greater extent, since the people occupying the most prominent place in the Martian visions, and making the conversation, in no wise enlighten us as to the civil and political organization of their globe, as to the fine arts and religion, commerce and industry, etc. Have the barriers of the nations fallen, and is there no longer a standing army up there, except that of the laborer occupied in the construction and maintenance of that gigantic net-work of canals for communication or irrigation? Esenale and Astané have not deigned to inform us. It seems probable from certain episodes that the family is, as with us, at the foundation of Martian civilization; nevertheless, we have no direct or detailed information in regard to this subject. It is useless to speculate. It is evident that the author of this romance did not care much for science, and that, in spite of her desire to comply with the wishes of M. Lemaître (see p. 92), she had not the least conception of the questions which arise in our day, in every cultivated mind, as to the planet Mars and its probable inhabitants.

Secondly: If, instead of quarrelling with the Martian romance about that which it fails to furnish us, we endeavor to appreciate the full value of what it does give us, we are struck by two points, which I have already touched upon more than once in passing—viz., the complete identity of the Martian world, taken in its chief points, with the world in which we live, and its puerile originality in a host of minor details. Take, for example, the family *fête* (p. 118). To be sure, the venerable Astané is there saluted by a caress of the hair instead of a hand-shake; the young couples while dancing grasp each other not by the waist but by the shoulder; the ornamental plants do not belong to any species known to us: but, save for these insignificant divergences from our costumes and habits, as a whole, and in general tone, it is exactly as with us.

The imagination which forged these scenes, with all their decoration, is remarkably calm, thoughtful, devoted to the real and the probable. The *miza*, which runs without a visible motor power, is neither more nor less extraordinary to the uninitiated spectator than many of the vehicles which traverse our roads. The colored globes placed in an aperture of the walls of the houses to light the streets recall strongly our electric lamps. Astané's flying-machine will probably soon be realized in some form or other. The bridges which disappear under the water in order to allow boats to pass (text 25) are, save for a technical person, as natural as ours which accomplish the same result by lifting themselves in the air. With the exception of the "evocative" powers of Astané, which only concern Mlle. Smith personally and do not figure in any Martian scene, there is nothing on Mars which goes beyond what has been attained or might be expected to be accomplished by ingenious inventors here below.

A wise little imagination of ten or twelve years old would have deemed it quite droll and original to make people up there eat on square plates with a furrow for the gravy, of making an ugly beast with a single eye carry the telescope of Astané to him, of making babies to be fed by tubes running directly to the breasts of animals like the female deer, etc. There is nothing of the *Thousand and One Nights*, the *Metamorphoses* of Ovid, fairy stories, or the adventures of Gulliver, no trace of ogres nor of giants nor of veritable sorcerers in this whole cycle. One would say that it was the work of a young scholar to whom had been given the task of trying to invent a world as different as possible from ours, but real, and who had conscientiously applied himself to it, loosening the reins of his childish fancy in regard to a multitude of minor points in the limits of what appeared admissible according to his short and narrow experience.

Thirdly: By the side of these arbitrary and useless innovations the Martian romance bears in a multitude of its characteristics a clearly Oriental stamp, upon which I have already often insisted. The yellow complexion and long black hair of Astané; the costume of all the personages—robes embroidered or of brilliant hues, sandals with thongs, flat white hats, etc., the long hair of the women and the ornaments in the form of butterflies for their coiffures; the houses of grotesque shapes, recalling the pagoda, kiosk, and minaret, the warm and glowing colors of the skies, the water, the rocks, and the vegetation (see Figs. 13 and 14), etc.: all this has a sham air of Japanese, Chinese, Hindoo. It is to be noted that this imprint of the extreme East is purely exterior, not in any wise penetrating to the characters or manners of the personages.*

All the traits that I discover in the author of the Martian romance can be summed up in a single phrase, its profoundly infantile character. The candor and imperturbable naïveté of childhood, which doubts nothing because ignorant of everything, is necessary in order for one to launch himself seriously upon an enterprise such as the pretended exact and authentic depictions of an unknown world. An adult, in the least cultivated and having some experience of life, would never waste time in elaborating similar nonsense—Mlle. Smith less than any one, intelligent and cultivated as she is in her normal state.

This provisional view of the author of the Martian cycle will find its confirmation and its complement in the following chapters, in which we shall examine the Martian language, from which I have until now refrained.

CHAPTER SIX

The Martian Cycle (Continued):
The Martian Language

OF THE VARIOUS automatic phenomena, the "speaking in tongues" is one which at all times has most aroused curiosity, while at the same time little accurate knowledge concerning it has been obtainable, on account of the difficulty of collecting correctly the confused and unintelligible words as they gush forth.

The phonograph, which has already been employed in some exceptional cases, like that of Le Baron,* will doubtless some day render inestimable service to this kind of study, but it leaves much still to be desired at the present moment, from the point of view of its practical utilization in the case of subjects not in their right mind, who are not easily manageable, and who will not remain quiet long enough while uttering their unusual words to allow the instrument to be adjusted and made ready.*

There are different species of glossolalia. Simple, incoherent utterances, in a state of ecstasy, interspersed with emotional exclamations, which are sometimes produced in certain surcharged religious environments, is another matter altogether from the creation of neologisms, which are met with in the dream, in somnambulism, mental alienation, or in children. At the same time this fabrication of arbitrary words raises other problems—as, for example, the occasional use of foreign idioms unknown to the subject (at least, apparently), but which really exist. In each of these cases it is necessary to examine further whether, and in what measure, the individual attributes a fixed meaning to the sounds which he utters, whether he understands (or has, at least, the impression of understanding) his own words, or whether it is only a question of a mechanical and meaningless derangement of the phonetic apparatus, or, again, whether this jargon, unintelligible to the ordinary personality, expresses the ideas of some secondary personality. All these forms, moreover, vary in shades and degrees, and there are, in addition, those mixed cases, possibly the more frequent, where all the forms are mingled and combined. The same individual, and sometimes in the course of the same spasm, also exhibits a series of neologisms, comprehended or uncomprehended, giving way to a simple, incoherent verbiage in common language, or vice versa, etc.

A good description and rational classification of all these categories and varieties of glossolalia would be of very great interest. I cannot think of attempting such a study here, having enough already to fully occupy my attention, by reason of having involved myself with the Martian of Mlle. Smith. This somnambulistic language does not consist, as we have already discovered, either in speaking ecstatically or in religious enthusiasm, nor yet in the use of a foreign language which really exists; it represents rather neologism carried to its highest expression and practised in a systematic fashion, with a very precise signification, by a secondary personality unknown to the normal self. It is a typical case of "glosso-poesy," of complete fabrication of all the parts of a new language by a subconscious activity. I have many times regretted that those who have witnessed analogous phenomena—as, for example, Kerner, with the *Seeress of Prevost*—have not gathered together and published in their entirety all the products of this singular method of performing their functions on the part of the verbal faculties. Undoubtedly each case taken by itself seems a simple anomaly, a pure arbitrary curiosity, and without any bearing; but who knows whether the collection of a large number of these psychological bibelots, as yet few enough in their total, would not end in some unexpected light? Exceptional facts are often the most instructive.

In order to avoid falling into the same errors of negligence, not knowing where to stop, in case I wished to make a choice, I have taken the course of setting forth here in full all the Martian texts which we have been able to gather. I will have them follow a paragraph containing certain remarks which that unknown language has suggested to me; but, very far from flattering myself that I have exhausted the subject, I earnestly hope that it will find readers more competent than myself to correct and complete my observations, since I must acknowledge that as a linguist and philologist I am very much like an ass playing the flute. It is expedient, in beginning, to give some further details regarding the various psychological methods of manifestation of that unknown tongue.

I. Verbal Martian Automatisms

I have described in the preceding chapter, and will not now return to it, the birth of the Martian language, indissolubly bound up with that of the romance itself, from the 2d of February, 1896, up to the inauguration of the process of translation by the entrance of Esenale upon the scene on the 2d of November following (see pp. 95–108). During several months thereafter the Martian language is confined to the two psychological forms of apparition in which it seems to have been clothed during the course of that first year.

First: *Verbo-auditive* automatism, hallucinations of hearing accompanying visions in the waking state. In the case of spontaneous visions, Hélène notes in pencil, either during the vision itself or immediately afterwards, the unintelligible sounds which strike her ear; but to her great regret many of them escape her, since she is sometimes only able to gather the first or the last phrase of the sentences which her imaginary personages address to her, or scattered fragments of conversations which she holds with herself; these fragments themselves often contain inaccuracies, which are ultimately rectified at the moment of translation, Esenale having the good habit of articulating very clearly each Martian word before giving its French equivalent. In the case of the visions which she has at the seances, Hélène slowly repeats the words she hears without understanding them, and the sitters make note of them more or less correctly.

Secondly: *Vocal* automatism ("verbo-motor hallucinations of articulation," in the cumbersome official terminology). Here again it is the sitters who gather as much as they can of the strange words pronounced in a state of trance, but that is very little, since Hélène, in her Martian state, often speaks with a tremendous volubility. Moreover, a distinction must be made between the relatively clear and brief phrases which are later translated by Esenale, and the rapid and confused gibberish the signification of which can never be obtained, probably because it really has none, but is only a pseudo-language (see pp. 97–98).

A new process of communication, the handwriting, made its appearance in August, 1897, with a delay of perhaps eighteen months as to the speech (the reverse of Léopold's case, who wrote a long time before speaking). It is produced, also, under two forms, which constitute a pendant to the two cases given above, and also complete the standard quartette of the psychological modalities of language.

Thirdly: *Verbo-visual* automatism—that is, apparitions of exotic characters before Hélène's eyes when awake, who copies them as faithfully as possible in a drawing, without knowing the meaning of the mysterious hieroglyphics.

Fourthly: *Graphic automatism*—i.e., writing traced by the hand of Hélène while completely entranced and incarnating a Martian personage. In this case the characters are generally smaller, more regular, better formed than in the drawings of the preceding case. A certain number of occasions, when the name has been pronounced by Hélène before being written, and especially the articulation of Esenale at the moment of translation, have permitted the relations between her vocal sounds and the graphic signs of the Martian language to be established.

It is to be noted that these four automatic manifestations do not inflict an equal injury upon the normal personality of Mlle. Smith. As a rule, the verbo-auditive and verbo-visual hallucinations only suppress her consciousness of present reality; they leave her a freedom of mind which, if not complete, is at least sufficient to permit her to observe in a reflective manner these sensorial automatisms, to engrave them on her memory, and to describe them or make a copy of them, while she often adds remarks testifying to a certain critical sense. On the contrary, the verbo-motor hallucinations of articulation or of writing seem to be incompatible with her preservation of the waking state, and are followed by amnesia. Hélène is always totally absent or entranced while her hand writes mechanically, and if, as seldom happens, she speaks Martian automatically, outside of the moments of complete incarnation, she is not aware of it, and does not recollect it.* This incapacity of the normal personality of Mlle. Smith to observe at the time or remember afterwards her verbo-motor automatisms denotes a more profound perturbation than that she experiences during her sensory automatisms.*

The Martian handwriting only appeared at the end of a prolonged period of incubation, which betrayed itself in several incidents, and was certainly stimulated by various exterior suggestions during a year and a half at least. The following are the principal dates of this development.

February 16, 1896.—The idea of a special handwriting belonging to the planet Mars occurs for the first time to Hélène's astonishment in a Martian semi-trance (see p. 99).

November 2.—Handwriting is clearly predicted in the phrase, "Astané will teach me to write," uttered by Hélène in a Martian trance, after the scene of the translation by Esenale (see p. 108).

November 8.—After the translation of text No. 3, Léopold, being questioned, replies that Astané will write this text for Mlle. Smith, but the prediction is not fulfilled.

May 23, 1897.—The announcement of Martian handwriting becomes more precise. "Presently," says Astané to Hélène, "thou wilt be able to trace our handwriting, and thou wilt possess in thy hands the characters of our language" (text 12).*

June 20.—At the beginning of a seance, a Martian vision, she demands of an imaginary interlocutor "a large ring which comes to a point, and with which one can write." This description applies to M. R., who has with him some small pocket-pens of this kind, capable of being adjusted to the end of the index-finger.

June 23.—I hand Hélène the two small pocket-pens which M. R. has brought for her, but they do not please her. After trying to use one, she throws it away and takes up a pencil, saying that if she must write Martian, the ordinary means will suffice as well as those peculiar pocket-pens. In about a minute she falls asleep, and her hand begins automatically to trace a message in Léopold's handwriting. I then ask that individual whether the pocket-pens of M. R. do not meet the exigencies of Martian, and whether Mlle. Smith will some day write that language, as has already been announced. Hélène's hand thereupon responds in the beautiful calligraphy of Léopold: "I have not yet seen the instrument which the inhabitants of the planet Mars use in writing their language, but I can and do affirm that the thing will happen, as has been announced to you.— LÉOPOLD."

June 27.—In the scene of the translation of text 15, Hélène adds to her usual refrain, "Esenale has gone away; he will soon return; he will soon write."

August 3.—Between four and five o'clock in the afternoon Hélène had a vision at her desk, lasting ten or fifteen minutes, of a broad, horizontal bar, flame-colored, then changing to brick-red, and which by degrees became rose-tinted, on which were a multitude of strange characters, which she supposes to be the Martian letters of the alphabet, on account of the color. These characters floated in space before and round about her. Analogous visions occur in the course of the weeks immediately following.

August 22.—Hélène for the first time writes in Martian. After various non-Martian visions Mlle. Smith turns away from the window (it rained hard, and the sky was very gray) and exclaims, "Oh, look, it is all red! Is it already time to go to bed? M. Lemaître, are you there? Do you see how red it is? I see Astané, who is there, in that red; I only see his head and the ends of his fingers; he has no robe; and here is the other (Esenale) with him. They both have some letters at the ends of their fingers on a bit of paper. Quick, give me some paper!" A blank sheet and the pocket-pen are handed to her, which latter she disdainfully throws down. She accepts an ordinary pencil, which she holds in her customary fashion, between her middle and index-finger, then writes from left to right the three first lines of Fig. 21, looking attentively towards the window at her fictitious model before tracing each letter, and adding certain oral notes, according to which there are some words which she sees written in black characters on the three papers—or, more correctly, on three white wands, a sort of narrow cylinder, somewhat flattened out—which Astané Esenale, and a third personage whose name she does not know but whose description corresponds with that of Pouzé, hold in their right hands. After which she again sees another paper or cylinder, which Astané holds above his head, and which bears also some words which she undertakes to copy (the three last lines of Fig. 21, p. 129). "Oh, it is a pity," says she, on coming to the end of the fourth line "it is all on one line, and I have no more room." She then writes underneath the three letters of line 5, and without saying anything adds line 6. Then she resumes: "How dark it is with you . . . the sun has entirely gone down" (it still rains very hard). "No one more! nothing more!" She remains in contemplation before that which she has written, then sees Astané again near the table, who again shows her a paper, the same, she thinks, as the former one. "But no, it is not altogether the

same; there is one mistake, it is there [she points to the fourth line towards the end] . . . Ah, I do not see more!" Then, presently she adds:
"He showed me something else; there was a mistake, but I was not able to
see it. It is very difficult. While I was writing, it was not I myself, I could
not feel my arms. It was difficult, because when I raised my head I no
longer saw the letters well. It was like a Greek design."

At this moment Hélène recovered from the state of obscuration, from
which she emerged with difficulty, which had accompanied the Martian
vision and the automatic copy of the verbo-visual text. But a little later in
the evening she only vaguely remembered having seen strange letters,
and was altogether ignorant of having written anything.

The very natural supposition that the three first words written were the
names of the known personages (Astané, Esenale, Pouzé), who bore them
on their wands, led to the discovery of the meaning of many of the Martian characters and permitted the divining of the sense of the three last
words.

The new alphabet was enriched by certain other signs on the following
days, thanks to the echoes of that seance in the ordinary life of Hélène,
who happened on several occasions to write not the true Martian as yet,
but French in Martian letters, to her great stupefaction when she found
herself after a while in the presence of these unknown hieroglyphics.

The first manifestation of that graphic automatism, being as yet concerned only with the form of the letters and not the vocabulary, dates
from the day after the following seance:

August 23.—"Here," wrote Hélène to me at noon, sending me some
memoranda from which I have taken the three examples of Fig. 22—
"here are some labels which I made it my business to make this morning
at ten o'clock, and which I have not been able to finish in a satisfactory
manner. I have only just now emerged from the rose-colored fog in which
I have been continuously enwrapped for almost two hours."

Three weeks later a complete automatic Martian handwriting was produced in a seance at my house, of which the following is a summary.

September 12, 1897.—At the end of a quite long Martian vision, Mlle.
Smith sees Astané, who has something at the end of his finger and who
signs to her to write. I offer her a pencil, and after various tergiversations
she slowly begins to trace some Martian characters (Fig. 23). Astané has
possession of her arm, and she is, during this time, altogether anaesthetic
and absent. Léopold, on the contrary, is at hand, and gives various indications of his presence.* At the end of the sixth line she seems to half
awaken, and murmurs, "I am not afraid; no, I am not afraid." Then she
again falls into a dream in order to write the four last words (which signify *Then do not fear,*" and which are the response of Astané to her
exclamation).

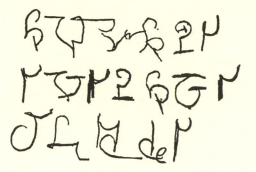

Fig. 21. Text No. 16; seance of August 22, 1897.—First Martian text written by Mlle. Smith (according to a visual hallucination). Natural size. (Collection of M. Lemaître.)—Herewith its French notation.

astane
esenale
pouze
mene simand
ini.
mira.

Fig. 22. Examples of isolated French words (*française, lumière, prairie*) automatically traced in Martian characters by Mlle. Smith in her normal handwriting. See also Fig. 1, p. 40.

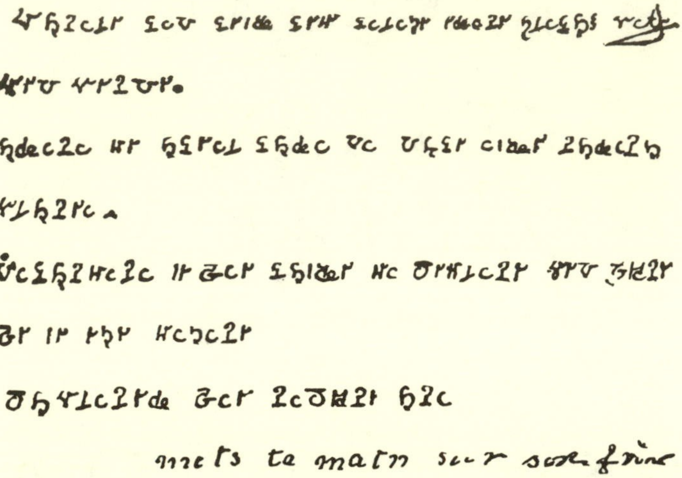

Fig. 23. Martian text No. 17; seance of September 12, 1897. Written by Mlle. Smith incarnating Astané (then Léopold for the French words at the end). See the translation, p. 143. Too many *l*'s at the end of the first line immediately produced the scrawls intended to strike them out. (Reproduction one-half natural size.)

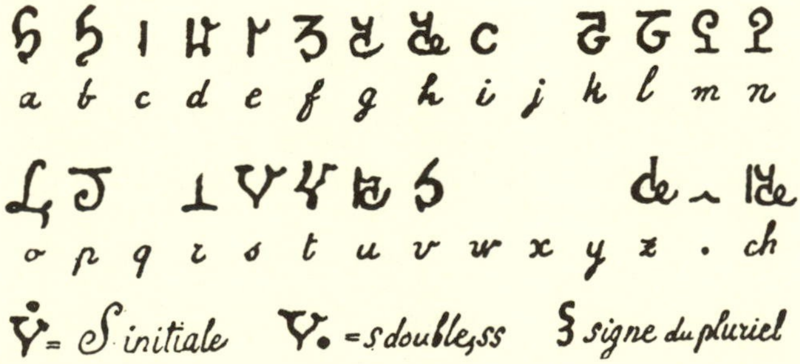

Fig. 24. Martian alphabet, summary of the signs obtained. (Never has been given as such by Mlle. Smith.)

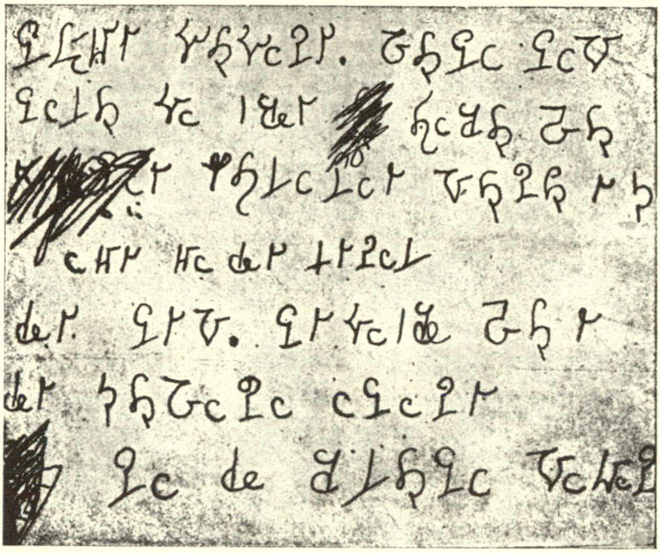

Fig. 25. Text No. 18 (October 10, 1897), written in pencil by Mlle. Smith incarnating Esenale. Reproduction in autotype two-thirds of the natural size.

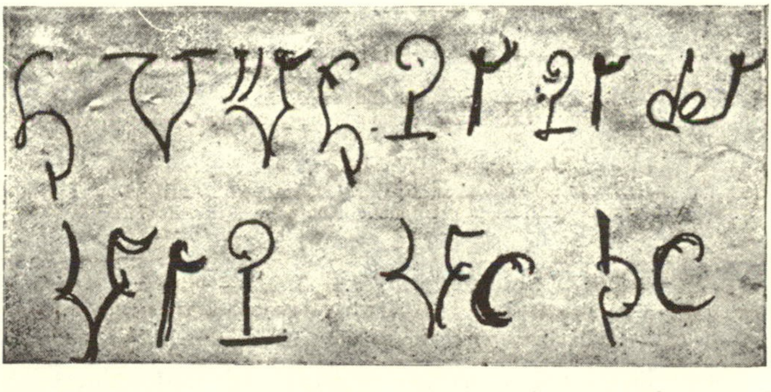

Fig. 26. Text No. 26 (August 21, 1898), which appeared in visual hallucination, and was copied by Mlle. Smith. Reproductions in autotype.

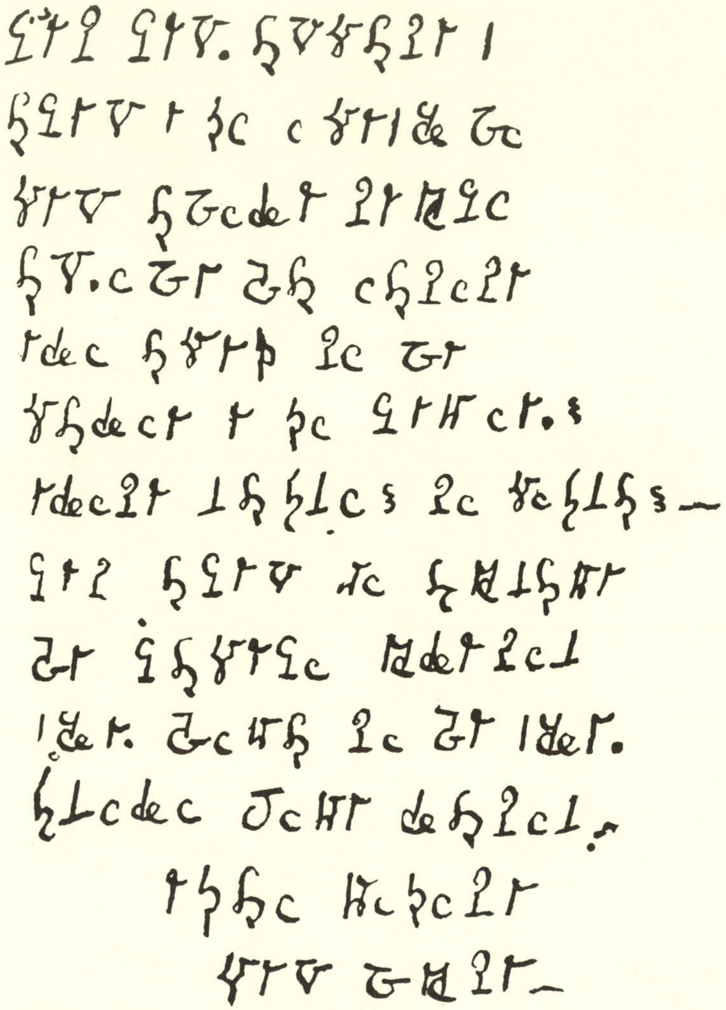

Fig. 27. Text No. 28 (October 8, 1898), written by Mlle. Smith, copying a text of Matêmi, seen in a visual hallucination. (The slight tremor of some of the lines in not in the original, but occured in the copying of the text in the ink, which was written in pencil and too pale for reproduction.)

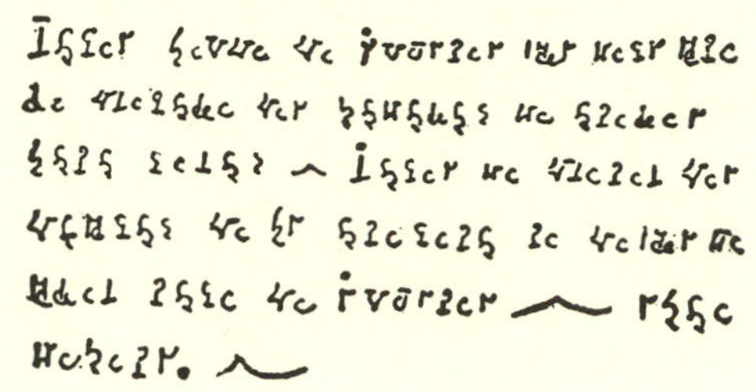

Fig. 28. Text No. 31 (October 27, 1898), written by Mlle. Smith, incarnating Ramié. Natural size.

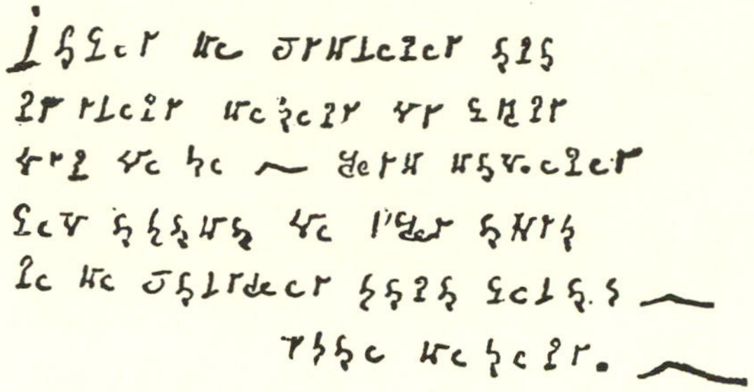

Fig. 29. Text No. 34 (November 2, 1898), written by Mlle. Smith. incarnating Ramié. Natural size.

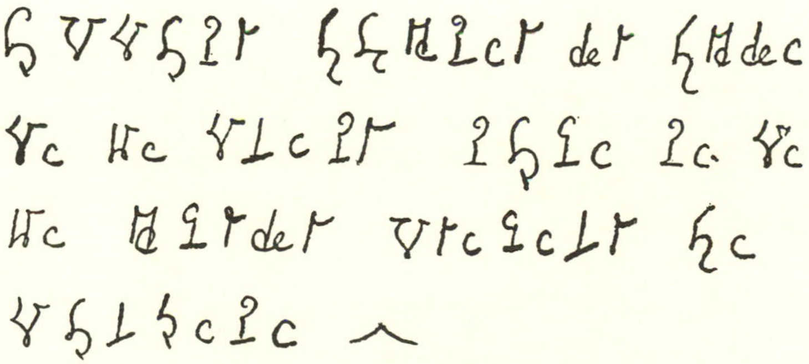

Fig. 30. Text No. 37 (March 24, 1899), written by Mlle. Smith, incarnating Astané. (Collection of M. Lemaître.) Owing to a defect of the stereotype plate a dot is lacking on the first letter.

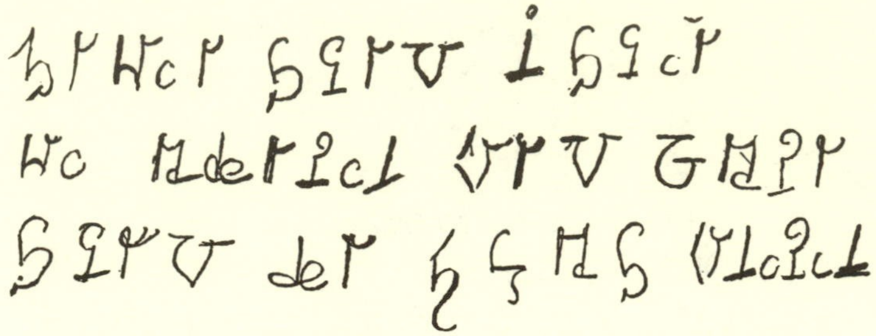

Fig. 31. Text No. 38 (March 30, 1899), written by Mlle. Smith copying a text of Ramié, who appeared to her in a visual hallucination. (Collection of M. Lemaître.)

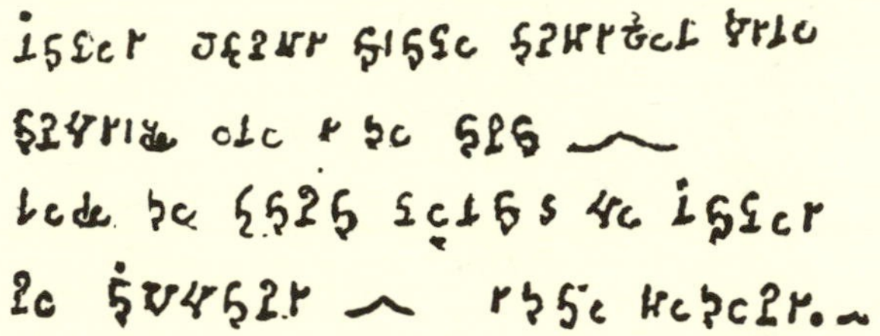

Fig. 32. Text No. 39 (April 1, 1899), written by Mlle. Smith, incarnating Ramié. (Collection of M. Lemaître.) Natural size.

Almost immediately Léopold substitutes himself for Astané and traces on the same sheet, in his characteristic handwriting (considerably distorted towards the end): *"Place thy hand on her forehead,"** by means of which he indicates to me that the time has arrived to pass on to the scene of translation by Esenale.

We may conclude from these successive stages that the Martian handwriting is the result of a slow autosuggestion, in which the idea of a special writing instrument, and its handling, for a long time played the dominant role, then was abandoned, without doubt, as impracticable to realize. The characters themselves then haunted for several weeks Hélène's visual imagination before they appeared to her on the cylinders of the three Martians in a manner sufficiently clear and stable to enable her to copy them and afterwards to be capable of subduing her graphomotor mechanism. Once manifested outwardly, these signs, which I have assembled under the form of an alphabet in Fig. 24, have not varied for two years.

Moreover, some trifling confusion, of which I shall speak a little later, shows well that the personality which employs them is not absolutely separated from that of Hélène, although the latter, in a waking state, might hold the same relation to Martian which she holds to Chinese— that is, she knows its general very characteristic aspect, but is ignorant of the signification of the characters, and would be incapable of reading it.

Hélène's Martian handwriting is not stereotyped, but presents, according to circumstances, some variations in form, especially in the size of the letters.

This may be established by Figs. 21 to 32, in which I have reproduced the greater part of the texts obtained by writing. When the Martian gushes forth in verbo-visual hallucinations, Hélène transcribes it in strokes of large dimensions, lacking firmness, full of repetitions (Figs. 21, 26, 31), and she always remarks that the original, which is before her eyes, is much smaller and clearer than her copy. In the texts which have come automatically from her hand—*i.e.*, supposedly traced by the Martians themselves—the handwriting is really smaller and more precise. Here again are some curious differences. Astané has a calligraphy less voluminous than that of Esenale, and Ramié has a much finer one than Esenale (Figs. 28 and 29).

It would be altogether premature for me to launch myself upon the study of Martian graphology, and, therefore, leaving that line to my successors, I take up the texts which have been collected in their chronological order.

II. The Martian Texts*

It is not always easy to represent a language and its pronunciation by means of the typographical characters of another. Happily the Martian, in spite of its strange appearance and the fifty millions of leagues which separate us from the red planet, is in reality so near neighbor to French that there is scarcely any difficulty in this case.

The dozen written texts[1] which we possess, and which Mlle. Smith either copied from a verbo-visual hallucination, or which were traced by her hand in an access of graphomotor automatism, are readily translated into French, since each Martian letter has its exact equivalent in the French alphabet. I have confined myself to placing accents on the vowels (there are none in the Martian writing), conformably to the pronunciation of Esenale at the moment of translation. It is only necessary to read the following texts aloud, articulating them as though they were French, in

---

[1] These are texts 16–20, 26, 28, 31, 34, 37–39. They are further distinguished by an asterisk.

order to secure the Martian words almost exactly as they proceed from the mouth of Mlle. Smith; I say *almost*, because there still remains, naturally, in the speech of Esenale, as in that of every one, a special mannerism of strengthening certain syllables and slurring others—in short, that of delicate shades of accentuation, which cannot be adequately represented, and which the hearers did not attempt to take note of at the seances.

In the auditive or vocal texts, those which have not been obtained by writing, I have adopted the more probable orthography, according to the pronunciation of Esenale, but (with the exception of words known by means of the written texts) I naturally cannot guarantee their absolute correctness.

The manner in which Hélène takes down in pencil the Martian phrases which strike her ear is not of great assistance to us in that respect, because, as I have said above (p. 125), she finds herself at the time of these verbo-auditive hallucinations in the situation of a person who hears some unknown words, and spells them as well as she is able, after a quite arbitrary and often faulty fashion. She writes, for example, "**hezi darri né ciké taisse,**" which, according to the pronunciation of Esenale and other written texts, should be "**êzi darié Siké tés**"; or, again, "**misse messe as si lé,**" instead of "**mis mess ass ilé.**" We cannot, therefore, depend upon the orthography of Hélèné, but I have naturally followed it in every case in which there seemed to be no good reason to depart from it. In stating that the following texts should be articulated like French, two remarks must be added: First, the final consonant, very rare in Martian, is always aspirated; the word **ten** is pronounced as in the French *gluten*; **essat**, like *fat*; **ames**, like *aloes*; **mis** and **mess**, like *lis* (flower), and mess (of an officer), etc. In the second place, for the different values of the *e* I have adopted the following rule: the *e* broad is always indicated by the accent grave *è*; the *e* medium, which is only found at the beginning and in the middle of a word, is marked with the acute accent *é*, the *e* short, by the acute accent at the end of a word (or before a final *e* mute), and by the circumflex at the beginning or in the middle; the *e* mute, or demimute, remains without accent.

The pronunciation, therefore, will be, for example, the *e*'s of the Martian words **mété, bénézee**, like those of the French words *été, répétée*; **êvé**, like *rêvé*, **tés**, as in *Lutèce*, etc.

There will be found in italics, underneath the Martian texts, their French equivalents, word for word, as given by Esenale in the manner described above (see pp. 108–109).[2] I have also indicated the kind of automatism—auditive, visual, vocal, or graphic—by means of which each

[2] A literal English translation of each text will be found immediately beneath the French equivalents of the Martian words.

text was obtained, also the date of its appearance, and (in parentheses) that of the seance, often quite remote, at which it was translated. I have also added such explanations as seemed to me to be necessary.

1. **métiche C.**   **médache C.**   **métaganiche S.**   **kin't'che**
   Monsieur C.   *Madame C.*   *Mademoiselle S.*   *quatre.*
   Mr. C.   Mrs. C.   Miss C.   Four.

Vocal. February 2, 1896. See above, p. 125.

2. **dodé   né   ci   haudan   té   mess   métiche   Astané   ké   dé**
   Ceci   est   la   maison   du   grand   homme   Astané   que   tu
   mé   véche
   as   vu.
   This is the house of the great man Astané, whom thou hast seen.

Auditive. About September 20, 1896 (translated November 2).—Heard by Hélèné at the same time at which she had the vision of Fig. 12 (see pp. 99 and 108).

3. **modé   iné   cé   di   cévouitche   ni   êvé   ché   kiné   liné**
   Mère   adorée,   je   te   reconnais   et   suis   ton   petit   Linet.
   Adored mother, I recognize thee, and am thy little Linet.

Words addressed to Mme. Mirbel by her son Alexis (Esenale) in a scene of incarnation altogether analogous to that described on p. 96.

4. **i   modé   météé   modé   modé   iné   palette   is**
   O   mère,   tendre   mère,   mère   bien-aimée,   calme   tout
   ché   péliché   ché   chiré   né   ci   ten   ti   vi
   ton   souci,   ton   fils   est   près   de   toi.
   Oh, mother, tender mother, dearly loved mother, calm all thy care, thy son is near thee.

Vocal. November 29, 1896 (translated same seance).—Spoken by Esenale and addressed to Mme. Mirbel, in a scene of incarnation analogous to the preceding. At the moment of translation, Esenale repeated, very distinctly, the last words, as follows: **né ci**, *est près* ["is near"], **ten ti vi**, *de toi* ("thee"). This was evidently an error, since it appears from numerous later texts that *est près de toi* corresponds to **né ten ti vi**; it follows that it would be natural to translate the word **ci** by *là, ici, or tout*, if these words had not been differently rendered in other texts. (A confusion of the adverb *là* with the article *la*, translated by **ci** in text 2, might also be suspected.)

5. **i   kiché   ten   ti   si   ké   di   êvé dé   étéche   mêné**
   Oh! pourquoi   près   de   moi   ne   te   tiens-tu   toujours,   amie

izé   bénézée
enfin   *retrouvée!*
Oh! Why dost thou not keep thyself always near me, friend, at last found again?

Auditive. December 4, 1896 (translated December 13). Fragment of a long discourse by Astané to Hélène, during an apparition which she had of him about nine o'clock in the evening, as she was about to go to bed. This sentence, which he uttered twice, is the only one which she has been able to recall with sufficient precision to note down immediately after the vision. She has the feeling of having understood Astané's whole discourse while he was delivering it, and thinks she would have been able to translate it into French, perhaps not word for word, but in its general sense. She expected to transcribe it the following day, but in the morning when she awoke she was unable to recall either the words of Astané or their meaning, not even that of this sentence, written on the previous evening. Heard again, as the second part of the following text, in the seance of the 13th of December.

6. **ti**   **iche**   **cêné**   **éspênié**   **ni**   **ti**   **êzi**   **atèv**   **astané**   **êzi**
   De   *notre*   *belle*   *"Espénié"*   *et*   *de*   *mon*   *être*   *Astané,*   *mon*
   érié   **vizé**   **é**   **vi . . .**   **i**   **kiché**   **ten**   **ti**   **si**   **ké**   **di**   **êvé**
   âme   *descend*   *à*   *toi . . ,*   *oh!*   *pourouoi*   *près*   *de*   *moi*   *ne*   *te*   *tiens-*
   dé   **étéche**   **mêné**   **izé**   **bénézée**
   tu   *toujours,*   *amie*   *enfin*   *rétrouvée!*
   From our beautiful "Espénié" and from my being Astané, my soul descends to thee—Oh! why dost thou not keep thyself always near to me, friend, at last found again?

Auditive. December 13, 1896 (translated same seance).—Heard in the far-away voice of Astané, Hélène having all the while a painful sensation, as though the skin of her face around her eyes, on the back of her wrists and hands, was being torn off. In the translation the word *Espénié* remains as it is, being a proper name; the left index-finger (Léopold) points heavenward, and says that it might be rendered by *terre*, *planète*, *demeure*.

7. **cé**   **êvé**   **plêva**   **ti**   **di**   **bénèz**   **éssat**   **riz**   **tès**   **midée**
   Je   *suis*   *chagrin*   *de*   *te*   *retrouver*   *vivant*   *sur*   *cette*   *laide*
   durée   **cé**   **ténassé**   **riz**   **iche**   **éspênié**   **vétéche**   **ié**   **ché**   **atèv**   **hêné**
   terre; je   *voudrais*   *sur*   *notre*   *Espénié*   *voir*   *tout*   *ton*   *être*   *s'élever*
   ni   **pové**   **ten**   **ti**   **si**   **éni**   **zée**   **métiché**   **oné**   **gudé**   **ni**   **zée**   **darié**
   et   *rester*   *près*   *de*   *moi;*   *ici*   *les*   *hommes*   *sont*   *bons*   *et*   *les*   *coeurs*
   grêvé
   larges.

I am sorry to find you again living on this wretched earth; I would on our Espénié see all thy being raise itself and remain near me; here men are good and hearts large.

Auditive. December 15, 1896 (translated January 17, 1897).—Words spoken by Astané to Hélène in a morning vision. The following fragment of the letter in which she sent me this text merits being cited as an example of those quite frequent cases in which Mlle. Smith, without knowing the exact translation of the foreign words, nevertheless divines their general signification and comprehends them by their emotional equivalent. "This morning, at a quarter before six, I saw Astané at the foot of my bed. The general sense of his language was at that moment quite clear to my mind, and I give it to you as I understood it—that is, in as clear a manner as possible, having noted it down afterwards: 'How much I regret your not having been born in our world; you would be much happier there, since everything is much better with us, people as well as things, and I would be so happy to have you near me.' That is about what it seemed to me to mean; perhaps some day we may be able to be sure of it."

8.

amès	mis	tensée	ladé	si—amès	ten	tivé	avé
viens	*un*	*instant*	*vers*	*moi, viens*	*près*	*d'un*	*vieil*
men—koumé		ié	ché	pélésse—amès	somé		têsé
ami	*fondre*	*tout*	*ton*	*chagrin:*	*viens*	*admirer*	*ces*
misaïmé—ké		dé	surès	pit	châmi—izâ	méta	ii
fleurs,	*que*	*tu*	*crois*	*sans*	*parfum, mais*	*pourtant*	*si*
borêsé	ti	finaïmé—		iâ	izi	dé	séïmiré
pleines	*de*	*senteurs!* . . .	*Mais*	*si*	*tu*	*comprendras!*	

Come towards me a moment, come near an old friend to melt away all thy sorrow; come to admire these flowers, which you believe without perfume, but yet so full of fragrance! But if thou couldst understand.

Auditive and vocal. January 31, 1897 (translated same seance).— Hélène, in hemisomnambulism, sees Astané, who tells her to repeat his words; she replies to him: "But speak plainly . . . I will gladly repeat them . . . but I do not understand very well . . ." Then she pronounces slowly and very distinctly the foregoing text, in groups of words, separated by a moment of silence (marked in the text by the sign—). It is remarked that these groups, with the exception of the sixth, correspond to the hemistiches of the French translation obtained in the same seance. After the sixth group Hélène remains silent for a long time, and finally says: "I cannot understand;" then utters the four last words, which are the reply of Astané to her objection.

9. ané   éni   ké   éréduté   cé   ilassuné   té   imâ   ni
C'est   ici   que,   solitaire,   je   m'approche   du   ciel   et
bétiné   chée   durée
regarde   ta   terre.
It is here that, alone, I bring myself near to heaven and look upon the earth.

Auditive. February 24, 1897 (translated March 14).—Reclining in her easy-chair, after the noonday meal, Hélène hears this sentence, while at the same time she has the vision of a house, constructed by digging into a Martian mountain, and traversed by a sort of air-shafts, and which represents Astané's observatory.

10. simandini   lé   lâmi   mêné   kizé   pavi   kiz   atimi
Simandini,   me   voici!   amie!   quelle   joie,   quel   bonheur!
Simandini, here I am! friend! what joy! what happiness!

Auditive. March 14, 1897 (translated same seance).—See following text.

11. i   modé   duméïné   modé   kêvi   cé   mache   povini
O   mère,   ancienne   mère,   quand   je   peux   arriver
poénêzé   mûné   é   vi   saliné   éziné   mimâ   nikaïné   modé
quelques   instants   vers   toi   j'oubie   mes   parents   Nikaïné   mère!
—i   men
—ô   ami!
Oh, mother, former mother, when I can arrive a few instants near thee, I forget my parents Nikaïné, mother!—Oh friend!

Vocal. March 14, 1897 (translated same seance).—From the beginning of this seance Hélèn complained of cold hands, then a great desire to weep, and of a buzzing in the ears, which kept increasing and in which she finally heard Astané address to her the Martian words of text 10. Immediately after she passes into full somnambulism; her respirations, very short and panting, rise to three per second, accompanied by synchronous movements of the left index-finger; then she stops suddenly with a long expiration, immediately followed by a deep inspiration: then her breast heaves, her face assumes an expression of suffering, and the left index-finger announces that it is Esenale (Alexis Mirbel) who is incarnated. After a series of spasms and hiccoughs, Hélène arises, and, placing herself behind Mme. Mirbel, takes her neck in her hands, bows her head upon hers, tenderly pats her cheek, and addresses to her the words of text No. 11 (except the two last words). Then she raises her head, and again, with panting respiration (accelerated to thirty inspirations in sixteen seconds), walks towards M. Lemaître (whose pupil Alexis Mirbel had been at the time of his death). She places her hands upon his shoulders, affectionately grasps his right hand, and with emotion and continued sobbing addresses to him the two words **i men**! After which she goes through the pantomime of extending her hand to Léopold and of allowing him to conduct her to a couch, where the translation of texts Nos. 10, 11, and 9 is obtained by the customary process, but not without difficulty.

12. **lassuné   ké   nipuné   ani   tis   dé   machir   mirivé**
     Approche,   ne   crains   pas;   bientot   tu   pourras   tracer
     iche   manir   sé   dé   évenir   toué   chi   amiché   zé   forimé
     notre   écriture,   et   tu   posséderas   dans   tes   mains   les   marques
     ti   viche   tarviné
     de   notre   langage.

Approach, fear not; soon thou wilt be able to trace our writing, and thou wilt possess in thy hands the signs of our language.

Auditive. May 23, 1897 (translated same seance).—Shortly after the beginning of the seance, Hélène, still being awake, has a vision of Astané, who addresses her in these words, which she repeats slowly and in a feeble voice. I give the text as it was heard and uniformly noted by several sitters, both at the moment of its utterance and at its subsequent translation. Many corrections, however, would be necessary, in order to make it correspond with the later written texts: **ké nipuné ani**, *et ne crains pas* ("and I am not afraid," or, "and I do not fear") should be changed to **kié nipuné ani**, *ne crains pas* (see text 17); **sé** or **cé** only stands here for *et*, which everywhere else is given as **ni**; **viche** is used in error for **iche** (unless the **v** was added for the sake of euphony, of which there is no other example) and **tis** for **tiche**.

13. (adèl)   **ané sini**   (yestad)   **i   astané   cé   fimès   astané   mirâ**
          C'est vous,   ô   Astané,   je   meurs!   Astané,   adieu!
     It is you, oh Astané, I am dying! Astané, farewell!

Vocal. Same seance as the preceding text, after which Hélène passes into full somnambulism, begins to weep, pants, holds her hand on her heart, and pronounces this sentence, mingling with it the two words *Adèl* and *yestad*, which are not Martian, but belong to the Oriental cycle; they also do not appear in the text as it was repeated at the time of its translation. This intrusion of terms foreign to the Martian dream is explained by the imminence of a Hindoo scene ready to appear, which occupied the latter half of the seance in which the Arab servant, Adèl, plays a leading role. The mingling of the two romances is greatly accentuated a few moments later, in a long discourse, devoid of *r*'s and very rich in sibilants, and spoken with so great volubility that it was impossible to gather a single word. At the time of the translation, at the close of the seance, this tirade was repeated with the same rapidity, preventing any notation; according to the French translation which followed, it concerned memories of the life of Simandini which Hélène recalled to Astané and in which there is much mention of the aforesaid Adèl (see Hindoo Cycle, Chap. VII.).

14.

eupié	zé	palir	né	amé	arvâ	nini	pédriné	évaï
Epuié,	*le*	*temps*	*est*	*venu;*	*Arva*	*nous*	*quitte,*	*sois*
diviné	lâmée	ine	vinâ	té	luné—pouzé		men	hantiné
heureux	*jusque*	*au*	*retour*	*du*	*jour.—Pouzé,*		*ami*	*fidèle,*
êzi	vraïni	né	touzé	med	vi	ni	ché	chiré	saïné—ké
mon	*désir*	*est*	*même*	*pour*	*toi*	*et*	*ton*	*fils*	*Saïné.—Que*
zalisé	téassé	mianiné	ni	di	daziné—eupié—pouzé
l'element	*entier*	*t'enveloppe*	*et*	*te*	*garde!—Eupié!—Pouzé!*

Eupié, the time has come; Arva leaves us; be happy till the return of the day. Pouzé, faithful friend, my wish is even for thee, and thy son Saïné.—May the entire element envelop thee and guard thee!—Eupie!—Pouzé!

Auditive. June 18, 1897 (translated June 20).—During a visit I made to Mlle. Smith she has a vision of two Martian personages walking on the shore of a lake, and she repeats this fragment of their conversation which she has heard. According to another text (No. 20), Arva is the Martian name of the sun.

15.

modé	tatinée	cé	ké	mache	radziré	zé	tarvini	va
Mère	*chérie,*	*je*	*ne*	*puis*	*prononcer*	*le*	*langage*	*où*
nini	nini	triménêni	ii	adzi	cé	zé	seïmiré	vétiche	i
nous	*nous*	*comprenions*	*si*	*bien!*	*Je*	*le*	*comprends*	*cependant;*	*ô*
modé	inée	kévi	bérimir	m	hed	kévi	machiri	cé	di	triné
mère	*adorée,*	*quand*	*reviendra-t-il?*		*Quand*	*pourrai-je*		*te*	*parler*
ti	éstotiné	ni	bazée	animina	i	modé	cé	méï	adzi
de ma dernière		*et*	*courte*	*existence?*	*O*	*mère,*	*je*	*t'ai*	*bien*
ilinée	i	modé	inée	cé	ké	lé	nazère	ani—mirâ
reconnue,	*i*	*modé*	*inée*	*cé*	*ne*	*me*	*trompe*	*pas!—Adieu*
modé	itatinée	mirâ	mirâ	mirâ
mère	*chérie,*	*adieu,*	*adieu,*	*adieu!*

My dearest, I cannot pronounce the language in which we understood each other so well! I understand it, however; oh! adored mother, when will it return? When shall I be able to speak to thee of my last and short existence? Oh! mother, I have well recognized thee, oh! adored mother, I am not mistaken!—Farewell, dearest mother, farewell, farewell, farewell!

Auditive. June 27, 1897 (translated same seance).—Mme. Mirbel being present, Hélène perceives Esenale, who remains in the vicinity of his mother and addresses these words to her. The "adieux" at the close were not spoken at that time, but were uttered by Esenale immediately following and as a complement of the translation; this is the only case (outside of text 36) in which he did not confine himself strictly to the texts already gathered and in which he permitted himself to introduce a new phrase, which otherwise does not contain a single unknown word: **itatinée**, *chérie*, is evidently a slip which should be corrected either to **tatinée**, *chérie*, or to it **atinée**, *ô chérie*. The precise French equivalent of **tri-ménêni** is probably *entretenions*.

*16. astané   ésenâle   pouzé   mêné   simandini   mirâ
     (Astané.   Esenale.   Pouzé.   Amie   Simandini,   adieu!)
     Astané. Esenale. Pouzeé. Friend Simandini, farewell!

Visual. August 22, 1897.—This text, for which there is no need of a translation, constitutes the first appearance of the Martian handwriting. See above, Fig. 21, and the résumé of that seance, pp. 127–128.

*17. taniré   mis   méch   med   mirivé   éziné   brimaɠ   ti   tès
     Prends   un   crayon   pour   tracer   mes   paroles   de   cet
     tensée—azini   dé   améir   mazi   si   somé   iche   nazina
     instant.   Alors   tu   viendras   avec   moi   admirer   notre   nouveau
     tranéï,—Simandini   cé   kié   mache   di   pédriné   tès   luné   ké   cé
     passage.   Simandini,   je   ne   puis   te   quitter   ce   jour.   Que   je
     êvé   diviné—patrinèz   kié   nipuné   ani
     suis   heureux!—Alors   ne   crains   pas!
     Take a pencil to trace my words of this moment. Then thou wilt come with me to admire our new passage. Simandini, I cannot leave thee this day. How happy I am!—Then fear not!

Graphic. September 12, 1897 (translated same seance).—See pp. 112 and 128 and Fig. 23.

*18. modé   tatinée   lâmi   mis   mirâ   ti   ché   bigâ   kâ
     Mère   chérie,   voici   un   adieu   de   ton   enfant   qui
     ébrinié   sanâ   é   vi   idé   di   zé   rénir—zé   mess   métich   kâ   é
     pense   tant   à   toi.   On   te   le   portera,   le   grand   homme   qui   a
     zé   valini   iminé—ni   z   [é]   grani   sidiné
     le   visage   mince   et   le   corps   maigre.
     My dearest, this is a farewell from thy child, who thinks so much of thee. The big man, who has a thin face and a slender body, will bear it to thee.

Auditive, then Graphic. October 10, 1897 (translated same seance).—Hélène has a vision of a Martian landscape, in which Esenale floats discarnate around the plants and speaks these words, which she repeats. (It is understood from the translation that this text was intended for Mme. Mirbel, who was then in the country, but to whom the person very clearly indicated by the final characteristic was about to pay a visit and could carry the message.) I then offer Hélène a pencil in the hope of obtaining this same text in writing; after various tergiversations and grimaces, denoting a state of increasing somnambulism, she finally takes the pencil between her index and middle fingers, tells Esenale that she still sees him and makes him sit down by her side, and then begins to write, completely absent and fascinated by the paper. The left index-finger (Léopold) informs us that it is Esenale himself who is writing by means of Hélène's arm. Twice she interrupts herself in order to say to Esenale, "Oh! do not go yet, stay a little while longer!" She appears nervous and agitated, and often stops writing to stab her paper with her pencil or to make erasures or scribble on it (see Fig. 25); in the **zé** of the last line, she forgets the **é** (this did not prevent Esenale from pronouncing the word correctly at the time of its translation).

*19. **m [en]   cé   kié   mache   di   triné   sandiné   téri**
(Amie,   je   ne   puis   te   parler   longtemps   comme
né   êzi   vraïni   zou   réch   mirâ   milé piri   mirâ
est   mon   désir;   plus   tard,   adieu   adieu.)
(Friend, I cannot speak to thee a long time, as is my desire; later, farewell, farewell!)

Graphic, then Auditive. October 24, 1897 (there has never been any translation of this text, two words of which are still unknown).—Hélène first sees the table illumined by a green light in which some designs appear which she copies, and which give this text, except the two last letters of the first word, the place of which remains blank. Immediately after she hears Martian spoken, which she repeats. It is the same text; then she has a vision of Astané, Esenale, and a little girl whose name she hears as Niké; but this soon gives way to other non-Martian somnambulisms. (See Fig. 25.)

*20. **Siké   évaï   diviné   zé   niké   crizi   capri   né   amé**
Siké,   sois   heureux!   Le   petit   oiseau   noir   est   venu
orié   antéch   é   êzé   carimi   ni   êzi   érié   é   nié   pavinée   hed
frapper   hier   à   ma   fenêtre,   et   mon   âme   a   été   joyeuse;   il
lé   sadri   dé   zé   véchir   tiziné   Matêmi   misaïmé   kâ   lé
me   chanta: tu   le   verras   demain.—Matêmi,   fleur   qui   me
amèz   essaté   Arvâ   ti   éziné   udâniᵷ   amès   tès   uri   amès
fais   vivre,   soleil   de   mes   songes,   viens   ce   soir,   viens
sandiné   ten   ti   si   évaï   divinée   Romé   ira   né   Siké
longtemps   près   de   moi;   sois   heureuse!—Romé,   où   est   Siké?—
atrizi   ten   té   taméch   épizi
Là-bas,   près   du   "taméche"   rose.
Siké, be happy! The little black bird came yesterday rapping at my window,

and my soul was joyful; he sang to me: Thou wilt see him to-morrow. Ma-têmi, flower which makes me live, sun of my dreams, come this evening; come for a long time to me; be happy!—Rome, where is Siké?—Yonder, near the "taméche" rose.

Auditive, then Graphic. November 28, 1897 (translated same seance).—Fragments of conversation heard during the vision of the Martian *fête* described on p. 118. Siké (a young man) and Matêmi (a young girl) form the first couple who pass by and walk off in the direction of a large bush with red flowers (**tamèche**); then a second couple exchange the last words of the text while going to rejoin the first. After this vision, which she contemplated standing and described with much animation, Hélène seated herself and began to write the same Martian phrases. It is ascertained from Léopold that it was Astané who held her hand (in holding the pencil between the thumb and the index-finger—that is, after the manner of Léopold and not that of Hélène as she had held it in writing text No. 17).* The writing being finished, Léopold directs that Hélène shall be made to seat herself on the couch for the scene of translation.

21. **véchési   têsée   polluni   avé   métiche   é   vi   ti**
    Voyons   cette   question,   vieux   homme;   à   toi   de
    bounié   seïmiré   ni   triné
    chercher,   comprendre   et   parler.
    Now this question, old man; it is for thee to seek, to understand and speak.

Auditive. January 15, 1898 (translated February 13).—Fragment of conversation between two Martian personages seen in a waking vision.

22. **astané   cé   amès   é   vi   chée   brimi   messé   téri**
    Astané,   je   viens   à   toi;   ta   sagesse   grande   comme
    ché   pocrimé   le . . .
    ton   savoir   me . . .
    Astané, I come to thee; thy great wisdom as well as thy knowledge to me. . .

Auditive. About January 25, 1898 (translated February 13).—Vision, at six o'clock in the morning, of a young Martian girl (Matêmi?) traversing a tunnel through a mountain and arriving at the house of Astané, to whom she addresses this utterance, followed by many others which Hélène could not grasp with sufficient distinctness to note them down.

23. [A] **paniné   évaï   kirimé   zé   miza   ami   grini**
    Panine,   sois   prudent,   le   "miza"   va   soulever;
    ké   chée   éméche   rès   pazé—[B] pouzé   tès   luné   soumini
    que   ta   main   se   retire!—   Pouzé,   ce   jour   riant . . .
    arvâ   ii   cen   zé   primi   ti   ché   chiré   kiz   pavi   luné—
    Arva   si   beau . . . le   revoir   de   ton   fils . . . quel   heureux   jour—

[C] saïné   êzi   chiré   izé   linëï   kizé   pavi   êzi   mané
Saïné,   mon   Jils,   enfin   debout!   quelle   joie! . . .   Mon   père
ni   êzé   modé   tiziné   êzi   chiré   êzi   mané   cé   êvé   adi
et   ma   mère . . .   Demain,   mon   fils . . .   Mon   père,   je   suis   bien
anâ
maintenant.

Paniné, be prudent, the "miza" is about to arise; remove thy hand! Pouzé, this laughing day . . . Arva so beautiful . . . The return of thy son . . . What happy day—Saïné, my son, finally standing! What joy! . . . My father and my mother . . . To-morrow, my son . . . my father, I am well now.

Auditive. February 20, 1898 (translated same seance).—Very complicated Martian vision. First, three small, movable houses, like pavilions or Chinese kiosks, going about on little balls; in one of these, two unknown personages, one of whom puts her hand out of a small oval window, which occasions, on the part of her companion, the observation of the first sentence (A) of the text; at this instant, in fact, these rolling pavilions (**miza**) assume an oscillatory movement, which makes a noise like "tick-tack," and then glide like a train upon rails. They go around a high red mountain and come into a sort of magnificent gorge or ravine, with slopes covered with extraordinary plants, and where they find white houses on an iron framework resembling piles. The two men then alight from their "**miza**," chatting together, but Hélène can only hear fragments (B) of their conversation. A young man of sixteen to eighteen years of age comes to meet them, who has his head tied up in a kind of nightcap, and having no hair on the left side. Martian salutations are exchanged; they mutually strike their heads with their hands, etc. Hélène complains of hearing very confusedly that which they are saying, and can only repeat ends of sentences (C). She has pain in her heart, and Léopold dictates to me by the left index-finger, *"Put her to sleep,"* which presently leads to the customary scene of translation of the text.

24. saïné   êzi   chiré   iée   êzé   pavi   ché   vinâ   ine   ruzzi
Saïné,   mon   fils,   toute   ma   joie,   ton   retour   au   milieu
ti   nini   né   mis   mess   assilé   atimi . . .   itèche . . .
de   nous   est   un   grand,   immense   bonheur . . .   toujours . . .
furimir . . .   nori
aimera . . .   jamais.

Saïné, my son, all my joy; thy return to our circle is a great, an immense happiness . . . always will love . . . ever.

Auditive. March 11, 1898 (translated August 21).—"Yesterday morning, on jumping out of bed," wrote Hélène to me, when sending me this text, "I had a vision of Mars, almost the same as that which I had before (at the seance of February 20). I saw again the rolling pavilions, the houses on piling, several personages, among them a young man who had no hair on one side of his head. I was able to note some words. It was very confused, and the last words were caught on the wing, when here and there something a little clear came to me. . . ."

25. | dé | véchi | ké | ti | éfi | mervé | eni |
|----|------|-----|----|-----|-------|-----|
| *tu* | *vois* | *que* | *de* | *choses* | *superbes* | *ici.* |

Thou seest what superb things (are) here.

Auditive. August 21, 1898 (translated same seance).—Waking vision of a river between two rose-colored mountains, with a bridge (like that in Fig. 9) which lowered itself into the water and disappeared in order to allow five or six boats to pass (like that in Fig. 13), then reappeared and was restored to its place. As Hélène describes all this, she hears a voice speaking to her the above Martian words of the text.

*26. | Astané | né | zé | ten | ti | vi |
|--------|-----|-----|-----|-----|-----|
| *Astané* | *est* | *là* | *près* | *de* | *toi* |

Astané is there, near to thee.

Visual. August 21, 1898 (translated same seance).—Following the preceding scene: Hélène perceives "in the air" (illumined and red—that of her Martian vision) some characters unknown to her, which she copies (see Fig. 26). I ask her, showing her the word zé (which elsewhere always stands for *le*), if she is not mistaken. She verifies it by comparing it with the imaginary model before her and affirms it to be correct.

27. | siké | kiz | crizi | hantiné | hed | é | ébrinie | rès | améré | é |
|------|-----|-------|---------|-----|---|---------|-----|-------|---|
| *Siké,* | *quel* | *oiseau* | *fidèle!* | *il* | *a* | *pensé* | *se* | *réunir* | *à* |
| **nini** | **éssaté** | **ti** | **iche** | **atimi** | **matêmi** | **hantiné** | **hed** | **né** | |
| *nous,* | *vivre* | *de* | *notre* | *bonheur!—Matêmi* | *fidèle,* | *il* | *est* | | |
| **hantiné** | **êzi** | **darié** | **siké** | **tès** | **ousti** | **ké** | **zé** | **badêni** | **lassuné** |
| *fidèle* | *mon* | *coeur!—Siké,* | *ce* | *bateau* | *que* | *le* | *vent* | *approche* | |
| **mazi** | **trimazi** | **hed** | **é** | **ti** | **zi** | **mazêté** | **é** | **poviné** | **é nini zé priàni** |
| *avec* | *force!* | *il* | *a* | *de* | *la* | *peine* | *à* | *arriver* | *à nous; le flot* |
| **é** | **fouminé** | **ivraïni** | **idé** | **é** | **ti** | **zi** | **mazêté** | **é** | **vizêné zé** |
| *est* | *puissant* | *aujourd'hui;* | *on* | *a* | *de* | *la* | *peine* | *à* | *distinguer le* |
| **chodé** | | | | | | | | | |

"chodé."

Siké, what (a) faithful bird! he has thought to reunite himself to us, to live of our happiness!—Matêmi faithful, my heart is faithful!—Siké, this boat which the wind brings near with force! it has some difficulty in reaching us; the current is strong to-day; one has some difficulty in distinguishing the "chodé."

Auditive. About the 4th of September, 1898 (translated October 16).—
Hélène heard and noted this phrase at the same time at which she had the
vision of the two young Martian people who were walking in a kind of
flower-garden, and saw a boat arrive, like that in Fig. 13. The meaning of
chodé has not been ascertained.

*28.

men	**mess**	**Astané**	**cé**	**amès**	**é**	**vi**	**itéch**	**li**	**tès**
Ami	*grand*	*Astané,*	*je*	*viens*	*à*	*toi*	*toujours*	*par*	*cet*
alizé	**néümi**	**assilé**	**kâ**	**ianiné**	**êzi**	**atèv**		**ni**	**lé**
élément	*mysterieux,*	*immense,*	*qui*	*enveloppe*	*mon*	*être*		*et*	*me*
tazié	**é**	**vi**	**med**	**iéeꝯ**	**éziné**	**rabriꝯ**	**ni**	**tibraꝯ.**	**men** **amès** **di**
lance	*à*	*toi*	*pour*	*toutes*	*mes*	*pensées*	*et*	*besoins.*	*Ami,* *viens* *te*
ouradé	**ké**	**Matêmi**	**uzénir**	**chée**	**kida**	**ni**	**ké**	**chée**	**brizi** **pi**
souvenir	*que*	*Matêmi*	*attendra*	*ta*	*faveur,*	*et*	*que*	*ta*	*sagesse* *lui*
dézanir.	**évaï**	**diviné**	**tès**	**luné**					
répondra.	*Sois*	*heureux*	*ce*	*jour.*					

Friend great Astané, I come to thee always by this element, mysterious,
immense, which envelops my being and launches me to thee by all my
thoughts and desires. Friend, come thou to remember that Matêmi will
await thy favor, and that thy wisdom will answer him. Be happy to-day.

Visual. October 3, 1898 (translated October 16).—At a quarter before
nine in the evening Mlle. Smith, desiring to obtain a communication from
Léopold for herself and her mother, sat down in an easy-chair and gave
herself up to meditation. Presently she hears the voice of Léopold telling
her that he cannot manifest himself that evening, but that something
much more interesting and important is being made ready. The room
seems to her to become completely obscured, except the end of the table
at which she is sitting, which is illumined with a golden light. A young
Martian girl in a yellow robe and with long tresses then comes and seats
herself beside her and begins to trace, without ink or paper, but with a
point on the end of her index finger, black figures on a white cylinder, at
first placed on the table, afterwards on her knees, and which is unrolled as
she writes. Hélène is near enough to see the characters clearly, and copies
them in pencil on a sheet of paper (see Fig. 27), after which the vision
vanishes and her mother and the room reappear.*

29.

sazêni	**kiché**	**nipunêzé**	**dodé**	**né**	**pit**	**léziré**	**bèz**
Sazeni	*pourquoi*	*craindre?*	*Ceci*	*est*	*sans*	*souffrance*	*ni*
neura	**évaï**	**dastrée**	**firêzi**	**zé**	**bodri**	**né**	**dorimé** **zé**
danger,	*sois*	*paisible;*	*certainement*	*le*	*os*	*est*	*sain,* *le*
pastri	**tubré**	**né**	**tuxé**				
sang	*seul*	*est*	*malade.*				

Sazeni, why fear? This is without suffering or danger, be peaceful; certainly
the flesh is well, the blood alone is ill.

Auditive. October 14, 1898 (translated October 16).—Morning vision of an unknown gentleman and lady, the latter having her arm, spotted with red, applied to an instrument with three tubes placed on a shelf fastened to the wall. These words were spoken by the man; the lady said nothing.

30.
modé	ké	hed	oné	chandêné	têsé	mûné	ten	ti
Mère,	*que*	*ils*	*sont*	*délicieux*	*ces*	*moments*	*près*	*de*

vi	bigâ	va	bindié	idé	ti	zâmé	tensée	zou	réche
toi!—Enfant,	*où*	*trouve*	*on*	*de*	*meilleurs*	*instants?*		*plus*	*tard*

med	ché	atèv	kiz	fouminé	zati
pour	*ton*	*être*	*quel*	*puissant*	*souvenir.*

Mother, how delightful they are, these moments near to thee!—Child, where finds one better moments? later for thy being what (a) powerful remembrance.

Auditive. October 22, 1898 (translated December 18).—"At a quarter-past six in the morning; vision of a pebbly shore; earth of a red tint; immense sheet of water, of a bluish green. Two women are walking side by side. This was all I could gather of their conversation."

*31.
Râmié	**bisti**	**ti**	**Espênié**	**ché**	**dimé**	**ûni**	**zi**
Ramié	*habitant*	*de*	*Espénié,*	*ton*	*semblable*	*par*	*la*

trimazi	**tié**	**vadâzéȝ**	**di**	**anizié**	**bana**	**mirâȝ.**	**Ramié**	**di**
force	*des*	*"vadazas,"*	*te*	*envoie*	*trois*	*adieux.*	*Ramié*	*te*

trinir	**tié**	**toumaȝ**	**ti**	**bé**	**animinâ**	**ni**	**tiche**	**di**	**uzir**	**nâmi**
parlera	*des*	*charmes*	*de*	*sa*	*existence*	*et*	*bientôt*	*te*	*dira*	*beaucoup*

ti	**Espênié.**	**évaï**	**divinée**
de	*Espênié.*	*Sois*	*heureuse!*

Ramie, dweller in Espénié, thy like, by the force of the "vadazas," sends thee three adieux. Ramie will speak to thee of the charms of his existence, and presently will tell thee much of Espenie. Be happy!

Graphic. October 27, 1898 (translated December 18).—"Ten minutes to one in the afternoon. No vision, but a severe cramp in the right arm and a strong impulse to take pencil and paper. I write, I know not why." (It is seen by the translation given two months later that the text refers to the first manifestation of Ramié and is an announcement of the ultra-Martian vision which came a few days later.) See Fig. 28. The term **vadazas**, which has never been explained, has not a Martian appearance, and appears to have been borrowed from the Hindoo cycle. As to *Espénié*, see text No. 6.

32.
anâ	évaï	maniké	é	bétiné	mis	tié	attanâ
Maintenant	*sois*	*attentive*	*à*	*regarder*	*un*	*des*	*mondes*

kâ	di	médinié	bétinié	tès	tapié	ni	bée	atèv	kavivé
qui	*te*	*entourent.*	*Regarde*	*ce*	*"tapié"*	*et*	*ses*	*êtres*	*étranges.*

danda   anâ
Silence   maintenant!
Now be attentive to behold one of the worlds which surround thee. Look at
that "tapié" and its strange beings. Silence now!

Auditive. November 2, 1898 (translated December 18).—Hélène has a
morning vision of a Martian (Ramié) who encircles her waist with one arm
and with the other shows her, while speaking these words, a strange tableau (*tapié*) containing extraordinary beings speaking the unknown language of the following text. At the moment the vision is effaced Hélène
writes, without perceiving that she has done so, text No. 34. (For further
details, see the following chapter on the Ultra-Martian.)

33. BAK   SANAK   TOP   ANOK   SIK
    sirima   **nêbé**   **viniâ-ti-mis-métiche**   **ivré**   **toué**
    rameau   *vertn*   *nom de un homme*   *sacré*   *dans*

      ETIP   VANE   SANIM   BATAM   ISSEM   TANAK
    viniâ-ti-misé-bigâ   **azâni**   **maprinié**   **imizi**   **kramâ**   **ziné**
    nom de une enfant   *mal*   *entré*   *sous*   *panier*   *bleu*

      VANEM   SEBIM   MAZAK   TATAK   SAKAM
    viniâ-ti-mis-zaki   **datrinié**   **tuzé**   **vâmé**   **gâmié**
    nom de un animal   *caché*   *malade*   *triste*   *pleure.*
    Branch green—name of a man—sacred—in—name of a child—bad—
    entered—under—basket—blue—name of an animal—hidden—ill—sad—
    weeps.

Auditive, as to the non-Martian text (see following chapter) which
Hélène heard spoken on the 2d of November by the strange beings of the
tableau of the preceding vision. Vocal, as to the Martian translation of this
text, which was given by Astané (incarnated in Hélène and speaking the
unknown language by her mouth, followed by its Martian equivalent for
each word), in the seance of the 18th of December, 1898. Immediately
after, Astané yielded his place to Esenale, who in turn repeated the Martian phrase, translating it word for word into French by the customary
process.

*34. **Ramié**   **di**   **pédrinié**   **anâ**   **né**   **ériné**   **diviné**
     Ramié   *te*   *quitte*   *maintenant,*   *est*   *satisfait,*   *heureux*
     té   **muné**   **ten**   **ti**   **vi.**   **hed**   **dassinié**   **mis**   **abadâ**   **ti**   **ché**
     du   *moment*   *près*   *de*   *toi.*   *Il*   *garde*   *un*   *peu*   *de*   *ton*
     atèv   **ni**   **di**   **parêzié**   **banâ**   **mirâξ.—evai**   **diviné**
     être   *et*   *te*   *laisse*   *trois*   *adieux. Sois*   *heureuse!*
     Ramié leaves thee now, is satisfied, happy for the moment near to thee. He
     retains a little of thy being and leaves thee three adieux. Be happy.

Graphic. November 2, 1898 (translated December 18).—Hélène only perceived after its accomplishment that her hand, which she felt "firmly held," had written this text at the close of the preceding vision (see Fig. 29).

35. [A]

attanâ	zabiné	pi	ten	té	iche	tarvini	mabûré
Monde	*arriéré,*	*très*	*près*	*du*	*nôtre,*	*langage*	*grossier,*

nubé	téri	zée	atèv	[B] Astané	êzi	dabé	fouminé	ni
curieux	*comme*	*les*	*êtres!—*	*Astané,*	*mon*	*maître*	*puissant*	*et*

ié	ti	takâ	tubré	né	bibé	ti	zé	umêzé
tout	*de*	*pouvoir,*	*seul*	*est*	*capable*	*de*	*le*	*faire.*

Hidden world, very near to ours, coarse language, curious like the beings.— Astané, my powerful master and all powerful, alone is capable of doing it.

Auditive. December 5, 1898 (translated December 18).—Working by lamp-light at seven o'clock in the morning, Hélène again had a vision of the Martian (Ramié) who had clasped her waist with one arm while showing her something with a gesture of the other (probably the tableau of the preceding vision, though Hélène did not see it) and uttering the first phrase of it (A). The second phrase (B) is the reply of this same Martian to a mental question of Hélène asking him to translate the strange language of the other day. (She must, therefore, have understood the meaning of the first phrase in order to have replied to it by her appropriate mental question.)

36. [A]

aé	aé	aé	aé	lassunié	lâmi	rêzé	aé	aé	aé
Aé,	*aé,*	*aé,*	*aé!—Approche;*	*voici*	*Rêzé . . .*	*aé,*	*aé,*	*aé,*	

aé	niké	bulié	va	né	ozâmié	zitêni	primêni—[B] ozâmié
aé,	*petit*	*Bulié . . .*	*où*	*est*	*Ozamié?*	*Zitêni,*	*Primêni . . . Ozamié,*

viniâ	ti	mis	bigâ	kêmâ	zitêni	viniâ	ti	misé	bigâ	kêmisi
nom	*de*	*un*	*enfant*	*mâle;*	*Zitêni,*	*nom*	*de*	*une*	*enfant*	*femelle;*

primêni	viniâ	ti	misé	bigâ	kêmisi
Priméni,	*nom*	*de*	*une*	*enfant*	*femelle.*

Aé, aé, aé, aé! Approach, here is Rêzé, . . aé, aé, aé, aé, little Bulié . . . where is Ozamié? Zitêni, Primêni . . . Ozamié, name of a male child; Zitêni, name of a female child; Primêni, name of a female child.

Auditive. March 8, 1899 (translated June 4).—Hélène heard the phrase (A) during the vision of which the description follows. At the translation, as the sitters did not at once understand that the three first words are proper names, Esenale adds the phrase (B) with its French signification. "I was unable to go to sleep yesterday evening. At half-past eleven everything around me was suddenly lighted up, and the vivid light permitted me to distinguish surrounding objects. I arose this morning with a very clear remembrance of that which I then saw. A tableau was formed in that light, and I had more before me than the interior of a Martian house—an immense square hall, around which shelves were fastened, or rather little tables suspended and fastened to the wall. Each of these tables contained a baby, but not at all bundled up; all the movements of these little infants were free, and a simple linen cloth was thrown round the body. They might be said to be lying on yellow moss. I could not say with what the tables were covered. Some men with strange beasts were circulating round the hall; these beasts had large flat heads, almost without hair, and large, very soft eyes, like those of seals; their bodies, slightly hairy, resembled somewhat those of roes in our country, except for their large and flat tails; they had large udders, to which the men present fitted a square instrument with a tube, which was offered to each infant, who was thus fed with the milk of these beasts. I heard cries, a great hurly-burly, and it was with difficulty that I could note these few words [of this text]. This vision lasted about a quarter of an hour; then everything gradually disappeared, and in a minute after I was in a sound sleep."

*37. **Astané**   **bounié**   **zé**   **buzi**   **ti**   **di**   **triné**   **nâmi**   **ni**
Astané   *cherche*   *le*   *moyen*   *de*   *te*   *parler*   *beaucoup*   *et*
ti   **di**   **umêzé**   **seïmiré**   **bi**   **tarvini**
de   *te*   *faire*   *comprendre*   *son*   *langage.*
Astané searches for the means to speak to thee much and to make thee understand his language.

Graphic. March 24, 1899 (translated June 4).—"Half-past six in the morning. Vision of Astané. I was standing, about to put on my slippers. He spoke to me, but I could not understand him. I took this sheet of paper and a pencil; he spoke to me no more, but seized my hand which held the pencil. I wrote under this pressure; I understood nothing, for this is as Hebrew to me. My hand was released; I raised my head to see Astané, but he had disappeared" (see Fig. 30).

*38. **fédié**   **amès**   **Ramié**   **di**   **uzénir**   **tès**   **luné**   **amès**   **zé**
Fédié,   *viens;*   *Ramié*   *te*   *attendra*   *ce*   *jour;*   *viens,*   *le*
boua   **trinir**
frère   *parlera.*
Fédié, come; Ramié will await thee to-day; come, the brother will speak.

Visual. March 30, 1899 (translated June 4).—Seated at her toilet-table, at half-past nine o'clock in the evening, Hélène found herself suddenly enveloped in a rose-colored fog, which hid one part of the furniture from her, then was dissipated, allowing her to see, at the farther end of her room, "a strange hall, lighted with rose-colored globes fastened to the wall." Nearer to her appeared a table suspended in the air, and a man in Martian costume, who wrote with a kind of nail fastened to his right index-finger. "I lean towards this man; I wish to place my left hand on this imaginary table, but my hand falls into empty space, and I have great difficulty in restoring it to its normal position. It was stiff, and for some moments felt very weak." Happily the idea occurred to her to take pencil and paper and copy "the characters which the Martian, whom I had seen several times before [Ramié], traced; and with extreme difficulty—since they were much smaller than mine—I succeeded in reproducing them" (the Martian text of Fig. 31). "All this lasted about a quarter of an hour. I went immediately to bed, and saw nothing more that evening, nor on the following day."

*39. **Ramié** **pondé** **acâmi** **andélir** **téri** **antéch**
Ramié, *savant* *astronome,* *apparaîtra* *comme* *hier*
iri **é** **vi** **anâ.** **riz** **vi** **banâ** **mirâ̰** **ti** **Ramié** **ni**
souvent *à* *toi* *maintenant.* *Sur* *toi* *trois* *adieux* *de* *Ramié* *et*
Astané. **évaï** **divinée**
Astané. *Sois* *heureuse!*
Ramié, learned astronomer, will appear as yesterday often to thee now. Upon thee three adieux from Ramié and Astané, Be happy!

Graphic. April 1, 1899 (translated June 4).— "Again, on going to bed at five minutes past ten, a new vislon of the personage seen day before yesterday [Ramié]. I thought he was about to speak, but no sound issued from his lips. I quickly take pencil and paper, and feel my right arm seized by him, and I begin to trace the strange handwriting attached hereto (see Fig. 32). He is very affectionate; his bearing, his look, everything breathes both goodness and strangeness. He leaves me really charmed."

40. **Ramié** **ébanâ** **dizênâ** **zivênié** **ni** **bi** **vraïni**
Ramié, *lentement,* *profondément,* *étudie,* *et* *son* *désir*
assilé **né** **ten** **ti** **rès** **kalâmé** **astané** **êzi** **dabé** **né** **zi**
immense *est* *près* *de* *se* *accomplir.* *Astané* *mon* *maître* *est* *là*
med **lé** **godané** **ni** **ankôné** **évaï** **bané** **zizazi** **divinée**
pour *me* *aider* *et* *réjouir.* *Sois* *trois* *fois* *heureuse!*
Ramié, slowly, deeply studies, and his great desire is near to being accomplished. Astané, my master, is there to aid me and to rejoice. Mayst thou be thrice happy!

Auditive. June 4, 1899 (translated same seance).—Hemisomnambulism, in which Hélène, without having a vision, hears a voice addressing words to her, from which, with some difficulty, she collected the preceding sentences.

41. To these texts, forming sentences, in order to complete the whole, some isolated words must be added, gathered on various occasions, the meaning of which is obtained with sufficient certainty, either from the French context in which they were framed, or from Hélène's description

of the objects which they designated. These words are **chèke**, *papier* ("paper"); **chinit**, *bague* ("ring"); **asnète**, *espèce de paravent* ("kind of screen"). **Anini Nikaîné,** proper name of a little girl (see p. 113), probably the Martian sister of Esenale, who floats beside her, invisible to her, and watches over her during an illness, after the fashion of spirit protectors. **Béniel,** proper name of our earth, as seen from Mars (which is called **Durée** in texts 7 and 9).

III. REMARKS ON THE MARTIAN LANGUAGE

Provided the reader has given some attention to the foregoing texts, if only to the two first, he undoubtedly will have been easily satisfied as to the pretended language of the planet Mars, and perhaps will be astonished that I have spent so much time upon it. But, as many of the *habitués* of the seances of Mlle. Smith—and, naturally, Mlle. Smith herself—hold seriously to its authenticity, I cannot absolve myself from stating why the "Martian" is, in my opinion, only an infantile travesty of French. Even in default of the astronomical importance which is claimed for it on the authority of Léopold, this idiom preserves all the psychological interest which attaches to automatic products of subconscious activities of the mind, and it well deserves some minutes of examination.

It is necessary at the start to render this justice to the Martian (I continue to designate it by that name, for the sake of convenience)—namely, that it is, indeed, a language and not a simple jargon or gibberish of vocal noises produced at the hazard of the moment without any stability. It cannot be denied the following characteristics—First: It is a harmony of clearly articulated sounds, grouped so as to form words. Secondly: These words when pronounced express definite ideas. Thirdly, and finally: Connection of the words with the ideas is continuous; or, to put it differently, the signification of the Martian terms is permanent and is maintained (apart from slight inconsistencies, to which I will return later on) from one end to the other of the texts which have been collected in the course of these three years.[3] I will add that in speaking fluently and somewhat quickly, as Hélène sometimes does in somnambulism (texts 4, 11, 15, etc.), it has an acoustic quality altogether its own, due to the predomi-

---

[3] If it is objected that the Martian lacks the essential character of a language—that is to say, a practical sanction by use; by the fact of its serving as a means of communication between living beings—I will not answer, like Mlle. Smith, that after all we know nothing about that, but will simply say that the social side of the question does not concern us here. Even if Volapük and Esperanto are not used, they are none the less languages, and the Martian has, in regard to its artificial construction, the psychological superiority of being a natural language, spontaneously created, without the conscious participation, reflective or willing, of a normal personality.

nance of certain sounds, and has a peculiar intonation difficult to describe. Just as one distinguishes by ear foreign languages which one does not understand, the whole dialect possessing a peculiar accent which causes it to be recognized, so in this case one perceives, from the first syllables uttered, whether Hélène is speaking Hindoo or Martian, according to the musical connection, the rhythm, the choice of consonants and vowels belonging to each of the two idioms. In this the Martian, indeed, bears the stamp of a natural language. It is not the result of a purely intellectual calculation, but influences of an aesthetic order, emotional factors, have combined in its creation and instinctively directed the choice of its assonances and favorite terminations. The Martian language has certainly not been fabricated in cold blood during the normal, habitual, French (so to speak) state of Mlle. Smith, but it bears in its characteristic tonalities the imprint of a peculiar emotional disposition, of a fixed humor or psychical Orientation, of a special condition of mind, which may be called, in one word, the *Martian* state of Hélène. The secondary personality, which takes pleasure in linguistic games, seems, indeed, to be the same, at its source, as that which delights in the exotic and highly colored visual images of the planet of red rocks, and which animates the personages of the Martian romance.

A glance at the *ensemble* of the foregoing texts shows that Martian, as compared with French, is characterized by a superabundance of *é*, *ê*, and *i's*, and a scarcity of diphthongs and the nasal sounds. A more accurate statistical table of sounded vowels which strike the ear in reading aloud the Martian texts on the one hand, and their translation into French on the other, gives me the percentages of Table I., which follows. But it is well known that the vowels are distinguished, from the acoustic point of view, by certain fixed characteristic sounds, and that they are distributed at different heights in the musical scale.

i and *é* are the highest, *a* and *o* occupy the middle place, *u* and *ou* are found in the lower part of the scale. In adding to the latter, therefore, the nasals, which are always hollow, and also *e* mute. Table I. divides itself into the three groups of Table II. from the point of view of height and sonorousness. It is, therefore, clear that the Martian is of a general tonality much higher than the French; since, while the two languages have almost the same proportion of middle vowels, the low, hollow, or mute sounds, which constitute almost one-half of the French vowels, amount to scarcely one-twelfth in Martian, in which the high sounds, on the contrary, represent in bulk three-quarters of the vowels, against one-third only in the French. On the other hand, researches in the field of colored audition have demonstrated that a close psychological connection exists, based on certain emotional analogies and an equivalence of organic reactions, between the high sounds and the bright or vivid colors, and the low

TABLE I
Statistics of Vowel Sounds

		Martian	French
a	%	16.3	13.7
e mute (like those of *casemate*)	"	3.6	20.8
e closed or half-closed (like those of *hébété, rêvé*) ..	"	36.9	14.3
e open (like that of *aloès*)	"	2.1	4.6
i	"	34.3	13.4
o	"	2.3	5.7
u	"	2.3	3.1
Diphthongs and nasals (*ou, oi, eu, an, in, on, un*) ..	"	2.1	24.5

or hollow sounds and the sombre colors. But this same correlation is found in the somnambulistic life of Mlle. Smith, between the brilliant, luminous, highly colored visions which characterize her Martian cycle and the language of the high and sonorous vowels which gushes forth in the same cycle. It is allowable to conclude from this that it is really the same emotional atmosphere which bathes and envelops these varied psychological products, the same personality which gives birth to these visual and phonetic automatisms. The imagination cannot, however, as is easily understood, create its fiction out of nothing; it is obliged to borrow its materials from individual experience. The Martian tableaux are, therefore, only a reflection of the terrestrial world, but of that part of it which possesses the most warmth and brilliancy—the Orient; in the same way, the Martian language is only French metamorphosed and carried to a higher diapason.

I admit, then, that Martian is a language, and a natural language, in the sense that it is automatically brought forth in the emotional state, or by the secondary personality, which is the source of all the remainder of the cycle without the conscious participation of Mlle. Smith. It remains for me now to mention some of the characteristics which seem to indicate that the inventor of this subliminal linguistic work had never known any idiom other than French, that it is much more sensible to verbal expression than to logical connection of ideas, and that it possesses in an eminent degree that infantile and puerile character which I have already pointed out in the author of the Martian romance. It now becomes necessary to examine rapidly this unknown language, from the point of view of its phonetics and its writing, its grammatical form, its syntax, and its vocabulary.

1. Martian Phonetics and Handwriting

Martian is composed of articulate sounds, all of which, consonants as well as vowels, exist in French. While on this globe languages geographically

TABLE II
Grouping from Point of View of Height

		Martian	French
Vowels, high (*i* and *e* sounded)	%	73.3	32.3
Vowels, middle (*a* and *o*)	"	18.6	19.4
Vowels, low or hollow (*u;* diphthongs and nasals; *e* mute)	"	8.0	48.4

our neighbors (not to mention those farther away) differ each from the other by certain special sounds—*ch*, German, *th*, English, etc.—the language of the planet Mars does not permit of similar phonetic originalities. It seems, on the contrary, poorer in this respect than the French. As yet I have not found in it the hissing *j* or *ge* (as in *juger*), nor the double sound *x*.* Martian phonetics, in a word, are only an incomplete reproduction of French phonetics.

The Martian alphabet, compared with ours, suggests a remarkable analogy. The graphic form of the characters is certainly novel, and no one would divine our letters in these designs of exotic aspect. Nevertheless, each Martian sign (with the single exception of that of the plural) corresponds to a French sign, although the inverse is not the case, which indicates that here again we are in the presence of a feeble imitation of our system of handwriting.

The twelve written texts upon which I base my comparison comprise about 300 words (of which 160 are different) and 1200 signs. There are altogether twenty-one different letters, all of which have their exact equivalents in the French alphabet, which also has five others which Martian lacks; *j* and *x*, of which the sounds themselves have not been observed, and *q*, *w*, and *y*, of which there is a double use, with *k*, *v*, and *i*. This reduction of graphic material manifests itself in two other details. First, there are neither accents nor punctuation marks, with the exception of a certain sign, resembling the French circumflex, used sometimes in the shape of a point at the end of phrases. In the second place, each letter has only one form, the diversity of capitals and small letters not seeming to exist in Martian. Of ciphers we know nothing.

There are still three small peculiarities to notice:

1. In default of capitals, the initials of proper names are often distinguished by a point placed above the ordinary character.
2. In the case of double letters the second is replaced by a point situated at the right of the first.
3. Finally, there exists, in order to designate the plural of substantives and of some adjectives, a special graphic sign, answering to nothing in the pronunciation and having the form of a small vertical undulation, which reminds

one a little of an amplification of the French s, the usual mark of the plural in French. These peculiarities, outside the ordinary form of the letters, constitute the sum total of ingenuity displayed in Martian handwriting.

It must be added that this handwriting, which is not ordinarily inclined, goes from left to right, like the French. All the letters are of nearly the same height, except that the *i* is much smaller, and that they remain isolated from each other; their assembly into words and phrases offers to the eye a certain aspect of Oriental hieroglyphic inscriptions.

The Martian alphabet never having been revealed as such, we are ignorant of the order in which the letters follow each other. It would seem as though the letters had been invented by following the French alphabet, at least in great part, if one may judge according to the analogies of form of the Martian characters corresponding to certain series of French letters: compare *a* and *b*; *g* and *h*; *s* and *t*; and also the succession *k, l, m, n*.*

It is in the phonetic value of the letters—that is to say, in the correspondence of the articulated sounds with the graphic signs—that the essentially French nature of the Martian may be seen. The only notable difference to be pointed out here between the two languages is the much greater simplicity of the Martian orthography, resulting in the employment of no useless letters. All are pronounced, even the final consonants, such as *s, n, z*, etc., which are generally silent in French. This gives the impression that the Martian handwriting is moulded on the spoken language, and is only the notation of the articulated sounds of the latter by the most economical means. In so far it realizes the type of a handwriting truly phonetic—that is to say, where each sign corresponds to a certain elementary articulation, constant and invariable, and vice versa. It is full, on the other hand, of equivocations, of exceptions, of irregularities, which make one and the same letter to have very different pronunciations, according to circumstances, and, reciprocally, which causes the same sound to be written in different ways without our being able to perceive any rational explanation for all these ambiguities—were it not for the fact that the very same thing is to be found in French!

Martian is only disguised French. I will mention only the most curious and striking coincidences, all the more striking from the fact that the field from which I have collected them is very limited, being confined to the dozen texts written and pronounced, which contain only 160 different words.

The simple vowels of the Martian alphabet correspond exactly to the five French vowels, *a, e, i, o, u*, and have the same shades of pronunciation.*

The Martian *c* plays the triple part which it also fulfils in French. The *s* has the same capricious character as in our language. It is generally hard, but between two vowels it becomes soft, like *z*.

2. Grammatical Forms

The *ensemble* of the texts which we possess does not as yet permit us to make a Martian grammar. Certain indications, however, warrant the prediction that the rules of that grammar, if it ever sees the light of day, will be only the counterpart of, or a parody upon, those of French.

Here, for example, is a list of personal pronouns, articles, possessive adjectives, etc., which have appeared hitherto:

je cé	*me* le, *moi* si	*ton* che	*ce* tès, *ces* têsé	*de* ti
tu dé	*te* di, *toi* vi	*ta* chée	*cette* tês, têsée	*des* tié
il hed	*se* rès, *lui* pi	*tes* chi	*le* (pron.) zé	*du* té
nous nini	*mon* êzi	*son* bi	*qui* kâ, *que* ké	*au* ine
vous sini	*ma* êzé	*sa* bé	*quel* kiz, *quelle* kizé	
ils hed	*mes* éziné	*ses* bée	*un* mis, *une* misé	
on idé	*notre* iche		*le, la les* (art.) zé, zi, zée.	

There are some texts where the feminine is derived from the masculine by the addition of an *e* mute, and the plural by the small, unpronounced sign, which has all the appearance of being a reminiscence of French *s*.*

Between these two languages there is another order of points of contact, of a more special interest, because it shows the preponderating role which verbal images have often played in the making of Martian to the prejudice of the intrinsic, logical nature of the ideas. I should say that at all times the Martian translates the French word, allowing itself to be guided by auditive analogies without regard to the real meaning, in such a way that we are surprised to discover in the idiom of the planet Mars the same peculiarities of homonyms as in French. It is also the case that two vocables identical as to pronunciation, but of entirely heterogeneous signification, as the preposition *à* and the *a* of the verb *avoir*, are rendered in Martian by the same word, *é*.*

Other curious coincidences are to be noted. In French the conjunction *et* only slightly differs, from the point of view of phonic images, from the verb *est;* in Martian also there is a great analogy between **ni** and **né**, which translate these two words. Between the past participle **nié** of the verb *to be* and the conjunction **ni** there is only the difference of an *é*, just as between their French equivalents *été* and *et*.

It must be admitted that all these coincidences would be very extraordinary if they were purely fortuitous.

3. Construction and Syntax

The order of the words is absolutely the same in Martian as in French. This identity of construction of phrases is pursued sometimes into the minutest details, such as the division or amputation of the negation *ne . . . pas* (texts 15 and 17), and also the introduction of a useless letter in Martian to correspond to a French euphemistic *t* (see text 15), **Kèvi berimir m hed,** *quand reviendra-t-il?* ("when will he return?")

If it is admitted hypothetically that the succession of words, such as is given us in these texts, is not the natural ordering of the Martian language, but an artificial arrangement, like that of juxtalinear translations for the use of pupils, the very possibility of that correspondence absolutely word for word would remain an extraordinary fact without a parallel, since there is not a single language that I know of in which each term of the French phrase is always rendered by *one* term, neither more nor less, of the foreign phrase. The hypothesis referred to is, moreover, inadmissible, since the Martian texts, of which Esenale gives the literal translation, were not previously arranged by him with that end in view; they are the identical words which Mlle. Smith heard and noted in her visions, often weeks and months before Esenale repeats them for the purpose of translating them, and which constitute the conversation, as such, taken from life, of the Martian personages. We must conclude from this that these in their elocution follow step by step and word by word the order of the French language, which amounts almost to saying that they speak a French the sounds of which have simply been changed.

4. Vocabulary

From an etymological point of view, I have not been able to distinguish any rule of derivation, even partial, that would permit the suspicion that the Martian words had come from French words, according to some law. Apart from the entire first text, where it is difficult to deny that the people of Mars have stolen French terms of politeness, at the same time distorting them, no clear resemblance is to be seen between Martian words and the French equivalents; at most, there are traces of borrowing, like **merve**, *superbe*, which might have been abridged from *merveille* (text 25), and **vechi**, an imitation of *voir*.

Still less does the Martian lexicon betray the influence of other known languages (at least to my knowledge). A term which suggests such similarity is hardly ever met with—*e.g.*, **modé**, *mère* ("mother"), and **gude** *bon* ("good"), cause us to think of German or English words; **animina** ("existence") is like *anima;* various forms of the verbs *être* and *vivre* "to be" and "to live," **êvé, évaï, essat,** recall the Latin *esse* or the Hebrew *évé*, and that passage of the Biblical story of the Creation where Eve is called the mother of all living beings. A linguist who happened to be at the same time a savant and a humorist would doubtless succeed in lengthening this list of etymologies, after the mode of the eighteenth century. But, *cui* *bono?* In that rarity of points of contact between the idioms of our terrestrial sphere and the Martian glossary, an argument might be found in favor of the extra-terrestrial origin of the latter, if, on the other hand, it did not seem to betray the influence of the French language from the fact that a notable proportion of its words reproduce in a suspicious manner the same number of syllables or letters as their French equivalents; note, for example, besides the terms of politeness already mentioned, the words **tarvine**, *langage*; **haudan**, *maison*; **dodé**, *ceci*; **valini**, *visage*, etc., and the great majority of the little words, such as **cé**, *je*; **ké**, *que*; **ti**, *de*; **dé**, *tu*; etc.

With the exception of such examples as these, it must be acknowledged that there is no trace of parentage, filiation, of any resemblance whatever between the Martian and French vocabularies, which forms a singular contrast to the close identity which we have established between the two languages in the preceding paragraphs.

This apparent contradiction carries its explanation in itself, and gives us the key to Martian. This fantastic idiom is evidently the naïve and somewhat puerile work of an infantile imagination, to which occurred the idea of creating a new language, and which, while giving to its lucubrations certain strange and unknown appearances, without doubt caused them to run in the accustomed moulds of the only real language of which it had cognizance. The Martian of Mlle. Smith, in other words, is the product of a brain or a personality which certainly has taste and aptitude for linguistic exercises, but which never knew that French takes little heed of the logical connection of ideas, and did not take the trouble to make innovations in the matter of phonetics, of grammar, or of syntax.*

The process of creation of Martian seems to have consisted in simply taking certain French phrases as such and replacing each word by some other chosen at random.* That is why, especially in the texts at the beginning, the structure of French words is recognized under the Martian. The author herself was undoubtedly struck by it, and from that time exerted herself to complicate her lexicon, to render her words more and more unrecognizable.

This research of originality—which, however, she has never extended beyond the purely material part of the language, never having an idea that there might be other differences in languages—represents an effort of imagination with which she must be credited. Homage must also be rendered to the labor of memorizing, which the making of a dictionary has necessitated. She has sometimes, indeed, fallen into errors; the stability of her vocabulary has not always been perfect. But, finally, after the first hesitation and independently of some later confusions, it gives evidence of a praiseworthy terminological consistency, and which no doubt in time, and with some suggestive encouragement, would result in the elaboration of a very complete language—perhaps even of several languages, as we may augur from text 33, to which we shall return in the following chapter.*

5. Style

It remains to investigate the style. If it is true that "manners make the man"—that is to say, not the impersonal and abstract understanding, but the concrete character, the individual temperament, the humor and emotional vibration—we ought to expect to find in the style of the Martian texts the same special stamp which distinguishes the visions, the sound of the language, the handwriting, the personages—in short, the entire romance, that is to say, the curious mixture of Oriental exoticism and of childish puerility of which the secondary personality of Mlle. Smith, at work in this cycle, seems to be composed. It is difficult to pronounce upon these matters of vague aesthetic impression rather than of precise observation; but, as well as I can judge, there seems to me to be in the phraseology of the texts collected an indefinable something which corresponds well with the general character of the entire dream. As these words are evidently first thought in French—then travesties in Martian by a substitution of sounds, the choice of which, as has been seen, apropos of the high tonality of this language, reflects the general emotional disposition—it is, naturally, under their French aspect that we ought to consider them in judging of their actual style. Unfortunately, we do not know how far the translation given by Esenale is identical with the primitive original; certain details seem to hint that there are divergences sometimes. However that may be, it is clearly to be perceived that the literary form of the majority of the texts (taken in French) is more akin to poetry than to prose. While no one of them is in verse, properly speaking, the large number of hemistiches which are met with, the frequency of inversion, the choice of terms, the abundance of exclamations and of broken phrases, betray a great intensity of sentimental and poetic emotion. The same character is found, with a strong shade of exotic and archaic originality, in the formulas of salutation and farewell ("be happy to-day," "three adieux to thee," etc.), as well as in many expressions and terms of phrases which rather recall the obscure and metaphorical parlance of the Orient than the dry precision of our language of to-day (*"il garde un peu de ton être; cet élément mystérieux, immense,"* etc.)

If, now, it is recollected that everywhere in literary history poetry precedes prose, imagination comes before reason, and the lyric style before the didactic, a conclusion according with that of the preceding paragraphs is reached. Which is, that, by its figures and its style, the Martian language (or the French phrases which serve it for a skeleton) seems to bring to us the echo of a past age, the reflex of a primitive state of mind, from which Mlle. Smith to-day finds herself very far removed in her ordinary and normal states of mind.*

IV. MLLE. SMITH AND THE INVENTOR OF MARTIAN

The preceding analysis of the Martian language furnishes its support to the considerations which the content of the romance has already suggested to us in regard to its author (p. 120). To imagine that by twisting the sounds of French words a new language capable of standing examination could actually be created, and to wish to make it pass for that of the planet Mars, would be the climax of silly fatuity or of imbecility were it not simply a trait of naive candor well worthy of the happy age of childhood.

The whole Martian cycle brings us into the presence of an infantine personality exuberant of imagination, sharing, as to their light, color, Oriental exoticism, the aesthetic tendencies of the actual normal personality of Mlle. Smith, but contrasting with it outside its puerile character in two points to be noted.

First: It takes a special pleasure in linguistic discussions and the fabrication of unknown idioms while Hélène has neither taste nor facility for the study of languages, which she cordially detests and in which she has never met with success.

Secondly: Notwithstanding this aversion, Hélène possesses a certain knowledge, either actual or potential, of German—in which her parents caused her to take lessons for three years—whereas the author of Martian evidently knows only French. It is, in fact, difficult to believe that, if that author had only a very slight knowledge of the German language (so different from the French by the construction of its sentences, pronunciation, its three genders, etc.), that some reminiscences of it, at least, would not have slipped into its lucubrations. I infer from this that the Martian secondary personality which gives evidence of a linguistic activity so fecund, but so completely subject to the structural forms of the mother-tongue, represents a former stage, ulterior to the epoch at which Hélène commenced the study of German.

If one reflects, on the other hand, on the great facility which Mlle. Smith's father seems to have possessed for languages (see p. 18), the question naturally arises whether in the Martian we are not in the presence of an awakening and momentary display of an hereditary faculty, dormant under the normal personality of Hélène, but which she has not profited from in an effective manner. It is a fact of common observation that talents and aptitudes often skip a generation and seem to pass directly from the grandparents to the grandchildren, forgetting the intermediate link.* Who knows whether Mlle. Smith, some day, having obtained Léopold's consent to her marriage, may not cause the polygot aptitudes of her father to bloom again with greater brilliancy, for the glory of science, in a brilliant line of philologists and linguists of genius?

Meanwhile, and without even invoking a special latent talent in Hélène's case, the Martian may be attributed to a survival or a reawakening under the lash of mediumistic hypnoses of that general function, common to all human beings, which is at the root of language and manifests itself with the more spontaneity and vigor as we mount higher towards the birth of peoples and individuals.

Ontogenesis, say the biologists, reproduces in abridged form and *grosso-modo* phylogenesis; each being passes through stages analogous to those through which the race itself passes; and it is known that the first ages of ontogenic evolution—the embryonic period, infancy, early youth—are more favorable than later periods and adult age to the ephemeral reappearances of ancestral tendencies, which would hardly leave any trace upon a being who had already acquired his organic development.* The "poet who died young" in each one of us is only the most common example of those atavic returns of tendencies and of emotions which accompanied the beginnings of humanity, and remain the appanage of infant peoples, and which cause a fount of variable energy in each individual in the spring-time of his life, to congeal or disappear sooner or later with the majority; all children are poets, and that in the original, the most extended, acceptation of the term. They create, they imagine, they construct—and language is not the least of their creations.

I conclude from the foregoing that the very fact of the reappearance of that activity in the Martian states of Hélène is a new indication of the infantile, primitive nature left behind in some way and long since passed by her ordinary personality, of the subliminal strata which mediumistic autohypnotization with her puts in ebullition and causes to mount to the surface. There is also a perfect accord between the puerile character of the Martian romance, the poetic and archaic charms of its style, and the audacious and naive fabrication of its unknown language.

CHAPTER SEVEN

The Martian Cycle (Concluded): The Ultra-Martian

ALL THINGS become wearisome at last, and the planet Mars is no exception to the rule. The subliminal imagination of Mlle. Smith, however, will probably never tire of its lofty flights in the society of Astané, Esenale, and their associates. I myself, I am ashamed to acknowledge, began, in 1898, to have enough of the Martian romance.

Once having satisfied myself as to the essential nature of the Martian language, I did not desire to make a profound study of it, and since the texts had made their appearance so slowly, for two years, as to threaten to continue during the remainder of my natural existence, as well as that of the medium, without coming to an end; finding, on the other hand, that the texts, considered as simple psychological curiosities, varied but little and were at length likely to become burdensome, I decided to try some experiment which, without drying up their source, might at least break through this monotony. Up to that time, without giving a positive opinion as to the Martian, I had always manifested a very real interest in these communications, as well as in Mlle. Smith in her waking state, and in Léopold in his incarnations. Both of these showed themselves fully persuaded of the objective verity of this language, and of the visions which accompanied it. Léopold had not ceased, from the first day, to affirm its strictly Martian authenticity. Hélène, without maintaining absolutely that it came from Mars rather than from any other planet, shared the same faith in the extra-terrestrial origin of these messages; and, as appeared from many details of her conversations and conduct, she saw in it a revelation of the loftiest import, which might some day cause "all the discoveries of M. Flammarion" to sink into insignificance. What would happen if I made up my mind to strike this strange conviction a telling blow, and demonstrate that the pretended Martian was only a chimera, a product, pure and simple, of somnambulistic autosuggestion?

My first tentative experiment, addressed to Léopold, had no appreciable influence on the course of the Martian cycle. It was at the seance of February 13, 1898. Hélène was profoundly asleep, and Léopold was conversing with us by gestures of the arm and spelling on the fingers. I categorically informed him of my certainty that the Martian was of terrestrial fabrication, and that a comparison with the French proved it so to be. As Léopold responded by emphatic gestures of dissent, I detailed to him some evidences, among others the accord of the two languages as to their pronunciation of *ch*, as to the homonym of the pronoun and article *le*. He listened to me, and seemed to understand my arguments but he refused to admit the force of these characteristic coincidences, and said: "There are some things more extraordinary," and was unwilling to give up the authenticity of the Martian. We stood by our respective opinions, and the later texts do not show any trace of our interview. It seemed, therefore, that it was not through the intervention of Léopold that a modification of the Martian romance was to be suggested.

I allowed some months to pass, then tried a discussion with Hélène while she was awake. On two occasions, in October, 1898, I expressed to her my utter skepticism as to the Martian. The first time, on the 6th of October, in a visit which I made to her outside of any seance, I confined myself to certain general objections to it, to which she replied, in substance, as follows: First, that this unknown language, by reason of its intimate union with the visions, and in spite of its possible resemblances to the French, must necessarily be Martian, if the visions are. Then nothing seriously opposes that actual origin of the visions, and, consequently, of the language itself; since there are two methods of explaining this knowledge of a far-off world—namely, communications properly *spiritistic* (*i.e.*, from spirits to spirits, without material intermediary) the reality of which cannot be held to be doubtful; *and clairvoyance*, that faculty, or undeniable sixth sense, of mediums which permits them both to see and hear at any distance. Finally, that she did not hold tenaciously to the distinctly Martian origin of that strange dream, provided it is conceded that it comes from somewhere outside herself, it being inadmissible to regard it as the work of her subconsciousness, since she had not, during her ordinary life, absolutely any perception whatever, any sentiment, not the shadow of a hint of that alleged interior work of elaboration to which I persisted in attributing it against all the evidence and all common-sense.

Some days later (October 16th), as Mlle. Smith, perfectly awake after an afternoon seance, passed the evening at my house, and seemed to be in the fulness of her normal state,* I returned to the charge with more of insistence.

I had until then always avoided showing her the full translation of the Martian texts, as well as the alphabet, and she only knew by sight, so to speak, the Martian handwriting, and was ignorant of the value of the letters.

This time I explained to her in detail the secrets of the language, its superficial originalities and fundamental resemblances to French; the frequent occurrence of *i* and *e*, its puerile construction, identical with French, even to the slipping in of a superfluous euphonic **m** between the words **bérmier** and **hed** in order to imitate the expression *reviendra-t-il?* its numerous caprices of phonetics and homonyms, evident reflexes of those to which we are accustomed, etc. I added that the visions seemed to me to be also suspicious through their improbable analogies with that which we see on our globe. Supposing that the houses, the vegetation, and the people of Mars were constructed on the same fundamental plan as those here below, it was nevertheless very doubtful whether they had the same proportions and typical aspect; in short, astronomy teaches us that on Mars the physical conditions—the length of the year, the intensity of weight, etc.—are all other than with us: the last point, in particular, should act on all the products, natural and artificial, in such a way as to alter greatly the dimensions as well as the proportions of height and size which are familiar to us. I observed, again, that there are doubtless on Mars, as on the earth, a great variety of idioms, and the singular chance which made Esenale speak a language so similar to French was very astonishing. I concluded, finally, by remarking that all this was easily explicable, as well as the Oriental aspect of the Martian landscapes and the generally infantile character of that romance, if it were regarded as a work of pure imagination, due to a secondary personality or to a dream state of Mlle. Smith herself, who recognized having always had "great taste for that which is original and connected with the Orient."

For more than an hour Hélène followed my demonstration with a lively interest. But to each new reason, after having appeared at first a little disconcerted by it, she did not hesitate to repeat, like a triumphal refrain and as an unanswerable argument, that science is not infallible; that no scientist has yet been on Mars; and that consequently it is impossible to affirm with any certainty that affairs there are not conformable to her visions. To my conclusion she replied that, as far as concerns Mars or anything else, her revelations did not, in any case, spring from sources within herself, and that she did not understand why I was so implacable against that which is the most simple supposition, that of their authenticity, or why I should prefer to it this silly and absurd hypothesis of an underlying self plotting in her, unknown to her, this strange mystification.

Maintaining all the while that my deductions appeared to me strictly correct, I felt bound to admit that science is not infallible, and that a voyage to Mars could alone solve all our doubts as to what takes place there. We parted good friends, but that conversation left me with a very clear impression of the complete uselessness of my efforts to make Mlle. Smith share my conceptions of the subliminal consciousness. But this, however, neither surprises nor grieves me, since from her point of view it is perhaps better that she thus believes.

The following shows, however, that my reasonings on that evening, sterile in appearance, were not without effect. If they have not modified Mlle. Smith's *conscious* manner of seeing, and, above all, the opinion of Léopold, they have nevertheless penetrated to the profound strata where the Martian visions are elaborated, and, acting there as a leaven, have been the source of new and unexpected developments. This result brilliantly corroborates the idea that the whole Martian cycle is only a product of suggestion and autosuggestion. Just as formerly the regret of M. Lemaître at not knowing that which passes on other planets had furnished the first germ of that lucubration, so now my criticisms and remarks on the language and peoples of that upper world served as a point of departure for new circuits of Hélène's subliminal imagination. If, in fact, the content of our discussion of the 16th of October, which I have above briefly summed up, is compared with the visions of the following months (see beginning with text 30), it is clear that these latter contain an evident beginning of an answer, and are an attempt to satisfy the questions which I raised. A very curious attempt is there made, naive and infantine, like the whole Martian romance, to escape the defects of which I complained on that occasion, not by modifying and correcting it—that would have been to reverse and to contradict herself—but by going beyond it in some sort, and by superposing upon it a new construction, an *ultra-Martian* cycle, if I may be permitted that expression, hinting at the same time that it unfolds itself on some undetermined planet still farther away than Mars, and that it does not constitute an absolutely independent narrative, but that it is grafted on the primitive Martian romance.

The suggestive effect of my objections of the 16th of October was not immediate, but became a work of incubation. Text 30, coming the following week, differed but slightly from the preceding, save for the absence of a euphonic letter, which, however, had been better in place between the words **bindié idé**, *trouve-t-on*, than in the **bèrimir m hed** of text 15, to which I had attracted Hélène's attention; possibly it is allowable to regard this little detail as a first result of my criticisms. The apparition, a little later, of a new Martian personage, Ramié, who promised Hélène some near revelations as to a planet not otherwise specified (text 31), proves that the ultra-Martian dream was in process of subconscious ripening, but it did not burst forth until the 2d of November (seventeen days after the suggestion with which I connect it), in that curious scene in which Ramié reveals to Mlle. Smith an unsuspected and grotesque world, the language of which singularly differs from the usual Martian. The detailed description of that strange vision, which Hélène sent me, is worth the trouble of citing (see also texts 32 to 35):

> I was awakened, and arose about twenty minutes ago. It was about a quarter-past six in the morning, and I was getting ready to sew. Then, for an instant, I noticed that my lamp was going out, and I ended by not seeing anything more. At the same moment I felt my waist clasped, strongly held by an invisible arm. I then saw myself surrounded by a rose-colored light, which generally shows

itself when a Martian vision is coming. I quickly took paper and pencil, which are always within reach on my toilet-table, and placed these two things on my knees, in case some words should come to be noted.

Hardly were these preparations concluded when I saw at my side a man of Martian visage and costume. It was, in fact, the personage [Ramié] who had clasped my waist with his left arm, showing me with his right hand a tableau, at first indistinct, but which finally outlined itself quite clearly. He spoke also some sentences, which I can note very well, it seems to me [text 32, where Ramié attracts the attention of Hélène to one of the worlds which surround him and makes her see strange beings.]

I saw then a section of country peopled by men altogether different from those which inhabit our globe. The tallest of all were three feet high, and the majority were an inch or two shorter. Their hands were immense, about ten inches long by eight broad; they were ornamented with very long black nails. Their feet also were of great size.

I did not see any tree, any bit of verdure. I saw a medley of houses, or rather cabins, of the most simple style, all low, long, without windows or doors; and each house had a little tunnel, about ten feet long [see Fig. 33] running from it into the earth.

The roofs were flat, supplied with chimneys, or tubes. The men, with arms and bodies bare, had for all clothing only a sort of skirt reaching to the waist and supported by a kind of suspenders thrown over the shoulders, which were apparently very strong. Their heads were very short, being about three inches high by six inches broad, and were close shaven. They had very small eyes, immense mouths, noses like beans. Everything was so different from what we are accustomed to in our world that I should have almost believed it to be an animal rather than a man I saw there, had there not suddenly issued from the lips of one of them some words, which, fortunately—I hardly know how—I was able to note down. This vision lasted a quarter of an hour. Then I found my waist liberated, but my right hand was still firmly held, in order to trace strange characters on the paper (text 34, adieux of Ramié to Hélène).

A little later there was a continuation, or an abortive repetition, of the same vision; the table did not appear distinctly, and Ramié (text 35) contented himself with teaching Hélène things concerning a world beyond, a near neighbor to Mars, and a coarser language, of which Astané alone could furnish a translation. This is, in effect, what took place two weeks later: Astané incarnated himself with gestures and peculiar spasmodic movements, and repeated (in Hélène's ordinary voice) the barbaric text, followed word by word by its Martian equivalents, which Esenale, in turn, succeeding Astané, interpreted in French, in his customary manner. Léopold also informed us, in reply to a question of one of the sitters, that this uncouth and primitive world was one of the smaller planets; but it

Fig. 33. Ultra-Martian houses. Drawn by Mlle. Smith after her vision of November 2, 1989.

is to be presumed that he would also have answered in the affirmative if he had been asked if it were called Phobos or Deimos; and, in short, one of the satellites of Mars would answer better than the asteroids to the globe "very near to ours," of which Ramié spoke.

Up to this point the ultra-Martian messages were confined to the preceding. The last texts obtained (37 to 40) seem to announce that the end has not been reached on that side, and cause us to hope for new revelations, when the astronomer Ramié, as the result of his having studied under the skilful direction of his master Astané, shall be in a position to make further discoveries in the Martian sky. Psychologically speaking, this amounts to saying that the process of latent incubation continues; a new ultra-Martian language is in a state of development in the subliminal depths. If it bursts forth some day, I shall hasten to bring it to the knowledge of the scientific world—in another edition of this book. For the present I limit myself to remarking how much the little ultra-Martian we possess already indicates the wish to answer my questions of the 16th of October.

I had accused the Martian dream of being a mere imitation, varnished with brilliant Oriental colors, of the civilized environment which surrounds us—and here is a world of terrifying grotesqueness, with black soil, from which all vegetation is banished, and the coarser people of which are more like beasts than human beings. I had insinuated that the people and things of that upper world ought really to have other dimensions and proportions than with us—and here are the inhabitants of that farther world veritable dwarfs, with heads twice as broad as they are high, and houses to match. I had made allusion to the probable existence of other languages, referred to the superabundance in Martian of *i* and *e*, impeached its syntax and its *ch*, borrowed from the French, etc.—and here is a language absolutely new, of a very peculiar rhythm, extremely rich in *a*, without any *ch* at all up to the present moment, and of which the construction is so different from the French that there is no method of discovering it.

This latter point, above all, seems to me to present in its apogee the character of childishness and puerility which clearly shows itself in that unexpected appendix to the Martian cycle, as in the entire cycle itself. Evidently the naïve subliminal philologist of Mlle. Smith has been struck by my criticisms on the identical order of the words in Martian and in French, and has endeavored to avoid that defect in her new effort at an unknown language.

But not knowing in just what syntax and construction consist, she has found nothing better to suit her purpose than the substitution of chaos for the natural arrangement of the terms in her thought and the fabrication of an idiom which had decidedly nothing in common with the French in this respect. Here is where the most beautiful disorder is practically a work of art. It has, moreover, succeeded, since, even with the double translation, Martian and French, of text 33, it is impossible to know exactly what is meant.

It is possibly the little girl *Etip* who is sad, and who *weeps* because the man *Top* has done *harm* to the *sacred* animal *Vanem* (which had *hidden, sick, under* some *green branches*), wishing to *enter in* to a *blue basket*. At least it could not have been the *branch*, the *man*, or the *basket* which was *sacred*, the child sick, etc.

The green branch is out of harmony with a world in which, according to Hélène's vision, there were neither trees nor verdure; but Esenale has not specified whether it means *vert* or *ver, vers*, etc., nor whether *caché* and *entré* are participles or infinitives. I leave this rebus to the reader and come to my conclusion, which will be brief, since it accords with the considerations already given at the end of the two preceding chapters.

The whole Martian cycle, with its special language and its ultra-Martian appendix, is only, at bottom, a vast product of occasional suggestions on the part of the environment, and of autosuggestions which have germinated, sprouted, and borne abundant fruit, under the influence of incitement from the outside, but without coming to amount to anything but a shapeless and confused mass, which imposes on one by its extent much more than its intrinsic worth, since it is supremely childish, puerile, insignificant in all aspects, save as a psychological curiosity. The author of this lucubration is not the real adult and normal personality of Mlle. Smith, who has very different characteristics, and who feels herself, in the face of these automatic messages, as though in the presence of something foreign, independent, exterior, and finds herself constrained to believe in their objective reality and in their authenticity. It seems, indeed, rather a former, infantine, less evolved state of Hélène's individuality, which has again come to light, renewed its life, and once more become active in her Martian somnambulisms.*

It is hardly necessary to add, in conclusion, that the whole spiritistic or occult hypothesis seems to me to be absolutely superfluous and unjustified in the case of the Martian of Mlle. Smith. Autosuggestibility set in motion by certain stimulating influences of the environment, as we come to see through the history of the ultra-Martian, amply suffices to account for this entire cycle.

The Hindoo Cycle

WHILE THE Martian romance is purely a work of fantasy, in which the creative imagination was able to allow itself free play through having no investigation to fear, the Hindoo cycle, and that of Marie Antoinette, having a fixed terrestrial setting, represent a labor of construction which was subjected from the start to very complex conditions of environments and epochs. To keep within the bounds of probability, not to be guilty of too many anachronisms, to satisfy the multiple demands of both logic and asthetics, formed a particularly dangerous undertaking, and one apparently altogether beyond the powers of a person without special instruction in such matters. The subconscious genius of Mlle. Smith has acquitted itself of the task in a remarkable manner, and has displayed in it a truly wonderful and delicate sense of historic possibilities and of local color.

The Hindoo romance, in particular, remains for those who have taken part in it a psychological enigma, not yet solved in a satisfactory manner, because it reveals and implies in regard to Hélène, a knowledge relative to the costumes and languages of the Orient, the actual source of which it has up to the present time not been possible to discover. All the witnesses of Mlle. Smith's Hindoo somnambulisms who are of the same opinion on that subject (several refrain from having any) unite in seeing in it a curious phenomenon of cryptomnesia, of reappearances of memories profoundly buried beneath the normal waking state, together with an indeterminate amount of imaginative exaggeration upon the canvas of actual facts. But by this name of cryptomnesia, or resurrection of latent memories, two singularly different things are understood. For me it is only a question of memories of her present life; and I see nothing of the supernormal in that. For while I have not yet succeeded in finding the key to the enigma, I do not doubt its existence, and I will mention later certain indications which seem to me to support my idea that the Asiatic notions of Mlle. Smith have a wholly natural origin.

For the observer inclined towards spiritism, on the contrary, the sleeping memory which is awakened in somnambulism is nothing less than that of a previous existence of Mlle. Smith, and that piquant explanation, which was first given by Léopold, profits in their eyes from the impossibility which I find in proving that it is anything else.

Doubtless, if one was familiar with all the incidents of Hélène's life from her earliest childhood, and if it were absolutely certain that her knowledge of India had not been furnished her from the outside, through the normal channel of the organs of sense, it would be necessary to seek elsewhere for the solution of the riddle, and to choose between the hypothesis of an atavic memory, hereditarily transmitted across fifteen generations, and actual telepathic communication with the brain of some Indian savant, or a spiritistic reincarnation. But we do not find ourselves in that position. There is nothing less known, in its details, than the daily life of Mlle. Smith in her childhood and youth. But, when all the feats of which the subconscious memory of our present life is capable are considered, it is not scientifically correct to have recourse to a pretended "anteriority," of which the only guarantee is the authority of Léopold, in order to explain the somnambulistic apparitions of facts of which Mlle. Smith in her waking state has no remembrance, I admit, but the origin of which may well have been hidden in the unknown recesses of her past life (reading, conversation, etc.).

The plot of the Hindoo romance, which I have already briefly hinted at on divers occasions, is as follows:

Hélène Smith was, at the end of the fourteenth century of our era, the daughter of an Arab sheik, possibly named Pirux, whom she left in order to become, under the name of Simandini, the eleventh wife of Prince Sivrouka Nayaka, of whom I have the honor to be the actual reincarnation. (I pray the reader once for all to pardon me the immodest role which has been imposed upon me in this affair against my will.)

This Sivrouka, who reigned over Kanara, and built there, in 1401, the fortress of Tchandraguiri, does not seem to have been a very accommodating person; although not bad at heart, and quite attached to his favorite wife, he had a wild humor and very uncouth manners. More could not be expected of an Asiatic potentate of that epoch. Simandini, nevertheless, passionately loved him, and at his death she was burned alive on his grave, after the fashion of Malabar.

Around these two principal personages are grouped some secondary figures, among others a faithful domestic named Adèl, and a little monkey, Mitidja, which Simandini had brought to India with her from Arabia; then the fakir Kanga, who occupies a much more important place in the Martian romance, in which we have seen him reincarnated as Astané, than in the Hindoo cycle.

Some other individuals, all masculine—Mougia, Miousa, Kangia, Kana —appear in obscure roles, concerning which nothing certain can be said.

The hypnoid states, in which this romance has manifested itself with Hélène, present the greatest variety and all degrees, from the perfect waking state (apparently), momentarily crossed by some visual or auditive hallucination, the memory of which is preserved intact and allows a detailed description, up to total somnambulism, with amnesia upon awakening, in which the most striking scenes of ecstasies or incarnations are unfolded. We shall see divers examples in the following pages.

I. APPARITION AND DEVELOPMENT OF THE ORIENTAL CYCLE

Without recurring to the strange and little-known visions which already haunted the childhood and youth of Mlle. Smith (see p. 20), I will retrace the principal stages of her Asiatic romance from the birth of her mediumship.

During the three first years there were but few manifestations of this sort, in the seances, at least, while as to the automatisms which developed at other times, especially at night, or in the hypnagogic state, we know nothing.

In November, 1892, two seances of the N. group are occupied with the apparition of a Chinese city—Peking, according to the table—in which a disincarnate spirit, a parent of one of the group, is found performing a mission to a sick child.*

In her seances of 1894, Hélène had on several occasions detached visions belonging to the Orient, as appeared from their content, or hints dictated by the table. She also saw Teheran; then the cemetery of the missions at Tokat (June 12th); a cavalier with a white woollen cloak and a turban bearing the name of Abderrhaman (September 2d); and, finally, an Oriental landscape, which depicted a ceremony of Buddhist aspect (October 16th). This latter vision, more especially, seemed to be a forerunner of the Hindoo romance, since the records of the seances of that period show an *ensemble* of characteristic traits which will be again met with in the later Hindoo scenes—*e.g.,* an immense garden of exotic plants, colonnades, rows of palm-trees, with enormous stone lions at the head; rugs of magnificent design, a temple surrounded by trees, with a statue, apparently that of Buddha; a procession of twelve women in white, who kneel, holding lighted lamps; in the centre another woman, with very black hair, detaches herself from the procession, balances a lamp, and burns a powder which expands into a white stone (the continuation of the romance shows this woman to be Simandini, of whom this was the first appearance).

February 17, 1895.—At the end of a rather long seance, the table dictates *Pirux sheik*, and replies to our questions that it refers to an Arab sheik of the fifteenth century. At this moment Hélène awakes, saying that she had seen a man with a black mustache and curly hair, wearing a cloak and a turban, who seemed to be laughing at and mocking her. The spelling out of Pirux was not very clear, and Léopold, when interrogated later, neither affirmed categorically, nor did he deny, that this name was that of the sheik, father of Simandini.

March 3.—Seance with six persons present, all having their hands upon the table. After a brief waiting, Hélène is surprised at no longer being able to see my left middle finger, while she can see all my other fingers quite clearly. My bunch of keys, which I then place upon my middle finger, likewise disappears from her view. This very limited, systematic, visual anasthesia authorizes the prediction, following numerous examples of former seances, that the phenomena about to appear will concern me. Presently begins a long vision, consisting of scenes which Hélène believes she has already partially seen before.

She describes a pagoda, which she draws with her left hand, with a few strokes of her pencil; then an avenue of palms and statues, a procession, and ceremonies before an altar, etc.

The principal rôles are played by a personage in sandals, a great yellow robe, a helmet of gold, ornamented with precious stones (first appearance of Sivrouka) and by the woman with black hair and white robe, already seen on the 12th of October (Simandini).

In the first part of the vision, Hélène, who follows that woman with ecstatic gaze, describing her to us sees her coming towards me, but at that moment the invisibility of my finger was extended to my entire person, and Hélène neither sees nor hears me. While she was fully conscious of the other sitters, she was astonished at seeing this woman make "on the empty air" certain gestures of laying-on of hands and benediction, which were made upon my head On several occasions I change my place, and seat myself in different parts of the room. Each time, after a few seconds, Hélène turns towards me, and, without perceiving me, sees the woman with black hair place herself behind my seat and repeat her gestures of benediction in space, at a height corresponding to that of my head.

As the vision continues, I do not play any further role, but it has to do with a ceremony during which the Hindoo woman with a diadem on her head burns incense in the midst of her twelve companions, etc.

During all this time the table, contrary to its custom, gave no explanation; but Hélène, having herself asked some questions, remarks that the imaginary woman replies to her by certain signs of her head and reveals to her many things that she had known in a former existence. At the moment of the disappearance of the vision, which had lasted more than an hour, Mlle. Smith hears the words ("Until presently"). The continuation, in fact, was not long delayed.

March 6.—Repetition and continuation of the preceding seance, with this degree of progress—viz., that the visual hallucination of the woman with the black hair was changed into a total coenaesthetic hallucination— *i.e.*, instead of a simple vision an incarnation was produced.* After a very impressive scene of benediction, Hélène gave herself up to a succession of pantomimes in which she seemed to take part in a fearful spectacle and to struggle with enemies (scene of the funeral pile). She ended by seating herself on the divan when she recovered her normal state, after a series of psychical oscillations, various attitudes, etc. The last of her phases of mimicry was to tear off and throw away all the ornaments which an Asiatic princess could wear—rings on all her fingers, bracelets on her arms and wrists, a necklace, diadem, ear-rings, girdle, anklets. Once awake, she had no recollection of the scene of benediction, but recalled quite distinctly the dreams corresponding to the other pantomimes. She saw again the black-haired woman, the Oriental landscape of the preceding seance, etc. In the course of her description the passage of the simple vision into the scene of incarnation was reflected in a change of the form of her narrative; she spoke to us of the woman in the third person, then suddenly adopted the first person, and said "I" in recounting among other things that she—or the black-haired woman—saw a corpse on the funeral pile, upon which four men, against whom she struggled, endeavored to force her to mount. When I drew her attention to this change of style, she replied that, in fact, it seemed as though she herself was that woman.*

Independently of the Hindoo romance, these two seances are interesting from a psychological point of view, because the change from a visual, objective hallucination into total coenaesthetic and motor hallucination occurs in it, constituting a complete transformation of the personality. This generalization of partial automatism at the beginning, this subjugation and absorption of the ordinary personality by the subliminal personality, does not always produce amnesia with Hélène, that unique impression which she might describe on awakening as being herself and some one else at the same time. (Compare, p. 75.) It must be noted that in the particular case of the identification of the black-haired Hindoo woman with Mlle. Hélène Smith of Geneva, the problem of the causal connection is susceptible of two opposite solutions (and the same remark will be equally appropriate in the case of Marie Antoinette).

For the believing spiritist it is because Mlle. Smith is the reincarnation of Simandini—that is to say, because these two personages, in spite of the separation of their existences in time and space, are substantially and metaphysically identical—that she really again becomes Simandini, and feels herself to be a Hindoo princess in certain favorable somnambulistic states. For the empirical psychologist it is, on the contrary, because the visual memory of a Hindoo woman (her origin is of no importance) grows like a parasite and increases in surface and in depth like a drop of oil, until it invades the whole impressionable and suggestible personality of the medium—this is why Mlle. Smith feels herself becoming this woman, and concludes from it that she formerly actually was that person (see p. 25). But we must return from this digression to the Hindoo dream.

March 10.—After various waking visions relating to other subjects,

Hélène enters into somnambulism. For twenty minutes she remains seated with her hands on the table, by means of raps struck upon which Léopold informs us that a scene of previous existence concerning me is being prepared; that I was formerly a Hindoo prince, and that Mlle. Smith, long before her existence as Marie Antoinette, had then been my wife, and had been burned on my tomb; that we should ultimately know the name of this Hindoo prince, as well as the time and place of these events, but not this evening, nor at the next seance. Then Hélène leaves the table, and in a silent pantomime of an hour's duration, the meaning of which, already quite clear, is confirmed by Léopold, she plays, this time to the very close, the scene of the funeral pile as outlined in the preceding seance.

She goes slowly around the room, as if resisting and carried away in spite of herself, by turns supplicating and struggling fiercely with these fictitious men who are bearing her to her death.

All at once, standing on tiptoe, she seems to ascend the pile, hides, with affright, her face in her hands, recoils in terror, then advances anew as though pushed from behind. Finally she falls on her knees before a soft couch, in which she buries her face covered by her clasped hands. She sobs violently. By means of her little finger, visible between her cheek and the cushion of the couch, Léopold continues to reply very clearly by yes and no to my questions. It is the moment at which she again passes through her agony on the funeral pile: her cries cease little by little; her respiration becomes more and more panting, then suddenly stops and remains suspended during some seconds which seem interminable. It is the end! Her pulse is fortunately strong, though a little irregular. While I am feeling it, her breathing is re-established by means of a deep inspiration. After repeated sobs she becomes calm, and slowly rises and seats herself on a neighboring sofa. This scene of fatal *dénouement* lasted eight minutes. She finally awakens, remembering to have seen in a dream the dead body of a man stretched on a funeral pile, and a woman whom some men were forcing to ascend the pile against her will.

There was nothing Oriental in the succeeding seances, and the Hindoo dream did not appear again until four weeks later.

April 7.—Mlle. Smith went quickly into a mixed state, in which the Hindoo dream was mingled and substituted, but only so far as concerns me, for the feeling of present reality. She believes me absent, asks other sitters why I have gone away, then rises and begins to walk around me and look at me, very much surprised at seeing my place occupied by a stranger with black curly hair and of brown complexion, clothed in a robe with flowing sleeves of blue, and with gold ornaments. When I speak to her she turns around and seems to hear my voice from the opposite side, whither she goes to look for me; when I go towards her she shuns me;

then, when I follow her, she returns to the place I had just left. After some time occupied in these manoeuvres she ceases to be preoccupied with me and my substitute in the blue robe, and falls into a deeper state. She takes on the look of a seeress, and describes a kind of embattled chateau on a hill, where she perceives and recognizes the before-mentioned personage with the curly hair, but in another costume and surrounded by very ugly black men, and women "who are good looking."

Interrogated as to the meaning of this vision, Léopold replies: *"The city of Tchandraguiri in Kanaraau"* (*sic*); then he adds, a moment later, *"There is a letter too many in the last word,"* and ends by giving the name *Kanara,* and adding the explanation *"of the fifteenth century."* Upon awaking from this somnambulistic state, which lasted two hours, Hélène recalls having had a dream of a personage with curly hair, in a blue robe, richly ornamented with precious stones, with a cutlass of gold, bent backward, suspended from a hook. She recollects having held a long conversation with him in a strange language which she understood and spoke very well herself, although she no longer knows the meaning of it.*

April 14.—Very soon passing into a deep sleep, Mlle. Smith leaves the table and gives herself up to a silent pantomime, at first smiling, then finishing in sadness and by a scene of tears.

The meaning of this is explained by Léopold as follows: Hélène is in India, in her palace of Tchandraguiri, in Kanara, *in 1401,* and she receives a declaration of love from the personage with the curly hair, who is the Prince Sivrouka Nayaka, to whom she has been married for about a year. The prince has flung himself upon his knees, but he inspires in her a certain fright, and she still regrets having left her native country in order to follow him. Léopold affirms that she will remember, on awaking, in French, all that the prince has said to her in Sanscrit, and that she will repeat to us a part of it, but not all, because it is too private. After awaking she seems in reality to recall clearly her entire dream, and tells us that she found herself on a hill, where they were building; that it was not exactly a city, nor even a village, since there were no streets; that it was rather an isolated place in the country, and that which was being built was not in the form of a house; it had holes rather than windows (a fortress and loop-holes).

She found herself in a fine palace, very beautiful as to its interior, but not its exterior. There was a great hall, decorated with greens, with a grand staircase at the end, flanked by statues of gold. She held a long conversation there, not in French, with the swarthy personage with the black curly hair and magnificent costume; he finally ascended the staircase, but she did not follow him.

She appeared to recall well the meaning of all that he said to her in their conversation in a foreign language, but seemed embarrassed by these memories, and would not consent to relate them to us.

May 26.—In the course of this seance, as Hélène, in a silent somnambulism, incarnates the Hindoo princess, I hand her a sheet of paper and a pencil in the hope of obtaining some text or drawing. After divers scribblings she traces the single word *Simadini* in letters which are not at all like her usual hand (see Fig. 34).

Then taking a fresh sheet, she seems to write on it with a happy smile, folds it carefully and thrusts it in her corsage, takes it out again, and rereads it with rapture, etc. Léoouka. On awaking she remembers having been "in such a beautiful palace," and of having received there a very interesting letter, but the contents of which she refused to disclose to us, being evidently too confidential.

I intercalate here two remarks apropos of the name Simadini, which is one of the first known examples of a handwriting of Mlle. Smith other than her own normal hand.

First: When, four months later, Léopold began to communicate in writing (pp. 63–65), a certain analogy in the formation of the letters, and the identical way of holding the pencil, caused us to believe that it was he who had already traced the word in Fig. 34. But he has always denied it, and we have never been able to discover the author of it. Secondly: I said above, (p. 124), that there had been divergences in the orthography of this name. Here, in substance, is a fragment of a letter which Mlle. Smith wrote me in the winter following (February 18, 1896), depicting to me the vexatious impressions which she still had concerning it.

> I am very sad, and I cannot tell why. I have a heavy heart, and for what reason I do not know myself. It came to such a pass to-day (you are going to laugh) that it seemed to me as though my left cheek had grown perceptibly thinner. I am sure that at this moment you would not recognize Simadini, so piteous and discouraged is her countenance! Think, that at the very moment in which I trace these words, I hear a voice speaking to me in my right ear: *Not Simadini, but Simandini!* What do you think that can be? It is very strange, is it not? Have we misunderstood that name? Or, perhaps, may it not be I who have misunderstood it?

Mlle. Smith here forgets that the name did not come to her on the first occasion by auditive hallucination, in which case it might be that she had misunderstood it, but by writing in somnambulism, which excludes any mistake of her ordinary consciousness. We must confine ourselves to registering as a fact, inexplicable hitherto, this correction of a graphic automatism by an auditive automatism at the end of several months. Between the two orthographies, I have adopted the second, which has undergone no further changes, and figures only in the Martian texts (10, 16).

June 16.—Fuller repetition of the scene of the letter of the Hindoo prince. Impossible to learn the contents of it. I suggest to her to remem-

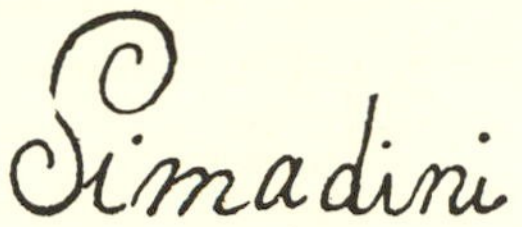

Simadini

Fig. 34.

ber and to relate them to us upon awakening, but Léopold replies: *"She will not reveal it. Why have you not gained her confidence sufficiently, that she may tell you everything without fear?"* and the suggestion had no effect.

June 30.—Somnambulism with silent pantomime, the meaning of which is given by Léopold: It is the scene of the betrothal of Simandini and Sivrouka at Tchandraguiri. There is first a phase of oppression, with sighs and gestures as of a struggle against various pretenders who wish to seize her; then laughter and ecstasy, provoked by the arrival of Sivrouka, who delivers her and drives off his rivals; finally, joy and admiration on accepting the flowers and jewels which he offers her.

I have reported, too much at length perhaps, though still greatly abridged, these first appearances of the Oriental romance, because they form a continuous series, in the reverse of the chronological order, conformably to a spiritistic theory which holds that in these memories of previous existences the mediumistic memory goes back and recovers the "images" of the more recent events before those which are more remote.* During this first period of four months, the Hindoo cycle made irruption into eight seances (about one-twentieth of those at which I have been present since I have had knowledge of them), and has manifested itself somewhat like the panorama of a magic lantern, unfolding itself in successive tableaux.*

This whole history can be summed up by a few principal tableaux: there was the scene of the death on the funeral pile, prepared in vision in the seance of the 6th of March and executed on the 10th; then the scene of the interior of the palace and the fortress in process of construction (7th and 14th of April); that of the love-letter (26th of May and 16th of June); finally, the betrothal (30th of June). There must be added to these the grand tableau at the beginning, first presented in vision the 3d of March, then realized three days later with the astonishing exclamation Atièyâ Ganapatinâmâ. The meaning of this scene has never been explained by Léopold, but seems to be quite clear. A species of prologue can be seen in it, or even apotheosis, inaugurating the entire romance; it is the Hindoo princess of four centuries ago recognizing her lord and master in flesh and blood, under the unexpected form of a university professor, whom she greets with an emphasis wholly Oriental in blessing him, very appropriately, in the name of the divinity of science and of wisdom—since Ganapati is an equivalent of Ganesâ, the god with the head of an elephant, patron of sages and savants.

It can be easily conceived that these two words of Oriental resonance, spoken aloud at a period at which the Martian was not yet born—and followed by all the conversations unfortunately unheard by us, which at the waking at the subsequent seances Hélène recalled having held in a strange language (in *Sanscrit,* according to Léopold) with the Hindoo prince of her dreams—would excite a lively curiosity and a desire to obtain longer audible fragments of this unknown idiom. It was only in September, 1895, that this satisfaction was afforded us, during a seance at which the Oriental romance, which had given no further sign of life since the month of June, made a new outbreak. Starting from that moment, it has never ceased during these four years to reappear irregularly, and, suffering some eclipses, accompanied on each occasion by words of a *Sanscritoid* aspect. But the plot of the romance has no longer the same clearness that it showed at the beginning. In place of tableaux linking themselves in a regular chronological order, they are often no more than confused reminiscences, memories, without precise bonds between them, which gush forth from the memory of Simandini. As the fragments of our youthful years surge up incoherent and pell-mell in our dreams, Mlle. Smith, too, finds herself easily assailed in her somnambulisms by visions connected with certain episodes, and not forming an entire continuation of supposed Asiatic pre-existence.

Some of these scenes concern her life as a young Arab girl. One sees her there, for example, playing joyously with her little monkey, Mitidja; or copying an Arab text (see Fig. 35, p. 193), which her father, the sheik, surrounded by his tribes, furnishes her; or embarking on a strange boat, escorted by black Hindoos, for her new country, etc. But much the larger number of her somnambulistic trances and her spontaneous visions have reference to her life in India and to the details of her daily existence. Her bath, which the faithful domestic Adèl prepares for her; her walks and reveries in the splendid gardens of the palace, all full of a luxurious vegetation and rare birds of brilliant colors: her scenes of tenderness and of affectionate effusions—always stamped, this is to be noted, with the most perfect propriety—towards the Prince Sivrouka, when he is kindly disposed; scenes of regret also and abundant tears for the memory of her far-off native land, when the capricious and brutal humor of the Oriental despot makes itself too severely felt; conversation with the fakir Kanga; devotions and religious ceremonies before some Buddhist image, etc., all this forms an *ensemble* extremely varied and full of local color. There is in the whole being of Simandini—in the expression of her countenance

(Hélène almost always has her large eyes open in this somnambulism), in her movements, in the quality of her voice when she speaks or chants Hindoo—a languishing grace, an abandon, a melancholy sweetness, a something of languor and of charm, which corresponds wonderfully with the character of the Orient, as the spectators conceive it to be, who, like me, have never been there, etc. With all this a bearing always full of *noblesse* and dignity conforms to that which one would expect of a princess; there are no dances, for example, nothing of the *bayadère*.

Mlle. Smith is really very wonderful in her Hindoo somnambulisms. The way in which Simandini seats herself on the ground, her legs crossed, or half stretched out, nonchalantly leaning her arms or her head against a Sivrouka, who is sometimes real (when in her incomplete trance she takes me for her prince), sometimes imaginary; the religious and solemn gravity of her prostrations when, after having for a long time balanced the fictitious brazier, she crosses her extended hands on her breast, kneeling and bowing herself three times, her forehead striking the ground; the melancholy sweetness of her chants in a minor key, wailing and plaintive melodies, which unfold themselves in certain flute-like notes, prolonged in a slow decrescendo, and only dying away at the end of a single note held for fully fourteen seconds; the agile suppleness of her swaying and serpentine movements, when she amuses herself with her imaginary monkey, caresses it, embraces it, excites it, scolds it laughingly, and makes it repeat all its tricks—all this so varied mimicry and Oriental speech have such a stamp of originality, of ease, of naturalness, that one asks in amazement whence it comes to this little daughter of Lake Leman, without artistic education or special knowledge of the Orient—a perfection of play to which the best actress, without doubt, could only attain at the price of prolonged studies or a sojourn on the banks of the Ganges.*

The problem, as I have already stated, is not yet solved, and I am obliged still to endeavor to discover whence Hélène Smith has derived her ideas in regard to India. It seems that the more simple method would be to take advantage of the hypnotic state of the seances to obtain a confession from Hélène's subconscious memory, and persuade it to disclose the secret; but my efforts in that direction have not as yet succeeded. It is doubtless incompetency on my part, and I will end, perhaps—or some one better qualified than I—in finding the joint in the armor. The fact is that hitherto I have always run up against Léopold, who will not allow himself to be ejected or ridiculed, and who has never ceased to affirm that the Sanscrit, Simandini, and the rest are authentic. All the trails which I have thought I have discovered—and they are already numerous—have proved false. The reader must pardon me for not going into the details of my failures in this regard.

If it was only a question of the Hindoo pantomime the mystery would not be so great: some recitations at school, newspaper articles concerning the incineration of the widows of Malabar, engravings and descriptions relative to the civil and religious life of India, etc.—in short, the varied sources of information which, in a civilized country and at our epoch of cosmopolitanism, inevitably meet some time or other the eyes or ears of every one of us and form part of the equipment (conscious or unconscious) of every individual who is not altogether uncultured, would more than suffice to explain the scene of the funeral pile, the prostrations, and the varied attitudes. There are, indeed, some well-known examples showing how small a thing a cunning intelligence, furnished with a good memory and a fertile and plastic imagination, needs in order to reconstruct or fabricate out of nothing a complex edifice, having every appearance of authenticity, and capable of holding in check for a considerable length of time the perspicacity even of skilled minds. But that which conscious and reflecting labor has succeeded in accomplishing in the cases referred to, the subliminal faculties can execute to a much higher degree of perfection in the case of persons subject to automatic tendencies.*

But two points remain, which complicate the case of the Hindoo romance and seem to defy—thus far, at least—all normal explanation, because they surpass the limits of a simple play of the imagination. These are the precise *historical* information given by Léopold, some of which can be, in a certain sense, verified; and the Hindoo *language* spoken by Simandini, which contains words more or less recognizable, the real meaning of which is adapted to the situation in which they have been spoken. But, even if Hélène's imagination could have reconstructed the manners and customs and scenes of the Orient from the general information floating in some way in cosmopolitan atmosphere, still one cannot conceive whence she has derived her knowledge of the language and of certain obscure episodes in the history of India. These two points deserve to be examined separately.

II. Sivrouka and M. de Marlès

*When Kanara, Sivrouka, Simandini, etc., successively made their appearance, slowly spelled out by Léopold, with the date of 1401, my companions of the seance and I hastened to investigate Brouillet, who brought to mind the province of Malabar in connection with the first of these names, but left us in utter darkness as to the others. The geography of Vivien Saint-Martin revealed the existence of no fewer than three Tchandraguiris—a hill, a river, and a small town in the district of Arcot-Nord (Madras). The latter—or rather its citadel on the summit of the hill—answered quite well to the description given by Hélène in her visions of the 7th and 14th of April, but the construction of this fortress dates back only to 1510, and this locality is very far removed from the Kanara where Léopold locates this entire story (see pp. 178–179).

As to Sivrouka and his surroundings, neither biographical dictionaries nor encyclopaedias were able to furnish me the least hint on this subject. Living historians or Orientalists to whom I addressed myself were of a discouraging unanimity in replying that they did not recognize even the names, the historic correctness of which they regarded as doubtful, and they did not at all remember having met with them in works of fiction.

"I have there," said a learned professor of history, showing me a good-sized bookcase, "numerous works on the history of India; but they relate only to the north of the peninsula; and as to what transpired in the south during the period to which you refer, we know almost nothing. Your names are unknown to me and do not recall to my mind any personage, real or fictitious."

"The very name of Sivrouka seems to me improbable as a Hindoo name" replied another, who was unable to give me any more information on the subject.

"I greatly regret," wrote a third, on receipt of Hélène's texts,

> not to have succeeded in getting upon the trail of the recollections of your medium. I cannot think of any book which would be likely to furnish the information. Tchandraguiri and Mangalore (where several scenes of the Hindoo cycle are located) are correct, but Madras (*id.*) did not exist in 1401. Its name and foundation do not go further back than the seventeenth century. That region was then a dependency of the kingdom of Vijayanagara, and a naïk in the service of those princes resided successively at Tchandraguiri and at Mangalore. I can make nothing of Sivrouka; the king of Vijayanagara, in 1402, was Bukkha II., or Bukkha called Siribukkha, Tiribukkha. But the naïk who so often changed his residence was evidently not a ruling prince. Was it a romance? Certain details caused me to doubt it. A romancer so careful in regard to local coloring as to introduce into his narrative Indian words, would not have given the title of the prince under the Sanscrit form *Nayaka*, but would have used the vulgar form naïk; he would not have made the wife, in speaking to her husband, call him by his name Sivrouka (as Hélène constantly does in this somnambulism). I have no recollection of having read anything of this kind, and I know of no work of fiction from which the story might have been taken.

It will be readily understood that I was annoyed at not being able to establish clearly my presumed Asiatic previous existence. However, while professional science was administering to me these cold douches, I continued, on my own account, to search the libraries at my disposal, and here one fine day I accidentally came across, in an old history of India, in six volumes, by a man named De Marlès, the following passages:

Kanara and the neighboring provinces on the side towards Delhi may be regarded as the Georgia of Hindustan; it is there, it is said, that the most beautiful women are to be found; the natives, however, are very jealous in guarding them, and do not often allow them to be seen by strangers.

Tchandraguiri, which signifies *Mountain of the Moon*, is a vast fortress constructed, in 1401, by the rajah Sivrouka Nayaka. This prince, as also his successors, belonged to the sect of the Djaïns.

At last! With what a beating heart did I fasten my eyes on that irrefutable historic evidence that my preceding incarnation, under the beautiful skies of India was not a myth! I felt new life in my veins. I reread twenty times those blessed lines, and took a copy of them to send to those pretended savants who were ignorant even of the name of Sivrouka, and allowed doubts to be cast upon his reality.

Alas! my triumph was of brief duration. It seems that the testimony of De Marlès is not of the highest order. This author is held in slight esteem in well-informed circles, as may be seen from the following passage in a letter of M. Barth, which merely expresses, in a vigorous and lively manner, an opinion which other specialists have confirmed:[1]

It is through a letter of M. Flournoy that I learn that there has existed since 1828 in Paris, printed in Roman characters, a history of India by De Marlès containing a statement that the fortress of Candragiri was built in 1401, and that its founder was Sivrouka Nayaka. What new facts there are in books one no longer consults! And that of De Marlès is, indeed, one of those that are no longer consulted. I found it yesterday at the library of the Institute. It would have been impossible to have done worse, even in 1828. But sometimes we find pearls in a dung-hill, and perhaps this Sivrouka Nayaka is one of them. Unfortunately, the author gives no hint as to the scources of his information; and later, in his fourth volume, in which he narrates the history of the twelfth to the sixteenth centuries, he does not say a word more either of Candragiri or of Sivrouka.

Here was a terrible blow to my Hindoo existence, which poor M. de Marlès had so well established for me.

Nevertheless, the hope still lingers that his information, although not reproduced by later writers more highly esteemed, may perhaps still be correct. This is quite possible, since science has not yet spoken its last word in this department, hardly even its first, if men still more competent may be believed, beginning with M. Barth himself.

"Up to the present moment," says he,

there is no trustworthy history of the south of the peninsula. . . . The Dravidian languages of India is a domain very unfamiliar to the majority of Indian

[1] De Marlès' *General History of India, Ancient and Modern, from the Year 2000 B.C. to our Own Times.* Pp. 268–269. Paris, 1828.

scholars. . . . There is nothing to draw upon but some works and monographs on the aboriginal chronicles and legendary traditions; and it would be necessary to know the Dravidian languages on the one hand and Arabic on the other, to be able to examine or even consult them with profit. The only works which we are able to follow are those which undertake to make this history by epigraphic documents, but these, thus far, say nothing of Simandini, of Adèl, of Mitidja, or even of Sivrouka.

This silence of epigraphy is certainly to be regretted; but who knows whether it will not some day enlighten us by proving De Marlès to be right—and also Léopold—by narrating to us the true story of the Hindoo princess, the Arabian monkey, and the slave Adèl! It costs nothing to hope! Already, thanks again to M. Barth, I have gained information concerning another Tchandraguiri than the one of the District of North Arcot mentioned by Vivien de Saint-Martin—i.e., a Tchandraguiri, situated in South Kanara, and in the citadel of which a hitherto unknown inscription has been discovered which must date back to the time of King Harihara II., of Vijayanagara, who reigned at the beginning of the fifteenth century.[2] Here is something approaching the somnambulistic revelations of Mlle. Smith. While awaiting their definite confirmation by new archaeological discoveries, traces of Sivrouka may be sought for in the earlier works upon which De Marlès must have drawn. Unfortunately these works are not easy to find, and are inconvenient to consult. Professor Michel, of the University of Liège, has had the kindness to run through those of Buchanan[3] and of Rennell,[4] but without result.

If De Marlès did not invent Sivrouka out of whole cloth, which is hardly supposable, it was very probably in the translation of Ferishta by Dow,[5] that he found his facts. I have, unhappily, not yet been able myself to consult that very rare work, which is not to be found in Geneva, so far as I am aware, nor to obtain accurate information regarding its contents.

The uncertainty which hovers over the historical problem extends, naturally, to the psychological problem also. It is clear that if certain inscriptions, or even some old work, should come some day to tell us not only of Sivrouka, but of Simandini, of Adèl, and the other personages who figure

---

[2] Robert Sewell. *Lists of Antiquarian Remains in the Presidency of Madras.* Vol i. p. 238 (1882.) Citation by M. Barth. I have not been able to consult this work.

[3] Buchanan. *A Journey from Madras through the Countries of Mysore, Canara, and Malabar, etc.* 3 vols. 4to. London, 1807.

[4] James Rennell. *Description Historique et Géographique de l'Indostan.* Translated from the English. Paris, an. VIII. (1800). 3 vols., 8vo and atlas 4to.

[5] Dow. *History of Hindustan.* Translated from the Persian of Ferishta. London, 1803. M. Michel suggests Wilks's *Historical Sketches of the South of India* (London, 1810) as having possibly served as a source of information for De Marlès. If some learned reader may discover any traces of Sivrouka antecedent to De Marlès, I shall be under great obligation to him if he will communicate the information to me.

in Hélène's Hindoo romance, but of whom De Marlès does not whisper a word, we should no longer care about the latter author, and the question would then be as follows: Could Mlle. Smith have had cognizance of these early works, and if not, how do their contents reappear in her somnambulism? But in the actual condition of things, and all allowance made for possible surprises in the future, I do not hesitate to regard as the more probable and more rational supposition, that it was really the passage of De Marlès, quoted above, which furnished the subliminal memory of Hélène the precise date of 1401—and the three names of the fortress, the province, and the rajah.

Various other traits of the visions of Mlle. Smith betray likewise the same inspiration. The scene in which she sees them engaged in building, and her description of that which is being built, suggest clearly the idea of a fortress furnished by the text. The translation *Mountain of the Moon* contributed to causing her to locate the scene upon a hill. The beauty of the women of the country, on which De Marlès dwells, has its echo in the remark of Hélène that the women whom she sees are "good looking." Finally, the princely character of Sivrouka, mentioned by De Marlès, is found throughout the length of the entire romance, and displays itself in the splendor of his costume, of the palace, of the gardens, etc.

It is possible that the names and the nationality of the other personages —Simandini, Adèl, the monkey, the sheik, etc.—may have been borrowed from some unknown work, which would be, for the Arabian portion of the narrative, the pendant to De Marlès for the Hindoo past.

This may be, but it is not necessary. It is permissible to regard, provisionally, the imaginations built up around Sivrouka, as an ingenious expedient, by means of which Hélène's imagination finds a way of binding to that central figure, and also of blending in a single whole, her other Oriental memories not specifically Hindoo.

The hypothesis which I am about to assume, which connects directly with De Marlès the data of Hélène's Asiatic dream, contained likewise in the work of that author, arouses, nevertheless, two objections. The first is drawn from the slight differences of orthography between the text of De Marlès and the words spoken by Léopold. This difficulty is only insurmountable by elevating the inerrancy of the subliminal memory to the plane of absolute infallibility, though the latter must be admitted to be ordinarily very much superior to that of the conscious memory. But the favorite comparison of the forgotten memories, reappearing in somnambulisms, to unchangeable, absolutely true photographic impressions, causes us readily to exaggerate the fidelity of the unconscious memory-images. The example of certain dreams—in which memories of childhood sometimes return with a startling clearness, but, nevertheless, altered or distorted in some details, conformably to later experiences or to recent events—suffices to show that automatisms of the memory are not always sheltered by influences of the imagination, nor absolutely free from error.

In this particular case there are two divergences between De Marlès and Léopold: the latter has substituted a *k* for the *c* in Nayaca, and has omitted the *n* in Tchandraguiri (compare pp. 179 and 185). Another mistake, which he immediately corrected, consisting in dictating first *Kanaraau*, was evidently a confusion such as frequently occurs in writing, occasioned by a too rapid passing from the word *Kanara* to the information following, and already about to come.* The spelling Nayaka, instead of Nayaca, is attributable to the termination of the word *Sivrouka*, which precedes it. Identity of pronunciation has produced identity of orthography.*

The second objection is of a negative character. It consists in the impossibility of showing where, when, or how Mlle. Smith obtained cognizance of the text of De Marlès.

I admit frankly that I know nothing about it, and I give full credit to Hélène for the indomitable and persevering energy with which she has never ceased to protest against my hypothesis, which has the faculty of exasperating her in the highest degree—and one readily understands that it would naturally do so. For it is in vain that she digs down to the very bottom of her memories; she does not discover the slightest trace of this work. And not only that, but how can one seriously suppose that she has ever had the slightest intimation of it, since she never studied the history of India, has neither read nor heard anything on the subject, the very name of De Marlès having been utterly unknown to her up to the day on which she learned that I suspected that author of being the source of the Hindoo romance? It must indeed, be admitted that the idea of the passage in question having come before the eyes or ears of Mlle. Smith through any ordinary channel seems a trife absurd. I only know in Geneva of two copies of the work of De Marlès, both covered with dust—the one belonging to the Société de Lecture, a private association of which none of the Smith family nor any friend of theirs was ever a member; the other in the Public Library, where, among the thousands of more interesting and more modern books, it is now very rarely consulted. It could only have happened, therefore, by a combination of absolutely exceptional and almost unimaginable circumstances that the work of De Marlès could have found its way into Hélène's hands; and how could it have done so and she not have the slightest recollection of it?

I acknowledge the force of this argument, and that the wisest thing to do is to leave the matter in suspense. But if the question must be decided, though there is scarcely any choice, extravagance for extravagance, I still prefer the hypothesis which only invokes natural possibilities to that which appeals to occult causes.

Possibly the work of De Marlès may have been heard of by Mlle. Smith without her normal consciousness taking note of it. Either when among her friends or acquaintances, or with her parents, she might have heard some passages read in her young days, etc. The fact that she has no conscious recollection of it proves nothing against such a supposition to any one who is at all familiar with the play of our faculties.

It goes without saying that my method of reasoning is the inverse of that which generally prevails in spiritistic circles. Witness the celebrated Aksakoff, as a single example, who, discovering that a curious typtological message was found already in print in a book which could not readily have come to the knowledge of the medium, and recognizing the fact that the message came from that book, says: "But in what way could the brain of the medium have been made aware of the contents of the book? There is the mystery. *I refuse to admit that it could have been through natural means. I believe it was by some occult process."**

Very well! this is plain language, and the frankness of the declaration charms me to such a degree that I cannot resist the temptation to appropriate it for myself in the case of Mlle. Smith and M. de Marlès, transposing only two words: *"I refuse to admit that it could have been through occult means. I believe it was by some natural process."* Evidently, in doubtful cases (which are in an enormous majority), in which the natural and the occult explanations are in direct opposition, without the possibility of a material demonstration as to which is true in fact, a decision must be reached in accordance with personal taste and feeling.* Between these two methodological points of view a reconciliation is scarcely possible. The reader may think what he will. But, right or wrong, I claim the first of these as my opinion, and regard the tendency of the supernatural and occult to substitute themselves, on account of the insufficiency of our knowledge, for the acquired rights of natural hypothesis, as an unjustifiable reversal of rôles.*

To those who shall find my hypothesis decidedly too extravagant—or too simple—remains a choice between the multiple forms of occult hypothesis. Shall it be Léopold who, in his all-powerful state of disincarnation, has read in the closed volume of De Marlès? Or has there, indeed, been a telepathic transmission of this passage from the brain of some unknown terrestrial reader to that of Mlle. Smith? Shall it be with her a case of clairvoyance, of lucidity, of intuition in the astral body; or, again, of trickery on the part of some facetious spirit? And if, taking the reincarnationist theory seriously, it is admitted that Sivrouka, 1401, and Tchandraguiri, are indeed really reminiscences of the past life of Simandini, how explain that curious coincidence in their choice and their spelling with precisely the designations used by M. de Marlès?*

III. The Arab Elements of the Oriental Cycle

Here is a problem for the partisans of the Oriental pre-existence of Mlle. Smith: How comes it that, recovering in her trances the use of the Hindoo which she formerly spoke at the court of Sivrouka, she has totally forgotten Arabian, which, however, had been her mother-tongue in that same previous existence, and which she was accustomed to use exclusively up to the time of her departure from her native land, in her eighteenth year?

If the emotions caused by her royal marriage had destroyed all memory of the past, one could understand how the idiom might have become obscured along with the rest in that loss of memory of her life as a young girl.

But such was not the case. She preserved very vivid memories of her father the sheik, of his tents gleaming in the sunlight, of the people, of the camels and landscapes of Arabia. In many seances and spontaneous visions she finds herself carried back to that first half of her Asiatic existence. But then she narrates in French that which is unfolded before her eyes, or gives herself up to a silent pantomime. She has never spoken or written anything at all resembling Arabian. Can it be supposed that already in her Hindoo life she had assimilated the language of her adopted country to the point of losing even the latent memories of her maternal language? That would be contrary to all known psychological analogies.

However, in saying that Hélène has never written or spoken Arabian I exaggerate. On one occasion she spoke four words of it. It is the exception which proves the rule. In fact, not only did she fail to accompany that single text with any pronunciation, but she executed it as a drawing, and apparently copied, without comprehending, a model which an imaginary person presented to her.

Here is a review of that incident:

October 27, 1895.—Shortly after the beginning of the seance Mlle. Smith has an Arabian vision: "Look at those tents! There are no stones here—it is all sand . . . [she counts the tents one by one] There are twenty of them. That one is beautiful. Don't you find it so, M. Lemaître—that largest one? It is fastened by cords and small stakes. . . ." etc. Then she describes the personages: The one who is smoking, seated in a corner, with his legs crossed; others all black (the table says they are negroes, and that the scene takes place in Arabia); then a man clothed in white, whom Hélène has the feeling of knowing without being able to recognize him; she places her finger upon her forehead, in the attitude of a person trying to remember, and the table (on which she has her left hand) informs us then that she lived in Arabia in her life as Simandini, and that she is trying to recollect those far-distant times. A quite long scene follows, in which her Arab reminiscences alternate and mingle with the consciousness of the real environment, though she neither sees nor hears us. At this point a state of mental confusion ensues, which seems to be very painful to her.

> M. Lemaître! M. Flournoy! are you there? Answer me, then. Did I not come here this evening? If only I could . . . however, I am not *en voyage*. . . . I really believe it is Sunday at last . . . I understand nothing more about it. I think my brain is so tired that all my ideas are mixed up . . . however, I am not dreaming. . . . It seems to me that I have also lived with them . . . [the sitters at the table], and with them [the Arabs of her vision]. . . . But I know them—all those men. Tell me, then, who you are! Did you arrive in Geneva lately? [They are, says the table, Arabs who lived five centuries ago, among them the father of Simandini.] Come nearer, then, come here. I want you to speak to me! M. Lemaître! Oh, that pretty little sketch! What is that sketch? [The table having said that it is a drawing which her father is presenting to her, and that she can copy it, a pencil and a sheet of paper are placed before her, the latter of which seems to be transformed into papyrus in her dream.] That green leaf is pretty. Of what plant is it the leaf? I think I have a pencil; I am going to try to make this sketch.

After the usual struggle between the two methods of holding the pencil (see pp. 63–65), she yields to Léopold's manner of holding it, saying, "So much the worse"; then traces, slowly and with great care, Fig. 35, from left to right, often raising her eyes to her imaginary model, as if copying a drawing. After which she goes profoundly asleep; then other somnambulisms come.

On awaking she recollects the state of confusion through which she had passed. "Wretched evening," said she. "I was unhappy. I felt that I was living here, as I always have, and I saw some things as though I were a foreigner. I was with you, but I was living elsewhere," etc.

This whole scene gives the distinct impression that the Arab phrase only existed in Hélène's recollection as a visual memory, without meaning or any verbal images. It was for her an incomprehensible piece of writing, a simple drawing, like Chinese or Japanese characters would be for us. Evidently it was a text which had come before her eyes at some propitious moment, and, having been absorbed by the subliminal imagination— always on the watch for matters of Oriental aspect—had been incorporated in a scene of the Asiatic dream.

Such, at least, is the supposition which seems to me the most plausible. For, to regard it as a fragment of Arabian, which Hélène could speak and write fluently if she were in an appropriate state of somnambulism—as Léopold pretended one day to be the fact—seems to me an hypothesis still more arbitrary, and little in accord with the other trance phenomena of Mlle. Smith.

Occasions have not been wanting to her in the five years during which

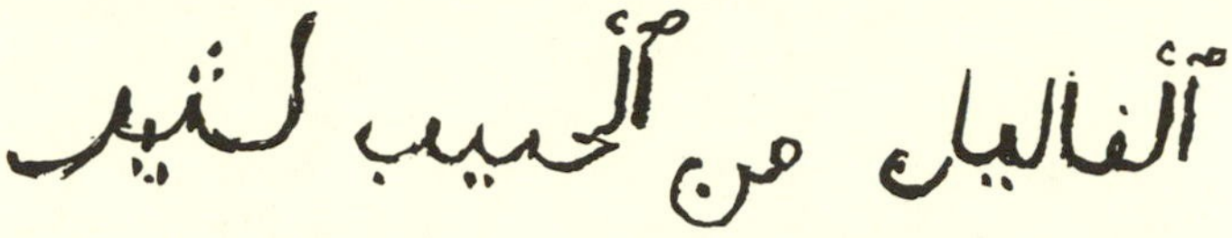

آلفاليل من آلحبيب كثير

Fig. 35. Arabian text drawn from left to right by Mlle. Smith in hemisomnambulism: elqalil men elhabib ktsir, *the little from the friend (is) much.* Natural size.

her exotic romances have been unfolding themselves to make use of her supposed philological reserves by speaking and writing Arabian, if her subliminal memory had so desired.

She has presented all degrees and kinds of somnambulism, and more visions of Arabia than could have failed to awaken by association the corresponding idiom, if it really was slumbering in her. The complete and total isolation of the text given above in the midst of this flood of Oriental scenes, seems to me, therefore, to testify strongly in favor of my supposition that it has to do with a visual flash, unique in its kind, accidentally encountered and stored up, and that the Asiatic secondary personality of Mlle. Smith is absolutely ignorant of Arabic.*

Concerning the other details of the Arab somnambulisms of Hélène, I have nothing to say; they do not go beyond the ideas which she could unconsciously have gathered from the surrounding environment; and to the other sources of her knowledge must be added whatever she might have heard from her father, who had at one time lived in Algeria.

The proper names connected with the Arab scenes, with the possible exception of Pirux, awaken certain associations of ideas, without making it possible to affirm anything with certainty as to their origin.*

IV. The Hindoo Language of Mlle. Smith

The nature of the Hindoo language of Hélène is less easy to explain clearly than that of the Martian, because it has never been possible to obtain either a literal translation of it or written texts. Besides, being ignorant of the numberless dialects of ancient and modern India, and not believing it to be incumbent upon me to devote myself to their study solely that I might be able to appreciate at their proper value the philological exploits of an entranced medium, I am not in a situation to allow myself any personal judgment in regard to this matter.

There is not even left to me the resource of placing the parts of the process as a whole before the reader, as I have done in the case of the Martian, for the reason that our ignorance of Hélène's Hindoo, added to her rapid and indistinct pronunciation—a real prattle sometimes—has caused us to lose the greater part of the numerous words heard in the course of some thirty Oriental scenes scattered over a space of four years.

Even the fragments which we have been able to note down present for the most part so much uncertainty that it would be idle to publish all of them. I have communicated the best of them to several distinguished Oriental scholars. From certain information which they have kindly given me, it appears that the *soi-disant* Hindoo of Hélène is not any fixed idiom known to these specialists; but, on the other hand, there are to be found in it, more or less disfigured and difficult to recognize, certain terms or roots which approach more nearly to Sanscrit than any actual language of India, and the meaning of which often very well corresponds with the situations in which these words have been uttered. I proceed to give some examples of them:

1. The two words, **atiêyâ ganapatinâmâ,** which inaugurated the Hindoo language on the 6th of March, 1895 (see p. 308), and which were invested at that moment, in the mouth of Simandini, with the evident meaning of a formula of salutation or of benediction, addressed to her late husband, inopportunely returned, were articulated in a manner so impressive and so solemn that their pronunciation leaves scarcely any room for doubt.

It is all the more interesting to ascertain the accord of my scientist correspondents upon the value of these two words; the first recalls to them nothing precise or applicable to the situation, but the second is a flattering and very appropriate allusion to the divinity of the Hindoo Pantheon, which is more actively interesting to the professional world.

M. P. Oltramare, to whom I sent these words, without saying anything as to their source, replied:

> There is nothing more simple than the word **ganapatinâmâ**; it means, *"who bears the name of Ganapati,"* which is the same as *Ganesa.* . . . As to **atiêyâ,** that word has not a Hindoo appearance; it might perhaps be **atreya,** which, it seems, serves as a designation for women who have suffered an abortion, an explication which, however, I do not guarantee [In order to affirm more concerning these words, it would be necessary to know] whether they are really Sanscrit, since if they belong to the vulgar languages, I excuse myself absolutely.

M. Glardon, who is more familiar with the vulgar languages and speaks Hindustani fluently, did not hint to me of any other meaning for **atiêyâ** and saw also in the other word "an epithet of honor, literally, 'named Ganapati,' familiar name of the god Ganesa."

M. de Saussure also found no meaning whatever for the first term, in which he inclines now to see an arbitrary creation of the Martian order, and he remarked that in the second, "the two words, **Ganapati**, well-known divinity, and **nâmâ**, *name*, are constructed together, in some inexplicable manner, but not necessarily false. It is quite curious," adds he, "that this fragment, which is mixed up with the name of a god, may be properly pronounced with a kind of solemn emphasis and a gesture of religious benediction. This denotes, indeed, an intelligent and intentional use."

According to this first brief specimen, therefore, Hélène's Hindoo appears to be a mixture of improvised articulations and of veritable Sanscrit words adapted to the situation. Later specimens only serve to corroborate this impression.

2. The next outbreak of Hindoo took place five months later (September 15, 1895), in the midst of a very long Oriental seance, in which I only refer to points especially interesting to us—to wit, Hélène's supposed Sanscrit, the French interpretation which Léopold gave of it, and the curious evidences of agreement of these two texts.

In one tender scene, with sighs and tears, in connection with Sivrouka, Hélène uttered in an exceedingly sweet voice the following words: **ou mama priva** (or **prira, priya**)—**mama radisivou**—**mama sadiou sivrouka** —**apa tava va signa damasa**—**simia damasa bagda sivrouka**. During the various phases which precede the awaking, I ask Léopold the meaning of these words. He at first refused to give it, saying, "Find it out yourself"; then, as I insist, "I would have preferred that you found it out yourself." I beg him to give at least the correct spelling of an Oriental text furnished us in so uncertain a manner, but he disappeared, saying he was ignorant of Sanscrit. By means of later questions which he answers by "yes" and "no," it is discovered that they are words of love from Simandini to her husband, who was about to leave her for a voyage to his principality. Then suddenly, as the awaking seems to be approaching, Léopold moves the index-finger feverishly, and commences to dictate impatiently: *"Hasten* [to spell] . . . My good, my excellent, my dearly loved Sivrouka, without thee where to find happiness?" His answers to our questions lead us to understand that this is the substantial meaning of all the Sanscrit spoken that evening (and given above), that it is not he, Léopold, who speaks this language to Hélène, because he does not understand it, but that it is indeed he who gives us the French equivalent for it, not by a literal translation of the words themselves, since he does not understand them, but by interpreting the inmost feelings of Mlle. Smith, with which he is perfectly familiar. Shortly afterwards Hélène awakes without recollection.

According to M. de Saussure there are certainly in this text some Sanscrit fragments answering more or less to the interpretation of Léopold. The most clear are **mama priya,** which signifies *my dear, my dearly loved,* and **mama sadiou** (corrected to **sâdhô**), *my good, my excellent*. The rest of the phrase is less satisfactory in its present condition; **tava** could well be *of thee*, but **apa tava** is a pure barbarism, if it is intended for *far from thee*. In the same way the syllable **bag** in **bagda** seems to mean, independently of the translation of Léopold, **bhâga**, *happiness*, but is surrounded by incomprehensible syllables.

3. In a subsequent seance (December 1, 1895), Hélène gave herself up to a varied series of somnambulistic pantomimes representing scenes in the life of Simandini, which were thought to be located at Mangalore, and in the course of which several Hindoo words escaped her, of which, unhappily, no interpretation could be obtained from Léopold. But here again, if one is not too difficult to satisfy, a meaning more or less adapted to the pantomime is finally discovered.

In the midst of a playful scene with her little monkey, Mitidja, she tells him in her sweetest and most harmonious tones (A), **mama kana sour** (or **sourde**) **mitidya.** . . . **kana mitidya** (*ter*). Later, answering her imaginary prince, who, according to Léopold, has just given her a severe admonition (the reason for which is not known), and to which she listened with an air of forced submission, and, almost sneeringly, she tells him (B), **adaprati tava sivrouka.** . . . **nô simyô sinonyedô** . . . **on yediô sivrouka.** Returning to a better feeling and leaning towards him, she murmurs with a charming smile (C) **mama plia** . . . **mama naximi** (or **naxmi**) **sivrouka** . . . **aô laos, mi sivrouka.**

In the fragment (A), one may suppose the **mama kana** to be a term of affection, taking the **kana** to be equivalent to the Sanscrit *kânta*, "beloved," or *kanistha*, "darling," unless it be translated, as M. Glardon does, **kana** (corrected to **khana**) **mitidya** *to eat for Mitidja*.

In the phrase (B), according to M. de Saussure, "the last words might, with some show of reason, make us think of the word **anyediuh**, *the following day*, or, *another day*, repeated twice; and, on the other hand, the first word might be transformed into **adya-prabhrti**, *starting from to-day*; which, combined with other syllables, themselves conventionally triturated, might give something like: **adya-pra-bhrti tava, sivruka** . . . **yôshin** . . . **na anyediuh, any ediuh**: *from to-day, of thee, Sivrouka, that I am* . . . *wife* . . . *not another day, another day*—which, besides (if it has any meaning at all,) has scarcely any connection with the scene"

In the phrase (C) the words **mama plia** evidently mean the same as the words above, **mama priya**, *my beloved*; **naxmi** might be **lakshmî**, *beauty and fortune*; and the last words might contain **asmi**, *I am.**

While, therefore, recognizing some words of pure Sanscrit, the whole appearance of these first texts presents, on the other hand, certain matters quite suspicious, from the point of view of construction, of the order of the words, and possibly also the correctness of the forms.

"*E.g.*," observes M. de Saussure, "I do not remember that one can say in Sanscrit, 'my Sivrouka,' nor 'my dear Sivrouka.' One can well say **mama priya**, *my well beloved*, substantively; but **mama priya Sivruka** is quite another thing: but it is *my dear Sivrouka* which occurs most frequently. It is true," adds my learned colleague, "that nothing can be affirmed absolutely, especially concerning certain epochs at which much bad Sanscrit was made in India. The resource always remains to us of assuming that, since the eleventh wife of Sivrouka was a child of Arabia, she had not had time to learn to express herself without error in the idiom of her lord and master, up to the moment at which the funeral pile put an end to her brief existence."

The misfortune is, in assuming by hypothesis the point of view of the romance, one exposes himself to another difficulty. "The most surprising thing," remarks M. de Saussure, "is that Mme. Simandini spoke Sanscrit, and not Pracrit (the connection of the first with the second is the same as that between Latin and French, the one springing from the other, but the one is the language in which the savants write, while the other is the spoken language). While in the Hindoo drama the kings, the brahmins, and the personages of high degree are observed habitually to use Sanscrit, it is questionable if such was constantly the case in real life. But, under all circumstances, all the women, even in the drama, speak Pracrit. A king addresses his wife in the noble language (Sanscrit); she answers him always in the vulgar language. But the idiom of Simandini, even though it be a Sanscrit very hard to recognize, is not in any case the Pracrit."

The numerous Hindoo speeches of Mlle. Smith during these latter years give rise to certain analogous observations, and do not throw any new light on their origin. I shall confine myself to a few examples, which I have chosen less for the sake of the Sanscritoid texts themselves, which are also always defective and distorted, than for the reason that the varied circumstances in which they have been produced afford a certain psychological interest.

4. Scene of Chiromancy. In the course of a long Arab seance, then Hindoo (February 2, 1896), Hélène knelt down by the side of my chair, and, taking me for Sivrouka, seized and examined my hand, all the while carrying on a conversation in a foreign language (without seeming to notice my actual words). It seems that this conversation contained some expression of anxiety in regard to my health, which had inspired several somnambulisms of Mlle. Smith during the preceding months (an example will be found on pp. 76–77).

At the same time at which she attentively examines the lines of my hand, she pronounces the following fragmentary sentences, separated by silences corresponding to the hallucinatory replies of Sivrouka: "**Priya sivrouka . . . nô** [signifying No, according to Léopold] **. . . tvandastroum** sivrouka . . . itiami adia priya . . . itiami sivra adia . . . yatou . . . napi adia . . . nô . . . mama souka, mama baga sivrouka . . . yatou." Besides sivra, which, Léopold says, is an affectionate name for Sivrouka, we can divine in this text other terms of affection: priya, *beloved*; mama soukha, mama bhâga, "*Oh, my delight, oh, my happiness!*" M. Glardon also calls attention to the word tvandastroum, which approaches the Hindustani *tandarast* (or *tandurust*), "who is in good health"—*tandurusti*, "health," coming from the two words *tan*, "physical condition," and *durust*, "good, true," of Persian origin. But he adds that it is possibly only a coincidence, and seems to me doubtful whether he would have thought of the connection if it were not found in a scene of chiromancy.

5. The Hindoo cycle, like the others, makes numerous irruptions into the ordinary life of Mlle. Smith, and affects her personality in most varied degrees, from the simple waking vision of Oriental landscapes or people up to the total incarnations of Simandini, of which Hélène preserves no memory whatever. One frequent form of these spontaneous automatisms consists in certain mixed states, in which she perceives personages who seem to her objective and independent, while continuing to have the feeling of a subjective implication or identification in regard to them, the impression of an indefinable *tua res agitur*. It then easily happens that the conversations she has with them are a mixture of French and a foreign language which she is wholly ignorant of, though feeling the meaning of it. The following is an example:

March 1, 1898.—Between five and six in the morning, while still in bed but wide awake, as she affirms, Hélène had "a superb Hindoo vision." Magnificent palace, with a huge staircase of white stone, leading to splendid halls furnished with low divans without cushions, of yellow, red, and more often of blue materials. In a boudoir a woman (Simandini) reclining and leaning nonchalantly on her elbow; on his knees near her a man with black curly hair, of dark complexion (Sivrouka), clothed in a large, red, embroidered robe, and speaking a foreign language, not Martian, which Hélène did not know, but which, however, she had the feeling of comprehending inwardly, and which enabled her to write some sentences of it in French after the vision. While she *listened* to this man speaking, she *saw* the lips of the woman open, without hearing any sound come from her mouth, in such a way that she did not know what she said, but Hélène had at the same time the impression of answering *inwardly, in thought,* to the conversation of the man, and she noted his reply. (This means, psychologically, that the words of Sivrouka gushed forth in auditive images or hallucinations, and the answers of Simandini-Hélène in psychomotor-spoken images of articulation, accompanied by the usual representation of Simandini effectuating the corresponding labial movements.) Here is a fragment of conversation noted by Hélène in pencil at the outset of the vision, in her ordinary handwriting, but very irregular, attesting that she had not yet entirely regained her normal state.

(Sivrouka.) "My nights without repose, my eyes red with tears, Simandini, will not these touch at last thy **attamana**? Shall this day end without *pardon, without love?*" (Simandini.) "Sivrouka, no, the day shall not end without pardon, without love; the **sumina** has not been launched far from me, as thou hast supposed; it is there—dost thou see?" (Sivrouka.) "Simandini, my **soucca, maccanna baguea**—pardon me again, always!"

This little scrap of conversation, it may be remarked in passing, gives quite correctly the emotional note, which is strong throughout the whole length of the Hindoo dream in the relationship of its two chief personages. As to the Sanscritoid words which are there mingled with the French, they have not an equal value. "**Sumina**," says M. de Saussure, "recalls nothing. **Attamana**, at most **âtmânam** (accusative of **âtmâ**) *l'âme*, 'the soul'; but I hasten to say that in the context in which **attamana** figures one could not make use of the Sanscrit word which resembles it, and which at bottom only signifies (*âme*) 'soul' in philosophical language, and in the sense of *'l'âme universelle,'* or other learned meanings."

6. The apparition of isolated Hindoo words, or words incorporated in a non-Hindoo context, is not very rare with Hélène, and is produced sometimes in auditive hallucinations, sometimes in her writings (see, *e.g.*, Fig. 37, p. 205); sometimes, again, in the course of words uttered in hemisomnambulism more or less marked. The list which has been collected of these detached terms shows the same mixture of pure Sanscrit and unknown words, which can only be connected with that language by some transformation so arbitrary or forced as to destroy altogether the value of such comparison.

To this second category belong, for example, **gava, vindamini, jotisse**, also spelled by Mlle. Smith. These terms, of whose signification she is absolutely ignorant, struck her ear in the course of a Hindoo vision which occurred in the morning when she first awoke. The last of these words recalls to M. de Saussure the Sanscrit *jyôtis*, "a constellation"; but then he would pronounce it *djiôtisse*, which hardly corresponds to the manner in which Hélène heard and wrote it. There must be added to these examples certain Hindoo words which have made irruptions into some Martian texts.

These are *Adel*, a proper name, and *yestad*, "unknown," in text 13; and (in text 31) *vadasa*, which, according to the rest of the sentence, seems to designate some divinities or some powers, and in which MM. de Saussure and Glardon suspect a mangled reminiscence of the Sanscrit term *dévâdâsa*, "slave of the gods."*

7. To crown these specimens of the Sanscrit of Hélène, let us cite her "Hindoo chant," which has made half a dozen appearances in the last two years, and of which Léopold deigned, on a single occasion, to outline the translation.

The utterances consist essentially of the Sanscrit word *gaya* "chant," repeated to satiety, with here and there some other terms, badly articulated and offering discouraging variations in the notes taken by the different hearers. I will confine myself to two versions.

One of them is by Hélène herself. In a spontaneous vision (May 18, 1898, in the morning, upon awaking), she perceived a man, richly dressed in yellow and blue (Sivrouka), reclining upon beautiful cushions near a fountain surrounded by palm-trees; a brunette woman (Simandini) seats herself on the grass, sings to him in a strange language a ravishing melody. Hélène gathers the following fragments of it in writing, in which may be recognized the disfigured text of her ordinary song, "**Ga haïa vahaïyami . . . vassen iata . . . pattissaïa priaïa.**"

The other version is that of M. de Saussure, very much better qualified than we are to distinguish the Hindoo sounds. He was quite near Hélène, who sang seated upon the ground, whose voice for the moment articulated so badly that several words escaped him, and he does not vouch for the accuracy of his text, which is as follows, as he wrote it to the measure: "**Gâya gaya naïa ia miya gayä briti . . . gaya vaya yâni pritiya kriya gayâni i gâya mamatua gaya mama nara mama patii si gaya gandaryô gâya ityami vasanta . . . gaya gaya yâmi gaya priti gaya priya gâya patisi. . . .**"

It was towards the end of this same seance that Léopold, undoubtedly with the idea of doing honor to the distinguished presence of M. de Saussure, decided, after a scene of Martian translation (text 14 by Esenale), to give us, in Hélène's voice, his interpretation of the Hindoo chant, which follows, *verbatim*, with its mixture of Sanscrit words: "Sing, bird, let us sing! **Gaya**! Adèl, Sivrouka,* sing of the spring-time! Day and night I am happy! Let us sing! Spring-time bird, happiness! **ityâmi mamanara priti**, let us sing! let us love! my king! Miousa, Adèl!"*

In comparing these translations of the Hindoo text, certain points of resemblance are discovered between them. Outside the two perfectly correct words, **gâya**, *song*, and **vasanta**, *spring-time*, the idea of *"let us love"* is discovered in **priti** and **briti** (Sanscrit *prîti*, the act of loving), and an approximate equivalent of *"my king"* in **mama patii**, recalling the Sanscrit *mama patê*, "my husband, my master."

It is, unfortunately, hardly possible to carry the identification further, except perhaps for *bird*, which, with some show of reason, might be suspected in **vayayâni**, vaguely recalling **vâyasân** (accusative plural of **vâyasa** *bird*).

As to the melody of this plaintive ditty, M. Aug. de Morsier, who heard

Fig. 36. Modulation of a Hindoo song. The final G of the three variations was held with perfect steadiness during fourteen seconds. The series A was often doubled and trebled before the continuation.

it at the seance of the 4th of September, 1898, has kindly noted it as exactly as possible (see Fig. 36).

The preceding examples suffice to give an idea of Hélène's Hindoo, and it is time to conclude.

It apparently does not belong to any actually existing dialect. M. Glardon declares that it is neither ancient nor modern Hindustani, and, after having put forth at the beginning, by way of simple hypothesis, the idea that it might be Tamil, or Mahratta, he now sees in it a *mélange* of real terms, probably Sanscrit and invented words. M. Michel, likewise, is of the opinion that the grotesque jargon of Simandini contains fragments of Sanscrit quite well adapted to the situation. All my correspondents are, on the whole, of exactly the same view, and I could not better sum up their opinion than by quoting the words of M. de Saussure:

> As to the question of ascertaining whether all this really represents Sanscrit, it is evidently necessary to answer, *No.* One can only say:
>
> First: That it is a medley of syllables, in the midst of which there are, incontestably, some series of eight to ten syllables, constituting a fragment of a sentence which has a meaning (especially exclamatory phrases—*e.g.*, **mama priya**, *mon bien-aimé* ("my well-beloved"); **mama soukha**, *mes délices* ("my delight").
>
> Secondly: That the other syllables, of unintelligible aspect, never have an anti-Sanscrit character—*i.e.*, do not present groups materially contrary or in opposition to the general figure of the Sanscrit words.
>
> Thirdly and finally: That the value of this latter observation is, on the other hand, quite considerably diminished by the fact that Mlle. Smith seldom launches out into complicated forms of syllables, and greatly affects the vowel *a*; but Sanscrit is a language in which the proportion of the *a*'s to the other vowels is almost four to one, so that in uttering three or four syllables in *a*, one could hardly avoid vaguely encountering a Sanscrit word.

It follows from this last remark of M. de Saussure that it ought not to be very difficult to fabricate Sanscrit after the mode of Simandini, if only one is possessed of some veritable elements which can serve as a model and give tone to the remainder. And there is no need to know very much of it, either, as M. Barth remarks: "Has Mlle. Smith been in communication with any person from whom she could have taken some scraps of Sanscrit and of history? That would suffice, in this case, for the original germ, even though it were but slight. Imagination would do the rest. Children are very frequently *onomatopoioi*."*

But it is, naturally, Mlle. Smith herself who furnishes us, in her own Martian, the fact most likely to throw light upon her Hindoo. It evidently is not difficult for a subconscious activity capable of manufacturing a language out of whole cloth to make another by imitation and by spinning out some real data. Also, as to the beginning of the Martian (a year later, as we have seen, to that of the Hindoo), M. de Saussure does not hesitate to make this comparison, and explains, *e.g.*, the initial Sanscritoid text, the famous phrase of benediction, **atiêyâ ganapatinâmâ**, by the same process of fabrication which shone forth in the words of Esenale or Astané.*

I am not convinced that the general process of replacing word for word the French terms by terms of Oriental aspect, which is certainly the process employed in the fabrication of the Martian, has been made use of in the case of Hélène's Oriental words. Léopold, who has laid so much stress on procuring us a quasi-magical means of obtaining the literal translation of the Martian, has never condescended to do the same thing for the Hindoo, but has confined himself to outlining for us some free and vague interpretations, which scarcely add anything to that which the pantomime permits us to divine. This leads us to think that an entire precise translation of the Hindoo is impossible—in other terms, that Hélène does not fabricate her *pseudo*-Sanscrit by following step by step a French plot, and by maintaining in her neologisms the meaning which has been once adopted, but that she improvises and leaves the result to chance, without reflection (with the exception of some words of true Sanscrit, the meaning of which she knows and which she applies intelligently to the situation).

It is not, then, to the Martian texts proper, in my opinion, that we must compare Hélène's Hindoo, but to that *pseudo*-Martian jargon spoken with volubility in certain seances, and which have never been noted with certainty nor translated by Esenale.

It is understood, too, that while Hélène's subliminal self can safely give itself up to the creation of a definite language in the freedom which the planet Mars affords, where there is no pre-existing system to be conformed to nor any objective control to fear, it would be very imprudent and absurd to repeat the process in connection with India: the few words of pure Sanscrit which were at its disposal kept it from inventing others, the falseness of which would be evident at the first attempt at a literal and *verbatim* translation. It, therefore, contented itself with these veridical elements, insufficient in themselves alone for the construction of complete sentences, being a jargon devoid of meaning, but in harmony through their dominant vowels with the authentic fragments.

Now how could these authentic fragments have come into the possession of Mlle. Smith, who has no recollection whatever (nor has her family) of ever having studied Sanscrit, or of having ever been in communication with Oriental scholars? This is the problem which my researches have encountered hitherto, and as a solution of which I can think of nothing more likely than that of a fortunate chance, analogous to that which enabled me to discover the passage of De Marlès. I am, for the time being, reduced to vague conjectures as to the extent of Mlle. Smith's latent knowledge of Sanscrit, and the probable nature of its manner of acquisition.

I had long thought that Hélène might have absorbed her Hindoo principally by *auditive* means, and that she had, perhaps, in her infancy lived in the same house with some Indian student, whom she had heard, across the street or through an open window, speaking aloud Sanscrit texts with their French translation. The story of the young domestic without education is well known, who, seized with a fever, spoke both Greek and Hebrew, which had been stored up in her mind, unknown to her, while she was in the service of a German savant. *Se non è vero è ben trovato.* In spite of the just criticisms of Mr. Lang,* apropos of its poorly established authenticity, this standard anecdote may be considered as a type of many other facts of the same kind which have since been actually observed, and as a salutary warning to distrust subconscious memories of auditive origin. But Indian scholars are rare in Geneva, and this trail has yielded me nothing.

I am really inclined to admit the exclusively *visual* origin of Hélène's Sanscrit. First, it is not necessary for her to have heard that idiom. Reading of texts printed in French characters coincides very well with a pronunciation so confused and badly articulated as hers; and, further, it alone can account for certain inexplicable errors of pronunciation if Mlle. Smith had acquired that language by ear.

The most characteristic of her errors is the presence in Hindoo of the French sound *u*, which does not exist in Sanscrit, but is naturally suggested by reading if it has not been previously ascertained that that letter is pronounced *ou* in the Sanscrit words in which it appears.*

Other observations militate in favor of the same supposition. Never in the seances has Simandini ventured to *write* Sanscrit, and it is in French letters that her name was given (see p. 181).

Still, Hélène subconsciously possesses a part, at least, of the De-

vanagari alphabet, since sometimes certain characters belonging to it slip
into her normal writing. But it is to be noted that her knowledge of this
kind does not seem in any way to go beyond that which might have resulted from a rapid glance at a Sanscrit grammar.

In certain cases this irruption of foreign signs (altogether analogous to
that which has been seen in the case of the Martian) is connected with an
access of spontaneous somnambulism and makes part of a whole troop of
images and of Oriental terms.

An interesting example is found in Fig. 37, which reproduces the end
of a letter which Hélène wrote me from the country. All the rest of this
six-page letter is perfectly normal, both as to handwriting and content,
but suddenly, tired by her effort of prolonged attention, she begins to
speak of her health, sleep overcomes her, and the last lines show the
invasion of the Oriental dream.

Kana, the slave, with his tame birds, and the brilliant plants of the
tropics, substitute themselves little by little for the actual room. The letter reached me unfinished and without signature, as is shown in Fig. 37;
Hélène closed it mechanically during her somnambulism, without knowledge of this unusual termination, at which she was surprised and annoyed
when I showed it to her later.*

Examination and comparison of all these graphomotor automatisms
show that there are in Hélène's subconsciousness some positive notions,
albeit superficial and rudimentary, of the Sanscrit alphabet. She knows
the exact form of many isolated characters, and their general value, in the
abstract, as it were, but she does not seem to have any idea of their concrete use in connection with other letters.*

In a word, these fragments of graphic automatisms betray a knowledge
of Hindoo writing such as a curious mind might be able to acquire by
perusing for some moments the first two or three pages of a Sanscrit
grammar. It would retain certain detached forms; first, the *a* and the *e*,
which, striking the eye at the commencement of the two first lines (containing the vowels, and usually separated from the following lines containing the consonants) of the standard arrangement of the Hindoo letters in
ten groups; then the series of ciphers, occupying a line by themselves and
easy to retain; finally, some other simple signs gleaned at hazard; but
there will probably not be retained any of the too complicated figures
resulting from the union of several characters in order to form words. This
supposed genesis entirely corresponds with the extent of the notions as to
Sanscrit writing of which Mlle. Smith's subconsciousness gives evidence.*

It will suffice in summing up, to account for Mlle. Smith's Hindoo language, that perhaps in the N. group, or in some other spiritistic environment of which I am ignorant, some one, for the sake of curiosity, may have
shown her and allowed her to glance over a Sanscrit grammar or lexicon,

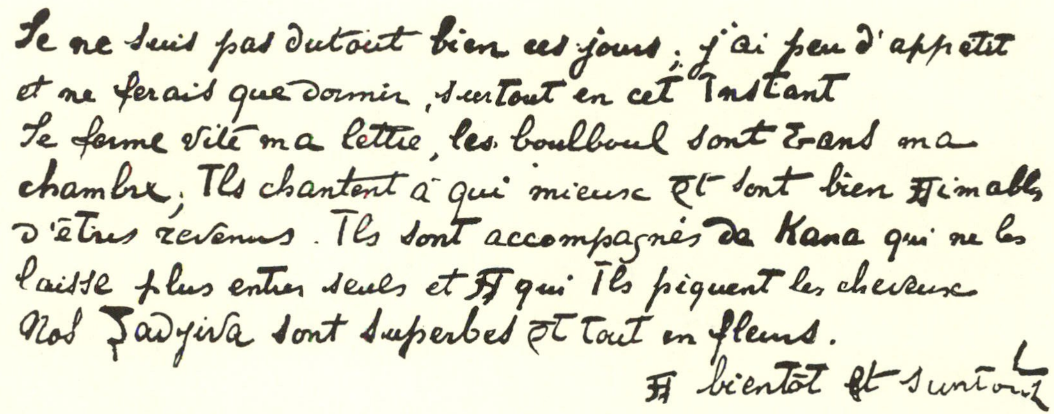
Je ne suis pas dutout bien ces jours; j'ai peu d'appetit
et ne ferais que dormir, surtout en cet instant
Je ferme vite ma lettre, les boulboul sont dans ma
chambre; Ils chantent à qui mieux et sont bien aimables
d'êtres revenus. Ils sont accompagnés de Kana qui ne les
laisse plus entrer seuls et à qui Ils piquent les cheveux
Nos radyiva sont superbes et tout en fleurs.
A bientôt et surtout

Fig. 37. Fragment. Final sentence of a letter of Mlle. Smith, finished (or rather remaining unfinished), during the irruption of a spontaneous access of Hindoo somnambulism. Note foreign words, *boulboul* (Persian name for nightingale), *Kana* (Hindoo slave of Simandini), and *radyiva* (Sanscrit name for blue lotus); also the Sanscrit letters *a, e, i, d, r,* taking the place of the French initials. Note also the change of the form of the *t*'s.

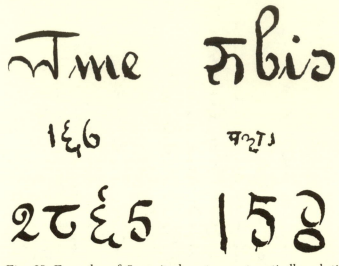

Fig. 38. Examples of Sanscrit characters, automatically substituted for French words and ciphers, in words and figures appearing in the normal writings of Mlle. Smith (*la*me, *ru*bis, *plis*, 2865, 154). Natural size.

immediately after a seance, during that state of suggestibility in which the exterior suggestions are registered very strongly in her case, often without leaving traces in her conscious memory. The fact will also be explained that Hélène has no memory whatever of it, is absolutely convinced that she never saw or heard the least fragment of Sanscrit or any other Oriental language.

I ought also to add that the information which I have up to the present time been able to gather has furnished me with no positive indication of the truth of my supposition, while, on the other hand, it has not tended to establish its falsity.*

V. The Sources of the Hindoo Dream

This paragraph will have no meaning whatever for those who hold the Oriental cycle to be in reality the reappearance in Mlle. Smith's somnambulistic states, of memories belonging to an anterior existence in which she was an Asiatic princess, and I myself naik of Tchandraguiri, Professor Seippel, an Arab slave, etc.

I shall confine myself in this case to an expression of regret that the chance which has united us afresh, after five centuries of separation, did not leave us in the midst of those tropical splendors instead of transporting us to the banks of the Rhône just where the fog is densest in winter. It is a severe punishment for our past misdeeds. But when one pushes his skepticism so far as only to see in the entire Hindoo dream a fantastic product elaborated out of certain scattered facts, as I have done in the preceding paragraphs, one is likewise punished for his want of faith by the obscure problems which are met with on the subject of the sources of this dream. I would say also that it is difficult to understand why the hypnoid imagination of Mlle. Smith gave itself up to such pranks, and distributed as it did the roles of this comedy.

It is easy to understand how a nature given to subconscious reveries, and such as I have described in the first chapters of this book, has taken pleasure in the fiction of the tragic destiny of Simandini, and also that she felt specially attracted towards the career of Marie Antoinette.

But M. Seippel, whom I quoted above, has nothing about him of the Arab, and still less of the slave, neither in outward appearance nor in character; and as to myself, let us say here, M. F.—if I may be permitted to substitute harmless initials for the always odious "I"—as for M. F., there is generally to be met with in him, under some diffidence, a certain mildness of manner and disposition which would scarcely seem to predestinate him to the energetic and wild role of a violent, whimsical, capricious, and jealous Oriental despot.

As to the psychological origins of the Hindoo dream—considered not so much in its Oriental decoration, but in its essential note, which is the relation of Simandini to Sivrouka (the pretended anteriority of M. F.)—two hypotheses can be framed, between which it is difficult to choose.

First: From the point of view of psychopathology I should be tempted to cause this entire somnambulistic romance to be included in that which Freud calls *Abwehr psychosen*,* resulting from a sort of autotomy which frees the normal self from an affective idea incompatible with it; which idea revenges itself by occasioning very diverse perturbations, according to the subjects, from disorders of innervation, coming to disturb the daily life (hysteria by somatic conversion of the affective coefficient of the repulsed idea), up to the case in which the self only escapes the intolerable contradiction between the given reality and the idea which besets it by plunging itself entirely into the latter (mental hallucinatory confusion, delirium, etc.).

Between these varied results may be found that in which the idea excluded from the consciousness becomes the germ of hypnoid developments, the point of departure of a secondary consciousness unknown to the ordinary personality, the centre of a somnambulistic life in which the tendencies which the normal self has driven far away from it may take refuge and give themselves free play.

This is, perhaps, the happiest solution, from a practical and social point of view, since it leaves the individual in a state of perfect equilibrium and free from nervous troubles, outside of the very limited moments in which the underlying processes break out in accesses of somnambulism.*

Such may be the case of the Hindoo dream and the origin of the attributing of the role of Sivrouka to M. F. Nothing, assuredly, in the normal life or being of Mlle. Smith would cause the suspicion that she had ever consciously felt towards the latter the absurd sentiments which good sense would have condemned in advance; but divers hints of her subliminal life, independently of the Hindoo cycle itself (certain dreams,* etc.), have sometimes seemed to betray a latent conflict, which the sane and reasonable self would have quickly gotten rid of by the banishment from the ordinary personality of the affective idea, inadmissible in the given conditions of reality. Hence, with a temperament accustomed to mediumistic doubling of personality and imbued with spiritistic doctrines, the birth and development, underneath the level of the normal consciousness, of this romance of a former existence, in which emotional tendencies incompatible with the present life have found on occasion a sort of theoretic justification and a free field for expansion.

Secondly: It may also be presumed, and I prefer to admit, that the sentiments of Simandini towards her fictitious rajah, far from being the reflection and somnambulic transposition of an impression really felt by Mlle. Smith in regard to some one real and determined, are only a fantastic creation—like the passion with which juvenile imaginations are sometimes inflamed for an ideal and abstract type while awaiting the meeting with a concrete realization more or less like it—and that the assimilation of Sivrouka to M. F. is only a coincidence due to the simple chance of Mlle. Smith having made the acquaintance of M. F. at the time when the Hindoo dream was about to begin. Two points strengthen this hypothesis of a contingent and superficial confusion between M. F. and Sivrouka. First, the Hindoo dream was evidently begun by a characteristic vision in which Simandini appeared, almost two months before the admission of M. F. to the seances (see pp. 15 and 175). Instead of supposing that the subconsciousness of Mlle. Smith foresaw already the probable arrival of this new spectator, and reserved for him in advance a leading role in the romance of former existence which she was in process of elaborating (which is not altogether impossible, it is true), it hardly seems as though M. F. could have stood for anything in the dream-personage of Sivrouka. In the second place, it is only in the light somnambulisms and her mixed or crepuscular states that Mlle. Smith happens to take M. F. for the Hindoo prince and to seat herself at his feet in attitudes of tenderness and abandon (without otherwise ever departing from the bounds of perfect propriety); as soon as the trance becomes profound and the Hindoo somnambulism complete, M. F. ceases to exist for her, as well as the others present, and she then is concerned only with an absolutely hallucinatory Sivrouka. This is the place to state that Hélène has never presented any phenomenon similar to—far from it—certain cases* in which have been seen the awakening in the hypnotic subject of gross and more or less bestial tendencies, for which the subjects would have blushed in their waking state. There is nothing of that nature in Mlle. Smith. Somnambulism does not detract in any way from the elevation of her moral sense. The same is true of her deepest trances or when she "incarnates" personages very different from her ordinary character—she never departs from that real dignity which is a trait of her normal personality.

To sum up—the hypothesis of a purely accidental identification, a kind of association by simple contiguity between the Hindoo prince and M. F., seems to me, on the whole, the most natural. It releases the latter, besides, from all responsibility (altogether involuntary, however) for the sentiments so profound, so disinterested, so worthy of a less tragic fate, which the imaginary personage of Sivrouka Nayaka inspires in the poor Princess Simandini.

CHAPTER NINE

The Royal Cycle

IF I WERE obliged to give this cycle a place proportioned to that which it occupies in the somambulic life of Mlle. Smith, a hundred pages would not suffice. But permit me to pass rapidly over facts concerning which I should only be obliged to repeat the greater part of the observations called forth by the preceding romances, which apply equally well, *mutatis mutandis*, to the personification of Marie Antoinette by Hélène.

The choice of this role is naturally explained by the innate tastes of Mlle. Smith for everything that is noble, distinguished, elevated above the level of the common herd, and by the fact that some exterior circumstance fixed her hypnoid attention upon the illustrious queen of France in preference to the many other historic figures equally qualified to serve as a point of attachment for her subconscious megalomaniac reveries.

In default of absolutely certain information on this point, I strongly suspect the engraving from the *Memoirs of a Physician*, representing the dramatic scene of the decanter between Balsamo and the Dauphiness, of having given birth to this identification of Hélène with Marie Antoinette, as well as to that of her secondary personality of Léopold with Cagliostro.

We have, in fact, seen that this engraving (pp. 60–61), so well calculated to impress the imagination, was shown to Mlle. Smith by Mme. B. at the end of a seance—that is, at a moment when one is never sure that Hélène's return to her normal state is complete, and in which her hypnoid personality, still on a level with consciousness, so to speak, is very prone to absorb the interesting suggestions which the environment may furnish. It was several months—a year and a quarter, possibly—after this incident (the precise date of which, in 1892 or 1893, it is impossible to determine) that announcement was made by the table, on the 30th of January, 1894, that Hélène was the reincarnation of Marie Antoinette. It is to be recollected that in the interval she had for some time believed herself to be the reincarnation of Lorenza Feliciani; it is, however, to be noted that these two successive identifications did not have the same guarantee or psychological signification. In fact, it was Mlle. Smith, in the waking state—that is, in her normal personality—who accepted the supposition of Mme. B., that she was the reincarnation of Lorenza;* but the table—*i.e.*, her subconsciousness—always remained silent on this point. On the contrary, the idea of having been Marie Antoinette does not seem to have occurred to Hélène's ordinary consciousness up to the time at which Léopold revealed this secret by the table. If any conclusion may be drawn from this, it is that, under the multiple suggestions of the engraving from Dumas' works and the suppositions of Mme. B., the hypnoid imagination of Mlle. Smith at first preferred to the role of Lorenza that of Marie Antoinette, which is undoubtedly more flattering and more conformable to Hélène's temperament, and then elaborated and matured it, very slowly, it is true, but not excessively so, in comparison with other examples of subliminal incubations of Mlle. Smith.

From the point of view of its psychological forms of manifestation, the Royal cycle from that time followed an evolution analogous to that of its congeners described in the preceding chapters. After some months, during which it unfolded itself in visions described by Hélène and accompanied by typtological explanations dictated by the table, the trance became more profound. Mlle. Smith began to personate the queen in pantomime, of which Léopold gave the exact signification by digital indications. Speech was added the year following, at a date which I cannot fix, but the first occasion on which I was a witness to it was on the 13th of October, 1895. Handwriting only made its appearance, as far as I am aware, two years later (November 1, 1897, see Fig. 39), when the royal incarnation attained its apogee and Hélène was in the habit of retaining in memory the somnambulistic role of Marie Antoinette for several hours. Since then the role has maintained itself at a very remarkable level of perfection, but it scarcely seems to me progressing, and seems likely to become stereotyped. The objectivity of the general type of queen must be distinguished in this brilliant personality, or at least that of a lady of great distinction, as well as a realization of the individual characteristics of Marie Antoinette of Austria. As to the first point there is almost nothing left to be desired. Mlle. Smith seems by nature to possess all that this role demands, and hypnoid autosuggestion finds no lack of material upon which to work.

When the royal trance is complete no one can fail to note the grace, elegance, distinction, majesty sometimes, which shine forth in Hélène's every attitude and gesture.

She has verily the bearing of a queen. The more delicate shades of expression, a charming amiability, condescending hauteur, pity, indifference, overpowering scorn flit successively over her countenance and are manifested in her bearing, to the filing by of the courtiers who people her dream. The play of her hands with her real handkerchief and its fictitious accessories, the fan, the binocle with long handle, the scent-bottle which she carries in a pocket in her girdle; her courtesyings, the movement, full of grace and ease, by which she never forgets at each turning around, to throw back her imaginary train; everything of this kind, which cannot be described, is perfect in its ease and naturalness. Special person-

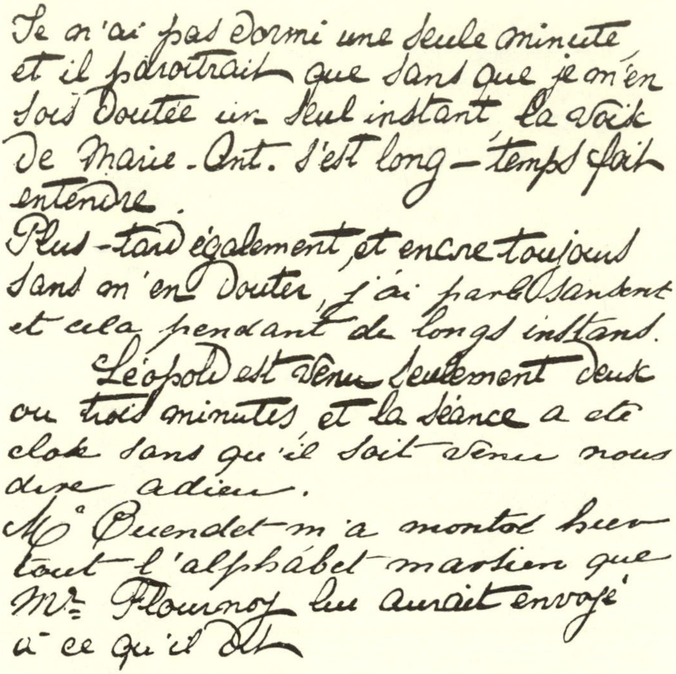
Je n'ai pas dormi une seule minute,
et il paraîtrait que sans que je m'en
sois doutée un seul instant la voix
de Marie-Ant. s'est long-temps fait
entendre.
Plus-tard également, et encre toujours
sans m'en douter, j'ai parlé sanskrit
et cela pendant de longs instans.
Léopold est venu seulement deux
ou trois minutes et la séance a ete
close sans qu'il soit venu nous
dire adieu.
Mr Cuendet m'a montré hier
tout l'alphabet martien que
Mr Flournoy lui aurait envoyé
à ce qu'il dit

Fig. 39. First known example of automatic irruption of the orthography and handwriting called that of Marie Antoinette among the normal writings of Mlle. Smith. Fragments of a letter of Hélène of November 1, 1897, narrating a seance during which she had successfully incarnated the queen of France and the Hindoo princess. (Collection of M. Lemaître.) See also p. 39.

ification of the unhappy Austrian wife of Louis XVI. is of a less evident, and moreover doubtful, accuracy. To judge of it from the only objective point of comparison at our disposal, the handwriting (see Figs. 39 to 41), the Marie Antoinette of Hélène's somnambulisms little resembles her supposed prototype, for there is less of difference between the autographs of Cagliostro and of Léopold (see p. 73) than there is between that of the real queen and that of her pretended reincarnation in Mlle. Smith, the latter having a rounded, inclined calligraphy, much more regular than in her normal state, instead of the angular and illegible writing which was characteristic of the queen of France, to say nothing of the glaring differences in formation of many letters. Some orthographic analogies (Hélène writes *instans, enfans, étois*, etc.) have nothing specific about them, and simply recall the general habits of the last century (see p. 70)

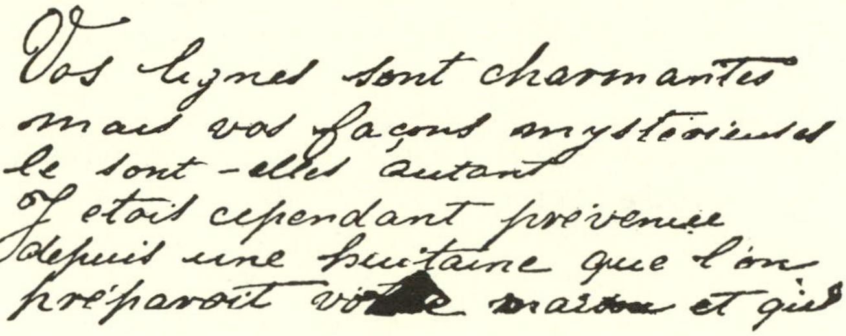
Vos lignes sont charmantes
mais vos façons mystérieuses
le sont-elles autant
J'étois cependant prévenue
depuis une huitaine que l'on
préparoit votre maison et qu'il

Fig. 40. Writing of Mlle. Smith incarnating Marie Antoinette. Seance of November 7, 1897. Beginning of a letter, written in ink and addressed to Philippe d'Orléans (M. Aug. de Morsier, who was not present at the seance). After the ink-stains of the last line, Hélène threw down her pencil, then began again and finished her letter in pencil in a still more regular and slanting hand than the above.

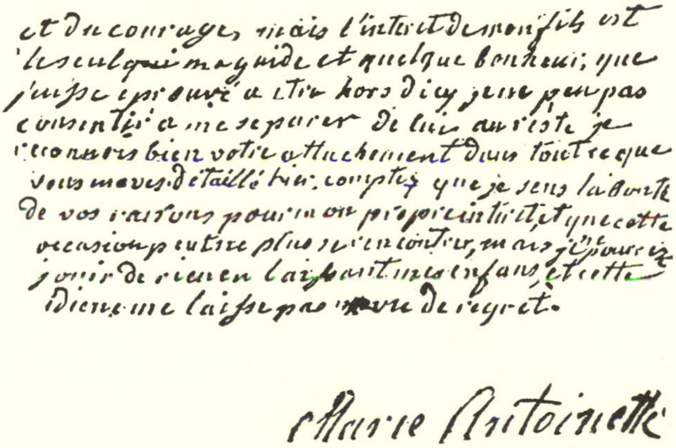
et du courage, mais l'interet de mon fils est
le seul qui me guide et quelque bonheur que
j'eusse éprouvé a etre hors d'icy je ne peux pas
consentir a me separer de lui au reste je
reconnois bien votre attachement dans tout ce que
vous m'avez détaillé hier. comptez que je sens la bonté
de vos raisons pour mon propre interet, et que cette
occasion peut ne plus se rencontrer, mais je ne pourrois
jouir de rien en laissant mes enfans, et cette
idée ne me laisse pas meme de regret.

Marie Antoinette

Fig. 41. Writing and signature of Marie Antoinette. Fragment of a letter written from the Temple to General de Jarnayes, and reproduced in the *Isographie des Hommes célèbres.* (Collection of fac-similes published under the direction of Duchesne, Sr., Paris, 1827–30.)

Not having discovered any indication as to Marie Antoinette's manner of speaking, I do not know whether the hypnoid imagination of Hélène has succeeded better than with the handwriting in adopting in her royal incarnatians certain intonations and a pronunciation which have nothing of German in them, and would rather recall the English accent. The timbre of her voice does not change, but her speech becomes trailing, with a slight rolling of the r's, and takes on something precise and affected, very pretty, but slightly irritating by its length. We already know that there is not an absolute wall of separation between Hélène's various trances. Just as is the case with the Martian and the Hindoo, the handwriting or the spelling of the queen sometimes slips into the correspondence of Mlle. Smith (see Fig. 39), and she also sometimes assumes the accent of Marie Antoinette, if not in the ordinary waking state (I do not know whether that is ever the case), at least outside her Royal cycle, especially in the phases of transition in which she begins or ends by incarnating Léopold, the Martians, etc. (see, for example, p. 81).

From the point of view of its content, the Royal cycle forms a collection of scenes and varied tableaux, like the Martian dream, lacking any continuous plot, and in which marked historic events scarcely hold a place—e.g., in it the queen is never seen to mount the scaffold as Simandini ascends her funeral pile. One does not always even know whether the spectacle before our eyes is supposed to be the repetition, the exact recollection, of unknown but real episodes in the life of Marie Antoinette, or indeed whether it has to do with new, actual incidents passing now between the reincarnated queen and her old acquaintances whom she discovers in the persons present at the seance or in the disincarnate spirits in mediumistic relationship with her. That depends on the case—e.g., on the 25th of December, 1896, Mlle. Smith, entranced, addresses touching exhortations to a lady present whom she took for the Princess Lamballe, which, according to Léopold, is a reproduction of the last evening which the unhappy queen, sustained by her companion in captivity, passed in this world. (It is true that at Christmas, 1792, the princess had already, three months previously, fallen a victim to the massacres of September.) Again the Abbé Grégoire dictates by the table, which bows significantly to Hélène, "*I desired to save you, but I was not able*"; or the sinister Hébert says to her by the same process, "*I was the cause of your death . . . I suffer; pray for me.*" Ought we to consider real the homage and the posthumous remorse which these two disincarnate spirits bring after the lapse of a century to their sovereign, finally recognized in the person of Mlle. Smith?

Generally it is impossible to decide whether the incident transpiring pretends simply to republish the past or constitutes a new fact.

The location of the royal scenes and visions is often undetermined. Many are located in the gardens or the apartments of the Petit Trianon, and the furniture which Hélène describes there is, indeed, always pure Louis XVI. More rarely Marie Antoinette is found at the Temple, or at certain rendezvous—innocent, but very imprudent—in some secret abode in Paris. She is never seen in Austria, since, unlike the Hindoo princess still filled with her Arab memories, she seems to have completely lost sight of her past as a young girl.

In the surroundings of the queen, the king is conspicuous by his absence; very rarely she makes some allusions to him with a marked indifference. The greater part of the personages known to that epoch, whom I refrain from enumerating, figure in it incidentally, but there are three who continually reappear and hold the first rank. There is, first, the Count of Cagliostro, *"mon sorcier,"* or *"ce cher sorcier,"* as the queen familiarly calls him, who never has enough of his visits and his conversations, which are very varied, including the discussion of philosophic subjects, such as the future life and the existence of God as well as the gossip of the last *fête* at Versailles. There is, secondly, Louis Philippe d'Orléans (Equality); while the third is the old Marquis de Mirabeau; all of whom, especially the first, have served as hallucinatory interlocutors towards Hélène in numerous scenes—up to the time at which, to the great amusement of the sitters, the somnambulistic monologue was transformed into real and lively conversation, in consequence of the introduction into the seances of M. Eugène Demole, then of M. Aug. de Morsier, in whom Marie Antoinette immediately recognized the two personages last above mentioned.

Since this unexpected meeting with her two contemporaries, reincarnated, like herself, the somnambulistic queen freely permits herself, on occasion, the pleasure of renewing the little suppers and joyous evenings of long ago. When a seance which has lasted from four o'clock until seven in the afternoon seems to have come to an end, and Mlle. Smith, after having awakened from a long series of Hindoo, Martian, and other scenes, has been invited to dine and refresh herself before taking up her household duties, it often happens that, perceiving M. Demole or M. de Morsier among the persons present, she gives a slight start, with a change of countenance, sometimes barely perceptible, but which there is no mistaking; then, in her very characteristic accent of Marie Antoinette, exclaims, "Oh, marquis, you have been here, and I had not noticed you before!" And then follows a somnambulistic vigil which may be prolonged until nearly ten o'clock in the evening, maintained by means of the suggestive amiability of her improvised companions in sustaining their roles of Mirabeau or Philippe d'Orléans.

They descend to the dining-room. The queen takes her place at the table alongside of the marquis (or of Philippe). She has eyes and ears for him alone, the other guests and the servants remaining shut out from her dream. She eats and drinks only that which he sets before her, and it is no sinecure to supply the wants of this august neighbor, since she possesses a truly royal appetite. The amount of food which she devours and the goblets of wine which she drinks off one after another, without suffering any inconvenience, are astounding, as in her normal state Mlle. Smith is sobriety itself and eats very little. After dinner they pass into the *salon*, with many compliments and obeisances, and Marie Antoinette takes coffee. On the first occasions of this kind, she also accepted a cigarette from Philippe and smoked it—Mlle. Smith never smokes in her waking state—but the remarks of the persons present upon the historical untruthfulness of this feature must have been registered, and bore fruit, since at the following seances she did not seem to understand the use of tobacco in that form; she accepted, on the other hand, with eagerness, a pinch of imaginary snuff, which almost immediately brought about by autosuggestion a series of sneezes admirably successful.

The evening passes in most varied conversation, until, evidently feeling fatigue, the queen becomes silent, closes her eyes, and goes to sleep in an easy-chair. At that instant Léopold, who gives no sign of life, and from whom no response can be obtained during the royal somnambulism, reappears and answers by the fingers or manifests himself in spontaneous gestures. Hélène's hand, *e.g.*, is raised, and makes passes on her forehead to accentuate the restorative sleep which is about to bring her back to her normal state. At the end of some time—half an hour or more—she awakes without any recollection of the evening, believing that she has not yet dined, and complaining of hunger and thirst, as if her stomachic sensibility participated in the amnesia and other modifications which accompany the change of personality. Nevertheless, at such times I have never seen her accept anything more than a couple of glasses of water, after which she feels wide awake.

In escorting her home, I was witness on one occasion to a return of the royal somnambulism. She was exceedingly desirous of going to the house of a well-known personage (whom she had perceived in her vision during the seance), who had been received at the court of Marie Antoinette, and who died in Geneva in the first quarter of this century; it was only upon arriving before the house in which he had lived, and as she was upon the verge of entering it, that I finally succeeded in awakening and restoring her to herself, without memory of the incident, and very much astonished at the unaccustomed streets in which we found ourselves.

It is useless to give a more circumstantial narration of these dinners and *soirées* of Marie Antoinette. They are very entertaining for the spectators, but lose much of their interest when related in their entirety. Their details are exactly what might be expected of a lively subliminal imagination, alert and full of verve, abundantly supplied, on account of the illustrious queen, with notions still more easily explicable, thanks to the intellectual atmosphere of France, than those of the Hindoo cycle.

Numerous anachronisms, however, slip into them, and her Majesty sometimes falls into the snares which the marquis or Philippe take a malicious pleasure in setting for her. She often escapes them when they are too clumsy, and, with a most comical display of temper, is at first confused, then curiously questions, or manifests uneasiness in regard to the mental state of her interlocutors when they introduce the telephone, the bicycle, steamships, or the modern scientific vocabulary into their eighteenth-century conversation. But, on the other hand, she herself employs terms still more malapropos, such as, "to derail" (figuratively), "metre" and "centimetre," etc. Certain words, such as "tramway" and "photography," have occasioned serious conflicts. Marie Antoinette first allows the treacherous word to pass unnoticed, and it is evident that she perfectly understood it, but her own reflection, or the smile of the sitters, awakens in her the feeling of incompatibility; she returns to the word just used, and pretends a sudden ignorance and astonishment in regard to it. Spiritism explains these blunders by accusing the Machiavelian companions of the queen of grossly abusing the suggestibility attached to the trance state by jumbling her ideas and throwing her into confusion. Psychology is not surprised that the subliminal imitation, however remarkable it may be, presents some little defects, and every one is in accord in regard to her thoughtless manner of expressing herself, in attributing these anachronisms to an accidental mingling of the memories of her ordinary personality and of the present life with those of the royal personality revived during the somnambulism. In her role as queen, Mlle. Smith gives evidence of a great deal of ingenuity. She is full of witty repartees, which disconcert her interlocutors, the style of which is sometimes perfectly after the manner of the epoch.

This ease and readiness of dialogue, excluding all reflective or calculating preparation, denote a great freedom of mind and a wonderful facility for improvisation. There are mixed with these, on the other hand, some witticisms and episodes which are not at all impromptu, but are the evident result of a preliminary elaboration in the course of the subconscious reveries and various automatisms which the royal romance causes to surge up in Hélène's ordinary life.

There are some scenes whose development or repetition can be followed in a series of seances and spontaneous visions as it passes through the other cycles. The following is one example among many:

At the end of a seance at which M. de Morsier was present (October 10, 1897), Mlle. Smith enters into her dream of Marie Antoinette. During dinner she makes several allusions to her son, the Dauphin, speaks of her daughter, tells of having demanded of her sorcerer the sex of her next child, etc.—matters all foreign to the conversation of Philippe, and which seem to announce some underlying scene ready to break forth. In fact, in the middle of the *soirée* the queen becomes absorbed and distrait, and finally falls on her knees in a dark corner of the *salon*; her monologue indicates that she is before the cradle where the little Dauphin and his sister are lying asleep. Presently she returns to seek Philippe and to conduct him to admire the sleeping children, to whom, in a very soft voice, she sings an unknown nursery rhyme ("Sleep in peace," etc.) of a plaintive melody analogous to that of the Hindoo chant; the tears gush from her eyes; tender kisses upon the imaginary cradle and a fervent prayer to the Virgin terminate this extremely touching maternal scene.

Several weeks after (the 1st of December), a new romance makes its appearance in a spontaneous access of visual, auditive, and graphic automatism, the recital of which Hélène sent me the following day. That evening, while alone with her mother, she had interrogated Léopold upon an affair in which she was greatly interested, and had obtained from him an answer: "As soon as his communication was ended, I saw everything disturbed around me; then at my left, at a distance of about thirty feet, a Louis XVI. *salon*, not very large, was outlined, in the middle of which was a square piano, open. Before this piano was seated a woman, still young, the color of whose hair I could not distinguish. Whether it was blond or gray I could not clearly see. She played and sang at the same time. The sounds of the piano, the voice even, reached me, but I could not catch the words of the song. A young girl and a boy stood on either side of the piano. Not far from them was seated a young lady holding an infant on her lap.[1] This charming vision lasted a very short time, not longer than ten minutes."

After the disappearance of the vision, Hélène had the idea of taking up her pencil.

> With pencil in hand, I was asking myself what I should write, when all at once I heard again the melody; then this time very distinctly, the words, but without any vision. The whole passed into my head, into my brain, and instinctively I pressed my hand to my forehead in order to hear and understand better. I felt myself compelled to hold the pencil in a manner different from my habitual way of holding it. Here are the words of the song heard and traced at that instant. As you see, the handwriting is not like mine; there are also some very glaring errors of orthography.
>
> Approchez-vous approchez-vous | enfans chéris approchez-vous | quand le-printemps sur nous ramène | ses frais parfums ses rayons d'or | venez enfanssous son haleine | gazouiller bas mes doux trésors | approchez-vous approchez-vous | enfans chéris approchez-vous | êtres chéris enfans bénis—approchez-vous de

[1] It will be readily understood that this vision represents Marie Antoinette with her three children and Madame Elizabeth.

votre mère | son doux baiser petits amis | calme et guérit toutes misères | approchez-vous approchez-vous | enfans chéris approchez-vous.[2]

Some months later the two preceding scenes were reproduced, with variations of detail, on the same evening, during which Marie Antoinette first conducts Philippe towards the fictitious cradle of her cherubs and sings to them her first song: "Sleep in peace," etc. Then she leads him to the piano, and, displaying an imaginary sheet of music beneath his eyes, obliges him to accompany her while she sings the "Song of Elizabeth."

M. de Morsier, who, fortunately, is not easily embarrassed, improvised an accompaniment to which the queen accommodated herself after some criticism, and to which she sings in a very sweet, pure voice some words which were found to be, word for word, identical with those automatically written by Hélène on the preceding 1st of December. In this example is seen the mixture of preparation, of repetition, and of impromptu, which are inferred from the varied incidents which constitute the royal *soirées*.

It is probable that if it were possible to be a witness of, or if Mlle. Smith could remember all the spontaneous automatisms which aid in nourishing the royal romance, nocturnal dreams, hypnagogic visions, subconscious reveries during the waking state, etc., there would be presented interminable imaginary conversations with the marquis, Philippe, Cagliostro, and all the fictitious personages who occasionally make their appearance in the somnambulistic scenes of Marie Antoinette.

It is by this underlying and unknown work, perhaps never interrupted, that the personality of the queen of France is slowly prepared and elaborated and which shines forth and displays itself with so much of magnificence in the *soirées* with Philippe d'Orléans and the Marquis de Mirabeau.

I have stated that, except these two gentlemen, who always form part of the royal dream when they are present (and even sometimes when absent), the others present at the seances are excluded. It is understood that they do not pass unperceived on this account.

In the same manner as in the negative hallucinations or systematic anaesthesia of hypnotized subjects, that which seems to be not felt is nevertheless registered; so, in like manner, it is altogether probable that nothing of that which passes around her escapes the fundamental individuality of Mlle. Smith. The royal personality which occupies the foreground of the scene and finds itself in an elective *rapport*, limited to Philippe and the marquis, merely causes the other personalities to be relegated to the

---

[2] I have respected the orthography as well as the complete absense of punctuation of this bit of automatic writing, confining myself to marking by vertical bars its evident separation into verses of eight feet. It is written in the inclined and regular hand called that of Marie Antoinette (like that of Fig. 40), but with a pencil too pale to permit its reproduction.

background without breaking their connection with the environment. There are many proofs of this. For example, in walking, Marie Antoinette never runs against any of the others present. The remarks and criticisms of the latter are not lost upon her, since very frequently her conversation betrays their influence after some minutes. At the same time, if anyone pinches her hand or tickles her ear, her lips, her nostrils, she seems anaesthetic; still, at the end of a few seconds she turns her head away, and if the tickling is persisted in, she experiences a kind of agitation accomodated to the circumstances of her dream, changes her position on some pretext, etc.

It is manifest, in short, that the excitations to which she seems to be insensible at the moment, far from having no effect, are stored up and produce, by their sum total, reactions which are retarded for some minutes and which are intelligently adapted to the somnambulistic scene, but with an intensity much more exaggerated than diminished by this period of latency.

Music also affects her, precipitating her out of the dream of Marie Antoinette into a common hypnotic state, in which she assumes passionate attitudes, which have in them nothing of the regal, and which conform to the varied airs which follow each other upon the piano.

In her phases as Marie Antoinette, Hélène has an accent characteristic of it; she recognizes me vaguely; she has some allochiria, a complete insensibility of the hands, and a large appetite; she does not know who Mlle. Smith is; if she is asked to give the actual date, she replies correctly as to the month and day, but indicates a year of the last century, etc. Then all at once her state changes; the royal accent gives way to her ordinary voice, she seems wide awake, all mental confusion has disappeared, she is perfectly clear as to persons, dates, and circumstances, but has no memory of the state from which she has just emerged, and she complains of a sharp pain in her finger (where I had pinched it while in her preceding phase). I took advantage one day of these alternations to offer her a pencil, and dictated to her the sentence of Fig. 42. In her normal moments she holds the pencil in her accustomed manner, between the index and middle fingers, and writes in her usual hand; during the returns of the royal somnambulism she holds it between the thumb and index-finger and assumes her handwriting and orthography known as that of Marie Antoinette, exactly as her voice is invested with the accent. It is to be presumed that all her other functions, if one could examine them, would show parallel analogous variations, the changing of the personality being naturally accompanied by connected changes not only of the memory and the sensibility, but of motility of the emotional disposition—in brief, of all the faculties of the individuality.

I must add that in each of her states Hélène has the memory of preced-

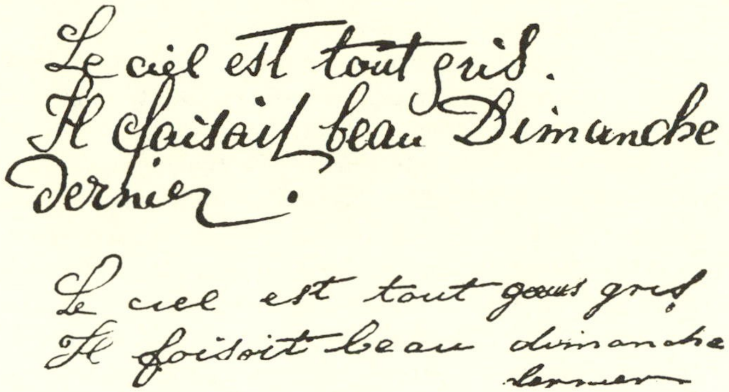

Fig. 42. Differences of handwriting of Mlle. Smith at the end of an incarnation of Marie Antoinette, according to whether she is in her normal state (upper lines, in her usual handwriting), or in a return of the royal dream (lower lines; note the word *foisoit*). Natural size. The tremor of some of the strokes is not in the original, but occurred in the reproduction in ink.

ing periods of the same kind, but not of another state: it was, for example, necessary to dictate anew, for the second test, the sentence of Fig. 42, which she did not remember having heard or written a few minutes previously. This separation into distinct memories is not, however, absolute, nor very profound: the personality of Marie Antoinette is, in short, a modification—of an intensity and extent which vary greatly with the seances—of the ordinary personality of Mlle. Smith, rather than an alternating and exclusive personality, of which so many striking cases have been observed.

For the mere spectators, the royal somnambulism is perhaps the most interesting of all of Hélène's cycles, on account of the brilliancy and life of the role, the length of time during which it may be sustained, the unexpected happenings which the presence of other real persons brings into it. It is truly a comedy.

But for the lovers of the supernormal it is the least extraordinary of the subliminal creations of Mlle. Smith, because the general environment, being in France, is so imbued with historic or legendary memories of the illustrious and unfortunate queen that there is nothing surprising in the hypnoid reconstruction of a personage so well known.

Finally, the psychologist and moralist who undertakes to reflect on the inner meaning of things cannot escape the impression of sharp contrast as compared with reality which this sparkling romance affords.

In themselves, Mlle. Smith's royal somnambulisms are almost always gay and joyous; but, considering their hidden source, in so far as they are the ephemeral and chimerical revenge of the ideal upon the real, of impossible dreams upon daily necessities, of impotent aspirations upon blind and crushing destiny, they assume a tragic signification. They express the sensation lived through, felt, of the bitter irony of things, of futile revolt, of fatality dominating the human being. They seem to say that all happy and brilliant life is only an illusion soon dispated. The daily annihilation of the dream and the desire by implacable and brutal reality cannot find in the hypnoid imagination a more adequate representation, a more perfect symbol of an emotional tonality, than her royal majesty whose existence seemed made for the highest peaks of happiness and of fame—and ended on the scaffold.

CHAPTER TEN

Supernormal Appearances

THE MEDIUMSHIP of Mlle. Smith is full of facts supernormal in appearance, and the question which offers itself for our solution is that of determining to what extent they are supernormal in reality.*

The title of this chapter, I must assert, is not to be understood in a partisan sense. The term "appearances" is not used in its unfavorable acceptation, as meaning that they are deceptive, and that there is nothing behind them. It is taken in a frank and impartial sense, to designate simply the exterior and immediate aspect of a thing, without prejudging its real nature, in order, by the very force of this neutrality, to provoke investigation destined to separate the true from the false, the pure gold from the dross. It is precisely this investigation which constitutes my present task.

A rather difficult task, for it is always risky to touch upon a subject which is an apple of discord among psychologists, and which has even been considered the "Dreyfus case of science."* The matter is complicated, too, in this particular case, by the absolute faith of Mlle. Smith and her friends in the supernormal character of her phenomena; a state of mind extremely worthy of respect, but which is not calculated to facilitate research, all desire of ordinary analysis and explanation being resented by them as an unjustifiable suspicion, interpreted as being an indication of invincible skepticism.

I. THE STUDY OF THE SUPERNORMAL

The term "supernormal" has been used for some years by the investigators of the Society for Psychical Research to take the place of the old word "supernatural," which has become impracticable on account of interloping connections, which finally caused its use to be limited to theological and philosophical environments. Mr. Myers, to whom the credit is due, if I am not mistaken, of coining this as well as many other new terms used today in the psychical vocabulary,* applies it to every phenomenon or faculty which passes beyond ordinary experience, and reveals either a degree of higher evolution not yet attained by the mass of humanity, or an order of transcendental things superior to the world of sense. In these two cases one finds one's self, indeed, in the presence of facts which are above the normal, but which are by no means to be taken as foreign or contrary to the true laws of human nature (as the word "supernatural" would imply).

It is to be observed that the definition of Mr. Myers lays stress upon the character of superiority of supernormal phenomena. I shall, however, separate this character from it in the present chapter, and in spite of the etymology, and for lack of any better term, shall simply use the word "supernormal" to designate facts which do not come within the actual framework of the science of to-day, and the application of which would necessitate principles not yet admitted—without occupying myself, however, with endeavoring to ascertain whether these facts are messengers of a superior economy or forerunners of a future evolution rather than the survival of a condition of things which has disappeared, or whether they are purely accidental, *lusus naturae*, denuded of signification.

It goes without saying that in treating of the supernormal we must admit theoretically its possibility, or—which amounts to about the same thing—fail to believe in the infallibility and perfection of present-day science. If I consider it, *a priori*, absolutely impossible for an individual to know, some time before the arrival of a telegram containing the news, of an accident by which his brother at the antipodes has been killed, or that another can voluntarily move an object at a distance without having a string attached to it, and contrary to the laws of mechanics and physiology, it is clear that I will shrug my shoulders at every mention of telepathy, and I shall not move a step to be present at a seance of Eusapia Paladino. What an excellent means of enlarging one's horizon and of discovering something new, by being satisfied with one's ready-made science and preconceived opinion, quite convinced beforehand that the universe ends at the wall opposite, and that there is nothing to be obtained beyond that which the daily routine has accustomed us to look upon as the limit of the Real! This philosophy of the ostrich, illustrated formerly by those grotesque monuments of erudition—over whom Galileo did not know whether to laugh or weep—who refused to put their eyes to the glass for fear of seeing something that had no official right to existence;* and. again, that of many brains petrified by the unseasonable reading of works of scientific vulgarization, and the unintelligent frequenting of universities—these are the two great intellectual dangers of our time.

If, on the other hand, the philosophical doubt degenerates in the presence of these scientific impossibilities into blind credulity; if it suffices that a thing be unheard of, upsetting, contrary to common-sense and to accepted truths, in order to be immediately admitted, practical existence, without speaking of other considerations, becomes unbearable. The convinced occultist ought never to allow the creaking of a piece of furniture to pass without assuring himself that it is not the desperate call of some great-grandaunt trying to enter into conversation with him; nor to complain to the police when he finds his house upset during his absence—for how is he to know that it is not some "elementals" from the world beyond who have done the deed? It is by the fortunate failure of consequences alone, and a continual forgetting of the doctrine, that one can continue to live in a universe constantly exposed to the capricious incursions of the "invisibles."

These opposite turns of the mind—the invincible fatuity of some and the silly superstition of others—inspire many people with an equal repugnance. The need of a happy medium between these opposed excesses has been felt for some time. Here are, for example, a few lines, which have lost nothing after the lapse of two centuries:

> What are we to think of magic and witchcraft [to-day we would say "occultism" and "spiritism"]? Their theory is obscure, their principles vague, uncertain, approaching the visionary; but—they are embarrassing facts, affirmed by grave men, who have seen them, or who have heard of them from persons like themselves; to admit them all, or to deny them all, seems equally embarrassing, and I dare to assert that in this, as in all extraordinary things which depend upon customary rules, there is a happy medium to be found between credulous souls and strong minds.

It is the voice of reason itself that the sagacious author of *Les Caractères* permits us to hear. We must, however, add that this "happy medium to be found" would not consist in a theory, a doctrine, a ready-made and entire system, from the height of which, as from a tribunal of arbitration, we would judge the "embarrassing cases" which reality places in the path of the seeker; for this system—however perfect it might be—would again be one more infallibility added to all those which already encumber the road to truth. The "happy medium" dreamed of by La Bruyère can be but a "method" always perfectible in its application and prejudging in nothing the results of investigation which go against the grain of the dogmatic points of view, equally authoritative and sterile, which characterize the two extremes of the "credulous souls" and "strong minds."*

To develop here this methodology of psychical research which might guide the investigator struggling with the apparent or real supernormal, would take me too far from Mlle. Smith. But I will briefly indicate its essence and general spirit, of which an excellent summary may be found in the following passage of Laplace:*

> We are so far from knowing all the agents of nature and their divers modes of action that it would not be philosophical to deny phenomena solely because they are inexplicable in the actual state of our knowledge. But we ought to examine them with an attention all the more scrupulous as it appears more difficult to admit them.

In writing these words Laplace hardly thought of telepathy, of the spirits, or the movements of objects without contact, but only of animal magnetism, which represented the supernormal of his time. This passage remains none the less the rule of conduct to be followed concerning all the possible manifestations of this multiform subject. Two inseparable facts, completing each other, as the faces of a medal, may be distinguished in it; but it is advisable, in order to place them the better in the light, to formulate them separately into two propositions representing the governing principles, the axioms of all investigations of the supernormal. The one, which I shall call "PRINCIPLE OF HAMLET,"* may be condensed in these words: *All is possible.* The other, to which it is but just to leave the name of "PRINCIPLE OF LAPLACE," is susceptible of many forms of expression. I shall express it thus: *The weight of the evidence should be proportioned to the strangeness of the facts.*

The forgetfulness of the "Principle of Hamlet" makes the "strong minds," for whom the limits of nature would not exceed those of their system, the simpleton popes of all times and of all kinds, from the burlesque adversaries of Galileo to the poor Auguste Comte, declaring that the physical constitution of the stars would never be known, and to his noble rivals of the learned societies, denying the aerolites or condemning railroads beforehand. In its turn, the ignorance of the "Principle of Laplace" makes the "credulous souls," who have never reflected that, if all is possible to the eyes of the modest seeker, all is, however, not certain, or even equally possible, and that some evidence would yet be necessary in order to suppose that a stone falling on the floor in an occult reunion arrived there through the walls by the aid of a dematerialization, rather than to admit that it came there in the pocket of a joker.

Thanks to these axioms, the investigator will avoid the doubly signalled danger, and will advance without fear into the labyrinth of the supernormal in advance of the monsters of the occult. However fantastic and magical the things may be which will spring up before his eyes or which will fill his ears, he will never be taken unawares, but, expecting all in the name of the "Principle of Hamlet," he will not be astonished at anything, and simply say: "Be it so! Why not? We shall see." On the other hand, he will not allow the wool to be pulled over his eyes, and he will not easily be satisfied in the matter of evidence; but, firmly intrenched behind the "Principle of Laplace," he will show himself all the more exacting as to the proofs, in proportion to the degree in which the phenomena or the conclusion, which they may wish him to accept, may be extraordinary and he will oppose a merciless *non liquet* to every demonstration which still seems suspicious or lame.

I wish to speak a word here of the inevitable role which the personal coefficient of the turn of mind and character plays in the concrete application of the "Principle of Laplace." This latter is of a vagueness and a deplorable elasticity which opens the door to all divergences of individual appreciation. If we could express in a precise manner and translate in ciphers, on the one hand, the *strangeness* of a fact, which makes it improbable; on the other hand the *weight of evidence* which tends to make it admissable; and finally, the demandable *proportion* between these two contrary factors, so that the second may counter-balance the first and secure assent—that would be perfect, and everybody would soon come to an agreement. Unhappily, the means to accomplish this result is not yet perceived.

We must pass now to the weight of the evidence. We may, up to a certain point, submit it to an objective judgment and to an impartial estimation by following the rules and methods of logic, in the broadest sense of the term. But the strangeness of the facts, or, as Laplace said, the difficulty in admitting them! Who, then, is to be the judge of them, and by what universal standard can we measure them?

We must recognize that we are here in presence of an eminently subjective and emotional factor, changeable from one individual to another.*

It is necessary to take some stand. in the matter of the supernormal there are too many interior and personal factors (intellectual idiosyncrasies, aesthetic temperaments, moral and religious sentiments, metaphysical tendencies, etc.) tending to determine the quality and intensity of the characteristic of the strangeness in the facts in litigation, to enable one to flatter himself upon a disinterested, objective, and *quasi*-scientific verdict upon their degree of probability or improbability. It is only when, after the accumulation of cases and evidences of similar character, a tacit agreement shall finally have been reached by those who have studied the subject, that the problem can be said to be solved, either by the relegation of pretended supernormal phenomena to the domain of vanished illusions and abandoned superstitions, or by the recognition of new laws and forces in nature. The phenomena considered till then as supernatural will cease to be so; they will form a part of established science, they will have nothing more in them that is strange, and will be admitted by everybody. As long as this mile-post is not reached, as long as the supernormal phenomenon is discussed as such, there are but individual opinions on this subject, subjective certitudes or probabilities, verdicts in which reality is only reflected as closely welded to the personality of their authors.

Two suggestions seem to me to spring from this. First, authors who take it upon themselves to give their advice upon the extraordinary facts coming to their knowledge ought always to begin by making their confession, so that the reader may the better distinguish the intimate factors which may have influenced them. It is true that we are not always thoroughly acquainted with ourselves, but it would be something to say frankly what we believe we have discovered in ourselves as to the position involuntarily taken by us, obscure inclinations for or against the hypothesis involved in the phenomena in question. This is what I shall try to do here by confining myself to the problems raised by the mediumship of Mlle. Smith, and without entering upon the boundless domain of "psychical research." I shall, therefore, begin each of the following paragraphs by giving my personal advice and my subjective sentiment on the point upon which Hélène's supernormal appearances touch.

It seems to me, in the second place, that the only rational position to take, concerning the supernormal, is, if not a complete suspension of judgment, which is not always psychologically possible, at least that of a wise probability, exempt from all dogmatic obstinacy. The fixed beliefs, the unshakable opinions as to the reality and the meaning of life, are certainly subjective conditions, indispensable to all properly moral conduct, to all human existence truly worthy of this name—that is to say, all that which pretends to be above the animal routine of inherited instincts and social slavery. But these firm convictions would be absolutely misplaced on the objective ground of science, and consequently also that of supernormal facts, which, though still situated outside of the scientific realm, hope shortly to be received within its pale. Practical necessities make us but too often forget that our knowledge of the phenomenal world never attains absolute certitude, and as soon as one passes beyond the brutal facts of the senses, the best-established truths, as well as the most thoroughly refuted propositions, do not rise above a probability which, however great or insignificant we may suppose it to be, never equals infinity or zero. The intellectual attitude which common-sense prescribes in the supernormal consists, for very strong reasons, in never absolutely and irrevocably denying or affirming, but provisionally and by hypothesis, as it were. Even in cases when, after having examined everything scrupulously, one imagines he has finally reached certitude, it must not be forgotten that this word is but a mode of expressing one's self; because, in point of fact, one does not rise above a probable opinion, and the possibility of an unsuspected error, vitiating the most apparently evident experimental demonstration, is never mathematically excluded.

This reserve is particularly indicated in cases of phenomena like those of Mlle. Smith, which often leave much to be desired concerning accessory information, which would be necessary in order to express one's self categorically on their account. My appreciation of these phenomena, far from pretending to an infallible and definite character, demands, therefore, from the start, the right of modification under the influence of new facts which may be produced subsequently.

For the sake of clearness I shall set off again in four groups the supernormal appearances with which I shall have to occupy myself in this chapter—viz., so-called physical phenomena, telepathy, lucidity, and spirit messages. The boundaries of these three last categories are but poorly defined and might easily be fused into one. But my division is but a kind of a measure of order, and not a classification.**

II. Physical Phenomena

This designation again covers several rather diverse categories of strange facts. I shall only speak of the two kinds of which Mlle. Smith has furnished samples (and which I have never personally witnessed)—that is to say, "apports" and "movements of objects without contact."

1. Apports[1]

Besides the unknown causes presiding over their aerial transportation, the arrival of exterior objects in a closed space, often coming from a considerable distance, implies, in order that they may pass through the walls of the room, either the subterfuge of a fourth dimension of space, or the penetration of the matter—that is to say, the passage of the molecules of atoms of the object (its momentary *dematerialization*) between the molecules or atoms of the wall. All these impediments to our vulgar conception as to the stability of matter, or what is worse, to our geometrical intuition, seem to me so hard to digest that I am tempted to apply to them the words of Laplace: "There are things that are so extraordinary that nothing can counterbalance their improbability." This is not to declare as false, *a priori*, all the stories of this kind, for we know that the true is not always the probable; but assuredly, even in the case of the good Mr. Stainton Moses, the weight of the proof does not, in my opinion, equal the strangeness of the facts.

So far as concerns the *apports* obtained at the seances of Mlle. Smith, they all took place in 1892–93, in the reunions of the N. group, where the obscurity favored the production of marvellous things in close relation with the visions and typtological messages.

I will cite from memory certain acoustic phenomena mentioned in the reports: The piano sounded several times under the touch of the favorite disincarnate spirits of the group; the same happened to a violin and to a bell; once we also heard metallic sounds that seemed to come from a small musical box, although there was none in the room. As to the *apports*, always received with delight by the members of the group, who are ever anxiously wishing for them and asking their spirit friends for them, they

---

[1] By this is meant the bringing or conveying of material objects into a closed space—the passage of one solid body through another.

were frequent and varied enough. In midwinter roses showered upon the table, handfuls of violets, pinks, white lilacs, etc., also green branches; among other things there was an ivy leaf having engraved upon it in letters, as though by a punching-machine, the name of one of the principal disincarnate spirits at play. Again, at the tropical and Chinese visions seashells were obtained that were still shining and covered with sand, Chinese coins, a little vase containing water, in which there was a superb rose, etc. These last objects were brought in a straight line from the extreme East by the spirits in proof of which they had the honor of a public presentation at a seance of La Société d'Etudes Psychiques de Genève, and were placed upon the desk of the president, where all, myself included, could satisfy themselves at their leisure as to their reality.*

2. Movements of Objects without Contact

The displacing, without contact and in the absence of all known mechanical processes, of objects situated at a distance (telekinesis), is very strange. However, it only upsets physiological notions, and does not, as is the case with the *apports*, go as far as to overthrow our conceptions in regard to the constitution of matter or our spatial intuitions. It only supposes that the living being possesses forces acting at a distance, or the power of putting forth at intervals a species of invisible supernumerary prehensile organs, capable of handling objects, as our hands do (ectenic forces of Thury, ectoplasms of Richet, dynamic members of Ochorowicz, etc.). Such are the ephemeral but visible pseudopodes that the amoeba puts forth in all directions.

It may be conceived that, as the atom and the molecule are the centre of a more or less radiating influence of extension, so the organized individual, isolated cell or colony of cells, is originally in possession of a sphere of action, where it concentrates at times its efforts more especially on one point, and again on others *ad libitum*. Through repetition, habit, selection, hereditary and other principles loved by biologists, certain more constant lines of force would be differentiated in this homogeneous primordial sphere, and little by little could give birth to motor organs. For example—our four members of flesh and blood, sweeping the space around us, would be but a more economic expedient invented by nature, a machine wrought in the course of better adapted evolution, to obtain at the least expense the same useful effects as this vague primitive spherical power. Thus supplanted or transformed, these powers would thereafter manifest themselves only very exceptionally, in certain states, or with abnormal individuals, as an atavic reapparition of a mode of acting long ago fallen into disuse, because it is really very imperfect and necessitates, without any advantage, an expenditure of vital energy far greater than the ordinary use of arms and limbs. Unless it is the cosmic power itself, the amoral and stupid demiurge, the unconsciousness of M. de Hartmann, which comes directly into play upon contact with a deranged nervous system, and realizes its disordered dreams without passing through the regular channels of muscular movements.

But enough of these vapory metaphysical or pseudobiological speculations to give an account of a phenomenon for which it will be time enough to find precise explanation when its authenticity shall be beyond dispute, if that time shall ever arrive.

Three groups of proofs, of a diverse nature, have gradually brought me to look upon the reality of these phenomena—in spite of the instinctive difficulty of admitting them—as an infinitely more probable hypothesis than its opposite.

First: I was first unsettled by the reading of the too-much-neglected memoir of Professor Thury,* which seems to me to be a model of scientific observations, the weight of which I could only overlook by rejecting, *a priori*—in the name of their strangeness—the possibility itself of the facts in question, which would have been against the Principle of Hamlet. The conversations which it was my privilege to hold with M. Thury have greatly contributed to arouse in me a presumption in favor of these phenomena, which the book would evidently not have done in the same degree if the author had not been personally known to me.

Secondly: Once created, my idea of the probability of these facts became rather strengthened than weakened by a number of foreign works of more recent date; but I doubt whether any, or all of these combined, would have been sufficient to create it. The displacement of objects without contact being once hypothetically admitted, it seems easier to me to explain Crookes's observations on the modifications of the weight of bodies in the presence of Home by authentic phenomena of this kind (in spite of the well-deserved criticisms that Crookes's publications brought upon him*) than to suppose that he was simply Home's dupe. The same is true with the cases of *Esprits tapageurs (Poltergeister)*, published by the Society for Psychical Research, the exclusive hypothesis of the "*naughty little girl*," without the addition of any trace of telekinesis, which seems to me a less adequate and more improbable explanation than that of real phenomena which would have tempted fraud.* Naturally all depends on the preconceived opinion one may have as to the general possibility or impossibility of these facts, and my feeling in regard to the matter would certainly be different without the preceding or following groups of evidence.

Thirdly: The probability of the movement of objects without contact has reached with me a degree practically equivalent to certitude, thanks to M. Richet, to whom I am indebted for my presence at his house last year at several seances of Eusapia Paladino, under conditions of control which gave no room for doubt—at least without challenging the combined witness of the senses of sight, hearing, and touch, as well as the average quantity of critical sense and perspicacity with which every ordinary intelligence flatters itself it is endowed; or, again, of suspecting the walls of M. Richet's study had been tampered with, and he himself, with his attending colleagues, of being impostors, in collusion with the amiable Neapolitan herself—a supposition which the most elementary sense of propriety would absolutely forbid me to entertain. From that moment I believed in telekinesis by constraint of the perception, *sensata et oculata certitudine*, to borrow the expression of Galileo,* who certainly did not mean by that an unreflecting adhesion to the evidences of the senses, like that of the casual onlooker at the tricks of the prestidigitator, but rather the final crowning of an edifice having for its rational framework the reasoned analysis of the conditions of observation, and of the concrete circumstances surrounding the production of the phenomenon.

In saying that I believe in these facts, I will add that there is no question here of a conviction, in the moral, religious, or philosophical sense of the term. This belief is for me devoid of all vital importance; it does not move any essential fibre of my being, and I would not feel the least inclination to submit to the slightest martyrdom in its defence. Whether the objects move or do not move without contact is absolutely indifferent to me. Should any one some day succeed in unveiling the physical tricks or the fallacious psychological processes which have led into error the best observers of telekinesis, from M. Thury down to M. Richet, with a number of other witnesses, myself included, I would be the first to laugh at the trick that art and nature had played upon me, to applaud the perspicacity of the one who discovered it, to congratulate myself, above all, in seeing supernormal appearances returning to the ordinary course of things.*

This is a disproportionally lengthy preamble to facts of which I shall have to speak here, for they are reduced to a few displacements of objects without contact (raising of tables, transporting or projecting of flowers and diverse things placed out of reach), of which Hélène and her mother were witnesses on several occasions at their house. I cannot be accused of stubborn skepticism, since I admit the reality of telekinesis. In the present case, however, all the stories which have been told me leave much to be desired from an evidential point of view. Without suspecting in any way the perfect good faith of both Mme. and Mlle. Smith, it suffices to recall the possibility of malobservation and errors of memory in the stories of supernormal events in order not to attribute a great evidential value to the absolutely sincere evidence of these ladies.

Incapacitated as I am from pronouncing judgment upon phenomena of which I was not a witness, I shall, however, put forth a fact which might militate in favor of their authenticity (their possibility having been first hypothetically admitted)—namely, that these phenomena have always been produced under exceptional conditions, at a time when Hélène was in an abnormal state and a prey to a deep emotion. On the one side, this circumstance increases the chances of malobservation, while, on the other, the day on which it shall be well established that (as divers observations cause us to think) certain abnormal and emotional states set at liberty in the organism latent forces capable of acting at a distance, it will be permitted us to suppose that perhaps something analogous has taken place in Mlle. Smith's case. Here is, as an example of these perplexing cases, a fact which happened to her during a period of general indisposition. Abridging the story, I reproduce it as Hélène sent it to me the following day:

> Last night I had a visit from M. H. I do not need to give you an analysis of my impressions; you will understand them as well as I do. He came to tell me that he had held a seance with a lady who was a stranger to me, and that this lady had seen Léopold, who had given her a remedy for the indisposition from which I was suffering. I could not refrain from telling him that Léopold had assured me that he manifested himself only to me, and that it would consequently be difficult for me to admit his alleged utterances to others.

But that is not the most interesting part of the story.

> While M. H. spoke to me I felt a sharp pain in my left temple, and, perhaps two minutes afterwards, my eyes, constantly directed towards the piano, on which I had placed two oranges the evening before, were entirely fascinated with I know not what. Then, suddenly, at the moment when we least expected it—we were all three (M. H., my father, and myself) seated at a reasonable distance from the piano—one of the oranges displaced itself and rolled to my feet. My father maintained that it had no doubt been placed too near the edge of the lid, and at a certain moment had fallen in a natural way. M. H. saw immediately in this incident the intervention of some spirit. I myself dared not pass my opinion on it. Finally, I picked up the orange, and we spoke of other things.
>
> M. H. remained about an hour; he went away exactly at nine. I went to my mother's room to give her a few details of M. H.'s visit. I described to her the fall of the orange, and what was my surprise when, on returning to the drawing-room and stepping up to the piano to take the lamp I had placed on it, I found the famous orange no longer there. There was but one left; the one I had picked up and replaced by the side of the other had disappeared. I looked for it everywhere, but without success. I went back to my mother, and while I spoke to her

we heard something fall in the vestibule. I took the lamp to see what might have fallen. I distinguished at the farthest end (towards the door of the entrance to the apartment) the much-sought-for orange!

Then I asked myself quite frankly whether I was in presence of some spiritistic manifestation. I tried not to be frightened. I took the orange to show it to my mother. I returned to the piano to take the second orange, so as not to be frightened in a similar way. But it, in its turn, had disappeared! Then I felt a considerable sensation of trembling. I returned to my mother's room, and, while we discussed the matter, we heard again something thrown with violence, and, rushing out to see what had happened, I saw the second orange placed in exactly the same spot where the other had been, and considerably bruised. Imagine how astonished we were! I took both oranges, and without losing an instant, went to the kitchen and put them in the cupboard, where I found them again the following morning; they had not moved. I did not go to bed without some fear, but fortunately I quickly went to sleep. My mother is sure that it is M. H. who brought some evil spirit into the house, and she is quite uneasy.

From the oral explanations of Mlle. Smith and her mother, and also from the location of the places, it follows that the oranges had been thrown at a distance of ten yards from the piano, through the wide-open parlor door leading to the vestibule, against the door of the apartment, as if to follow and strike fictitiously M. H., who a few moments before had left by this door.

One has undoubtedly always the right of discarding at the outset, as presenting too little guarantee of genuineness, the extraordinary stories of a person subject to hallucinations. In the present case, all that I know of Mlle. Smith and her parents keeps me from doing so, and persuades me that her story is thoroughly exact, which, however, does not amount to saying that there is anything of the supernormal about it. One has, in fact, the choice between two interpretations.

First: In the hypothesis of veritable telekinesis, the following is the manner in which the adventure would be summed up: the emotion due to the unexpected and unpleasant visit of M. H. had brought about a division of consciousness. The feeling of irritation, anger, and repulsion against him had condensed themselves into some secondary personality, which, in the general perturbation of the entire psychophysiological organism, had momentarily recovered the use of these primitive forces of action at a distance, entirely removed from the will, and without the participation of the ordinary self, and thus automatically accomplished outwardly the instinctive idea of bombarding this ill-bred visitor. Notice is to be taken of the painful aura at the temple and the fascination of gaze, which, according to Hélène's story, preceded the first signs of the phenomenon, the orange falling and rolling at her feet.

Secondly: But the most natural supposition is certainly that Mlle. Smith, by the ordinary use of her limbs, had taken and thrown these projectiles in an access of unconscious muscular automatism.* It is true that this would not agree with the presence of her father, mother, or M. H., who did not see her make the supposed movements. But an absent-mindedness of even normal witnesses will seem easier to admit than the authentic production of a supernormal phenomenon.

These episodes which have happened to Mlle. Smith and her mother since I have known them are very few, amounting to half a dozen at the most, and I will not dwell longer upon this subject. Hélène is not conscious of possessing any faculty of movement at a distance, and she always attributes these phenomena to spirit intervention. Léopold, on the other hand, has never acknowledged that he is the author of them. He claims that Hélène possesses within herself supernormal powers, and that, in order to succeed, she would only have to set them to work, but that she did not wish to do so. All my suggestions and repeated entreaties with Léopold and Hélène—either awake or in a state of somnambulism—in the hope of obtaining in my presence some physical phenomenon, have been in vain up to the present time.

III. Telepathy

One may almost say that if telepathy did not exist one would have to invent it. I mean by this that a direct action between living beings, independent of the organs of the senses, is a matter of such conformity to all that we know of nature that it would be hard not to suppose it *a priori*, even if we had no perceptible indication of it. How is it possible to believe that the foci of chemical phenomena, as complex as the nervous centres, can be in activity without giving forth diverse undulations, x, y, or z rays, traversing the cranium as the sun traverses a pane of glass, and acting at a distance on their homologues in other craniums? It is a simple matter of intensity.

The gallop of a horse or the leap of a flea in Australia causes the terrestrial globe to rebound on its opposite side to an extent proportional to the weight of these animals compared to that of our planet. This is little, even without taking into account the fact that this infinitesimal displacement runs the risk at every moment of being neutralized by the leaps of horses and fleas on the other hemisphere, so that, on the whole, the shocks to our terrestrial globe resulting from all that moves on its surface are too feeble to prevent our sleeping. Perhaps it is the same with the innumerable waves which coming from all other living beings, shock at every moment a given brain: their efforts are counterbalanced, or their resultant too slight to be perceived. But they exist nonetheless in reality, and I confess I do not understand those who reproach telepathy with being strange, mystical, occult, supernormal, etc.*

As to the knowledge whether this theoretical telepathy offers results open to experimental demonstration—that is to say, whether this chain of intercerebral vibrations into which we are plunged exercises any notable influence on the course of our psychic life; and whether, in certain cases, we happen to feel emotions, impulses, hallucinations, which the psychological state of one or another of our own kind exercises directly upon us, across the ether and without the ordinary intermediary of the channel of our senses—that is a question of fact arising from observation and experience. We know how much this question has actually been discussed, and how difficult it is to solve it in a decisive way, as much on account of all the sources of errors and illusions, to which one is exposed in this domain, as on account of a probably always necessary concurrence of very exceptional circumstances (which we do not as yet know how to accomplish at will), in order that the particular action of a determined *agent* should sweep away all rival influences, and betray itself in a manner sufficiently marked and distinct in the life of the *percipient*. Everything considered, I strongly lean towards the affirmative. The reality of telepathic phenomena seems to me difficult to reject in presence of the cluster of very diverse evidences, entirely independent of each other, that militate in its favor.* Undoubtedly none of these evidences is absolutely convincing when taken separately; but their striking convergence towards the same result gives to their entirety a new and considerable weight, which tips the scale, in my opinion, while awaiting an inverse oscillation, which may some day destroy this convergence, or explain it by a common source of error. Besides, I understand very well why those to whom telepathy remains a mystic, and to our scientific conceptions heterogeneous, principle, should obstinately resist it. But, seeing nothing strange in it myself, I do not hesitate to admit it, not as an intangible dogma, but as a provisional hypothesis, corresponding better than any other to the condition of my certainly very incomplete knowledge of this department of psychological research.

Although predisposed in favor of telepathy, I have failed in finding striking proofs of it in Mlle. Smith, and the few experiments I have attempted with her on this subject offered nothing encouraging.

I tried several times to make an impression upon Hélène from a distance and to appear before her during the evening, when I thought she had returned to her home, which is a kilometre distant from mine. I obtained no satisfactory result. My only case of striking success, lost among a number of nonsuccesses, can be explained by mere coincidence as well, and, after taking all the accessory circumstances into consideration, does not deserve a lengthy discussion.

As to spontaneous telepathy, a few indications would make me think that Mlle. Smith sometimes involuntarily submits to my influence. The most curious is a dream (or a vision) that she had one night at a time when I had suddenly fallen ill during a stay in the country some twenty leagues distant from Geneva. She heard the ringing of a bell at her door, then saw me entering, so emaciated and apparently so tired that she could not refrain from speaking to her mother on the following morning of her uneasiness concerning me. Unfortunately these ladies took no note of the exact date of this incident, and Hélène did not speak of it to M. Lemaître until three weeks later, when he told her about my illness, the beginning of which dated back to the approximate time of the dream. The evidential value of this case is weak. On other occasions Mlle. Smith announced to me that, to judge from her dreams or vague intuition in a waking state, I was to have on a certain day an unexpected vexation, a painful preoccupation, etc. But the cases in which she was right were counterbalanced by those in which she was wrong. It does not appear that Hélène's telepathic relations with other persons are closer than with me, and among the cases known to me there is not one that deserves the trouble of being related. An exception must, however, be made on behalf of a M. Balmès (pseudonym), who was for some time employed in the same business house as Mlle. Smith, and concerning whom she had several really curious phenomena. This M. Balmès was himself "a sensitive medium" of a very nervous and vibrating nature. He was working in the story above that of Hélène, and stopped sometimes to talk concerning spiritism with her. Their relations, which they did not extend beyond the office, ended there. There never seemed to be any personal sympathy or special affinity between them, and it is not known how to account for the telepathic bond that seemed to exist between them. The following are examples:

1. One morning M. Balmès lent a newspaper to Hélène in which there was an article on spiritism. He himself had received this paper from one of his friends, M. X., a Frenchman who had been in Geneva for some three weeks only and who did not know Hélène even by name. This M. X. had marked the interesting article in red and had added on the margin an annotation in black. During her noon meal at home Hélène read the article rapidly, but for lack of time did not read the annotation marked in black. Having returned to her office she began again to work. However, at a quarter-past three her eyes fell on the annotation of the paper, and as she was taking up her pen to make some calculation in her note-book, "I do not know," she wrote to me,

> either how or why I began to draw on this writing-tablet the head of a man entirely unknown to me. At the same time I heard the voice of a man, of a high, clear, and harmonious quality, but unfortunately I could not understand the

words. A great desire came over me to run and show this drawing to M. Balmès. He examined it, and seemed astonished, for the head drawn in ink was no other than that of his friend who had lent him the paper marked in pencil. The voice and the French accent were, as it seems, entirely correct also. How was it that at the sight of an annotation I found myself in communication with a stranger? M. Balmès, in presence of this curious phenomenon, hastened that very evening to his friend and learned that at the time when I drew his portrait there was a very serious discussion in progress concerning him (M. Balmès) between M. X. and other persons.

Strictly speaking, this case may be normally explained by supposing: First, that Mlle. Smith, without consciously noticing or remembering him, had seen M. X. during his short stay in Geneva, walking in the street with M. Balmès, and that the paper, which she knew had been lent to M. Balmès by one of his friends, had, by means of a subconscious induction, awakened the latent memory of the face and voice of the stranger whom she had seen with him. Secondly, that there is but a fortuitous coincidence in the fact that M. X. spoke of M. Balmès at precisely the hour when Hélène traced the face and heard the voice of the aforesaid M. X. in an access of automatism, set free at the sight of his annotation on the paper.

In the telepathic hypothesis, on the contrary, the incident would have been explained somewhat as follows: The conversation of M. X. concerning M. Balmès (which was, as it appears, of an excited nature) had telepathically impressed the latter and awakened in him subliminally the remembrance of M. X. M. Balmès, in his turn, without consciously suspecting it, had transmitted this remembrance to Mlle. Smith, who was already predisposed to suggestion on that day by the loan of the paper, and with whom the said remembrance broke forth into a graphic, auditive, and impulsive (the desire of showing her drawing to M. Balmès) automatism. The subconscious strata of M. Balmès had thus served as a link between M. X. and Mlle. Smith.

2. "Some eight days after the preceding case, being a few minutes after noon in an open streetcar, I saw before me this same M. Balmès talking to a lady in a room apparently close to the street-car. The picture was not very clear. A kind of mist seemed to extend over the whole, which was, however, not strong enough to hide from me the personages. M. Balmès, especially, was quite recognizable, and his somewhat subdued voice made me overhear these words: 'It is very curious, extraordinary.' Then I felt a sudden, violent commotion, and the picture vanished at the same time. Soon I found myself again riding in the street-car, and, according to the progress which it had made, I understood that the vision had lasted but three minutes at the most. Notice must be taken of the fact that during

these few minutes I did not lose for a single moment the consciousness of my situation; I knew and felt that I was riding home, as I was in the habit of doing each day, and I felt entirely like myself, without the slightest mental disturbance.

"Two hours later I went up to M. Balmès. Approaching him frankly—yes, even a little abruptly—I said to him: 'Were you satisfied with the short visit you made a few minutes after twelve, and would it be indiscreet to ask what you found so *curious*, so *extraordinary*?' He seemed confused, astonished, pretended even to be vexed, and looked as if he wished to ask me by what right I permitted myself to control his actions. This movement of indignation passed as quickly as it came, to give way to a sentiment of the greatest curiosity. He made me tell him in detail my vision, and confessed to me that he really had gone at noon to call upon a lady, and that they had discussed the incident about the newspaper. He had really pronounced the words that I had heard: 'It is curious, extraordinary,' and, strange to say, I also learned that at the end of these words a violent ringing of the bell had been heard, and that the conversation between M. Balmès and his friend had suddenly come to an end by the arrival of a visitor. The commotion felt by me was, therefore, nothing more than the violent ringing of the bell, which, putting an end to the conversation, had also put an end to my vision."

3. At the beginning of a seance one Sunday afternoon at a quarter to four, I handed to Hélène a glass ball, of the kind used for developing clairvoyance by means of gazing into a crystal. Shortly afterwards she saw in it M. Balmès and his friend, and above their heads an isolated pistol, but which seemed to have nothing to do with them. She told me then that M. Balmès had received the day before at his office a telegram which very much upset him, and which obliged him to leave Geneva that very evening for S. She seemed to apprehend some misfortune about to befall M. Balmès, but soon fell asleep. By his digital dictations Léopold tells us that he sent her to sleep to save her some painful visions seen in the crystal, and that she, Hélène, has a mediumistic consciousness in regard to all that is passing at S., and that the pistol is connected with M. Balmès. It was impossible to learn more, and the remainder of the seance was taken up with other matters.

M. Balmès, who returned to Geneva on the following Monday, and whom I saw the same evening, was very much struck with Hélène's vision, for, on Sunday afternoon he really took part in a scene which came near being tragic, and in the course of which his friend X. had offered him a pistol which he always carried with him. Mlle. Smith and M. Balmès did not hesitate to see in this coincidence a highly characterized supernormal phenomenon.* This case offers, however, some difficulty—viz., that the incident of the pistol at S. did not take place till more than two hours after

Hélène's visions, and that M. Balmès, as he affirms, had no premonition of the affair at the time when Hélène had her vision. It follows from this that there was a kind of anticipated telepathy, a premonition experienced by another than the interested principal, and this raises the great question of the supernormal knowledge of future events. I find it easier to admit that, although M. Balmès did not consciously foresee the incident of the pistol, he foresaw subconsciously the event, and that this idea passed telepathically to Hélène. Perhaps this case might be explained without having recourse to the supernormal at all. Mlle. Smith, knowing M. Balmès' character, and up to a certain point his personal circumstances, having been present the evening before when M. Balmès received the telegram, and foreseeing (as she said at the seance), the gravity of the situation, could easily imagine the intervention of a fire-arm in the affair. Besides, no detail of the vision indicates that the pistol seen in the glass ball corresponds to that of M. X.

How far the delicate sense of probabilities can go, and how often spontaneous inferences, with people of a quick imagination, are correct, one never knows. Undoubtedly we often see a supernormal connection where there is, in reality, only a striking coincidence, due to a happy divination and prevision, which is very natural. I ought to add that this manner of evicting the supernormal and reducing the vision of the pistol to a mere creation of the subliminal fantasy, seems inadmissible to Hélène, who remains absolutely certain that this was a convincing case of telepathy.*

IV. LUCIDITY

All the facts of lucidity (clairvoyance, second-sight, etc.) which are attributed to Mlle. Smith may be explained by telepathic impressions proceeding from living persons. This means that I not only admit from the start the *possibility* of such phenomena by virtue of the "Principle of Hamlet," but, since telepathy is not, in my opinion, anything very strange, I shall feel no subjective difficulty in accepting the reality of Hélène's supernormal intuitions, provided that they present some serious guarantee of authenticity, and do not explain themselves still more simply by normal and ordinary processes.

Léopold, who appears in almost all of these veridical messages—whether he recognizes himself as the author or whether he accompanies simply by his presence their manifestation through Hélène—has never deigned to grant me one under entirely satisfactory conditions, and he censures my insistence as vain and puerile curiosity. As to the innumerable phenomena with which others more fortunate than myself have been gratified, they have always offered this singularity: when they appeared to be really of a nature calculated to furnish a decisive and convincing proof as to their supernormal origin, I never succeeded in obtaining a written, precise, and circumstantial account, but only uncertain and incomplete tales, too intimate and too personal to be divulged by those interested in them; and, again, when my friends were quite willing to write out a detailed account and to answer to my demand for exact information, the fact reduced itself to such a small matter that it was beyond my power to see anything of the supernormal in it.*

Taking everything into consideration, I am inclined to believe that Mlle. Smith, in truth, possesses real phenomena of clairvoyance, not, however, passing beyond the possible limits of telepathy; only, in order that they may be produced, it is necessary that Léopold—that is to say, the special psychic state of Hélène which is necessary for the reception and externalization of these telepathic impressions—be aided from the outside by the influence of certain favorable temperaments, more frequently met with among convinced spiritists than among persons who are normal, and that he be not impeded, on the other hand, by the paralyzing presence of hostile temperaments, such as that of a critical observer. It is greatly to be regretted that the naive believers who inspire and succeed in obtaining magnificent phenomena of lucidity usually care so little for the desiderata of science, and, above all, refuse to submit themselves to an examination which might explain the phenomena in a natural manner; while the investigators in search of "convincing" proofs are not inspiring and obtain almost nothing.*

However it may be, I shall give a few examples of Mlle. Smith's proofs of lucidity, which are not very varied, and can be divided into the three categories of the medical prescriptions and diagnoses, of lost objects found again, and of retrocognitions of events more or less remote.

I. Medical Consultations

In promising specimens of extraordinary facts of this kind I have gone too far. Many such have been told me—as, for instance, Léopold dictating an unknown and complicated recipe of a hair tonic for a gentleman living abroad, a single bottle of which was sufficient to bring forth a full growth of hair on a head which had become bald before middle age; or, again, Léopold, being consulted about the health of a lady living at a great distance from Geneva, revealing both the veridical nature of her illness, which was unknown till then to her physicians, and its origin, which was due to certain unsuspected but perfectly true incidents connected with her childhood, and, finally, the treatment, which was crowned with success. But the absence of written testimony and precise information as to the concomitant circumstances of these marvellous cures reduce them to the rank of amusing stories, the value of which cannot positively be estimated. As to better-attested episodes, it is true I have been able to obtain authentic stories, but they are those in which the probability of a super-normal element has been reduced to a minimum—imperceptible to me. I will cite but one case.

M. and Mme. G. having invited Mlle. Smith during the month of August to pass a day with them in the country, a few leagues distant from Geneva, took advantage of the visit to hold a seance in order to consult Léopold on the health of one of their children. I will tell the incident from a written account sent me by Mme. G. soon afterwards:

"Our little girl was suffering from anaemia, and fell frequently into a state of weakness, in spite of intervals of improvement. Dr. d'Espine had been recommended to us for the time of our return to Geneva. The medium [Mlle. Smith] knew nothing of this; we had taken the precaution to keep it from her." The seance begins with a few kind words from Léopold, whom M. G. then asks whether he would do well in consulting Dr. d'Espine. "And I," replied Léopold, "can I do nothing for you? Ungrateful people!" But when he was asked to indicate some treatment, he replied: "Wait till your return to Geneva." Then, upon being asked whether an egg mixed with brandy would be good for the child, he replied that the egg would be good, but the brandy was not necessary in her case. Then he recommended that the child be taken for an hour's walk in the open air everyday. As to the prescription relating to her food, he repeated: "I told you to wait till your return to Geneva."

On their return to Geneva in the middle of September, M. and Mme. G. held a second seance. This time Léopold was more exact; he advised: "Not too much milk, but rather a few glasses of good pure wine at each meal." Then he added: "Treat the anaemia first and you will triumph over the throat trouble, which would finally weaken her too much. Her blood is so weak that the least cold, the slightest emotion, I will go so far as to say that the expectation of a pleasure even, would be sufficient to bring the angina to a crisis. You ought to have foreseen that." "Léopold," M. G. notes here, "has enabled us to put our finger upon such of the details as we did not know how to explain. At each sentence my wife and I looked at each other with stupefaction." Léopold ordered also many green vegetables, warm salt-water douches of three minutes' duration in the evening, and: "The principal thing now is five drops of iron in half a glass of water twice a day before the meal. Do this and you will see the result in a month." In two weeks' time the little girl was hardly recognizable.

I have cited this case because it is among those that have most struck M. and Mme. G., and upon which they build their conviction of the independent existence and supernormal knowledge of Léopold, and because it shows how little is needed to kindle the faith among spiritists. I forgot to say that the G. family was well known by Mlle. Smith, and that during the whole winter and the preceding spring she had held weekly seances at their home. There is but one thing that astonishes me, and that is, that Léopold, at the time of the first improvised consultation, should have been taken unawares up to the point of postponing his orders until later, and adhering to such commonplace things as a walk in the open air and the suppression of brandy. In the second seance one sees the effect of a month's incubation. Léopold has had time to recover in Hélène's memory the remembrance concerning the little girl who was anaemic and subject to sore throat; also the prescription which, in the given case, surely proved most efficacious, but which hardly denotes a supernormal knowledge. One does not even need here telepathy to explain messages which are amply accounted for by the subconscious functions of Mlle. Smith's ordinary faculties.

Examples of this kind, drawn from Mlle. Smith's mediumship, might be almost indefinitely multiplied; but *cui bono*? Once more, I do not claim that Léopold has never given any medical consultation surpassing Hélène's latent knowledge and implying supernormal powers of clairvoyance. I only say that I have not yet succeeded in finding a single case where the proofs reached the height of that conclusion.

2. Objects Recovered

I do not know any case in which Mlle. Smith has indicated the situation of an object which had been hidden, and as to the location of which she could have had no information through natural channels. All her discoveries consist, so far as I have been able to judge, in the return, under a spiritistic and with a dramatic aspect, of memories either simply forgotten or properly subliminal, which depended upon the incidents concerned having first belonged to the ordinary consciousness, or their having always escaped it and having been from their origin registered in the subconsciousness.

These are facts of cryptomnesia pure and simple—*i.e.*, explicable by a normal psychological process very common in its essence, while the picturesque embellishments added by the mediumistic imagination give to these teleological automatisms a certain mysterious and supernormal appearance which in other surroundings would certainly create for Hélène—or rather for Léopold—a place alongside St. Anthony of Padua. I confine myself to two examples. Mlle. Smith being charged with the duty of making ready the merchandise sent out from her department, was handed a telegram one day from a customer who asked that four yards of No. 13,459 be despatched to him immediately. "This brief order," said Hélène, "was not calculated to hasten the forwarding of the goods. How could I readily find this No. 13,459, in the midst of six or seven thousand others in the store? Pondering, telegram in hand, I was wondering how I could find it, when a voice outside of but very near me said to me: 'Not there, but here,' and involuntarily I turned round, without knowing why, and my hand laid itself mechanically on a piece of goods which I drew towards me, and which actually bore the No. 13,459."

It is not necessary to be a medium to know by experience these happy reminiscences or inspirations which sometimes come to free us from embarrassment by shining forth like a light at an opportune moment; but that which in the case of ordinary persons remains in the feeble condition of an idea or internal image, among mediumistic temperaments assumes readily the fixed and vivid form of an hallucination. Instead of simply "suddenly recollecting" in the case of the No. 13,459, as would have happened to anyone else, Hélène hears an exterior voice, and perceives her hand moving involuntarily in a given direction. It is noted that this automatism assumed an auditive and motor form which is the pendant of the vocal and visual automatism which I have referred to on p. 41. It is to this same class of facts, well known and almost common to-day, that the following example likewise belongs, although the subliminal imagination had surrounded it with the form of an intervention on the part of Léopold.

One Sunday evening, on returning home, Mlle. Smith noticed that she had lost a small breastpin which had been fastened to her corsage, and which she greatly valued as a souvenir. The following day she returned to look for it where she had been the evening before, but in vain, and a notice which she caused to be inserted in the "lost" columns of a daily newspaper gave no result. Here I leave the narration of the story to her:

> Persuaded that my pin was really lost, I did my best to think no more about it, but this was a difficult matter, since one night I was awakened suddenly by three raps struck against my bed. Somewhat frightened, I looked around, but saw nothing. I tried to go to sleep, but again many raps were struck, this time near my head. I seated myself on my bed (I was agitated), trying to discover what was happening, and hardly had I seated myself when I saw a hand shaking my lost breastpin before my eyes. This vision lasted only a minute, but that was long enough for it to make a deep impression upon me.

The following Tuesday evening (ten days after the loss of the trinket) Hélène held a seance at the house of M. Cuendet, at which two other persons were also present. She told of the loss of her pin and the curious vision above described; then all seated themselves at the table. After a typtological dictation upon an altogether different subject, the following incident occurred, the account of which I have borrowed from notes taken by M. Cuendet (it was in 1894, and I only knew Mlle. Smith by reputation at the time):

We notice that from the beginning of the seance Mlle. Smith describes to us our familiar spirit [Léopold] as holding a lantern in his hand. Why? The table is shaken anew, about to tell us something. The following is then dictated to us by it: "*Arise. Take a lantern. Extend your walk to the Municipal Building. Take the path which crosses the meadow, and which ends at the Street of the Baths. In the middle of the path, to the left, a few yards distant, a block of white stone will be found. Starting from the block of stone, only one yard away from it, towards the setting sun, the pin so much sought for will be found. Go, I accompany you.*"

I copy verbatim this communication, which was obtained letter by letter. I add nothing, take nothing from it. General stupefaction! We hesitate! Finally, we all four rise, we light a lantern and set out. It was twenty minutes to ten o'clock.

We walk slowly; we arrive at the Municipal Building, and take the path which leads from it to the Street of the Baths. In the middle, to the left, some yards distant, we, in fact, find the block of stone indicated. We search for a moment without result, and begin to fear we shall find nothing. Finally, towards the setting sun, a yard from the block of stone, I find buried in the grass, covered with sand, and consequently badly soiled, the pin indicated.

Some one had evidently stepped on it, as it was slightly bent. Mlle. Smith uttered an exclamation of surprise, and we all four returned to the house, to recover from our very natural emotion.

This case has remained in the eyes of Mlle. Smith and her spiritistic friends as one of the most striking and irrefragable proofs of the objective and independent reality of Léopold. For the psychologist it constitutes a very beautiful and interesting example of cryptomnesia, well worthy to figure among the very instructive cases collected by Mr. Myers,* in which the memory of a subliminal perception (*i.e.*, registered immediately without striking the normal personality) appears as a revelation in a dream of ordinary sleep, or under some other equivalent form of automatism. Here is "Léopold"—the subconsciousness of Hélène—who, having felt the pin fall and noticed where it rolled, first manifested himself in a passing nocturnal vision, and then took advantage of the next spiritistic gathering to restore completely her latent memories. It is not necessary to see anything intentional in this restitution, the simple play of association of ideas sufficing to explain that the memory of the situation of the pin stored up in a subliminal stratum and stimulated by a desire to recover the lost object might have mechanically reappeared at the moment of the seance, thanks to mediumistic autohypnotization, and gushed forth under the dramatic form, naturally appropriate to the environment, of an apparently supernormal piece of information furnished by Léopold.*

3. Retrocognitions

The apparently supernormal revelations in regard to the past, furnished at the seances of Mlle. Smith, can be divided into two groups—namely, whether they concern universal history, or deal with private interests relative to the families of the sitters.

First: The messages of the first group abound, under the form of visions accompanied by typtological explanations, in Hélène's seances of 1894, but have almost wholly come to an end since I made her acquaintance, and I have never been witness of any. According to the reports which I have seen, all these retrocognitions have reference to the history of Protestantism, or that of the French Revolution—*i.e.*, to two classes of facts which are among the best known in France to-day.

It goes without saying that the firmly convinced spiritistic group in which these messages were received have never had a doubt that the apparitions which Hélène perceived were the veritable personages they asserted themselves to be, habited as they were in the costume of the period to which they belonged. communicating by means of the table, and speaking in the first person (except when Léopold acted as showman and dictated in his own name the explanations asked for).

But as the content of these messages is always the *verbatim* reproduction or almost exact equivalent of information which is to be found in historical and biographical dictionaries, I cannot avoid being inclined to the impression that we here are concerned with common facts of cryptomnesia.

If the intervention of the supernormal be absolutely insisted upon in this case, it can only be manifested under the form of a telepathic transmission from the sitters to the medium. In favor of that supposition two facts may be urged: first, that Mlle. Smith passed in that group as devoid of all historical knowledge, and was very much surprised at these revelations of facts totally unknown to her; secondly, that there were regularly in attendance at these seances one or more members of the teaching body, who by their general education possessed, without any doubt whatever, either consciously or in a latent manner, all the historical knowledge, which, after all, was not very great, displayed by Léopold.

But these arguments are not of much weight in my opinion. To begin with the second: as the sitters had their hands on the table at the same time with the medium, according to the spiritistic custom, they could themselves, without any telepathy, properly speaking, and simply by their slight, unconscious muscular contractions, have directed, unknown to themselves, the movements of that piece of furniture, Mlle. Smith only augmenting these shocks proceeding from her neighbors.*

As to the supposed ignorance of Mlle. Smith, it is not at all so great as has been imagined, and the historical revelations obtained at her seances do not in any degree surpass the level of that which she could have absorbed, consciously or unconsciously, at school and in her surroundings.

Moreover, the hypothesis which appears to me the most probable, and on which I rest, is that the messages come essentially from Hélène herself—I ought rather to say from her subliminal memory; that, however, does not exclude a certain amount of cooperation on the part of the sitters, whose conversation, on the one hand, and their unconscious muscular action upon the table, on the other, have often maintained and directed the course of the subconscious ideas of the medium and the automatic unfolding of her latent memories.*

Secondly: Retrocognition of family events, which are exhibited in Mlle. Smith's seances, have generally the savor of the unknown for the sitters, from the fact that they concern incidents of the past which have never been printed save in the memories of certain aged persons or of a few lovers of local anecdotes.

I do not hesitate to see in these stories of other days, gushing forth invisions and in dictations by the table in the course of Hélène's hemisomnambulisms, narratives heard in her childhood and long since forgotten by her ordinary personality, but which reappear by the aid of mediumistic autohypnotization, bringing the deepest strata to the surface; the simple play of association, in an entirely natural manner, then causes the memories relative to the families of the persons present at the seance to be poured forth. There is nothing whatever of the supernormal in all this, in spite of the dramatic form, the piquant and unexpected art, the amusing embellishments, of which the subliminal imagination bethinks itself—or I should rather say Léopold, in his role of historiographer and scene-shifter of the past.

The judgment which I have pronounced is the result of a course of inductive reasoning based on the retrocognitions of Mlle. Smith concerning my own family. I trust it may be allowable for me to enter upon some details designed to justify my opinion.

I note first that all these retrocognitions with which Léopold honored me took place in the first six seances which I had with Hélène, after which there has not been a single one in the whole five years which have since elapsed. This argues in favor of a limited group of latent memories, which my introduction to the seances set free, a sort of subliminal sac or pocket which was emptied once for all on the first occasions of my presence.

In the second place, this knowledge only concerns outside details, susceptible of striking the attention of the gallery and of being carried from mouth to mouth. Since family histories have no great interest for the ordinary reader, I will confine myself to citing, by way of example, the vision which so astonished me at my first meeting with Hélène (p. 9), and which has already been published by M. Lemaître. I reproduce his narrative, giving real names:

> The medium [Mlle. Smith] perceives a long trail of smoke, which envelopes M. Flournoy. "A woman!" cries the medium, and, a moment after, "Two women . . . quite pretty, brunettes . . . both are in bridal toilet! . . . This concerns you, M. Flournoy!" [The table approves by a rap.] They remain motionless; they have white flowers in their hair and resemble each other a little; their eyes, like their hair, are black, or, at all events, very dark. The one in the corner appears under two different aspects; under both forms she is young—perhaps twenty-five years old; on the one hand she remains with the appearance already described (bridal toilet), and on the other she appears very luminous in a great space, a little more slender of visage, and surrounded by a number of pretty children, in the midst of whom she appears very happy; her happiness manifests itself by her expression, but still more in her surroundings. Both women seem ready to be married. The medium then hears a name, which at first escapes her, then returns little by little. "An! . . . An! . . . Dan . . . Ran . . . Dandi . . . Dandiran!"
>
> "To which of these two women does this name belong?" demands M. Flournoy—"to the one you see under two aspects, or to the other?" Answer: "To the one who is presented under two forms." The medium does not see the other woman as distinctly as the first, but all at once distinguishes a tall man by her side, who only passes by, when the table dictates: "I am his sister; we will return!" after which the scene changes and we pass to another subject.

This vision revolves altogether around the facts that my mother and her sister were married on the same day;* that they were brunettes, quite pretty, and looked alike; that my father was tall; that my aunt married M. Dandiran and died while still young, without children; all matters which should have been of public notoriety in a small city like Geneva. But the same is true of all the other retrocognitions of Mlle. Smith; their content is always veridical, but at the same time is also such as could not fail to be known to a host of people. This causes me to doubt whether there is at the base of these phenomena a really supernormal faculty of retrocognition.*

A third striking feature is, that all Hélène's retrocognitions concerning me are relative to the family of my mother, and are connected with two quite precise and brief periods, the first of which is many years previous to Mlle. Smith's birth. This limitation as to times and persons seems to me significant.*

To clear up the matter, if possible, I addressed myself to the last representative of the present generation of my family, Professor Dandiran, of Lausanne, and laid the case before him. He did not immediately remember whether my grandparents Claparède had any communication, nearly half a century before, with the Smith family, but on the following day he wrote me:*

One understands that I had a reason for not addressing myself first to Mme. Smith herself; but I must do her the justice to state that when I questioned her in turn, she very obligingly gave me all the information I desired, and which was in perfect accord with the statements of M. Dandiran.

Without entering into details wearisome to the reader, it will be sufficient for me to state that all the retrocognitions in which I was involved were connected with two periods in which Mme. Smith had relations with my mother's family, periods separated by an interval during which these relations were suspended by the fact of M. and Mme. Smith making a sojourn of several years in a foreign country. It would have been possible for Hélène to know directly the facts of the second period, at which time she was about five or six years of age. As to the first period, which was many years prior to her birth (the time of the double marriage of my mother and her sister in 1853), it is evident that Mme. Smith has had many opportunities at a later date to narrate these facts to her daughter; and it would have been altogether natural for her to have done so.

Ab uno disce omnes. Although I am less familiar with the retrocognitions of Mlle. Smith concerning other families, everything contributes to prove to me that they are explicable in the same manner. In two cases, at least, proof has been obtained that the mother of Mlle. Smith was found to have been in direct and personal communication with the families concerned, exactly as was the case with my grandparents, and this circumstance is sufficient to account for the knowledge, very astonishing at first sight, contained in the revelations of Léopold.

To sum up—pure cryptomnesia seems to me to furnish a sufficient and adequate explanation for Hélène's retrocognitions, both as to family events as well as historic facts.

And no more in this domain of knowledge of the past than in those of recovered objects and medical consultations have I thus far succeeded in discovering in her the least serious indication of supernormal faculties.

V. INCARNATIONS AND SPIRIT MESSAGES

The time having arrived to speak of spiritism, I feel ill at ease and embarrassed by my surroundings, for divers reasons, some of which I will set forth, without, however, endeavoring to explain them at length, since my aim is simply, as has been seen above (p. 227), to indicate my subjective ideas as to the standing of that doctrine, in order that the reader may share, if he pleases, in my appreciation of the phenomena of this class presented by Mlle. Smith. I confess, in the first place, that spiritism is a subject which has the faculty of arousing my mirth, and develops a spirit of playfulness. I really do not know why this should be the case, since that which concerns the dead and the great beyond ought not to be a matter for joking. Perhaps the cause is to be found in the nature of the intermediaries, and the character of the messages with which the spirits are accustomed to favor us. However it may be, I have ordinarily much difficulty in preserving a serious countenance in the presence of manifestations of "disincarnates."

But I reproach myself bitterly with this facetious humor when I reflect that it is indulged in at the expense of conceptions and beliefs which supported the first steps of our race on its painful ascent, the survival or atavic reapparition of which is yet, even to-day, a source of moral strength, of happy certitude, of supreme consolation for a host of my contemporaries, many of whom I have learned to know, and who, moreover, inspire me with respect as well as admiration by their uprightness of life, their nobility of character, the purity and elevation of their sentiments.*

In the second place, I have often had the deceptive experience that, when it comes to a discussion of it, spiritism possesses a great advantage for its defenders, but which is most inconvenient for those who would investigate it closely—of being fugitive and incapable of being grasped on account of the fact of its double nature—a science and religion at the same time—which never permits it to be wholly and entirely the one or the other.

When we come to analyze and criticise, according to strict scientific methods, the positive facts upon which it pretends to base its fundamental argument—the reality of communication with the spirits of the departed, through the intervention of mediums—as soon as the adepts begin to unpack for you their stock of theories (I was about to say their stock theories!) they are astonished at the lack of ideal on the part of these terrible materialist-scientists, who are intent upon searching for the "hidden rat" in the demonstrations of spiritism, instead of falling on their knees before the splendor of its revelations.*

A third cause of my uneasiness whenever obliged to approach this subject is the fear of being misunderstood or misinterpreted, thanks to the naïve and simple classification which prevails in the environment which the "disincarnates" frequent.

Spiritism or materialism—these are the brutal alternatives to which one finds himself driven in spite of himself. If you do not admit that the spirits of the dead reveal themselves by raps on the table or visions of the mediums, you are, therefore, a materialist! If you do not believe that the destiny of the human personality is terminated at the grave, you are a spiritist! This mode of nomenclature and labelling is surely puerile. Moreover, no one willingly consents to be thrust into the company of those with whom, no matter how honorable they may be, he is not in sympathy.

I also wish to state that I absolutely repudiate the above alternative. There is greater variety of choice in the cabinet of human thought. In the last century, for example, outside the spiritism of Swedenborg and the materialism of Baron d'Holbach, there was yet the criticism of one named Kant, who made some noise in the world and whose vogue is even now not absolutely extinct. I should not fear to range myself among his followers. And in our own times, if it was necessary for me to choose between Büchner and Allan Kardec, as the spiritist seems sometimes to believe, I would not hesitate to choose—in favor of M. Renouvier, or my deceased compatriot Charles Secrétan.

I hold to no other philosophy, and it suffices me, in order to repulse the whole of materialism and spiritism, to be the disciple—unworthy, but convinced—of the Nazarene, who replied to the materialists of his time, not by spiritistic evocations, but by the simple words, "God is not the God of the dead but of the living, for all live unto Him."* I am not sure whether this argument convinced the Sadducees, but it pleases me by its simplicity, and I have no desire for any other.

If God exists—I should say, if the supreme reality is not the unconscious and blind force-substance of conventional monism, but that sovereign personality (or *supra* personality) which in the clear consciousness of Christ made its paternal presence to be continually felt—if God exists, it is not, apparently, in order to play the role of a perpetual undertaker of funereal pomp that he consents to exist, or to allow to fall forever into nothingness the poor creatures who wait upon Him.

They may disappear from before our eyes, but they do not disappear from before His; for they are dead to us, but for Him, and, consequently, in actual reality, they are living. Otherwise He would not be God. This is all I need. I see nothing clearly, it is true, as to the concrete conditions of that other existence, of which the manner even, if it were revealed to me, would probably remain a sealed book to my intelligence, hampered by the bonds of space and time. But of what importance is it? That which I am ignorant of, God knows; and while waiting for Him to call me to rejoin those who have preceded me, He is great enough for me to leave to Him the mysterious fate of our personalities. "Since all live unto Him," I ask no more than that, and as for the pretended demonstrations of spiritism, true or false, I do not care a farthing.

Or I would prefer them to be false. And if they are true, if it is actually a law of nature that during long years to come, after this terrestrial existence, we must drag ourselves miserably from table to table and medium to medium, the best of us (not to speak of the others) displaying without shame the proofs of our mental decrepitude in pitiable nonsense and wretched verses—oh, so much the worse!

It is one misery and shame the more added to all those of which this satanic world is made up, a new calamity coming to crown the physical and moral ills of a world against which the Christian continually protests as he repeats *"Thy kingdom come,"* an additional scandal condemned to disappear when "His kingdom shall have come."

There is nothing in common between the empirical, spatial, and temporal survivals which spiritism pretends to establish and that "eternal life" proclaimed by the Prophet of Nazareth. These things, said Pascal, are not of the same order. That is why I am not a spiritist.

Here rises a last point, which worries me when I ought to speak my mind in regard to spiritism in the presence of spiritists. "You do not personally hold," it has been often objected to me,

> to these communications of the living with those who have gone before us into the great unknown, and you cry out against spiritistic demonstrations. It is all very well for you, who are a mystic, and to whom the existence of God in Jesus Christ seems a sufficient guarantee of the destinies of human personality and its ultimate palingenesis. But every one has not the same temperament, and does not take so blithely his ignorance of the kind of life which awaits him beyond the tomb. To believe in God, and to abandon to Him with closed eyes the fate of those who leave us, carrying away with them the best portions of our being, is all very well, but it is very difficult. The times of the psalmist who could say *"Though He slay me, yet will I trust Him"* are no more; and as for Christ, He was certainly a very remarkable medium, but His simple affirmation would scarcely be taken to-day for gospel words. The solid and the palpable are necessary to the "fools" of our epoch. They are not capable of admitting a higher world than that of sense, unless they are enabled to touch it with their finger by means of messages and the return of the dead themselves. Whence it results that every attack, every hostile attitude towards spiritism tends directly to break down the only rampart which might henceforth be efficacious against materialism and its disastrous consequences—infidelity, egotism, vice, despair, suicide, and, finally, the destruction and annihilation of the entire social organism. On the other hand, when science at length shall recognize and consecrate spiritism officially, thereupon, simultaneously with the tangible certainty of another life, courage and strength will return to the hearts of individuals, devotion and all virtues will begin to flourish once again, and an elevated humanity will soon see heaven descend upon the earth, thanks to the connection established and daily practised between the living and the spirits of the dead.

My embarrassment is easily seen. On the one hand, I do not in any way admit the foregoing objection. I do not think that the gospel has had its day or is above the reach of "fools," since it was for them that its author designed it. I believe, on the contrary, that the Christian faith, the faith of Christ or faith in Christ, is, in its inmost essence, a psychological reality, a personal experience accessible to the most humble, a fact of consciousness which will survive when all theological systems shall have been forgotten and all the clergy shall have been abolished. That vital and regenerating power will save our civilization (if anything can save it) by means of the individuals whom it shall have regenerated, without owing anything to spiritistic theories or practices. Inversely, I do not share the optimism of those who would make of spiritism a social panacea, and who imagine that when the moral consciousness on the one side and the religious consciousness on the other have ceased to make themselves heard, the messages of the "disincarnates" will have better success. ("If they hear not Moses and the prophets, neither will they be persuaded though one rose from the dead.")

But, on the other hand, there are individual cases which are interesting and which certainly merit consideration.*

All things are possible, and was it not of the revenants that Hamlet was thinking in his celebrated apostrophe, from which I have taken this principle?

These are the things which perplex me: while waiting to find a way out of them, and by way of summing up, it seems to me indispensable to separate distinctly spiritism-religion, which is an assemblage of beliefs and practices dear to many, from spiritism-science, a simple hypothesis designed to explain certain phenomena arising from observation. The first tells me nothing, or rather it amuses me or repels me according to circumstances; but the more elevated sentiments, and those worthy of all respect, which it inspires in its adepts, impose upon me the duty of passing it by and ignoring it here. The second, on the contrary, does not fail to interest me, as it does all who are curious in regard to natural phenomena.

For the question, Do human or animal individualities continue to intervene in an effective manner in the physical, physiological, or psychological phenomena of this universe after the loss of their corporeal and visible organism? is not an ordinary one. If there are facts which peremptorily establish an affirmative answer, what problems will arise, what an unexpected field of investigation will it not open up to our experimental sciences! And even if the hypothesis is false, how captivating the study of the singular phenomena which have been able to give it birth, which simulate the return of the dead to our observable world! It is understood, therefore, that, even despoiled of all the emotional accessories in which it so easily wraps itself in the heart and imagination of men, the empirical question of immortality and spiritistic interventions, apparent or real, preserves its scientific importance, and merits being discussed with the calm serenity, independence, and strictness of analysis which belong to the experimental method.

It goes without saying that, *a priori*, the hypothesis of *spirits* to explain the phenomena of mediums has in it nothing of the impossible or the absurd. It does not even necessarily contradict, as is sometimes imagined, the directing principle of physiological psychology—the psychological parallelism,—which demands that every mental phenomenon shall have a physical correlative. For, in spite of our habit of considering the molecular or atomic phenomena of the brain, the katabolism of the nerves, as the true concomitant of conscious processes, it may well be—it is even very probable—that these molecular movements do not constitute the ultimate physical term immediately paralleling the mental world, but that the real physical correlatives (spatial) of the (non-spatial) psychological phenomena should be sought for in the vibrations of imponderable matter, the ether, in which the ponderable atoms and molecules are plunged somewhat like grains of dust in the atmosphere, in order to make a sensible though somewhat inaccurate comparison.

The ethereal body, perispiritistic, astral, fluid, etc., of the occultists, and of many thinkers who are not believers in occultism, is only a notion scientifically absurd when it is made to be an equivocal and cloudy intermediary between the soul and the body, an unassignable *tertium quid*, a plastic mediator of which nothing is known as to its being material or spiritual or something else. But conceived as a system of movements of the ether, it contains nothing absolutely anti- or extra-scientific in its nature; the connection between the subjective facts of consciousness and the objective, material facts, remains essentially the same whether one considers the material world under the imponderable form of ether or under the ponderable form of chemical atoms, of physical molecules, and of anatomical elements. Nothing, then, would be radically opposed, from the point of view of the natural sciences, to the existence of disincarnate spirits wandering through space.*

The foregoing will doubtless please my spiritistic friends. Here are two facts which will please them less. First: I separate myself from them when they pass prematurely from mere abstract possibilities to the affirmation of actualities. Perhaps the outcome will prove them right some day; perhaps in the near future, but we have not yet reached that point. I freely admit that never have circumstances been so favorable for the spiritistic doctrines as at present. The authentic return of George Pelham and other deceased persons, through Mrs. Piper entranced, as intermediary, seems to be admitted by so many acute observers, the phenomena observed for fifteen years past in the case of this incomparable medium are at times so marvellous and surrounded with such solid scientific guarantees—the case is, in a word, so unheard of and astounding in all respects, that those who are only acquainted with it from a distance, by printed reports and oral narratives of immediate witnesses, feel themselves in a poor position for formulating their doubts and reservations upon this subject.*

I fear, in the second place, for mediums and practical spiritists, that when their hypothesis shall have been scientifically demonstrated the result may be very different from that which they now imagine it will be.

It might well happen that the cult of the table, mechanical writing, seances, and all other mediumistic exercises, may receive their death-blow from the official recognition of spirits by science. Suppose, in fact, that contemporaneous researches should at last have proved clearly that messages actually come from the disincarnate; it has already followed from the same researches that in the most favorable cases the veritable messages are very difficult to distinguish from those which are not authentic.*

This subject, decidedly, is fatal to me. I lose myself in digressions when discussing it—very useless they are, too, since the verdict which the future will pronounce upon the theory of spirits, with or without an ethereal body, matters little as far as the actual examination of the messages furnished by Mlle. Smith is concerned. Even having become scientifically verified, spiritism will never absolve us from bringing to the analysis of the pretended communications less care and rigor than while it was only an undemonstrated hypothesis; each particular case will always demand to be scrutinized by itself, in order to make the distinction between that which in all probability only arises from many non-spiritistic causes, and the residue eventually proceeding from the disincarnate.

I ought to state at the outset that, as far as Hélène's mediumistic phenomena are concerned, their careful analysis has not revealed to me in them any evident vestige of the other world, not even of traces of a telepathic transmission on the part of the living. I have only succeeded in perceiving in them very beautiful and instructive examples of the well-known tendency of the subliminal imagination to reconstruct the deceased and to feign their presence, especially when the favorable suggestions of the surrounding environment incites them to do so. Not being infallible, and bearing in mind Hamlet's principle, I will guard myself well from affirming that these subliminal imitations and simulacra are absolutely free from any spirit collaboration; I content myself with repeating that I have not discovered any, and that it seems to me in the highest degree improbable, and with leaving it to others to demonstrate its reality, if they think they are able to do so. Some examples taken from the principal incarnations of Mlle. Smith will enable me to show after a more concrete fashion my manner of regarding them.

1. Case of Mlle. Vignier

This case has no evidential value whatever, since (as has been seen, p. 330), there were formerly relations between the Vignier family and

Mme. Smith which suffice to explain the veridical knowledge manifested by Hélène in this incarnation.

I give an abridged recital of it, nevertheless, for the sake of certain points of psychological interest. None of the spectators had any suspicion of these relations at the time of this scene, which was absolutely enigmatical to all of them.

In a seance at my house (on March 3, 1895, after a Hindoo vision, described p. 175), Mlle. Smith saw an unknown lady appear, of whom she gave the following description: "A nose bent and hooked like the beak of an eagle; small gray eyes, very close together; a mouth with three teeth only; a wicked smile, mocking expression; simple dress; a collar not of the fashion of to-day; she draws near to this portrait,[2] and gazes at it not ill-naturedly."

The name of this person is asked, and the table (Léopold) commences to spell: "*Mademoiselle*"—but refuses to go further, while Hélène sees the apparition laughing, "with a sly air"; as the name is insisted on, the table dictates: "*That does not concern you*," then she begins to jump and skip as though glad of an opportunity to mock us.

Presently Hélène falls asleep and enters into somnambulism; she leaves the table and moves towards the portrait in question, before which she remains fixed, completely incarnating the unknown lady of her vision. I take down the portrait and place it in its frame upon an easy-chair; immediately she kneels before it and contemplates it with affection; then, taking the frame in her right hand, while the left, very much agitated, plays with the cord, she ends, after many vain attempts, by saying with a great stammering, "*J—j—je l'aimais b—b—beaucoup: je n'aime pas l'autre— j—j—je ne l'ai jamais aimée l'autre—j'amais bien mon neveu—adieu!— je le vois.*" ("I liked it very much: I do not like the other one: I never liked the other one I was very fond of my nephew. Adieu! I see him.)

It was impossible to obtain any explanation of this incomprehensible scene, until, having slipped a pencil and a writing-tablet into Hélène's hand, she scribbled feverishly, in a hand not her own, these two words "*Mademoiselle Vignier*"; then she fell into a cataleptic phase, from which she awakened without memory at the end of half an hour.

This name of Vignier evoked in me far-off memories and vaguely recalled to my mind the fact that Professor Dandiran (who had married, as we have seen, my mother's sister) had an ancestress of that name; was it she who returned to express to me by means of Mlle. Smith her affection for my mother, whose portrait she had so attentively regarded, and her regrets, perhaps, that her nephew had not been preferred to my aunt?

On the other hand, M. Cuendet recollected a Mlle. Vignier who had

---

[2] A small oil-portrait of my mother.

been a friend of his family, but who did not correspond at all with the description of Hélène's visions; he promised to obtain information, and, in fact, wrote me on the following day: "Dear Sir,—Here is some information on the subject of our seance of yesterday. This morning I asked my mother: 'Did you ever know another Mlle. Vignier than the one who was your friend?' After an instant of reflection: 'Yes,' replied she; 'I did know another. She was M. Dandiran's aunt, of Lausanne, his mother's sister. She stammered, and was not always very good-natured, she had three large teeth which projected, and a hooked nose.' It is useless to state to you that this was the first time I had heard her spoken of."

This information, coinciding with my remembrances and Hélène's vision, was later confirmed by M. Dandiran, who gave me the following information:

> Your aunt, Mlle. Vignier, who died about thirty-five or forty years ago, loved her nephew very much; but she was made very angry by his marriage, and the sentence uttered before my mother's portrait could not have referred to a difference of sentiment in regard to the two sisters, for whom she always had an equal affection. This sentence, on the contrary, is wonderfully well explained by the following facts: My mother and her sister having become betrothed at the same time, oil-paintings of both, of natural size, were made by the same painter. These portraits were not of equal merit, and Mlle. Vignier, who was herself something of an artist, always considered that of my mother excellent, while the other, that of my aunt, she did not like at all. Mlle. Vignier was very lively, and M. Dandiran finds that the epithet "sly" and the table dictating *"That does not concern you,"* very well express her character; she was, however, not at all malicious or mocking at heart, but it is true that persons who knew her slightly could easily have gained that impression of her. She had three or four prominent teeth and stammered badly. In her photograph she wears a white collar, has a nose long and arched, but the eyes are rather large and wide apart. She always wore gold eye-glasses, of which the medium did not speak.

If the reader has had patience to read these details, he will have remarked that the distinctive traits of Mlle. Vignier in the vision and her incarnation by Hélène (the stammering, the teeth, the shape of the nose, the ill-natured air) coincide with those spontaneously indicated by M. Cuendet, who had known her slightly; and that while M. Dandiran, better posted as to his aunt's character, finds the note of maliciousness or want of good-nature false, he acknowledges that people outside of her family could have been deceived concerning it. That is to say, has not the imagination of Mlle. Smith produced the exterior memory, the description according to public notoriety, as it were, which Mlle. Vignier left behind her? And if it be recalled that at the period at which the two *fiancées* were painted, Mme. Smith was in communication with my maternal grandparents through the only sister of Mlle. Vignier, there would be a probability amounting almost to a certainty that these are contemporary remembrances, narrated some time or other to Hélène by her mother, and which furnished the material for this somnambulic personification.

In this example, to which I might add several analogous ones, the apparent *spirit control* is reduced to latent memories of recitals formerly heard by Hélène.

In other cases, in which, for lack of information, it has hitherto been impossible to discover this wholly natural filiation of facts, simple analysis of the circumstances and of the content of the communications indicates that, in all probability, they proceed from reminiscences and impressions appertaining to living individuals much rather than from disincarnates. In other words, these messages and personifications too evidently reflect the point of view of the medium or other living persons for it to be permissible to regard them as due to the intervention of deceased persons, whose attitude towards them would, in all probability, be wholly different.

2. Case of Jean the Quarryman

We have here to deal with a very curious spirit message concerning Mme. Mirbel, in which I cannot fail to see actual memories of the latter— transmitted I know not how (but not necessarily in a supernormal manner) to Mlle. Smith—rather than an authentic communication from a pretended disincarnate.

In a seance at which Mme. Mirbel was not present, Hélène had the hallucination of a very strong odor of sulphur; then the vision of a quarryman from the foot of Salève, in which she perceived and described in detail an unknown man, who, by the dictations of the table, was declared to be Jean the Quarryman, and charged the sitters with an affectionate message for Mme. Mirbel. The latter, interrogated on the following day, recognized in the very circumstantial description of this man, and under all the features of Hélène's vision, perfectly correct facts connected with her childhood, and which had passed away from the habitual circle of her ideas for more than twenty years. It concerned a workman employed in her father's quarries, and who, when she was a little girl, had always evinced a special affection for her.

Let us suppose—in the absence of all proof that Mlle. Smith had ever heard these remembrances of Mme. Mirbel's childhood mentioned—that recourse must be had to the supernormal in order to explain the case. It still would not amount to an intervention of the deceased quarryman; and M. Lemaître was perfectly right, in my opinion, in clinging to telepathy and in hazarding the idea of an etheric influence, to which Hélène was subjected by Mme. Mirbel, who at the hour of this seance happened to be half a kilometre distant from the place of the seance. Without going out of the domain of telepathy, I still would prefer the hypothesis of a previous transmission in the course of one of the seances at which Mme. Mirbel was present to that of telepathy at a great distance at the time of the seance. It is, in fact, not contrary to that which is believed to be known of mental suggestion, to admit that Hélène's subliminal, in the state of Esenale, for example, could in some way draw from Mme. Mirbel's subliminal the latent memories which there lay buried for some time before being ready to reappear at a seance at which she had some reason to think Mme. Mirbel would again be present.

Whatever the mode of its transmission may have been, the content of this vision seems to me to indicate clearly that it has its origin in the personal memories of Mme. Mirbel rather than in the posthumous memory of Jean the Quarryman. All the presumptions in this case are, to my mind, in favor of a memory of Mme. Mirbel, and not of a veritable communication from the other world. The personal aspect of the messages supposed to be dictated by the quarryman do not constitute an obstacle to my interpretation or a guarantee of spiritistic authenticity, this aspect being the form that the automatisms habitually assume among mediums.*

5. Case of the Syndic Chaumontet and of the Curé Burnier

The following case is the last. It is a very recent one, in which the spiritistic and the cryptomnesiac hypotheses exist face to face, apropos of signatures written by Mlle. Smith in somnambulism which do not lack similarity to the authentic signatures of the deceased persons to whom they are supposed to belong.

In a seance at my house (February 12, 1899), Mlle. Smith has a vision of a village on a height covered with vines; by a rocky road, she sees descending from it a little old man, who has the air of a *quasi* gentleman; he wears shoes with buckles, a large felt hat, the collar of his shirt is unstarched, and has points reaching up to his cheeks, etc. A peasant in a blouse, whom he meets, makes reverences to him, as to an important personage; they speak a patois which Hélène does not understand. She has the impression of being familiar with the village, but vainly searches her memory to discover where she has seen it. Presently the landscape fades away, and the little old man, now clothed in white and in a luminous space (*i.e.*, in his actual reality of a disincarnate), appears to draw near to her. At this moment, as she leans her right arm upon the table, Léopold dictates by the index-finger: "*Kiss her arm.*" I execute the order; Hélène's arm at first resists strenuously, then yields suddenly. She seizes a pencil, and in the midst of the customary struggle relative to the manner of holding it (see p. 248), *"You are holding my hand too tightly,"* says she to the imaginary little old man who, according to Léopold, wishes to make use of it in order to write. *"You hurt me very badly; do not hold it so firmly. . . . What difference does it make whether it is a pencil or a pen?"* At these words she throws away the pencil and takes up a pen, and, holding it between the thumb and index-finger, slowly traces in an unknown hand: *"Chaumontet, syndic"* (see Fig. 44).

Then the vision of the village returns; at our desire to know the name of it she ultimately perceives a sign-post on which she spells *"Chessenaz,"* a name which is unknown to us. Then, having by my advice asked the little old man, whom she still sees, at what period he was syndic, she hears him answer, "1839."

It is impossible to learn more; the vision vanishes and gives way to a total incarnation of Léopold, who, in his deep Italian voice, speaks to us at length of various matters. I take advantage of it in order to question him upon the incident of the unknown village and syndic; his replies, interrupted by long digressions, may be summed up about as follows: "I am searching. . . . I traverse in thought the ascent of this great mountain pierced through at its foot by something, the name of which I do not know; I see the name of Chessenaz, a village on a height, and a road which ascends to it. Search in this village; you will certainly find the name (Chaumontet); seek to examine his signature; this proof you will find there; you will find that the handwriting was that of this man."

To my question whether he sees this in Hélène's memories and whether she has ever been at Chessenaz, he replies in the negative as to the first point and evasively as to the second: "Ask her; she has a good memory for everything. I have not followed her in all her wanderings."

Awakened, Hélène could not furnish us any information. But the following day I found on the map a little village called Chessenaz, in the Department of Haute-Savoie, twenty-six kilometres, in a straight line, from Geneva, and not far from the Crédo. As the Chaumontets are not rare in Savoy, there was nothing unlikely in the fact of a person of that name having been syndic there in 1839.

Two weeks later I made a visit to Mme. and Mlle. Smith—there was no seance held—when Hélène suddenly assumed the voice and accent of Léopold, without being aware of the change, and believing me to be joking when I sought to cause her to notice it. Presently the hemisomnambulism becomes accentuated; Hélène sees the vision of the other day, the village and then the little old man (the syndic) reappear, but the latter is accompanied this time by a *curé* with whom he seemed on good terms and whom he called (which she repeats to me all the while with Léopold's Italian accent), *"My dear friend Burnier."* As I ask whether this *curé* could not write his name with Hélène's hand, Léopold promised me by a digital dictation that I should have that satisfaction at the next seance; then he begins to talk to me of something else by Hélène's mouth, she being now entirely entranced

At the following seance at my house (the 19th of March), I remind Léopold of his promise. He answers at first by the finger: "*Do you very much desire that signature?*" and it is only upon my insisting that he consents. Hélène then is not long in again seeing the village and the *curé*, who after divers incidents takes hold of her hand as the syndic had done, and traces very slowly with the pen these words, "*Burnier greets you*" (Fig. 44); then she passes into other somnambulisms. The moment had arrived to clear up the matter. l wrote at hazard to the mayor's office at Chessenaz. The mayor, M. Saussier, had the kindness to answer without delay: "During the years 1838–39," stated he to me, "the syndic of Chessenaz was a Chaumontet, Jean, whose signature I find attached to divers documents of that period. We also had as *curé* M. Burnier, André, from November, 1824, up to February, 1841; during this period all the certificates of births, marriages, and deaths bear his signature. . . . But I have discovered in our archives a document bearing both signatures, that of the syndic Chaumontet and that of the *curé* Burnier. It is an order for the payment of money. I take pleasure in transmitting it to you." I have caused to be reproduced in the middle of Fig. 44 the fragment of this original document (dated July 29, 1838), bearing the names of these two personages; the reader can thus judge for himself in regard to the quite remarkable similarity which there exists between these authentic signatures and those automatically traced by the hand of Mlle. Smith.

My first idea was, as may be supposed, that Mlle. Smith must some time or other have seen some certificates or documents signed by the syndic or by the *curé* of Chessenaz, and that it was these forgotten visual flashes, reappearing in somnambulism, which had served her as inner models when her entranced hand retraced these signatures. One may likewise imagine how angry such a supposition would make Hélène, who has no recollection whatever of having ever heard the name of Chessenaz nor of any of its inhabitants, past or present. I only half regret my imprudent supposition, since it has availed to furnish us a new and more explicit manifestation of the *curé*, who, again taking hold of Mlle. Smith's arm at a later seance (May 21st, at M. Lemaître's) comes to certify to us as to his identity by the attestation, in due and proper form, of Fig. 43. As is there seen, he makes it twice; being deceived as to the signature, he incontinently, with disgust, crosses out that which he had so carefully written, and recommences on another sheet; this second draft, in which he has omitted the word "*soussigné*" ("undersigned") of the first, took him seven minutes to trace, but leaves nothing to be desired as to precision and legibility. This painstaking calligraphy is very like that of a country *curé* of

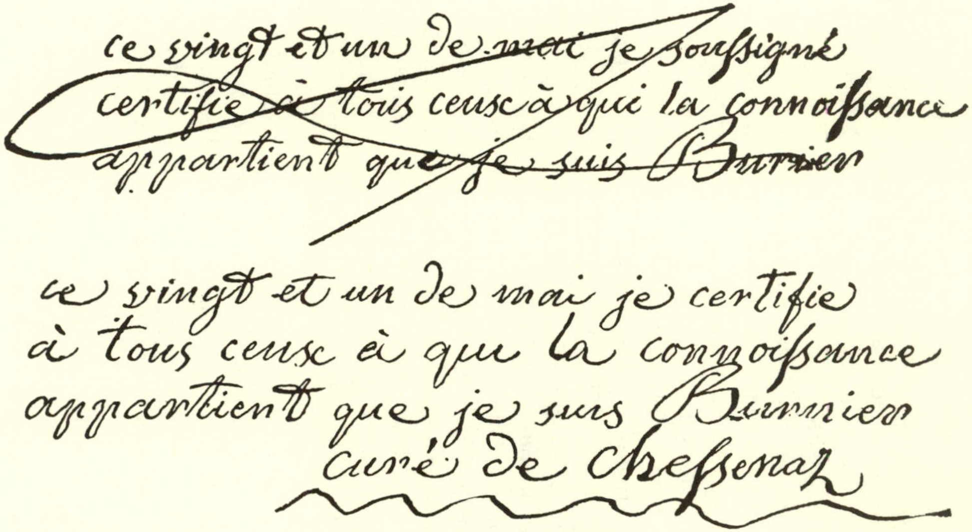
ce vingt et un de mai je soussigné certifie à tous ceux à qui la connoissance appartient que je suis Burrier

ce vingt et un de mai je certifie à tous ceux à qui la connoissance appartient que je suis Burnier curé de Chessenaz

Fig. 43. Certificates written (May 21, 1899) by Mlle. Smith while in a trance. The one above was feverishly crossed out in finishing the faulty signature. The one below was afterwards written in seven minutes. Natural size. (From the collection of M. Lemaître.)

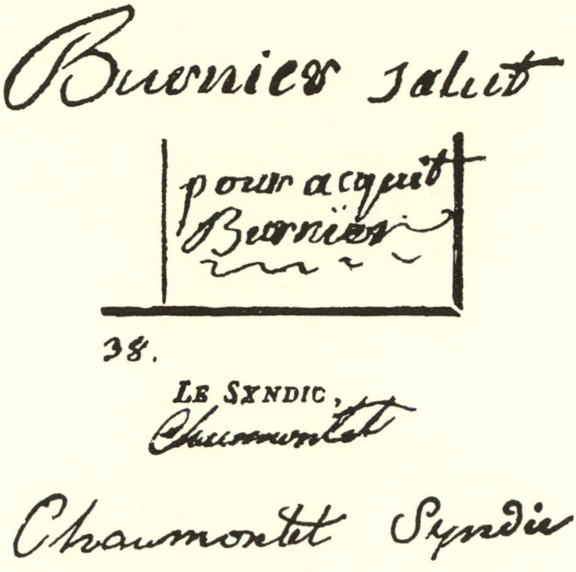

Fig. 44. Comparison of the signatures of the syndic Chaumontet and of the curate Burnier, with their pretended signatures as disincarnates given by Mlle. Smith in somnambulism. In the middle of the figure, reproduction of a fragment of an order for payment of money of 1838. Above and below, the signatures furnished by the hand of Hélène. Natural size.

sixty years ago, and in default of another specimen for comparison, it presents an undeniable analogy of hand with the authentic receipt of the order for payment of money of Fig. 44.

Neither Mlle. Smith nor her mother had the least notion in regard to the *curé* or the syndic of Chessenaz. They nevertheless informed me that their family formerly had some relatives and connections in that part of Savoy, and that they are still in communication with a cousin who lives at Frangy, an important town nearest the little village of Chessenaz. Hélène herself made only a short excursion in that region, some dozen years ago; and if, in following the road from Seyssel to Frangy, she traversed some parts of the country corresponding well to certain details of her vision of the 12th of February (which she had the feeling of recognizing, as we have seen, p. 259), she has not, on the other hand, any idea of having been at Chessenaz itself, nor of having heard it mentioned. "Moreover," says she, "for those who can suppose that I could have been at Chessenaz without remembering it, I would affirm that even had I gone there I would not have been apt to consult the archives in order to learn that a syndic Chaumontet and a *curé* Burnier had existed there at a period more or less remote. I have a good memory, and I positively affirm that no one of the persons around me during those few days while I was away from my family ever showed me any certificate, paper—anything, in a word—which could have stored away in my brain any such memory. My mother, at the age of fourteen or fifteen, made a trip into Savoy, but nothing in her remembrances recalls her ever having heard these two names uttered."

The facts are now presented, and I leave to the reader the privilege of drawing such conclusion from them as shall please him.

This case seemed to me worthy to crown my rapid examination of the supernormal appearances which embellish the mediumship of Mlle. Smith, because it sums up and puts excellently in relief the irreconcilable and hostile respective positions of the spiritistic circles and mediums on the one side, perfectly sincere but too easily satisfied—and investigators somewhat psychological on the other, always pursued by the sacrosanct terror of taking dross for gold. To the first class, the least curious phenomenon—an unexpected vision of the past, some dictation of the table or the finger, an access of somnambulism, a resemblance of handwriting—sufffices to give the sensation of contact with the unknown and to prove the actual presence of the disincarnate world. They never ask themselves what proportion there could well be between these premises, however striking they may be, and that formidable conclusion. Why and how, for example, should the dead, returning at the end of a half-century to sign by the hand of another person in flesh and blood, have the same handwriting as when alive?

The same people who find this altogether natural, although they have never seen any absolutely certain cases of it, fall from the clouds when the possibility of latent memories is invoked before them, of which the present life furnishes them, moreover, daily examples—which they have not, it is true, ever taken the trouble to observe.

The psychologists, on the contrary, have the evil one in them in going to look behind the scenes of the memory and the imagination, and when the obscurity prevents them from seeing anything, they have the folly to imagine that they will end by finding that which they are seeking—if only a light could be had.

Between these two classes of temperaments so unlike, it will, I fear, be very difficult ever to arrive at any satisfactory and lasting understanding.

CHAPTER ELEVEN

Conclusion

THIS VOLUME reminds me of the mountain which gave birth to a mouse. Its length would be excusable if only it marked a step in advance in the field of psychology or physiology, or as to the question of the supernormal. As such is not the case, it is unpardonable, and nothing more is left me to do except to make clear its deficiencies in this triple aspect.

First: From the physiological point of view, it is apparent that Mlle. Smith, as is doubtless true of all mediums, presents during her visions and somnambulisms a plenitude of disturbances of motility and sensibility, from which she seems entirely free in her normal state.

But these trifling observations do not suffice to solve the neuropathological problem of mediumship, and the question still remains open as to whether that term corresponds to a special category of manifestations and to a distinct syndrome, or whether it merely constitutes a happy euphemism for various scientific denominations already in use.

To endeavor to fix the connections of mediumship with other functional affections of the nervous system, it would first be necessary to possess exact intelligence on a number of important points still enveloped in obscurity. In regard to some of these, such as the phenomena of periodicity, of meteorological and seasonal influences, of impulses, and of fatigue, etc., we have only very vague and incomplete hints. And we know almost nothing of other still more essential questions, such as the relations of equivalence and substitution between the various modalities of automatism (nocturnal visions, crepuscular states, complete trances, etc.), the effect of spiritistic exercises, and especially of that of the seances upon nutrition or denutrition (variations of temperature, of urotoxicity, etc.), which would permit the comparison of spontaneous seizures and those excited by mediumship with those of the more serious nervous affections, the phenomena of heredity, similar or reversed, etc.

Let us hope that a near future will establish some good mediums and their observers in practical conditions favorable to the elucidation of these various problems, and that the day will come when the true place of mediumship in the framework of nosology will be discovered.

Secondly: From the psychological point of view, the case of Mlle. Smith, although too complex to be reduced to a single formula, is explicable *grosso modo* by some recognized principle, the successive or concurrent action of which has engendered her multiple phenomena. There is, in the first place, the influence, so often verified, of emotional shocks and of certain psychic traumatisms upon mental dissociation. By means of these the birth of hypnoid states may become the germ either of secondary personalities more or less strongly marked (we have seen that the first manifestations of Léopold in the childhood of Hélène are attributable to this cause) or of somnambulistic romances, which hold the same relation towards the normal state as does that exaggeration of stories and indulgence in reveries to which so many are addicted—perhaps all of us.

We must also take into consideration the enormous suggestibility and auto-suggestibility of mediums, which render them so sensitive to all the influences of spiritistic reunions, and are so favorable to the play of those brilliant subliminal creations in which, occasionally, the doctrinal ideas of the surrounding environment are reflected together with the latent emotional tendencies of the medium herself. The development of the personality of Léopold-Cagliostro, starting from the moment at which Mlle. Smith began her seances, is easily explained in this manner, as well as the Martian dream and the previous existences of the Hindoo princess and the queen of France.

And, finally, we must note the phenomena of cryptomnesia, the awakening and setting to work of forgotten memories, which easily account for the elements of truth contained in the great preceding constructions and in the incarnations or casual visions of Mlle. Smith in the course of her seances.

But besides this general explanation how many points of detail there are which remain obscure! For example, the precise origin of Hélène's Sanscrit, and many of her retrocognitions, for want of information concerning the thousand facts of her daily life whence the ideas which nourish her somnambulism may have been drawn! And how difficult it is to gain a correct idea of her case as a whole, on account of the crudity of our actual notions as to the constitution and organization of the human being, of our almost total ignorance of psychological ontogeny!

Without mentioning Hélène's ephemeral incarnations (in which I have shown there is no reason for seeing anything beyond the imitations due to autosuggestion), the divers more stable personalities which manifest themselves in her hypnoid life—Léopold, Esenale, and the actors of the Martian romance, Simandini, Marie Antoinette, etc.—are only, in my opinion, as I have hinted on many occasions, the varied psychological states of Mlle. Smith herself—allotropic modifications, as it were, or phenomena of polymorphism of her personality. For no one of these personalities corresponds sufficiently with her ordinary personality by intellectual faculties, the moral character, separation of memories, to justify the hypothesis of a foreign *possession*.

But the theory of psychic polymorphism is still very imperfect, and inadequate to explain the embryological shades which shine forth in Hélène's subliminal products—the retrograde perspective which they open as to the different stages or periods of her evolution. The Martian cycle, with its unknown language, evidently betrays an eminently puerile origin and the display of an hereditary linguistic aptitude, buried under Hélène's ordinary self; whereas the Hindoo romance denotes a more advanced age, and that of Marie Antoinette seems to have sprung from still more recent strata, contemporaneous with the actual normal personality of Mlle. Smith. The primitive nature and different ages of the various hypnoid lucubrations of Mlle. Smith seem to me to constitute the most interesting psychological fact of her mediumship. It tends to show that the secondary personalities are probably, in their origin, as the idea has been sometimes suggested, phenomena of reversion of the ordinary actual personality, or of momentary returns of inferior phases, long since passed, and which normally should have been absorbed in the development of the individuality, instead of breaking forth again in strange proliferations.*

Thirdly: As to the supernormal, I believe I have actually found a little telekinesis and telepathy. As to lucidity and spiritistic messages, I have only encountered some brilliant reconstructions, which the hypnoid imagination, aided by latent memory, excels in fabricating in the case of mediums. I do not complain of this, since for psychology, which is not especially enamoured of the marvellous, these admirably successful imitations are also interesting and instructive on account of the light which they throw upon the inward workings of our faculties.

Of course Mlle. Smith and her friends see things in a very different light. With Hélène everything, or almost everything, is supernormal, from the reminiscences of her lives as Marie Antoinette and Simandini, to the Martian and the incarnations of Cagliostro, of Mlle. Vignier, or of the *curé* of Chessenaz.*

And now let us admit, hypothetically, that I have not been able to see the supernormal, which was plainly before my eyes, and that it is this blindness of mine alone which has prevented me from recognizing the real presence of Joseph Balsamo, my own mother, the Hindoo princess, etc.—or, at all events, the presence of real, disincarnate, independent spirits. It is, of course, to be regretted, but then it is I alone who will be in disgrace on the day when the truth shall be made manifest.

For, as to progress in our knowledge of things, everything is to be feared from easy credulity and obstinate dogmatism, but that progress will not be arrested or seriously retarded by possible errors, committed in good faith, through an exaggerated severity of application and a too strict observance of the principles themselves of all experimental investigation;

while, on the contrary, the obstacles and the difficulties which the necessities of the method multiply along its path have always been a strong stimulant, producing new movements forward and more durable conquests based on better demonstrations.

It is better, then, to follow my advice—in the well-understood interest of and for the advancement of science, in a domain where superstition is always ready to give itself free play—it is better to err through excess of caution and strictness of method than to run the risk of being sometimes deceived; it is better to allow some interesting fact to escape for the moment, rather than to open the door to the follies of the imagination by a relaxation of necessary caution.

As to Mlle. Hélène Smith, supposing that I have failed to recognize in her phenomena which are really supernormal (which, in that case, will some day be better set forth by other observers), she will, nevertheless, accomplish more in the way of discovering the real truth, whatever it may be, in submitting herself disinterestedly to my free criticisms, than by doing as so many useless mediums have done, who, afraid of the light, in their foolish eagerness for the triumph of a cause very dear to their hearts, have shunned close investigation, and would have us rely upon their word alone.

They forget the saying of Bacon, which is ever being confirmed: *"Truth is the daughter of time, not of authority."*

Appendix One

The Making of Martian: The Creation of an Imaginary Language

Mireille Cifali

IN 1900 a work appeared, *From India to the Planet Mars*,[1] stirring the spiritist milieu at the start of the century and capturing the attention of some scholars interested in psychology and linguistics. It was written by a Genevan, the doctor and psychologist Théodore Flournoy,[2] with a subtitle that indicates more precisely its contents: "A Study of a Case of Somnambulism with Glossolalia."

Catherine Élise Müller—named Hélène Smith in this work—said to be glossolalic, considers herself to be a medium capable of conversing with the dead. She pretends to have been, in a previous life, a princess of ancient India with the name of Simadini and married to prince Sivrouka, sensibly reincarnated in the person of Théodore Flournoy. Moreover she knows how to speak Sanskrit and proves it by pronouncing it before an audience of credulous admirers and incredulous examiners. She was also Marie-Antoinette and speaks a royal French. But above all, perniciously, she has the privilege of transferring herself onto distant planets from which she brings back the language of the inhabitants, notably Martian.

Théodore Flournoy, the psychologist, and eminent linguists—Ferdinand de Saussure for example—were struck by the linguistic marvels that Élise Müller produced. They scrutinized with the greatest care the linguistic corpus furnished by the young lady. Their results were recorded in *From India to the Planet Mars*. Did Élise know Sanskrit—she who had not studied? Certain people confirmed it. But must one then believe in the immortality of the soul and in the reality of the phenomenon of reincarnation? The Martian language that she claimed to know, could she not just have made it up? How would she go about it? We could take recourse to

---

[1] T. Flournoy, *Des Indes à la Planète Mars* (Paris: Seuil, 1983) [new edition].

[2] See M. Cifali, "Théodore Flournoy, la découverte de l'inconscient," in *Le Bloc-Notes de la psychanalyse* 3 (1983): pp. 111–31; "Les chiffres de l'intime" (postface) in Flournoy, *Des Indes*, pp. 371–85.

this book and, from the glossolalic text, seek to provide further interpretations. A modern linguist might without any doubt find in it various linguistic curiosities.[3] Such, however, is not our purpose.

Auguste Lemaître is one of the principal participants in the mediumistic seances convened around Élise Müller, whom he calls "my" medium. It is he who draws up the records of each of the seances when they are held at his residence, and who copiously writes them out with his schoolmasterish handwriting in exercise books. The records, which we have had the luck to retrieve at the descendants' of Lemaître, are a *literal* account of the seances.[4] They are signed each time by all the participants. Flournoy used them to construct his book, but he never published them as such. He merely provides summaries and only extracts certain passages useful to his argument.

We now have the complete text of around sixty seances spread very unevenly between October 24, 1894 and May 18, 1901: two hundred and sixty pages in seven notebooks. As regards the meetings that took place in Théodore Flournoy's apartment and from which he made records, we unfortunately have not discovered the slightest trace. This is so much the more regrettable since it was at these meetings that Élise Müller spoke Sanskrit in the presence of Ferdinand de Saussure, who had been invited for the occasion.

We have studied the records of Auguste Lemaître for a long time in an attempt to understand the reconstruction carried out by Théodore Flournoy throughout the writing of his work. It seemed important to us to reconsider the question of the Martian language, not so as to restore the text, but in order to determine the *conditions of its enunciation*. It will be, we hope, from another vantage point that we shall be able to reveal the procedure which permitted the fabrication of Martian. The present approach in no way renders null and void the study of the Martian articulation undertaken by Flournoy or by the linguist Victor Henry;[5] it simply wishes to recreate the theatre that saw it take place and unfold.

On Mars

The Martian adventure begins on November 25, 1894—with an important detail: Théodore Flournoy does not yet figure among the participants in this seance, from which the following extract is taken:

> From the beginning, Melle. Müller senses a vivid gleam at a distance, high up. Then she feels a swinging that goes to her head after which it seems to her as if

[3] See for example M. Yaguello, *Lunatic Lovers of Language: Imaginary Languages and their Inventors*, trans. C. Slater (London: Athlone Press, 1991).

[4] Private archives of the descendants of A. Lemaître, Geneva.

[5] V. Henry, *Le langage martien* (Paris: Maisonneuve, 1901).

her head is empty and that she no longer has a body. She finds herself in a thick fog which changes gradually from blue to bright pink and then to grey and black. She floats, she says; and the table resting on only a single leg begins to take on a very strange floating movement, like whorls constantly repeating the same turning. Then Mlle. Müller sees a star that continually grows and grows and becomes "larger than our house." Melle. Müller feels that it rises. Then the table conveys through spelling:

—*Lemaître, this is what you would like so much!*

Melle Müller who was ill at ease feels better. She discerns three enormous spheres, of which one is very beautiful. "What is it that I walk on?" she asks herself and the table answers, *On land. Mars.* (Laughing): "How funny, these cars! Hardly any horses or people that are on the move. Imagine different kinds of armchairs that slide but don't have wheels. It is the tiny wheels that produce the sparks. People sit in their armchairs. Some of them, the larger ones, hold four to five people. To the right of the armchairs a kind of handle stick is attached, fitted with a button that one presses with the thumb to put the vehicle in motion. There are no rails. One also sees the people walking. They are built like us and hold onto each other with the little finger. The clothing is the same for both sexes: a long blouse tight around the waist, very large trousers, shoes with very thick soles, no heel and of the same colour as the rest of the outfit which is in shammy, white with black designs."

Thus begins the Martian voyage. Lemaître does not know "how to explain" Élise's first words: "*Lemaître, this is what you would like so much.*" Someone reminds him of a conversation during the summer of 1893, in the course of which he is supposed to have said: "It would be very interesting to know what happens on other planets!" And here it is granted: "If this is the response to the wish of last year . . . then well and good!" he rejoices. One must note that all his listeners at that moment are given over to the spiritual powers of Élise Müller. Moreover she provides what is expected, i.e., to see, hear and explore. She excels in painting with words. The text of the seance continues. It is a kind of canvas Élise Müller paints before a blind public.

Théodore Flournoy gains admission to the seances on December 9, 1894 and his presence transforms their style as well as the minutes. The new reporter constantly breaks the thread with his countless suggestions. Élise's monologue is interrupted by the incessant questioning that names and determines the answers. Another change due to the presence of Flournoy: the Martian visions are suspended for fifteen months. It is only on February 2, 1896 that the traveller resumes her voyage, a fact for which Flournoy provides two possible explanations. Firstly he holds himself to be the involuntary cause—the Hindu romance in which he plays an essential role having completely occupied the spirit of Élise Müller. In the second place, he invokes "a period of latent incubation necessary for the perfection of the Martian dream and for the preparation of the new language which was to reveal itself."[6]

These two explanations are plausible. But one needs to spell out that the birth of Martian follows the "battle" that was joined around Sanskrit, the language of the transference,[7] which allowed Élise to converse passionately with Sivrouka-Flournoy. The distinguished scholars, gathered to determine whether this is really Sanskrit, doubt its purity. Élise does not fail to take notice. Hence the hypothesis that she takes recourse to Martian as a new linguistic marvel. Besides, she has discovered that the scholars are particularly interested in the production of language. The advent of Martian is in some way the response to their scientific interest.

IS IT HUNGARIAN?

Between November 25, 1894 and February 2, 1897—the date of the first Martian words—Élise Müller above all speaks Sanskrit, above all in the course of her Hindu "romance." We do not have in our possession the records of the seances that would allow us to know which questions were put to her and which commands were addressed to her, so we can only infer from two sources: the work of Flournoy and an article which Lemaître wrote in 1897.[8]

By comparing the two linguistic productions, Flournoy proposes the following: "The nature of Hélène's Hindu language," he writes, "is less easy to bring to clarity than that of Martian, for it has never been possible to obtain neither a literal translation nor written texts of it." And he continued by another route, abashed:

> There is not even left to me the resource of placing the parts of the process as a whole before the reader, as I have done in the case of the Martian, for the reason that our ignorance of Hélène's Hindu, added to her rapid and indistinct pronunciation—a real prattle some times—has caused us to lose the greater part of the numerous words heard in the course of some thirty Oriental scenes scattered over a space of four years.[9]

These few words cause us to think, without great risk of being mistaken, that Hélène-Élise is pressured to translate and write, but that she resists it, that she is urged to pronounce with care in order to facilitate a transcription, known to be difficult.

---

[6] This volume, p. 295.

[7] See M. Cifali, "Une glossolalie et ses savants: Élise Muller alias Hélène Smith," in *La linguistique fantastique* (Paris: Clims-Denoel, 1985), pp. 236–44.

[8] A. Lemaître, "Contribution à l'étude des phenomenes psychiques," in *Annales des sciences psychiques* 7 (1897): pp. 65–88.

[9] This volume, above, pp. 193–194.

Auguste Lemaître speaking of *his* medium—we emphasize the use of the masculine gender[10]—never cites the name, and much less does he indicate that it is a woman. Of the Sanskrit which she speaks, he also points out its basically melodic nature:

> There were also incarnations and sayings pronounced in a language similar to Sanskrit, with a melodious accent, which permits me to contend that had Greek not existed, then Sanskrit would have been the most beautiful language ever to have come from human lips.[11]

Élise's prowess to which he bears witness to the reader does not fail to amaze:

> Try, you who have learned foreign or ancient languages, try to learn Sanskrit and to speak it, try above all to place the accent, the harmonious intonation which characterizes it, then apply yourselves to acquire it with no wavering, with volubility. Well! The medium from whose mouth these amazing words flowed, like as many pearls, had no knowledge at all of languages, it had never been taught the Greek and Latin roots, and still less those of Sanskrit.[12]

There is, however, no doubt that the entire Hindu romance feeds on the play of questions and answers into which Élise is dragged. Here is a brief example of it to do with the seance of March 10, 1885. The meeting began at 8 p.m., and it is now 9:15.

> Mademoiselle gets up. Will she go towards Flournoy? (Always the little finger:) Yes. Must Flournoy get on the sofa? Yes. M. Flournoy sits there. Does Mademoiselle see the funeral pyre? Yes. She walks backwards in the direction of the dining room door. Is Mademoiselle on the verge of a precipice? No. Are men there, like the other day, that push her towards the pyre? Yes. Is it the messieurs present here? No. M. Flournoy: Can I go to meet her in order to protect her? No reply. Is there a body on the funeral pyre? Yes. Is it lit? No. Will it be so soon? Yes. Will the widow throw herself onto it? No. Will they put her there by force? Yes. Mademoiselle joins her hands. Does she supplicate? Yes. Will she die? Yes. Soon? Yes. Will Mademoiselle fall? Yes. Is it necessary to let her fall? Yes. Will she fall backwards? No. Forwards? Yes. M. Flournoy: Must I lay down on this funeral pyre? No reply. Is my [Flournoy's] anteriority there? Yes. Mademoiselle retreats again, and we ask why? It is because they lay hold of her.

The dance of questions is irresistible. She lets herself be taken there and the gentlemen participate in the choreography. We may suppose that during the entire Hindu romance she is requested, in the same fashion, to render her Sanskrit accessible to the ear, then to translate it so that it

---

[10] [*Son médium, médium* being masculine in French.—Trans.]

[11] Lemaître, "Contribution," p. 83.

[12] Ibid.

could be committed to writing. It is in this context that the birth of Martian is prepared, finding its "incubation," as Flournoy writes, supported by the sustained interest among the scholars in the phenomenon of language.

We can catch a glimpse of the direction of their questioning regarding the language at another seance. On May 26, 1895, Élise speaks the first words in a foreign language, and here is how her tentative report is welcomed by Auguste Lemaître:

> At 8:50 Mademoiselle experiences a heartbeat that, so she says, she has never felt. At the same time she has allochiria, but she distinguishes perfectly between tokens in different colors that Flournoy presents to her. Mademoiselle experiences an unknown trembling from top to toe. The table expresses the wish to speak and Mademoiselle being a bit tired asks me [A.L.] to spell. We get: *Koos* . . . Is it Hungarian? [Table:] Yes. New sign from the table; I [A.L.] spell *Oluu* . . . and after a short silence: *opoq* . . . Are these three words? [Table:] Yes. She continues: *Unly.* Does this sentence: "Koos oluu opoq unly" have a meaning? [Table:] Yes. Is it Léopold who has dictated it? Yes. Is he alone? Yes. Is the sentence addressed to Mademoiselle? Yes. Have we too much light? Yes. We turn down the lamp. Will Mademoiselle have a vision? Yes. Related to someone present? Yes.

"Are these three words? Does the sentence have a meaning? Is the mother tongue of Élise's father Hungarian?" The scholars want her to reflect on language. In a manner they impose a school exercise upon her. The important thing certainly is that she speaks, but above all that she translates, divides up into segments, pronounces clearly, corrects herself. Martian is evidently Élise's response to the prearranged frame of questions. The participants will get what they require, even if they should have to wait a little to obtain it. And what they collect no longer depends on the spirit but on a scientific context. The articulation of a melodic sentence does not satisfy them. However, the production of Martian seems really to be nothing but that, initially. Proof is provided by the famous scene from February 2, 1896 concerning which Flournoy writes:

> We are constrained to believe that these first outbursts of Martian, characterized by a volubility which we have rarely met with since then, were only a pseudo-Martian, a continuation of sounds uttered at random and without any real meaning, analogous to the gibberish which children use sometimes in the games of "pretending" to speak Chinese or Indian.[13]

But in turn we hear:

> I don't understand this language . . . You are not too warm in this dress? (Little finger: She will speak a language to us, not a terrestrial one, but a language

[13] This volume, above, p. 97.

spoken on Mars) . . . I don't understand . . . You want me to get in there, oh
no! . . . Speak French to me! . . . I don't understand anything! . . . Speak so
that I understand you! You call yourself that! . . . Is it easy to learn? . . . In the
name of Heaven, where are you coming from? . . . I seem to have seen it . . .
Not a hat, it is like a plate! . . . You believe that I shall learn easily; I don't like
learning foreign languages . . . Is there another coming? Then I'll hardly understand anything at all . . . What is this stick doing? . . . I won't get over there,
you get over there . . . It is soft! . . . Ah! I understand, it is only that which
causes movement. (She steps back to let him pass.) Do you understand me
when I chat to you? . . . How do you understand me when I don't understand
you! Speak to me in French all the time . . . I shall never be able to retain all
that. What does that mean? . . . I need to tell them this entire story, that will
interest them . . . Well then! (Mademoiselle proceeds towards the dining room)
Careful! You will get yourself wet, how will you get in, it's full of water! . . . It's
an impossible language! . . . Speak, what do you call it? . . . What language! Is
it Chinese? If at least I could comprehend what you're telling me here! . . .
Sure, I shall speak, but on one condition: you tell me what that means! . . . You
know French well, you have spoken French on two occasions! . . . What are you
saying there? You are only a person here . . . a woman! . . . There is someone
who speaks French, but where is he? Go find him! . . . Speak slowly, I shall
repeat . . . *Michma mitchmou minimi tchouanimen mimatchineg masichinof
mézavi patelki abrésinad navette naven navette mitchichénid naken chinoutoufiche* . . . (These words were pronounced roughly with the sounds transcribed
here; but in the quick conversation which followed, it was impossible to grasp
anything; I noted in passing some words and here they are separately : *teké-*
. . . *katéchivist* . . . *magetch* or *méketch* (several times in the course of the
dialogue) . . . *kéti* . . . *chiméké*).

On that day Élise Müller refused to provide the translation which was
demanded of her. She even remained deaf to Flournoy's suggestion: "After your awakening, when I knock three times on the table, you will remember all that you have said in Martian and you will repeat it in French
to Madame Mégevant". One needs to resort to trickery for her finally to
deliver. At the end of the seance in fact:

Mademoiselle hears our questions with a natural charm, answering us in Martian. I [A.L.] profit from posing the following questions to her, to which I already knew the answers in French. *Quest*: Which persons were present at the
seance on Wednesday at M. Cuendet ? *Rep. Métich* Cuendet, *Médache* Cuendet, *Metich* Senn, *Métaganich* Müller. So you weren't that many, how many
were you? *Reply* (smiling): *Kintch* (that which should mean *four*) and a moment
later Mlle. repeats in the following order: *Métich* Cuendet, Senn, *Médache*
Cuendet, *Métaganich* Müller. Note that one does not repeat Métich in front of
a series of names.

We thus have four Martian words with translation.

The encounter here is exemplary. Mademoiselle says that she does not like to learn foreign languages, but she produces a melodic sentence, and Auguste Lemaître underscores "the great volubility," "her complete lack of hesitation."[14] To them what matters is the translation, and their triumph consists in having been able to get four of these words with their French equivalent out of her. On our part, we do not remain insensitive to Élise's "monologic dialogue." These sentences are truncated, the text is chopped up, the dialogue with an absent interlocutor is constantly interrupted by silences. The points of suspension, exclamation marks, and question marks are mixed up. We are a thousand miles from the descriptions and narratives which would have flourished in the initial mediumistic seances.

SILENCE, WRITING, AND PRODUCTION

After this first attempt on February 2, 1896, the participants are evidently in a hurry "to know more." Théodore Flournoy now laments that "the following seance, unfortunately, did not fulfil the promises with which it began." It is even "almost entirely deficient"—which is to say that Élise expounded neither her Martian language nor her translation as she had announced; she is content, according to Flournoy, with chatting "in French with the sitters, but mingling with it here and there a strange word (such as *méche, chinit, chèque,* which, according to the context, seem to signify 'pencil,' 'ring,' 'paper')."[15] In fact, here is how that happened:

> 8:59 "Oh! such heat!" she exclaims. Is it better like that? we ask her. She replies: "Who was unwell?" She seems to have come to her senses. But turning towards M. Roch, she kneels before the table where he writes and says to him laughing: "What is this stick (it is about a pencil)? One doesn't write like that!" I [A.L.] bring a table towards her to ask her to show us how one should write, and quickly she shouts: *I don't want this mèche!* While laughing all the time she calls M. Flournoy and says to him: *Come and see how he writes!* And catching sight of her ring which she had deposited at the beginning of the seance she says: *Help, chinit!* Her amazement before the pencil continues. We try to give her a long one, a short one, but she turns them over in her hand and throws them away. I present her with a feather dipped in ink. She removes this ink with the tip of her index finger which she runs over the paper making blobs. We insist that she should write, but she replies: *I can't, everything has been taken away from me!* She crumples the paper between her fingers and with her nail she cuts out a very regular square from the rectangular sheet. At a point where we have hidden away the paper which she had she says: *My paper is not this one, this is another small chèque!*

14 Lemaître, "Contribution," p. 87.
15 This volume, above, p. 98.

Disappointment, most certainly, for the audience: Élise does not comply with the request for writing. Flournoy merely glosses that "the importance of this seance is in the fact that the idea stands out clearly (which was not to be realized until a year and a half later) of a mode of handwriting peculiar to the planet Mars."[16] Whose idea is it of "standing out clearly" and what kind of writing is actually in question?

The preceding records are dated February 16. The health of Élise Müller has been seriously jeopardized: struck by long illness, she is kept in bed. Hence the seances are to be suspended for six months; they resume in the autumn. And this will be the outburst of Martian and of its translation, which one may think of as being the unique result of the slow "incubation" of the medium. Nothing, in effect, within the work of Flournoy permits the denial of this interpretation.

Nothing, except that we suppose it is during this six-month break that Auguste Lemaître writes his article "Contribution à l'étude des phénomènes psychiques," appearing in March-April 1897 in the *Annales des sciences psychiques*.[17] Between the summer of 1896—the presumed date of its composition—and the date of its publication, the delay is of importance. What makes us believe that it is during this period that the article was written? Firstly, when speaking of Martian in his article, Lemaître only refers to the seance of February 2, 1896. Now if he had written this article in the autumn or even later he would have had other Martian texts at his disposal and he would have been eager, no doubt, to provide his reader with them to read. What supports us in this thesis is furthermore that this first article by Lemaître is to be followed in the May-June issue of the journal by the "Remarques sur les expériences de M. Lemaître" by M. E. Lefébure, Professor at l'École Supérieure des Lettres d'Alger, to which the Genevan replies, indicating with regard to the unknown language that "he had only been able to capture four words with translation" at the moment when his first article went to press.[18] On the other hand, Lemaître points out that *since then* Martian has reappeared in several seances of which he "had not been able to transcribe everything—far from it." He adds, that "when the medium spoke it with speed, it seemed like these animated conversations which Russian or Romanian students have with each other."[19]

If we insist on reconstructing the chronology of events, it is because we suspect that the outburst of Martian came after Lemaître's text.[20] We like-

---

[16] Ibid.

[17] Lemaître, "Contribution."

[18] E. Lefébure, "Remarques sur les expériences de M. Lemaître," *Annales des sciences psychiques* 7 (1897): pp. 176–80; A. Lemaître, "Reponse," *Annales des sciences psychiques* 7 (1897): pp. 181–88.

[19] Lemaître, "Réponse," p. 182.

[20] However, an enigma remains: Lemaître only refers to the seance of February 2 at the

wise measure the impact of this text in the evocation of a "monstrous beast" who writes. Speaking Martian, its translation, and the announcement of a writing appear at the same time, in the autumn of 1896. Here is a fragment of the seance of November 8:

> Asténé [a Martian figure], I would like to come often to you. I feel less heavy, less oppressed, calmer, more peaceful. I feel much better at your place than at my place. But you will easily carry off this vile beast from here . . . Oh no, I don't think it could be intelligent . . . Oh no, I don't want to see it, I don't want it to come near me. It is very ugly; they have prettier ones at our place . . . It is she who knows how to write all that; I will only believe it when I see it! . . . So make her write! . . . Ah! she doesn't understand; it is from habit that she writes! . . . Her eyes aren't beastly, when one sees her . . . She is sweet, this beast! . . . Is it she who lowers the telescope [*lunette*]? (I [A.L.] had written the match [*l'allumette*]). . . Does she know how to unscrew it? . . . She gives it to you. Then she deserves hanging. It's crazy! . . . But have you taught her to be intelligent? . . . It must have taken you a lot of time . . . No? . . . It doesn't matter, it's a pity she should be so ugly! I only like pretty things! . . . You will show me your lantern.

Who is the "vile beast" that Élise Müller is afraid of, or jokes about? Who says one must "be intelligent"? "Make her write," Élise says to the beast. "Write," the participants say to Mademoiselle, since one of them is already given the task, and all the seances are committed to writing.

We are certain that Élise has read Lemaître's article shortly after he has written it or even during its composition, just as she read the records. She must have retained the hypothesis expressed in it: "Rigorously, one could account for this extraordinary language by attributing it to a double of the medium or, in scholarly terms, a splitting of the personality. *Children at times amuse themselves by fabricating a language from nothing.*"[21]

This hypothesis Lemaître takes—without citing its author—from Flournoy, who already speaks thus about the first Martian words as being a playful and childish creation. Élise most certainly knows it—she would either have heard it from the mouth of Flournoy or have read it in Lemaître. Is it wrong to think that from then on she will manage to refute it by fabricating a language according to a model that their questions provide, that is to say, by delivering a word for word translation and committing it to writing? Flournoy admits to this when he writes, "It is necessary at the start to render this justice to the Martian . . . namely, that this is, indeed, a language and not a simple jargon or gibberish of vocal noises

---

moment when his article goes to press. It is hardly plausible that his article appearing in March-April 1897 was already typeset in the preceding autumn. On the contrary, one might think that it was already written and that Lemaître did not complete it with the new seances.

[21] Lemaître, "Contribution," p. 87. Our emphasis.

produced at the hazard of the moment without any stability."[22] We are in the presence of "a typical case of 'glosso-poesy,' of complete fabrication of all the parts of a new language by a subconscious activity," he concedes.[23] But he maintains his comparison with a children's game.

FROM WORD TO WORD

From the autumn, Élise Müller consequently speaks in Martian. During the seance of November 2, she herself stages the scenario of the translation. Léopold—her double patron—gives Flournoy instructions: he is to place his hand on the forehead of Élise and utter the name of Ésenale, an inhabitant on Mars who is the incarnation of a son of one of the participants, Alexis Mégevand (Mirbel in *From India to the Planet Mars*). The submission to this ritual is the condition for Élise agreeing to translate what Flournoy calls a "long monologue, constantly interrupted by silences" and whose continuation is only secured "having constant recourse to the name of Ésenale as the magic word, alone capable of extracting each time a few words from Hélène's confused brain."[24]

During the seance of November 8 in which Flournoy did not participate, the scenario repeats itself. Is the young woman on the alert? In effect, she only resolves to translate by taking even further precautions:

> The left index finger then says that we shall have some Martian, since we will have the translation of it. My [A.L.] left thumb tells me that by uttering the name of Ésenale I shall obtain the translation, it also tells me that the Martian will be pronounced sufficiently slowly for me to be able to transcribe it.

From then on, Élise is no longer satisfied with being voluble and producing harmonious intonations. She is worried about the transcription of her speech, concerning which she knows she is being difficult. The seance of November 8, 1896, beginning at 4:40 p.m. and finishing at 6:15, shows this:

> 5:50 p.m. Mademoiselle gets up and turns towards Mme. Mégevand, in front of whom she genuflects. She takes her right hand and caresses it in a friendly way several times over. After that she utters a Martian sentence roughly like the following: *Mon déiné cé dji sé vouitch ni évé chéé quiné liné*. When the sentence is completed whilst Mlle. continues to caress the hand of Madame Mégevand, I [A.L.] say "Ésenale" and we get it word for word. I had not divided the words as they should be. It is with a low voice that Mademoiselle gives the following interpretation:

---

[22] This volume, above, p. 154.
[23] Ibid., p. 124.
[24] Ibid., p. 108.

Mondé, Mother—*iné*, dear—*cé* (or *si*), I—*di* (or *dji*), you—*séveouitch*, recognise—*ni*, I—*évé*, am—*ché* (or *chéé*), your—little—Liné.
(One needs to point out that *quiné* and *Liné* were not repeated in the word for word.)
The sentence thus translates : *Dear Mother, I recognise you, I am your little Linet.*

While Élise unfolds the phantasmatic scenario of its translation, the scholars on their part insist on gaining accuracy. How do they do it? Flournoy gives a hint in a note:

> The "word for word" is not always directly as strict. . . . Ésanale often interprets several words at a time. . . . But in instances of hesitation on the correspondence between the Martian and French terms, he is made to repeat the doubtful words separately so that at the end of the reckoning one truly possesses the exact word for word.[25]

Each time it is necessary to caress the forehead of Élise and repeat the name of Ésanale. It is not her who translates, but the young man from whom she repeats the phrases. When submitting to the demand for rigour, she dissects what she has just uttered, as Auguste Lemaître points out on November 29, 1896:

> Translation: Mlle. sometimes repeats the Martian words, at other times she continues without repeating them. I [A.L.] make a point of repeating certain words in order to know how to separate them. The sentence in French becomes . . .

Most often, one has to wait for some hours to reach that point and so be able to undertake an analysis of the text at which one has finally arrived. A Martian glossary is built up, and its syntax pinned down. The curious scholars compel Élise to a difficult exercise concerning the "unknown language." The dialogic context to which she is subjected strangely resembles the relational structure belonging to the "schoolmasterish monologue" addressed to disobedient children to be reared or taught.

PRODUCTION OF TEXT AND DISSOCIATION OF ÉLISE

"Mademoiselle" perseveres from seance to seance, and even *outside*. Flournoy and Lemaître collect the textual productions. We could confine ourselves to recalling them without drawing attention to what goes on all around, and notably the progressive dramatization of the seances. We see, for example, what takes place on December 13, 1896. Flournoy is absent. Élise complains: they "tear off her skin in flakes from top to bottom on the back and wrists to the end of both hands"; "they take away the skin of her eyes"; they "shake her blood"; they "whip her blood." She comes and goes unflaggingly between the Martian and the Hindu scene: the name of Sivrouka comes up again on repeated occasions as if a struggle was taking place to the point where the participants ask themselves "if by chance M. Flournoy would have made a suggestion to Mademoiselle through Florrisant or otherwise." We are in the presence of an anarchic succession of offended monologues. Élise no longer knows who is "I," who is "you," who is "they," as she addresses herself to Léopold at the time of the seance of December 13:

> Oh yes, Léopold, life, what a sad comedy! In fact, I am very glad for you to have . . . One never has two happy hours . . . always being tormented by a mass of unpleasant things . . . Well, in any case you always look after me. And then one must believe that it is probably for my own good. One needs to look at things in that way, we have got to admit it . . . With him, that's a totally different matter . . . Yes, I'll go tomorrow, that's it . . . At first, yes, it is you who have gained victory in this matter . . . It is you who have made me write it, and at the moment where I expected it the least, I had to pick up the pen . . . First these utterances, they are not mine . . . He seemed satisfied, even delighted, but I really made him feel it was me . . . I have done well, on the whole you have done well because it was not me who wrote; you have instructed me, thanks! . . . And then you believe that this is not what I think.

Quite often we no longer know who speaks: is it Élise or is it really Flournoy making suggestions to her? Is it Léopold through the voice of Élise? On January 17, 1897, Élise at last obeys a suggestion of Flournoy's: her voice changes into "a strong, deep, hollow voice joined by a great laughter, vulgar and prolonged," that of Léopold who speaks through her mouth. This scene, which Lemaître classifies as "grotesque," signifies the slow dispossession of Élise. By being the object of different suggestions, by being pestered with questions, she is woman and then man; she is again the other. Nothing stops her in her propensity for moving on to a third. Flournoy nevertheless multiplies the suggestions, to which she surrenders, like in the seance of February 21, in order to lose herself further still.

> From then on M. Flournoy made several suggestions to her which she obeyed exactly. M. Lemaître plays some sad or joyful music on the piano: in the first instance she goes towards M. Flournoy to cry, in the second she laughs. Otherwise she beats the time with her left hand or with her head, even with her eyelids as M. Flournoy has suggested to her. M. F. makes her kneel down in front of him or beat him, tells her to go and take a rose on the knees of Mme. Lemaître, to prick herself on the finger on this imaginary rose, etc. The feeling

of being pricked and of blood trickling down is most gripping. On several occasions Mlle. groans when showing us her finger.

Thus the production of the Martian texts progresses in keeping with the dissolution of she who, meanwhile, continually attempts to respond to that which she knows to be the firm belief of Théodore Flournoy. In effect, during the seance of February 21 she transmits the following, through the table that dictates her thought: "that which Mademoiselle begins to perceive comes to her neither from Léopold, nor from her own depths, nor from anybody present."

WRITINGS

We have already foreshadowed the fact that the article by Lemaître was not, from the time of its writing, without effect on the outburst of Martian in the autumn. Now we may ask ourselves if the publication of this article in April-May 1897, followed by the reply by Lemaître in May-June, had repercussions on Élise's production. Between March and May we no longer have any records at our disposal: two months of interruption, for which nothing gives any hint, neither Lemaître in his records nor Flournoy in his work. The seances resume on May 9, 1897, and here—could this be mere chance?—Élise's preoccupation with writing becomes more specific. On May 30, 1897, we can read:

> (According to me [A.L.] who writes) I believe that at this moment you fulfil the position of a writer (Pleasant position, is it not?) Everything depends on what you write (But who are you then?) Marie! (What is the king doing?) I think that the king is sleeping at the moment—M. Lemaître, what time do you make it? Oh! it's not really late. I slept (M. Roch says Madame to her; she responds:) M. Roch, in treating me like a Madame you make a fool of me, since for the moment I am really a mistress. I don't know if I've been cold, but it hurts here on my right side (actually the left) Ah! now it's on the left side (actually the right).
>
> (With the voice of Léopold:) I don't know what's the cause of it, but I feel very bad on this side! But what are you then writing, M. Lemaître? Ah! I feel so bad, I feel very bad on this side. (M. Roch tells her that he will relieve her of her pain by magnetizing it.) I have never heard it said that you magnetize; M. Lemaître, M. Roch pretends that he knows how to magnetize. But he hasn't understood a bit of it, M. Lemaître, put in the *biography that you are writing*, that you bore me, also put that M. Roch pretended to know the area where I felt pain and he placed his finger on the side! At the moment, sure the pain is gone, but it comes here from the right side (actually the left).[26]

[26] Our emphasis.

This preoccupation of Élise Müller with writing does not date, as we know, from this period. It concurred quite exactly with the first words spoken in Martian during the month of February 1896. And we bear in mind her dialogue, in the autumn of 1896, with the "nasty beast."

Flournoy very accurately retraces the history of staging the Martian writing: it "only appeared at the end of a prolonged period of incubation, which betrayed itself in several incidents, and certainly stimulated by various exterior suggestions during a year and a half at least."[27] However, he never calls to mind the public battle surrounding her during the first eight months of 1897. We resume this chronology.

In the course of the summer Élise never stops announcing the writing will come soon. Thus on June 27, 1897:

Come here, Ésenale! . . . Ah! There is Asténé! Come close to me . . . not behind the armchair! . . . There he is! . . . Ésenale is there! They see each other but don't speak to each other. Asténé is aged, Ésenale is young . . . It doesn't absorb—the ink—this material! It is a material where the ink dries immediately, a kind of blotting paper! . . . A stiffer material . . . You are writing on that! Do they not have paper at your place? . . . It is a material you can roll, it dries immediately . . . It is not in ink . . . M. Flournoy wants me to write with this thing (allusion to a kind of pen made from a nib or a pencil attached to a ring through which one puts a finger, so that it writes in Martian) . . . It is heavy, it is material . . . but I can understand this blade, this piece of metal which marks . . . It is movable, one can press at the tip . . . It is beautiful this writing . . . All that sums up a long conversation . . . Would you teach me to write? . . . They make out that you one day said, I will write, is that true? . . . Yes, I do well believe what one tells me . . . Stay a bit, stay Ésenale! Listen, that's Ésenale who speaks: *Modè tatiné cé ké mache radziré zé.* . . .

"Soon he will write," Élise confirms during this seance. In July she has a vision on the tram. Here is how Auguste Lemaître reports it: "Mademoiselle met Léopold on the tramway who urged her not to obstruct (on the contrary rather) the work which M. Flournoy considers undertaking with his subject."[28]

On August 19 Flournoy writes a letter to the *Annales des sciences psychiques* in order to indicate that he dissociates himself from the interpretations by his friend Lemaître and that he is preparing another work:

I am so much more inclined to renounce my responsibility for the ideas raised in passing by my excellent colleague and friend M. Lemaître, since I hope soon to return to the curious phenomena of his medium in order to provide a purely

[27] This volume, above, p. 126.
[28] Records from July 11, 1897.

psychological interpretation without recourse to spiritist notions of incarnation, anteriority, etc.[29]

On August 22 Élise Müller supplies a sample of Martian writing. Long after this date she will still produce texts, with their translation and writing. But while she had, up to the present moment, succeeded in preserving her everyday life as a salesperson in a silk shop, she now makes a mistake at her place of work. She replaces the number ten (the tenth month of the year) with the number three: "Without knowing why, writes Lemaître, she constantly substitutes the number 3 for the number 10 on the shop's dockets where she should indicate October by its number in the order of the year (10th month)."[30] *Mars* [March] is the third month.

The rest we know. In October of the following year, in 1898, Flournoy expresses his "utter skepticism" to her concerning the area of Martian.[31] This should not come as a surprise to her. Never mind that, she takes recourse to ultra-Martian, then to Uranian, and on to Lunarian. She accedes to trilingual translations: Ultra-Martian text with Martian and French translations.[32] While Élise Müller is uneasy about responding to Théodore Flournoy's scientific quest, her linguistic productions do not in fact dry up.

THE LANGUAGE OF SCIENTIFIC ILLUSION

In the phenomenon that occupies us here, Flournoy sees a "infantile travesty of French."[33] Subsequently, all those who will lean on the glossolalic case of Élise will undertake, in the same way, to dismantle the mechanics of Martian which, according to Guilhem Teulié, "from a linguistic point of view is nothing but a literal translation of French through the aid of neologisms."[34] Jean Bobon, for his part, resumes the appraisals of Flournoy: the glossolalic productions are "puerile in their form and in their basis, strongly tinted by affect, varying in their vocabulary and not in their internal structure, *they bear witness to a regression to an infantile stage of personality.*" Élise's case "incontestably forms a part of psychopathology," according to the same author.[35]

How did Élise Müller go about creating Martian? The linguists cer-

[29] Flournoy, "Lettre à l'adresse du directeur," *Annales des sciences psychiques* 7 (1897): p. 255.

[30] Seance of October 24, 1897.

[31] This volume, above, p. 166.

[32] Flournoy, "Nouvelles observations sur un cas de somnambulisme avec glossolie," *Archives de psychologie* 1 (1901): pp. 101–255.

[33] This volume, above, p. 154.

[34] G. Teulié, "Une forme de glossolalie," *Annales médico-psychologiques* (1938): p. 50.

[35] J. Bobon, "La glossolalie ludique psychonévrosique," in *Introduction historique à l'étude des néologismes et des glossolalie en psychopathologie* (Paris: Masson, 1952), p. 64.

tainly have their reasons for arguing that it is only a disguised form of French. It seems to us that the principal question has to be posed otherwise. The Martian language is not merely that of Élise. Is it not created by those who are questioning? When Élise begins to speak it, Sanskrit as well as Martian are remarkable in their melodic character, their musicality. Élise, Lemaître stresses, does express herself with "an incredible volubility having a very exotic, inimitable and never-failing accent."[36] Whereas Sanskrit resists questioning and remains a language of love in which the name of Sivrouka can be pronounced with softness and passion, Martian yields to suggestions without which there would be no construction.

We know that the phenomenon of glossolalia is always social and needs to be sustained by others, by ideology—religious or spiritual—which gives it a frame, authorizes it, valorizes it, and furnishes it with an external meaning. It requires an Institution that awaits the production by the subject in order then to interpret it. In a religious context, "speaking in tongues" has its writings, its masters, and its examples. In the spiritist context, similarly, its comprehension is of a straightforward nature; it rests on the immortality of the soul, on reincarnation—that is to say, the capacity for being "other" in another life, or being visited by someone dead, a spirit, etc., something that makes it possible. We are each time in contexts where use is made of suggestion.

Élise Müller, by passing from a spiritist to a scientific context, is subjected to different suggestions, the power of which, however, remains the same. Without this passage, she would possibly not have developed her speaking in tongues. She would probably only have achieved through it a "classical" glossolalic production, a melody coming from elsewhere. In his work *From India to the Planet Mars*, Flournoy certainly does not conceal that he multiplies the suggestions. By reading the minutes from the seances, we are, however, surprised by their profusion and above all by their steadfastness. And we remain struck with astonishment when they come close to farce, when they manipulate Élise and make of her a true puppet, a pure object of observation.

Flournoy takes no account of these suggestions in his analysis: Élise's "infantile" productions are her own creation. By restoring certain texts from the seances we have, on the contrary, wanted to show that Martian was at the least her creation for him, and also the mirror of his conception of language, the result of his desires, the other side of himself.

The linguist Victor Henry, for his part, ponders judiciously as to why Sanskrit and Martian do not know, or hardly know, the letter *f*. Is it because, for Élise, the f symbolizes the French that she does not want to

---

[36] Lemaître, "Réponse," p. 184.

speak?[37] We could also very well say that by its absence the f reveals the omnipresence of Flournoy, whose initial it is.

A VISIONARY OF LANGUAGE

We can further show the impact of the scientific context on the production of Martian through another opposition. Whereas Élise uses Sanskrit in order to converse directly with Sivrouka, she only speaks in Martian in order to repeat what she has heard. This enunciation, translated on May 23, 1897, testifies to this: "Come nearer, don't fear; soon you will be able to write in our writing, and you will have our language at the tip your fingers."

She is content with repeating fragments of conversations in Martian, audible to her only: "Speak, I'll repeat it to them, that should interest them." She seeks to understand, but in a way she remains at a distance in order to prove, probably, that the foreign language does not come from her, that this language really exists in the mouth of her invisible interlocutors.

Beforehand, she only depicted Martian landscapes. She now attributes a language of which she is the interpreter to the people inhabiting these landscapes. She invites us to the scene provided by actors, evoking for the audience a plot played out beyond the stage by invisible protagonists with whom she does not stop conversing. Beforehand, she described landscapes with plenty of detail and colors; her speech was concerned with representing a reality. The dialogue turned out successfully. Actually, the texts of the seances take the form of an endless dialogue, as if dedicated to excess. Élise takes complete part in this dialogue. But this is not at all the case when she formulates her Martian enunciations.

In the Hindu romance, the Sanskrit work forms a love transference by Élise onto Sivrouka-Flournoy. The Martian itself is sustained by their rivalry around knowledge and observation: in it, Élise is definitively effaced as a subject of enunciation. Martian is not only the staging of an "ability to speak," as Michel de Certeau defines glossolalia;[38] it is the caricature of a linguistic production where the meaning has been reduced to signification, to the word-for-word.

Many have questioned themselves and will still question themselves about the pathology of Élise Müller. Must one consider her a hysteric, or even a psychopath? Should one not liken her glossolalic productions to "speaking in tongues" such as happens in certain deliria? We believe that wanting to pin it down in whatever classification is to revert to pushing

[37] V. Henry, *Le langage martien*, p. 22ff.
[38] M. de Certeau, "Utopies vocales: Glossolalie," *Le discours psychanalytique* 7 (1983): pp. 10–18.

her to the front of a stage in a role created by her alone, and which varies from one seance to the other. Without denying her predispositions, it seems more just to us to restore the theatre of its performance, where the drama is played out; we also owe it to the audience.

We shall finish with this: Lefébure asks himself in his article if the medium spoken about is not a painter. "He sees in pictures, he writes, and if he is not a draughtsman by profession, he is at least so by instinct," so it seems to him.[39] Élise's father was a polyglot. Élise Müller always maintained that she did not like learning foreign languages and after she had come out of the storm provoked by the publication of *From India to the Planet Mars*, she became an inspired painter.[40] The glossolalic production thus only lasts as long as the time of the prompting observation.

Translated by Michael Münchow.

[39] E. Lefébure, "Remarques," p. 179.
[40] W. Deonna, *De la Planète Mars en terre sainte* (Paris: Boccard, 1932).

Appendix Two: Passages Abridged from the 1900 Translation

THE PASSAGES that follow make up the large majority of those that were omitted from the 1900 translation. The translations are mine, except for pp. 44, 148–189, 193, and 259–267, which have been translated by Natalie Baron, whom I would like to thank. I would also like to thank Natalie Cohen for providing a rough draft of pp. 190–255.

Ed.

P. 12

I knew later, through the documents that were supplied to me on the seances of the spiritist group of Mme. N., that there Hélène was sometimes asleep for several moments in the course of 1892. But these somnambulisms, during which the table continued to dictate certain indications, never took hold of the development of the scenes performed as those to which we have been present from 1895, and they seem to have as quickly ceased through no longer having been reproduced during two and a half years.

P. 13

NOTE: See on this subject the instructive inquiry and the statistics of Learoyd, "The continued story," *American Journal of Psychology* 7: 86.

P. 19

NOTE: See the inquiry of Learoyd cited above, p. 13. See also on subconscious reveries, the chapter of P. Janet, in *Névroses et Idées Fixes* (Paris, 1898), 1: 390.

P. 31

NOTE: It is not one of the least scandalous barbarisms of our so-called civilization that these houses of commerce and these large shops where the 'sense of business' seems to have banished all notion of humanity, and where one sees feminine constitutions, in contempt of the most elementary physiology, condemned for hours in a quasi-immobility in the upright position, and exposed to the thunderbolts of the honorable patron for each moment of rest taken stealthily and by contraband on some miserable stool.

P. 34

NOTE: I insist once and for all on the fact that Hélène does not belong at all in the class of professional somnambulists, nor the persons who occasionally mint money with their mediumship. (Having said in passing, these two categories of workers, of whom I have no reason to speak ill of moreover, seem to me much less numerous with us, even all proportions kept, than in most cities and many other countries.) Mlle. Smith, who largely makes her living in the place where her intelligence and her aptitudes enable her to, and whose family moreover is well off, never draws out any pecuniary profit from her seances or consultations. Such a trade of faculties, which have a sort of religious value and significance in her eyes, would be absolutely repugnant to her character.

P. 44

Sometimes, her fingers are equally rigid, sometimes they stay actively or passively mobile. On occasions, such rigidity does not occur until the very instant when her forearm is touched, at which time it increases proportionally with the exertion made to relax it. These very attempts are manifested in Hélène a few seconds or moments later, in her previously sensitive and mobile arm, or in complaints of fatigue, or pain. If one of her hands, completely unfeeling and hidden by a screen, is pricked simultaneously in three or four places, or an M or an H, for example, is traced on it, or if one of her fingers is pinched, and she is asked at the same time to think of a random number or letter, her response corresponds exactly to the impression just received on her sensationless hand. This occurrence is familiar to M. Binet, who demonstrates that retained unconscious sensations nevertheless recall associated images or ideas, and impose them, as if involuntarily, onto the ordinary conscience, which one believes to be making a random choice. Similarly, the fingers of her sensationless hand begin to twitch, to be given to shaking, or to tap on the table. Hélène watches her fingers, "which are moving by themselves," with surprise; it amuses her at first, then irritates her as she cannot control them, and thus she vainly tries to restrain them with her other hand. Their automatic movements shortly resolve themselves into regular communicative taps, by which Léopold shows his presence. Alternatively, they spread through her whole hand and arm and, after various spasmodic contortions similar to miniature seizures, end up in passionate attitudes or significant gestures that relate to the ensuing somnambulist dream.

P. 44

For example, I have seen Hélène trying with all her might to lift her hands from the table, and managing only merely to pull them to its edge, where the top joints of her three longest fingers remain as if nailed down. The table, by shaking under this minimal contact, shows it to be impossible for her to entirely release her grip, just as she would rather not have a certain incident which she laboured to keep quiet loudly related.

Similar phenomena, and every temperamental anaesthesia, convulsive tic, paralysis, all sorts of sensations which Hélène complained about, often take place on her face, in her eyes, mouth, neck, etc. In the middle of such disturbances, the presence and grouping of which are utterly inconsistent, the vision breaks loose and somnambulism is introduced with equally variable modifications of other functions: tears, sobs, sighs, repeated hiccoughs, esophageal noises, various changes in the rhythm of breathing, etc.

P. 56

Here are two examples of these typtological dictations addressed by Victor

Hugo to Mlle. Smith and conserved in the verbal proceedings of the N. group: 9th December, 1892:

> Love, divine essence, fathomless mystery,
> Rejects nothing, it is the sky on the earth.
> 19th February 1893
> Love, charity, will be your entire life;
> Enjoy and make enjoy, but never be haughty.

P. 60

NOTE: Following the vacillating recollections of different witnesses, Léopold had already manifested a first time, a few days before the date below, in a seance of Hélène's held with several persons of the N. group, but outside of the regular meetings of this group, and without verbal proceedings.

P. 61

Two points remain that are obscure and impossible to elucidate in this genealogy. To begin with, what was this vision of Hélène where Léopold showed her a carafe with a baguette? If it really represented the scene of the chateau of Tavernay, one could conclude that Léopold truly had the distinct consciousness of being Cagliostro before Mme. B. uttered the idea, and that this vision was an indirect means of making it known; but this would not at all prove that he could not have drawn this consciousness in some former suggestion unknown to us. But does this vision accord well with this celebrated scene, or was it not of something totally different? One must give up knowing; neither the memories of Mme. B., nor above all those of Hélène, who never retains for a long time the exact memory of her seances when awake, permit further settling of this question.

Finally, from where comes this name of Léopold and why would Cagliostro masquerade as him instead of presenting himself openly as at M. and Mme. Badel and at many other spiritist tables? No one knows. There is not anyone, to my knowledge, in Mlle. Smith's entourage bearing this name and from whom it could come. M. Cuendet, starting from the idea this is truly a pseudonym intentionally adopted by the real Joseph Balsamo to be able, on occasion, to assert his identity while hiding it at Mlle. Smith's seances, made the ingenious hypothesis that the choice of this assumed name was determined by its symmetric construction on the three famous initials L*P*D, which would represent the specification of the Illuminati (*lilia pedibus destrue*), which Alex. Dumas had once inscribed at the head of one of his most impressive chapters and on the chest of Joseph Balsamo who is the central figure in it. I do not ask for better; in admitting that the second personality of Hélène could have believed itself to exist before the suggestion of Mme. B. of which I have just spoken, and before manifesting for the first time under the name of Léopold, it would be psychologically very plausible that, through the capricious game of the association of ideas, the subconscious imagination of Hélène would have, in effect, passed from the fascinating image of the famous Cagliostro to the memory of the chapter where Dumas revealed him in his essence, then to the three letters in bold type which crowned this amazing chapter, and from there, finally, to the only first name for which these letters could so to speak be taken.

On the other hand, Hélène categorically affirmed, and her mother as well, that she had never read nor even seen the *Mémoires d'un médicin* before the epoch when Léopold-Cagliostro revealed himself. As for asking Léopold himself, this hardly advances the question. The first times that I questioned him on this subject, he replied that this name was an arbitrary pseudonym for which he had not found a reasoned explanation. Later (the seance of February 28, 1897), when M. Cuendet informed him of his hypothesis, he immediately accepted it and through energetic gestures of approbation congratulated the author for having finally found the truth. But this adhesion proves nothing, because it is a prominent trait of Léopold (which he shares with most of the subliminal personalities) that, not knowing to say very much himself when one asks him precise information on a certain subject, he acquiesces all the more quickly to everything which, in what one proposes to him, can flatter his *amour-propre* and tally with his nature or role. Additionally, interrogated again on the origin of his name in a much more recent seance (February 12, 1899) he seemed to have no recollection of the hypothesis of M. Cuendet, and he explains that he took as a pseudonym the first name of one of his friends from the last century, who was very dear to him, and who was part of the house of Austria though he didn't play any historical role—it is impossible to make him more precise. It is totally evident that he does not exactly know himself why he became him, and signed his messages with the first name of Léopold rather than any other, nor even why he adopted and kept a completely useless pseudonym since his claimed identity hasn't been a secret for anyone for six or seven years when he took the trouble to divulge it.

To sum up, Mme. B., who is moreover a convinced spiritist and a profound admirer of the mediumistic faculties of Mlle. Smith, had the impression "to have been good for something," by her remarks and suppositions, in the fact that Léopold gave himself for Joseph Balsamo and that Hélène at first believed herself to be Lorenza Feliciani and then later, Marie Antionette. It is equally to Mme. B., who spoke freely of Victor Hugo, that other following references of the name of the first temporary guide of Mlle. Smith go back.

P. 61

NOTE: This same affirmation is evidently the result of an exterior suggestion; see p. 54 the verbal proceedings of the seance of August 26, 1892. When one knows how the questions and responses are made in spiritist seances, one would know not to have any doubt that it is the assistants themselves who, to explain the dominating and jealous character of this new spirit, asked him if he had already perhaps known Hélène in some anterior existence. As is only fair, Léopold hastened to subscribe to a supposition that furnished his essential character (proceeding from his real psychological origins) such an excellent legitimation, and so conforms to the ambient spiritist ideas.

P. 61

NOTE: See C. Richet, "La Personnalité et la mémoire dans le somnambulisme," *Revue Philosophique* 15 (1883): 226.

P. 63

NOTE: Here is a song, textually dictated by the table, of this preaching and moralizing Léopold. (We consider that the count of Cagliostro has had much time to sooth and improve himself since he has been disembodied.)

> "When often near you I sound your thoughts,
> When at the bottom of your hearts I stop myself an instant,
> Searching amidst all you elevated souls,
> Of souls without detour helping themselves and in accord with themselves
> I was confused by all your miseries,
> Of this lack of peace and then of charity,
> And I ask God in a humble prayer
> To unite you all with a holy friendship."

P. 71

NOTE: The manner in which Léopold excuses himself from not replying to my questions in Italian is not worth the effort of being cited to show how he can sometimes be ingenious and wily. He holds that he knows Italian perfectly, but then he makes as if he is ignorant, because if he makes use of it, I would not fail to pull out a new argument against his real and independent existence, by saying that it is all simply the brain of Hélène that fabricates this language through having it often heard spoken around her! I agree that he is not mistaken and knows me pretty well, but, all the same, I did not expect this reason!

P. 71

To suppose that this would be of a rigorous historical truth right down to the smallest details, "This solemn language, these majestic gestures, this unctuous and at times severe accent"[1] corresponds too well to the figure of the great Coptic such as the dramatic pages of Dumas have forever engraved in the popular imagination—without speaking of the well-known portrait of Cagliostro—in order that there would be place to see in this thrilling incarnation anything other than a vivid reflection of preexisting ideas, a very interesting objectification of a type formed by the most natural means in the subliminal thought of Mlle. Smith.

[1] A. Dumas, *Mémoires d'un médecin*, introduction, chap. 3.

P. 72

One understands that, in these conditions, one must give up discriminating between that which Léopold could draw from the unconscious memories of Mlle. Smith, and that which he would have had to derive from the fluid or astral memory of the true Balsamo.[2]

[2] Mlle. Smith reckons that I exaggerate the richness of her therapeutic arsenal and do too much honor to her knowledge. She affirms that, through the intermediary of her daughter, Léopold has often ordered substances, the curative properties of which she is ignorant of, and remedies of which she has never even heard the name. I will report in the chapter of "Supernatural appearances" several examples of these cases where Léopold had truly posed diagnoses or given prescriptions inexplicable by ordinary ways. One must perhaps remark, on the point which occupies us here, that the established reality of these supernormal phenomenon do not prove that they must have been due to the intervention of Joseph Balsamo in person, rather than to telepathy, clairvoyance, or a completely other occult, but not properly spiritist cause.

P. 72

I have nothing to add on the relations of Léopold and Balsamo, except for an early remark that one will understand better after having gone over the cycles of Mlle. Smith. The emotional tie that unites Léopold to Hélène, or Cagliostro to Marie-Antoinette, is very distinctive: from he to her, it is a sentiment as violent as disinterested, a melange of platonic admiration, of religious devotion, of paternal solicitude; from her to him, it is much more profound, without a trace of love properly speaking, but a high esteem, a little gratitude, a need to consult on material questions as on the gravest problems of moral philosophy, a very great confidence never perhaps reaching a blind submission. Now, singular coincidence, this is, as much as one can judge, exactly the same emotional note that finds itself between the Hindu sorcerer Kanga actually reincarnated in the Martian magician Astané, and the princess Simandini reincarnated in Mlle. Smith. This rapprochement provokes thought. One says well that history repeats itself, nevertheless, this tendency to symmetry, these returns to a same phrase with different modulations, this permanence of an identical motif under various embellishings, is, in general, the fact of art, of poetry and music—in one word, of the creative imagination, rather than the brutal unfolding of reality. I avow that I really would regret a little the day when I would have to see in the mediumship of Mlle. Smith the authentic revelation of real experiences, rather than the beautiful subliminal poem that I have admired up to now.

P. 74

NOTE: Dr. Azam, *Hypnotisme, double conscience, etc.* (Paris, 1887).

P. 74

It is suitable nevertheless to say beforehand a few words of another side of the close connection that exists between the two personalities; I wish to speak of their very diverse and nuanced melange, since the clear-cut dualism is implied in their simultaneous presence and perhaps their quarrels, up to their total fusion in one and the same consciousness.

P. 75

The opposite of this complete division (in appearance) is fusion. One can say that there is a real fusion, although not felt, between Hélène and Léopold in all the incidents of the ordinary life of the former, which, even though it doesn't manifest itself, is nevertheless there, as is proved in subsequently returning to these incidents in some automatic message. Besides this unfelt fusion or identity, there are also cases of felt fusion, of coalescence experienced and felt by Hélène between her coenaesthesia and that of Léopold.

P. 75

It is, in sum, a spontaneous incarnation, with consciousness and memory, and she would certainly not describe otherwise her coenaesthetic impressions, if, at the end of the seances where she had personified Cagliostro in tensing her muscles, swelling her neck, straightening her bust, etc., she retained the memory of that which she had experienced during this metamorphosis.

P. 75

NOTE: See the interesting auto-observation of M. Hill Tout ("Some Psychical Questions Bearing on the Question of Spirit-Control," *PSPR* 11 [1895]: 309), who continues to have consciousness of himself and to observe himself during his incarnations. In the same way that he feels himself become his own deceased father while still remaining himself, Mlle. Smith feels herself become Léopold without ceasing to be herself. M. Hill Tout has put into light well the objection that such facts arouse against the spiritist interpretation; one will see from another angle further on the support that they seem to lend in certain cases to the doctrine of "anteriorities."

P. 77

Hélène described to me by the menu all the treatment and the drugs that Léopold had prescribed for me in her dream, without doubting that it was the exact repetition (as for the content, but not word for word) of that which she had already said to me in the waking seance.[1]

[1] One has often noted the role of the ordinary dream as intermediary between somnambulisms initially followed by forgetting, and the appearance of their memories in the waking state of the following days. See Janet, *Névroses et Idées fixes*, I: 184 and following.

P. 80

No doubt, without spiritualism, the same reflections would not have been equally present to her, and would not have placated her and brought her comfort as well as the intervention of Léopold did. In developing automaticity, the practice of mediumship only achieves here, as in most cases, the dissociation of the elements that in the normal state are the deepest, more inextricably mixed with the ordinary personality, and to give an air of independence, of a strange provenance, to certain intimate and profound tendencies of the individual.

P. 80

at least even though it would not be pointless, the essential point being perhaps much more in the manner that we welcome the Ideal and submit to its exigencies, than in the intellectual or affective, external or internal, vehicle of appearance that it employs to reveal itself to us.

P. 89

NOTE: The discoveries of Schiaperelli and of many others over twenty years, and the scientific discussions which proceeded from them, had numerous echoes in the popular and everyday press. It is sufficient to recall the articles of vulgarization like that of M. Flammarion on the "Inondés de la Planète Mars" (*Figaro*, June 16, 1888) or of the caricatures like those of Caran d'Ache, "Mars est-il habité?" (*Figaro*, February 24, 1896) to understand at which point the idea of Martian humanity now had to be made a part of everyone's current notions.

P. 94

if the young man appeared in this neighboring world of ours, it is because he was actually reincarnated there at the end of his terrestrial life. This is the subconscious reason, very natural from the spiritist point of view, which has furnished one of the principal themes for the rest of the story.

P. 94

Of this sudden change in the course of the subliminal dreams of Mlle. Smith, I was probably the involuntary cause. It is, in effect, at this time, that M. Lemaître asked her permission to invite me to the seances that she gave at his home. She consented, not without several conflicts, it seemed to him, between the fear of exposing herself to the shock of a critical and perhaps malevolent eye of a university professor who was passing by to be imbued with a deplorable incredulity towards mediumistic faculties, and on the other hand, the secret hope, which finished by taking it away, to come to convince this recalcitrant skeptic, which would not be a triumph to disdain for the spiritist cause. One understands thus that before having even made the personal acquaintance of Mlle. Smith, I could play a role in her conscious or subconscious preoccupations that afterwards was accentuated again, which seemed to me to result from diverse indications: firstly, the retrocognitions concerning my family, which formed the principal part of the visions of Hélène at the first seances of Hélène that I attended; then the prompt transformation of her partial automatisms into complete somnambulism under the influence of my presence (see p. 11); the numerous counsels full of solicitude that Léopold lavished on me; finally and above all, the blossoming and rapid development of the Hindu romance where I occupied the place of honor as one will see. Be that as it may, my admission to the seances of Hélène, from the meeting (December 9, 1894) that followed the first apparition of the Martian romance marked the beginning of a long suspension of this romance, of which the second explosion did not take place until February 1896.

It may be nevertheless that another cause had contributed to this eclipse, and that it is necessary to see not only the effect of a strange diversion, but, at the same time, a period of latent incubation necessary to perfect the Martian dream and the preparation of the new language that came to reveal itself there. I did not know of any other exterior incident that could have induced Mlle. Smith to make the people up there speak in an original idiom; but it can be produced, and moreover an idea so natural could well have been landed by the subconscious thought of Hélène itself and become the initial autosuggestion of Martian language. One saw that in November 1894, Alexis Mirbel, although finding himself on Mars with Raspail, spoke in French with his mother via the intermediary of a table in the salon of M. Lemaître. There, there was an amusing lack of coherence and logic that would be of importance in an ordinary dream, but that detonates in a spiritist vision and calls for later explications or corrections. It is to this that the subliminal imagination of Hélène had to apply itself to in silence, while externally producing the Hindu cycle and many other things. It certainly profited from this respite of more than a year to ripen the Martian romance and to make several alterations there.

P. 96

NOTE: Compare the case of Mlle. Anna O. understanding her German entourage, but only speaking English without suspecting it. Breuer and Freud, *Studien über Hysterie* (Wien, 1895), p. 19.

P. 109

NOTE: The "word for word" is not always directly as strict as in the seance resumé here below. Esenale often interprets several words at a time; for example (text 24): *Saïné ézé chiré Saïné* my child, *iée ézé pavi* all my joy, *ché vinna* your return, etc. But in instances of hesitation in the correspondence of Martian and French terms, one makes him separately repeat the doubtful words, so that at the end of the reckoning one truly possesses the exact word for word.

P. 111

One cannot even clearly reconstitute the relations of paternity or of fellowship of the crowd whom one sees march past in the course of this series of disparate episodes.

I naturally only speak of those of whom we know through the seances of Mlle. Smith or by the spontaneous visions that she often remembers sufficiently to subsequently recount. But this does not prejudge anything on the hidden depth from where all these data rise up. It could be possible that in spite of the fact of this fragmentary and disconnected appearance, continuity exists in the secret retreats where the Martian romance is elaborated. What we take for momentary creations without connections between them would then only be the points of emergence, eruptions, of an underground level, conscious in itself though unknown to the ordinary Ego, conspiring in an uninterrupted manner under the habitual level of the normal waking state.

There are mediums with whom automatic communications rise up at intervals more or less long, following on without lacunas or encroachments, and constitute a whole, each new message exactly taking up the point, sometimes to the word and to the comma, where the preceding had stopped. One can ask oneself if the work is truly created by puffs, at the same instant where they spring in to the consciousness of the subject; or if they are unceasingly going on in the obscurity of the cerebration called unconscious, to bring to light by packets, from time to time, the accumulated products of this permanent incubation, like the serial story writer who continually produces, but only periodically publishes, the results of his elucubrations. In the case of the Martian of Mlle. Smith, the question is more embarrassing since her visions lack continuation and, placed end to end, do not form a whole, but a pell-mell or a mosaic of pieces and morsels seeming to come from several different edifices, as one would make an idea in traversing the texts joined in a chapter following the chronological order of their appearance.

One can very well see in this succession of meshing communications only capricious improvisations born in the chance of the moment without any pretension to a systematic connection, of which the points of resemblance or of contact, the common Martian character, would simply hold to only those that were inspired by a certain state of the soul, a particular emotional disposition, reproducing itself a little from one time to another nearly always identically; entirely as we resume again the same genre of dreams, falling in the same category of nightmares, each time we find ourselves in certain determinate organic or psychic conditions: the return of the same circumstances well enough explains the birth of analogous dreams, and there isn't any reason to suppose that they would have been subconsciously continuing in the interval.

But one can also suppose that the chaos of the Martian cycle is only apparent and results from the fact that we only have a minimal part of the total oeuvre. The romance would then form a well-connected ensemble in the subconscious creative imagination of Hélène, still unfinished perhaps, but of which the diverse threads are held and unfold in good order. A psychologist gifted with a double sight that would permit him to be present at all that takes place in the psychic individuality of Mlle. Smith could thus follow the uninterrupted progress of this Martian construction. He would see it slowly building during the day, below the level and without the knowledge of the ordinary personality of Hélène, totally absorbed in her professional preoccupations; feeding many of her nocturnal dreams unfortunately lost to waking; surging by instants in strange images and incomprehensible conversations, to astonished ears and eyes, in the abandon of her short recreations and in her crepuscular phases, early in the morning or late in the evening, where the transition between sleep and the waking state is made; deploying itself finally with more fullness in the somnambulistic visions and spiritist meetings. Unfortunately, double sight is much more rare with psychologists than with the professional super-lucid pythonesses, and on the subliminal arcana of our subjects we only have thin runaways, vague glimmers, which the seances which they give us furnish us with, and the too rare memories that remain to them of their spontaneous ecstasies, when again they consent to us to take part. One must then renounce the resolution of the problem of the subconscious coherence or incoherence of the Martian reveries.

P. 111

NOTE: This name, which I leave in the orthography without accents which Léopold gave him in his verses cited on p. 100, was always pronounced *ezenale* by Mlle. Smith. Its origin is unknown, like those of all the Martian names.

P. 112

at the end of which Hélène had only succeeded in grasping three precise words in the midst of a Martian conversation too indistinct to be integrally noted. Like the schoolboy who finds it quite sufficient to go just to the end of his strict tasks and to already close his ears before the end, Esenale only consented to search in his dictionary (or only recalls) the ends of phrases, neither more nor less, which one is entitled to ask him; his obligatory version finished, he flies off, with a sigh and a spasm of Hélène, and every attempt to recall him remains useless.

P. 113

At first she supposes, contrary to the doctrine, that memories are clearer in the first moments of post-mortem "disengagement" than after a period of rest, since the spiritists insist unceasingly on the state of confusion that follows disincarnation and only dissipates in the course of time. Afterwards, the memory of Léopold, falsified by his need of harmonization, completely denatured the facts; one has only to refer to the two first sessions (pp. 91 and 95) to establish that Alexis Mirbel did not at all appear as discarnate, but that he was fully there in the reality of his Martian existence, hearing a discussion of Raspail, or meeting Mlle. Smith on her landing on Mars, and astonishing her by his big-boy appearance, etc. What a lot of contradictions of detail finally for Léopold not to be tempted to totally purge this romance of Alexis Mirbel! How, in reality dead on our globe in July 1891, could he, at the same time as being immediately reborn on Mars, find himself there already aged five or six, as he pretended (p. 96), in the seance of February 2, 1896, as the years of this planet are nearly double ours? How, in this same seance, does he not know hardly any of the French that he spoke fifteen months previously, and which he recommences one and a half years later to know sufficiently to fill the office of translator, but not enough to say a word of affection or goodbye to his poor mother? Etc.

People will reply to me without doubt—and I have nothing to rejoin—that my ignorance of the finenesses of occult philosophy is the sole cause of the difficulties on which I stumble, difficulties that would not exist at all for an intelligence less engulfed in the grossness of this empirical world. It would suffice, for example, for everything to arrange itself for the better and according to the explication of Léopold, to admit that in absolute reality, of which ours would be the reversed image, that the seance of February 2, 1896 had taken place before that of November 25, 1894; it is totally natural then that in the first, Alexis Mirbel, living on Mars, would no longer know French, and that, if he recovers its use in the second, it is because he is again discarnate, the conference room being able to pass for a "fluid table" that he must not take for a reality. One sees that by this simple inversion of the course of time during a year or two, which is not harder to swallow than the mysteries of the astral or of the fourth dimension of space, the story of Esenale becomes very intelligible: while those who are not sufficiently wised up to accept it have only the sad resource of attributing to the caprices of the dream and to the chance of the association of ideas the apparent contradictions in which they drown themselves.

I ask myself if at bottom the subliminal thought of Mlle. Smith is so inaccessible that one could believe in the difficulties that worry me, and if this is not the secret sentiment of all these impossibilities, revived, much rather than dissipated, at the end of the explications attempted by Léopold on September 12, 1897, which finished by removing from the repertoire the role of Alexis Mirbel and by giving to the Martian romance a turn more disengaged from all historical attachment with our terrestrial world.

There is nothing much to add on Esenale, whose functions of discarnate interpreter condemn to remain in the wing, I wish to say, aside from the Martian realities perceptible to the living of up there. Only the mediumistic gaze of Mlle. Smith sometimes catches sight of him, who returns to float fluidly in the gardens of Mars, and amongst his ancient companions, invisible for them as are, for us other nonmedium terrestrials, the innumerable souls who constantly wander in our surroundings, impalpable swarms of powers of the air or of shadows of Hades, filling our houses and our fields with their mysterious presence.

P. 114

NOTE: In the spiritist symbolism familiar to the groups where the mediumship of Hélène was developed, this aspect of "inanimate statues" signified that the appearing personages were now incarnate and living, and that the vision does not refer to themselves in their present state, but to ancient events where they played a role. That which the medium has before her eyes is not an actual reality, but only "the image or the fluidist tableau" of the past.

P. 119

We only have, on the subject of this new arrival, the visions accompanying several recent texts. This is too little to pronounce with certitude on his account. Meanwhile I strongly suspect from the point of view of his psychological origin that he is only a lining, a hardly modified echo of Astané, as the latter is of Léopold, that is to say at bottom a third edition of the principal type created by the imagination of Mlle. Smith to return to her dominant emotional tendency. As he presents himself to us up till now . . .

P. 120

That which is more significant, and decisive to my understanding, is that he appeared to bear to Mlle. Smith exactly the same nuance of affection as Astané and Léopold, and tends in returning to place her by his simple presence in the same ecstatic state of well being (text 39).

If the distinctive trait of each of our fellowmen, in relation to us, above all resides in the sentiment that they inspire in us and those which we believe we inspire in them . . .

P. 120

It seems that Astané had delegated his powers to Ramié, in that which concerns the exploration, I was going to say the creation, of the Ultra-Martian world, just as he had himself received from Léopold that which touches on the planet Mars. The fact that Astané and Ramié sometimes figure together, coexisting in the same vision, in the same way as very often Léopold and Astané do, isn't an objection to their essential identity, because an analogous fact presents itself in dreams, where one sometimes walks and converses with one's double. The meeting of one's double, in a waking state, is an adventure that is not very rare with mediums: it happened to Hélène, in a seance where she was hardly entranced and was freely conversing with the assistants, that she would see herself appear in two copies a few meters in front of herself, such that, as she would express and describe it very well at the time, there were in all "three Hélène Smith girls" in the room.

P. 120

I leave to partisans of the first hypothesis, if it happens, the trouble of drawing out of all these communications the consequences that they bear relative to the distance between the human civilization and that up above, and I restrict myself to wish them that the discovery of some other mode of investigation, preferably not mediumistic, will come without delaying too long to independently confirm the correctness of their deductions.

P. 120

As it is certainly not the scruple of deluding us nor the fear of being mistaken that stops him, since these sentiments would have been as natural in the linguistic domain where one will see that they were hardly retained, I conclude that truly the problems of the physical and natural sciences do not exist for him.

P. 122

It is as if the scholar of whom I have just spoken, having seen several photographs or colored engravings of these far countries, but without knowing anything more precise of their costumes and their inhabitants, had conserved in the eye a confused impression of the whole ensemble of forms and tonalities so different from our land, then amused himself to spread this superficial varnish of exoticism on the images of the new world that one had burdened him with creating, so as to give to it as original an appearance as possible.

P. 123

NOTE: The content of this chapter was communicated to the Société de physique et d'histoire naturelle of Geneva in its session of April 6, 1899 (*Archives des sciences physiques et naturelles* [1899]:90).

P. 123

NOTE: *PSPR* 7 (1897): 278.

P. 123

NOTE: An attempt of this genre has been made at a seance of Mlle. Smith, thanks to the obligence of M. Eugene Demole who had brought his recording phonograph; but it did not succeed.

P. 126

I would not know if she ever found herself in the case of mediums who consciously see their hand writing without their participation, nor in that, much more rare, it is true, of subjects who hear themselves with astonishment proffer without wanting to unknown speeches that they can gather.[1]

[1] See the curious auto-observation of Le Baron, "A case of Psychic Automatism including 'Speaking with Tongues'" published by William James, *PSPR* 7 (1897): 277.

P. 126

This difference is understood—it is all the same curious that it would not be universally spread—when one muses on the capital role that our motor sensations and images play in the constitution of our personality, as against the visual and auditive givens that above all serve the intellectual and objective representation of non-Ego. The chains of *visa* and *audita* can thus develop themselves automatically without broaching much the ordinary Ego of Hélène, which finds itself, on the contrary, gravely disorganized when a group of her kinesthetic centers, above all those serving speech and writing, which we all always hold so close, is seized by a second personality.

P. 126

June 18. In a visit which I made to Hélène, we speak of Martian and, at my request, she takes a crayon to see if some signs would automatically come. She finds that the crayon has a tendency to take its place by itself (through unconscious movements of her fingers) on the back of her index finger, as if it wished to fix itself there, then she believes she sees a ring encircling the bottom of her finger and ending with a sharp point. She writes nothing, but before long she lets go of the crayon and pushes it far from her with little flicks, then she little by little enters into a Martian vision where she hears text 14.

P. 128
for example, as one of the assistants, on seeing her form these bizarre letters, speaks of comparing them with the diverse oriental alphabets to see if they came from there, Léopold dictated by a finger: Your researches will be totally useless.

P. 134
NOTE: It is to be noted that Léopold wrote these words while keeping the crayon in the position that Astané held it, that is to say between the index and the middle finger (Hélène's mode), instead of taking it in the ordinary manner, between the thumb and index, as he usually does.

P. 135
NOTE: Text 14 and a list of a hundred Martian words have already been published by M. Lemaître in his "Réponse à M. Lefébure" (Annales des sciences psychiques 7 [1897]:181.

P. 145
Mlle. Smith appeared above all completely absorbed and insensible during this operation; meanwhile, the conversation of several assistants seems to trouble her a little, and Léopold finished by giving three violent blows of his left fist on the table to make silence, after which the writing executes itself more rapidly (on average twelve characters per minute).

P. 148
Hélène is unaware of the meaning of these letters, "which look like the numbers two to seven," and she says that the original on the cylinder was both smaller and neater than her copy. She held her pencil as usual between her index and middle finger, and has the impression throughout of being in a normal waking state, albeit fascinated by the presence of the young girl. However her mother, who was present during the automatic writing, thinks that, "they were making her write, for she looked peculiar and was making small pencil strokes, and following the text with her left index finger, etc."

P. 157
I talk only about the texts proper collected together above, because in spoken discussions during various seances that were impossible to record, there were certainly js; but there again, I did not notice a single sound alien to the French language, and the particular acoustic style of the jargon merely resulted in a profusion of infrequently heard French combinations, such as the phoneme tch, which is only found again in texts 1 and 3.

P. 158
Moreover, we notice peculiar connections between letters which are far apart in

the French alphabet, such as when *u* and *g* are brought together, *z* and *h*, *f* and *v*, in the same way that *c* and *i* seem to have become confused in the transition from French to Martian. On the whole, if we attempt to categorize these odd letters according to a similarity in shape, we find that they fall into five fairly distinct groups. The first of these includes only *c* and *r*, being the only letters to be formed only by straight lines. The second, comprising of *e* and *d*, is a sort of transition group towards the next two categories; letters characterised by the presence of a fat loop or belly, either towards the left (*a b f n p v*), or towards the right (*i g h k l m z n*). The final group in which there are neither straight lines nor dominant loops but simply various curves, includes *o*, *s* and *t*. Still to be looked at are certain pairs of letters which are nothing but the reverse, or mirror image, of each other; *m* and *n*, *l* and *p*, imperfectly *f* and *k*. Although inexact, cases of horizontal symmetry must then be added to these examples of vertical symmetry, such as *l* and *m*, *n* and *p* (as in French with the letters *d* and *q*, *b* and *p*).

P. 158

The most interesting aspect of this relationship is the *e*, which has no less than four or five different values, as in French the three *e*'s in *Esenale*, for example, are respectively pronounced as those in *médecine*, those in *êvé* as those in *rêvé*, the ending of *amés* as that of *kermès*, etc. The diphthongs and nasals in Martian are pronounced and written exactly as in French, even if the only examples we may use to judge are: *ou*, *an*, *on*, which come up in the written text.

The Martian *c* plays a triple role, as it does in French (with others still). It is guttural and equivalent to the *k* sound in *carimi*, *crizé*, where it is pronounced as in *car*, *cri*. It takes the hissing sound of the hard *s* before an *e* (it has not yet been before an *i* in a word) in the word *cé*, which is pronounced as in *agacé*. Finally, together with an *h*, it forms the hushing sound *ch* of which I will speak again.

The *s* has the same idiosyncrasies as with French. It is generally strong, but between two vowels it becomes soft like the *z*; at least if it is not in a pair, in which case it remains hard. For example, in the words *somé*, *astané* and *mis* it is pronounced as in the French words *somme*, *astres*, and *fils* while in *ésenale* and *misaïmé*, it whistles like the *z* of *êzé*, *épizi*, exactly like in French where the *s* and the *z* have the same sound in *visage* and *gazeuz*; but it becomes strong again when it doubles, in *essate* and *dassinié* as in *essai* and *assiginer*.

Alternatively, if we start from the articulated sounds and examine their representation in Martian writing, we come across singularities existing in French. The strong guttural, which has many means of expression in French, has two more in Martian: the *c* and the *k*; Martian economizes unwaveringly only with the *q* by replacing it with a *k* (see, for example, the words *ka* and *ké*, meaning "*qui*" [who] and "*que*" [what]). Even so, the strong sibilant, ordinarily written as a single *s* (except between the two vowels), is translated as a *c* before an *e*; and the soft sibilant is represented generally by *z*, although sometimes by a single *s* between two vowels.

Moreover, sounds that are phonetically as simple as many others, and could claim a different letter as happens in many other terrestrial languages, are found to have in Martian exactly the same complex symbol as in French. The sound *ou*, for example, which in German is a single letter, has followed the French manner:

it is written and pronounced in *pouzé* and *bounié*, etc., as in *poule*. The same goes for the nasals *an* and *on*, the only two to figure in the written texts, where they are spelled in *sandiné*, *pondé*, etc., as in *santé* and *pondre*. Lastly the strong hushing sound that French alone in the world, I think, represents by the union of *c* and *h*; it is written *sh* in English, *sch* in German, *c* in Italian etc., and to which many oriental have far more logically given a single simple symbol like the sound itself; it is found equally represented in Martian as *ch*, which is pronounced in *ché*, *métiche*, etc., as in *chez* and *fétiche*.

The small detail in the spelling of this fairly frequent ending, *che*, betrays in a significant way the influence of old customs and shows that the so-called Martians who are writing through the hand of Hélène are at bottom more accustomed to the French style than their own language. By skimming through the various written texts, one notices that the sound *ch* in the last syllable of a word now with a final *e* (*iche*, *mache*), now without the *e* (*métich*, *antéch*), although in both of these cases, the pronunciation is exactly the same, and resembles the French endings in *riche*, *tache* and *mèche*. Where does this difference in spelling come from, which nothing in the pronunciation explains, which is even more strange, given that in French the sound *ch* not followed by an *e* has a completely different sound and becomes guttural (*varech*, *almanach*)? I think that it must be interpreted as a simple *lapsus calami* owing to a fortuitous resemblance between the Martian letter *h* and the French letter *e*. The correct and complete spelling would always be *che* (*méticha* and *antéche*); but it happens that the Martian *h* finishes in a closed ring similar to the French *e*, a coincidence that may easily lead to confusion: suppose that the Martian personality of Hélène was distracted while writing the final *ch*, and her hand mistakes the ring for the shape of the final *e* and forgets to add the Martian *e*, which is actually still missing. It is the inverse and opposite of cases where the underlying dream troubles the normal waking personality and slips, in Martian characters, into Hélène's French writing (see fig. 1, p. 40 and fig. 22, p. 129). What confirms this explanation is a case when the same error with the letter *z*, also finished by a circle in the shape of an *e*. In the Martian article *zé*, which is mentioned a number of times in the written text, the final *e* cannot really be left out, for the double reason that in a word of two letters it is more difficult to forget one of them that in a longer word—and above all that the *é*, which is not silent but closed—would upset the internal structure of the word. However, at the end of text 18 we see an example of this absence of the final *e*, so that the article *é*, which in other places afterwards has been fully written, finds itself reduced to the letter *z*. Esenale obviously let himself be foiled by the deceitful ring that he had just traced through the hand of Hélène, as he had already done two lines above in the word *métich*, although on other occasions in the same text he had not fallen prey to this error (see fig. 25, p. 131).

P. 159

Thus *diviné heureux* has the feminine form *divinée heureuse*; *ié tout* becomes *iée toute* and *iéeΣ toutes* (texts 7, 24, 28, etc.). In much the same way, the ending *ir* indicative of a future tense is similar to the French ending *ra* (*uzir*, *dira* [will say]; *dézanir*, *répondra* [will reply]; *trinir*, *parlera* [will speak]; etc.). In such words, the vowel, of average pitch, has been replaced by the highest pitch of all, in accordance with the high-pitched Martian tone. In any case these examples are sufficient proof, just as the structure in the series *cé amès, je viens* [I come]; *amès, viens* [come]; *né amé, est venu* [has come]; *dé améir, tu viendras* [you will come] is sufficient proof that Martian is an inflected, even an analytical language, albeit singularly similar to French.

P. 159

In the same way, the small word *le* [the/he/it] is always translated by *zé*, in its double role of article and pronoun (see for example in the same text 20: the [*le*] small bird, you will see it [*le*]). Similarly the diversely used *que* [that/it etc.] is always replaced by *ké*. The French word *si* [yes/if/very] becomes *ii* in the sense of both *oui* [yes] and *tellement* [very]. The preposition *de*, which is part of so many different constructions, is invariably translated as *ti*, and the personal pronoun *te* as *di*, regardless of whether it is a dative or an accusative. It is fruitless to continue with these examples (which the reader will easily be able to find more of if he so desires), which reveal that these small words: conjunctions, pronouns, prepositions, etc., which in our very analytic French idiom, constitute the essential articulation of the French language. They replace the case of the declension and are translated always only by their verbal appearance, without any regard to their logical function. Martian slavishly follows French and has no discernible feeling of the sort that M. Bréal[1] has described as the survival of inflections. It is clear to anyone who has studied even the smallest amount of a foreign language, such as German or English, that it is not advisable to translate the two *nous* [we, to us] with the same meaning in the phrase, *nous nous comprenions* [we understood each other], as Martian does in *nini nini triménêni*. In short, it is evident that these extraterrestrial visitors are thinking only in French, and have modeled their language on exclusively French words, be it interior, auditory, or motor.

[1] M. Bréal, *Essai de Sémantique* (Paris 1897), p. 55.

P. 161

probably not even suspecting the existence of all these beautiful things nor the possibility of such refinements. The naive inventor of Martian has taken it upon herself to make solely a dictionary, but that as extraordinarily as possible, conforming to infantile and undeveloped notions that can see nothing in a foreign idiom but an incomprehensible mass of words. The inventor is unaware that what characterizes a language and makes it different from any other, is not its vocabulary, but its internal structure.

P. 161

But this job of artificial fabrication is in reality far more wearing and difficult than one who had not tried to invent one would have thought. One involuntarily gets stuck in the rut of rhythm and of number; one allows oneself to translate brief terms with other brief terms, and long ones with other long ones. Sometimes, without even noticing, one keeps certain vowels or consonants from the original word; all in all, one realizes that one has counterfeited or distorted the old, rather than newly inventing.

P. 162

I have spoken about the inconsistencies that occur in the Martian vocabulary, above all in the first occasions. Many are only outward discrepancies and are due to either Hélène or the listeners occasionally mistaking the sounds that they were hearing. However, while benefiting Martian in every doubtful case, there are a few where there are certainly no mistakes, and which reveal shifts in the words or their precise meanings. For example, in text 4, *tout* is said *is* (no hesitation is possible with the pronunciation *ice*), while in text 7, two weeks later, it will permanently become *ié* and in the feminine *iée* (text 24). In the same way, the word *kiné*, *petit* [small] (3), is later transposed into niké (20) and amiché: *mains* [hands] (12), has become *éméche*: *main* [hand] (23), unless one is trying to see an eccentric method of distinguishing between the plural and the singular! The article *la* [the], which is spoken *ci* in text 2 (such was what Hélène heard and wrote down and what Esenale had clearly pronounced at the time of the translation) and which later became *zi* (27, 31). The adverb *là* [there], as a result of the verbal confusion of which I have already given examples (p. 159), fell prey to the same fate (compare 4 and 40), and, what is more, it appears as *zé* in written text 26. This is an undeniable mistake on Astané's part, because *zé* always means *le* [the]. The negation *ne*, clearly pronounced and written *ké* in the first texts, has been pronounced and written *kié* since text 17, perhaps to distinguish it from *ké* [that]. In other cases, the lack of continuity can be explained by a momentary lapse in remembering the correct French equivalent and the substitution of a synonym. For example, the word *instant*, which is said *tensée* (8 and 17), is used in another occasion (11) to translate *mûné*, whose correct meaning is moment (34). In the same way, the word *triménêni* (15) should probably have been translated as *entretenions* [we maintained] rather than *comprenions* [we understood], for in the same passage (15) and various other texts (8, 37), the verb *seïmiré* is given as the correct Martian equivalent of *comprendre* [to understand]. In the same way, *azini*, translated by *alors* [so] as is *patrinèz*, seems rather to mean *puis* [then] or *ensuite* [next] (17). These examples of total inconsistency are rare—that is to say, two words with a completely different structure used to express the same idea. One of them is found in a comparison of two occasions seven months apart, when Esenale says to his mother that he *recognizes* her (3) and that he has *recognized* her (15), the two forms of the same verb expressed by two words as different as *cévouitche* and *ilinée*.

Another sort of variation is very obvious in the way French monosyllables, *je*, *de*, etc., are rendered as when their *e* elides and is replaced by an apostrophe before the next word. On the first occasion, Martian appears always to take the French word as a block, like one unit: *tive*: *d'un*; *ilassuné*: *m'approche*; *zalisé*: *l'élément*; *mianimé*: *t'enveloppe*; *méi*: *t'ai*, etc. (passim in the first fifteen texts). In the later texts on the other hand (since 29), there is always a distinction between the two words, and Esenale separates them in Frence as in Martian: *ti mis*: *de un*; *lé godoné*: *me aider*; *zé brodi*: *le os*; *de anizié*: *te envoie*, etc. There has therefore been a sort of progress in the analytical faculty of the Martian philologist. Such a progress could have been spontaneous, but I am tempted to like a fairly substantial part of the discussion that I have had with Léopold about Martian, namely the confusion between the article and pronoun *zé le*, etc. (see the following chapter); a discussion that happened precisely in the interval between the two series of texts and that must have drawn Hélène's subliminal attention towards the proper value of these small words, which became part of the following word, from a verbal point of view, after elision. Moreover, this analytical process did not supress other inconsistencies; for, if we can understand *zalisé*, *l'élément*, as the contraction of the article *zé* and the noun *alisé* (compare texts 14 and 28), the formation of *ilassumé*, *méi*, etc. cannot be explained when *me* becomes *cé*, *te di*; nor the discrepancy between *tive* and *ti mis*.

Without doubt this list of contradictions and variations could be enlarged. But when all is said and done, these minor imperfections amount to very little when compared to the truly remarkable overall consistency of the Martian vocabulary.

P. 163

There would be many minor points to be made about the style of the Martian texts, which, as is to be expected, vary noticeably according to the character in play. Esenale talks differently to his mother than Astané to Simadini, and the language of the lover Siké, is, aptly, much more flowery ("sun of my thoughts," etc.) than that of the wise astronomer Ramié, even though the latter has none of the scientific dryness characteristic of this planet, and is probably a likeness of M. Flammarion rather than the late Le Verrier. But these remarks lead me astray from the point. I confine myself to a single aim: the use of *f* the word *Métiche*—incontestably derived from the French *Monsieur* (see text 1)—with the meaning of *homme* [man] (texts 2, 7, 21, 31; in text 18 it has been put into a position to be translated, above all by Esenale, as *monsieur*). In this confusion, I am inclined to see two very different meanings; not a complete suppression of social inequalities on Mars, but a reminder of the tender age when children still called everyone they saw on their way or in picture books "ladies and gentlemen." This would be another minor indication of the infantile origin of the Martian literature.

P. 163

[that] it could really be said that one had inherited a blank instead of the family talent. However, it must be good that this disadvantaged chain possesses such gifts—until they are transmitted—in the form of latent germs, undeveloped potentialities, which in appearance, are apparently dead. The anatomophysiological substratum representing this latent disposition in an organism matters very little here. This substratum waits to hatch on the more favorable terrain of some alternatively or better constituted descendant; it suffuces that in one way or another these invisible abilities are present in the individual, and thus we can understand that they occasionally throw out fugitive glimmers in certain exceptional circumstances, such as a hypnoid state.

P. 164

NOTE: For an example of the application of this biological point of view onto psychology, see M. G. Stanley Hall's very interesting and suggestive study on fears, phobias, and various obsessions, which are so common in childhood, most of which he explains as short-lived reproductions of racial states of the soul, so to speak, atavistic reminiscences of conditions dating from the first ages of humanity, even animality: "A Study of Fears," *American Journal of Psychology* 8 (1897): 147

P. 166

NOTE: The result indeed proves that what was there was only an outward semblance, and that in reality Hélène still found herself in a suggestible state, which continued until some time after the seances, and perhaps did not completely end until the night's sleep.

P. 171

Just as in pathology when neoplasms are most likely to use those cells remaining in an embryonic state as their starting point, which (under the influence either of external stimulation or some as yet undiscovered internal circumstances) suddenly begin to proliferate and differentiate themselves in an abnormal manner; so, in psychology, it seems that certain distant and primitive elements within the individual, infantile layers still capable of plasticity and mobility are particularly suited to generate these bizarre subconscious growths, like some sort of tumor, or psychic excrescence, which we call second personalities. Moreover, we have no more clear an idea of etiology than that of organic neoplasms. Stimulations from ambient milieus—such as emotional shocks, moral traumas, spiritist or other suggestions—all these causes remain inadequate explanations without the presence of indispensable internal conditions. At the moment we know next to nothing of these latter, for the terms hypnoid predisposition, tendency to disaggregation, ability to split, suggestibility, etc., do nothing so much as increase the number of names for the fact itself, without actually removing our ignorance about its innermost nature and its real reason for existing.

We could easily push the comparison further between such anatomical tumors that are sometimes malignant, sometimes benign, contained, or diffused, etc.— and these psychological parasites, restricted or pervasive, either harmless like the Martian dream, or dangerous as in a morbid fixed idea, either ignored by the normal person or troubling them with automatic interruptions, etc. But it is not right to compare the two and we would be falling prey to a naive illusion in believing that it is helpful in decoding such a complex and delicate puzzle as mental phenomena by comparing them to cortical neurons and their protractive, retractive, coaptive, reptative, and *tutti quanti* movements, their dendritic or cylindrical continuations. Nor shall I reckon to have added anything whatsoever to an explanation of the Martian cycle by recalling—that which without saying is a priori for physiological psychology—that the infantile subpersonality that created this cycle must be represented, in the brain of Mlle. Smith, by networks of fibers or a system of particular dynamic associations. Those out of use (or dispersed to form part of other combinations) when the real personality of Hélène is dominant, start to function more or less completely when she returns to her Martian state. The existence of these anatomophysiological correlatives of our mental life is self-evident, but their inevitably vague and uncertain representation is utterly useless for the understanding of psychical facts. Thus it has to be acknowledged on trust that this cerebral mechanic is always implied, yet we ought never to talk about it as long as we have nothing more precise to say.

P. 175

(This irruption of Chinese here, when we are not really expecting it, is in all likelihood due to the influence of a small Chinese vase that Hélène had noticed in the salon of Mme. B***, (of whom I have spoken, p. 118). Mme. B***, when I visited her, herself showed me this oriental vase and told me that Hélène, noticing it one day, had picked it up and examined it with curiosity and inquired about its origin. It was shortly after this incident that the Chinese visions manifested themselves.)

P. 176

The seance had hardly started when Mlle. Smith stopped hearing us while continuing to look at us, and said to us: "Go on, chat! Talk!" She could still read and understand my written communications to her, but the level of possession increased. She seemed to be absorbed with some inner vision. Shortly afterwards she entered a state of somnambulism, during which she moved onto the corner of the settee where I was sitting, pressed my head hard with her hands, made vain efforts to speak, then little by little released my head, and raising her hands majestically above as if to bless me, suddenly uttered in a solemn voice these two words separated by several sighs: *Atiétyâ . . . Ganapatinâmâ.*

P. 177

She also remembers awakening for an instant, able to distinguish us, while at the same time seeing herself dressed in oriental clothing and bedecked with jewels; but she does not remember the scene when she divested herself of these ornaments.

P. 179

(The curious game of the beginning—in which in my opinion systematic anaesthesia and allochria combined in a sort of delayed attraction that makes her go and sit down in a corner of the room or on the piece of furniture I had just vacated—could be considered as an autosuggestion due to the following circumstance: in the afternoon of that same day, Mlle. Smith had been present at a seance held by the Société Psychique de Genève, where the president knew all about the fact that "exceptional somnambulists can find the influence of people in a room when they are no longer there, and follow their trail, feeling their traces and seeing their fluid image on the furniture where they had been.")

P. 181

NOTE: This theory (I don't know if it is very well known outside the local circles where I encountered it) might have a real psychological foundation. One knows that MM. Breuer and Freud, in their cathartic method—which consists in reawakening latent memories of psychic traumas suffered by their patients, to give them an emotional free rein—rediscover through this the most recent incidents and then gradually work back to the earlier ones. It is possible that something similar occurs to the mediums in stories of anteriories. If the story is elaborated in their subconscious reveries, while following the normal course of events, one sees that, once finished, they unwind in an inverted sense in the seances, which are a form of release or natural catharsis for these subliminal tangles.

P. 181

of which the definition was not immediately perfect, but underwent a process of trial and error in guessing. The scenes of the story are not exactly divided up into the different seances, but often touch upon several, voluntarily taking the form of simple visions, having attained their perfection of concrete and living reality in a scene of somnambulistic personification.

P. 183

NOTE: Naturally, the preceding description only applies to good seances, in which nothing hinders the development of the complete purity of the Hindu dream. However, the somnambulism is often neither deep not frank enough; vague memories of real life, the influence of the Martian romance, of Marie-Antoinette, or visions concerning those present, etc., would come and interfere with the oriental cycle; thus one is present at confused scenes, in which these different chains of heterogeneous images intertwine and mutually paralyze each other.

P. 184

I have recalled above (p. 61) the virtuosity with which a hypnotized subject will adopt the character that one prescribes to them, and will become, in the blink of an eye, a fireman, a wet-nurse, an old man, a rabbit, and anything else one wishes by an extraordinary and sudden concretion of all the images or experiences stored up inside themselves relevant to the role in question. And nevertheless, it is not the subject who chooses the character, it is the hypnotist who imposes it from the outside without any knowledge of their tendencies or natural aptitudes. If, despite this constraint, the hypnotic imagination never finds itself starved, and if it instantaneously takes the best parts of a frequently insubstantial body of information regarding the imposed subject, must one then be astonished by the perfection that can obtain to the realization of a character that the subconscious Ego has freely adopted on the grounds that it corresponds to its tastes and inclinations, for the execution of which it has had the leisure of trying out and storing up, over years, the materials that are directly relevant to its intention, amid all those offered to it by everyday experiences?

Nobody ordered Mlle. Smith to play the role of a Hindu princess or a queen of France, in the way that M. Richet ordered Mme. B. to transform herself into a priest or general. If then she becomes Simandini or Marie-Antoinette in somnambulism, it is because these figures correspond better than others to her congenital inclinations, express her latent tendencies, and incarnate a quirk or secret ideal of her being. There can be, in consequence, no doubt that the instinctive selection made by each living being constantly from among the impressions of every sort that assail it, noticing and retaining some and leaving others, conforms to its inborn aptitudes, to its character and temperament, in a word, to its entire individuality; no doubt then that this selection was not carried out with Mlle. Smith following the same tendency, this same quirk of spirit that would later determine the choice of her somnambulist incarnations. If she so admirably personifies the Hindu princess, it is because, ever since she was a little girl, just as a magnet will separate iron filings from dust, she has instinctively noted and remembered all that which in the thousand encounters of daily life has to do with the Orient.

Snatches of conversation, glimpses of shop windows, stories of missions, illustrated journals, foreign tourists seen in the street, posters, and fairground shows perhaps, and who knows what else, all these innumerable forms of the truant schooling to which we owe all the knowledge that official schooling does not teach us, that is to say, nine-tenths of what we actually possess—these are the sources from which Hélène could draw, without doubting the remarkable knowledge of India that inspired her asiatic somnambulisms.

Inversely, if she had looked around herself and carefully stored up that which especially evoked the exotic, having as a contrary reaction neither attention nor memory for that which concerned, for example, German or mathematics, it is because such was the nature and inclination of her spirit. The individual personality, be it the result of heredity, of accident, or of free pre-empirical determination in the manner of Schopenhauer, is an ultimate notion beyond which one cannot go in our experimental sciences. I should like very much to see in this the legacy of an anterior existence, which moreover only serves to defer the difficulty. But, even allowing that Mlle. Smith was really an Arab-Hindu princess of the fifteenth century—a pleasantly poetic hypothesis—in order to explain her so strong taste, I almost said nostalgia, for oriental splendours in her bland Genevan existence today, it is no less clear that this taste is sufficient to take account of the attention she paid without her knowledge, in the ambient milieu, to everything that could be added to her exotic dream, and later put into practice in the form of the Hindu romance in her hypnoid states favored by spiritist seances. There is then no need for true and authentic reminiscence of a past life, of the mysterious reappearance of concrete memories from five centuries ago, in order to explain the creation of the character of Simandini, for it is, from my point of view, much more suitable to pay direct homage to the extravagant subliminal fantasy of Mlle. Smith.

P. 184

When you have been as hopeless as I am at history and geography, it is not lucky to come across a medium whose subliminal is so packed with the rarest and most subtle knowledge of this area.

P. 189

in the fifteenth century. But this information itself, in the free translation of the date 1401 of Marlès, and the foresaid correction, not to mention many of the other examples, show well enough that Léopold is not solely a repeating machine, delivering with a blind servility that which he has stored up. He is an original personality who reflects, reasons, invents and whose spontaneity, as with all of us, even leads him to certain chances of error. His memory is hardly perfect. He can be mistaken, and the fact that he doesn't write foreign words like a gifted author, does not prove that they do not come from him.

What is more, the two differences with which this is concerned appear simply to indicate that Léopold's sort of verbal memory, of the endophasic type, is not visual (in which case the mistake would be of greater consequence), but rather audito-motor as with most people. Each of these errors is explained in the most natural fashion.

P. 189

As for forgetting the *n* in *Tchandraguiri*, that is to say, confusing the nasal *an* with the single vowel *a*, one finds another example, exactly the same, occurring in the name of the princess, primarily written Simadini and later rectified to Siman-dini, as seen on p. 181. This simply proves that, in her interior speech and the conservation of the memory of words, the individuality of Léopold-Hélène forgot or neglected the verbo-visual images, and kept primarily to verbo-auditive or verbo-motor images like most other people. Certainly, if Léopold had dictated *Nayaca* in spite of the analogy with *Sivrouka*, I would see in that another indication that his model is Marlès; all the same, if he had dictated one of the actual scholarly spellings of *Tchandraghiri* or *Candragiri*,[1] such a striking divergence from Marlès, who writes consistently in the ancient style and vulgar pronunciation, would seem to me to be a grave impediment in my hypothesis. However, given that the facts are as they are, I do not think that these two insignificant differences that I have just exposed and sufficiently explained can be begrudged me.

[1] The former adopted by Vivien de Saint-Martin, for example, the latter by M. Barth, as was noted earlier.

P. 190

NOTE: A. Aksakof, *Animisme et Spiritisme*, French tr. by Sandow (Paris, 1895), p. 411.

P. 190

Or, if one invokes logic, it should be recognized that two incompatible and contradictory kinds of logic have existed ever since spiritism began, one which is used by adepts and the other by those who dabble. Naturally enough this does not promote understanding between the two camps, each accusing the other of bad faith, *parti pris*, ignorance of scientific methods, etc. At bottom both of them are equally sincere, convinced, and respectful of that which the different structure of their brain or the opposed structure of their understanding oblige them to regard as the absolute rules of all impartial research. I would not dream of joining so hazardous a debate, for one cannot be simultaneously judge and jury; I will content myself, before taking a position, to summarize and clarify the arguments by expressing the principals that implicitly serve as the base of these two logics.

The one says that the doubt—that is to say, the lack of absolute proofs, the absence of memories, the obscurity of the past, the ignorance of precise circumstances, in brief all the negative arguments hinged on the unreliability of evidence —ought to profit from natural and ordinary explanations that will always be provisionally admitted until proof to the contrary; and that the *onus probandi*, the burden of demonstration, in good method lies with any new, occult or supernormal hypotheses. Conversely, the other logic proclaims that current and normal explanations must be proved in each individual case, and that it is the occult, supernormal, or mysterious causes that it is legitimate to make benefit from the obscurity of the facts and that ought to always be provisionally admitted until proof to the contrary.

P. 190

I shall therefore allow that in the particular case of Mlle. Smith and the passage in Marlès, provisionally and until proof to the contrary, that in spite of the lapses in her conscious memory, Hélène had knowledge of the contents of this passage via the usual channels of sight and hearing; perhaps, I am apt to think, during some state of distraction, of reverie or drowsiness, etc., thanks to which the information escaped her normal personality to settle immediately in her hypnoid strata. I would not be astonished if Marlès's remark on the beauty of Kanaran women was the hook, the tiny detail that caught her subliminal attention, which, quite naturally, held on to this unique passage along with two or three consecutive lines, to the exclusion of all the much less interesting surrounding context.

P. 190

Was it perhaps a kindness on the part of Léopold, who knows and foresees everything, to thus translate for us into the Christian and to spell for us in French the historical information contained in the Hindu memories of the princess, so that we would have less difficulty in recognizing and verifying the Marlès text when we happened, by some happy accident to put our hand on this forgotten author? My head truly spins at the thought of all these possibilities, and from fear only seeing extravagances there in my turn, I shall quickly pass to another subject.

P. 193

This supposition is corroborated by evidence that I was able to gather about the probable origin of this cliché. When I showed it to my colleague Professor Montet, he told me that it was an Arabic proverb, phrased in the N. African manner, meaning: "A little of a friend is a lot." Hélène's subliminal imagination was obviously unaware of this meaning, otherwise it would not have missed embellishing it into a pretty scene that it made possible, rather than reproducing it in basically very insignificant circumstances. After M. Montet had reminded me that the Muslim decoration is made up largely from proverbs or adages of this sort, to form ornamental motifs, I devoted myself to assiduous researches to find the source: objet d'art, fabrics and carpets, illustrated books, etc., to find out where Hélène could possibly have seen this text. It was in vain, and I began to despair of finding anything, especially as the aforementioned text was naturally traced, in handwritten characters, while in the ornamental inscriptions that I came across, the Arabic lettering was nearly always stylized, interlaced, twisted in a thousand different ways to an artistic end—when chance put me on a different track.

I was discussing these phenomena with Dr. E. Raspin one day, who has on several occasions been called to the Smith family, and I was showing him my documents when, examining the text in question, he cried out, "That looks like my handwriting!" and showed me how the four words were written in a large and straight and horizontal format, whereas true Arabs write obliquely, and more or less askew. It must be said that Dr. Raspin, an Arabic scholar in his spare time, had a few years previously traveled to the north of Africa. On his return, he published the story of one of his excursions[1] and, before distributing this booklet out among his friends and acquaintances, he inscribed on each copy as a dedication, some Arabic proverb (without a French translation), borrowed from a collection of grammatical exercises he had studied. Now Mlle. Smith's somnambulist text, in the way that it is punctuated, can be seen to be precisely one of these proverbs: it is the very one at the top of the list in the same grammatical text book.[2] Hence the more than likely supposition that Hélène had at one time seen a copy of Dr. Raspin's pamphlet with this manuscript dedication, and moreover was more affected as she knew the author personally. Dr. Raspin believes that it is highly probable that he sent one of the booklets to either Mlle. Smith or her parents; unfortunately, because this took place ten years ago and he did not take note of who he gave his booklets to, the supposition cannot be confirmed, and even less can he remember what Arab proverb he would have inscribed in Hélène's copy. As before, because neither Hélène in her waking state, nor Léopold when questioned during her somnambulisms and most certainly not her mother, Mme. Smith, have the slightest memory of having ever received or seen Dr. Raspin's booklet, it is better to make an abstraction of this possibility. It does not seem improbable that a copy bearing this proverb was seen by Hélène, either during the course of a visit to a friend or in Dr. Raspin's waiting room, as she could well have gone to during this time (the exact dates are impossible to give after so long a period has elapsed). In my opinion this latter conjecture appears to be more particularly apt in explaining why the Arab inscription was noticed and kept in the subliminal or hypnoid consciousness, without the participation of the ordinary personality, naturally preoccupied and absorbed with the imminent medical consultation.

It is not until the inaccuracies of Hélène's text are compared with the model of the Machuet grammar, which are only explained as the reproduction of Dr. Raspin's habitual errors, in which one sees here another curious proof that the text is a slavish imitation of his writing, if we do not take the enlargement into account:

A spelling mistake in the first word (the absence of a link between the *a* and the *l* of *elqalil*), a mistake which I was in the habit of making at the start of my studies in Arabic, made me realize that I must have written this proverb from memory. I also used to miss out one of the letters from the last word (the *i* of *ktsir*), and to correct myself afterwards; this explains the configuration of this word in the text in question. The only difference would be in the size of the writing; Mlle. Smith's is more exaggerated than mine. However it could be that I had written in that size in this particular case.

In my library I found the copy of the same book that Dr. Raspin had sent me in 1887; it has at its beginning on a corner of the cover an Arabic proverb that attracts attention from a distance, which is not the same as Mlle. Smith's, but which has the same horizontal writing. It is true that this writing is a third smaller than that of fig. 35, but this difference in size cannot be important; for nothing proves that a visual memory is always reproduced graphically in the exact dimensions of the original; on the contrary, one could point out that from the example of the verbo-visual Martian texts, Hélène has a marked propensity to write on a notably larger scale than the imaginary models she is copying. Thus everything pushes me to conclude from the hypothesis with the most likely presumptions, that Hélène's only rich Arab text is the visual memory of Dr. Raspin's dedication. But I hasten to recognize that this has not yet been definitively demonstrated, in order to leave a small door open to those who will instinctively prefer a different, less probable, but occult, explanation, to this very simple, but natural supposition.

¹ Dr. E. Raspin, *En Kabylie* (Paris, 1887). (Extract of the *Annuaire du Club Alpin Français* 8 [1886]).

² Machuet, *Méthode pour l'étude de l'arabie parlé*, 3d ed. (Alger 1880), p. 270.

P. 193

The name of the little monkey, Mitidja, seems to have been borrowed from the well-known plain near Algiers. Adèl, the name of the faithful slave, means *justice* in Arabic and denotes certain juridical functions in Algeria. Simadini, later corrected to Simandini, reminds me of a family of long established Grison merchants in Geneva, MM. Semadeni, who could easily have had business contacts with Hélène's father, and also of the little town of Simaud in the Comitat of Arad in Hungary. Unless again this word represents either the Indianized form of an Arab name ending in *eddin*, or a memory of the Sanskrit *símantiní*, "which," says M. Saussure, "was perhaps here and there a proper name although it was usually a poetic word for *woman*." But all this brings us to the Hindu language.

P. 196

But, M. de Saussure adds, "it should be understood that all kinds of continuous sense, there where I amuse myself to find it, is for the moment a simple game."

P. 199

Among these examples of isolated words that are pure Sanskrit, one can above all cite *radyiva* (fig. 37) evidently equivalent to *râdjîva*, "the blue lotus." Also *pitaram* (accusative of *pita* "father"), which appears, but in error from the point of view of tense, in the following phrase: "Mon pitaram m'avait confiée à lui"—from a Hindu scenario where Hélène-Simandini speaks about the faithful slave Adèl who her father the Arab sheik had given her when she left for India. But the most remarkable specimens are the two words *sumanes* and *smayama*, which particulary struck M. de Saussure. The first "is irrefutably a graphic reproduction of Sanskrit *sumanas*, 'friendly,' cited a little in all the grammars and even serves here and there as the model for declension." It should be noted however that, for all these grammars equally, this word is pronounced *soumanas*, whereas Hélène specifically says *sumanas*, which seems to designate a plant in the phrase: "They were the most beautiful sumanas in our garden." As for *smayamana*, it escaped Hélène (and it was immediately noted as such by M. Lemaître) in a French conversation, while she was looking at an album of pictures of the Orient that would naturally have awakened the Hindu dream on the edge of consciousness. According to M. de Saussure, this word, which means *smiling*, is perhaps one that Mlle. Smith "produced as the best way of making Sanskrit; firstly because it has four syllables, and thus has a greater chance of being exact than a two or three syllable word; also because of the consonantal grouping *sm*, because it is very rare for Mlle. Smith to tackle a Sanskrit word presenting two consonants at once; finally for this fact, much more rare, that *smayamâna* bears a grammatical and not simply lexicographical character, being a participle similar to the Greek *lego-memo-s*." One understands, in effect, the interest of this word, which represents an already very complicated form, when one considers Hélène's habitual ignorance of "Sanskrit," an ignorance not only of inflections but of all types of formations.

P. 200
NOTE: Here Hélène appears to be addressing M. P. Seippel and myself (who are reincarnations of Adèl and Sivrouka respectively!) as if to invite us to sing.

P. 200
NOTE: The same game, aimed at M. Seippel and M. de Saussure (reincarnation of Miousa).

P. 202
In his early years my brother thus invented a whole language to himself. My grandmother, who was remarkably intelligent, could still recite *verbo tenus* in her extreme old age, a little chant comprising a dozen lines that she wrote as a child. It was during the wars of the Revolution: troops constantly marched through Alsace, and she was mortified because she did not know a single word of French. So she set about making up this little speech using assonances that sounded French, but of which the first words demonstrate a germ of sense. This began with: *I cannot speak in French*; then came a dozen lines of syllables added at random, with a French word here and there, for example *vinaigre* [vinegar], *manger* [to eat]; everything finishes with: *a toujours beni perpense sa tavirettement*. My grandmother often recited this singular morsel, which I regret that I hadn't noted. I have described it to M. Barth because of his interest in such subjects.

P. 202
"Rightly or wrongly," he wrote to me

but I am now disposed to see in the *sivroukian* phrases something analogous with Martian, scattered only at intervals of shreds of Sanskrit. As a simple illustration of my idea: suppose that Samandini would want to say this phrase: *I bless you in the name of Ganapati*. Placed in the sivroukian state, the only thing that does not occur to her to state, or rather to *pronounce*, is this in French words, but these are nevertheless French words that remain the theme or substratum of that which she says; her spirit works by the law that all familiar words are rendered by a substitute of an exotic aspect. It doesn't really matter what: above all it must not have the look of French to her own eyes, and she is content to replace the place that is marked for each French word in her spirit with new sounding figures at random. I add that the substitution will sometimes therefore be completely arbitrary (as is the case with Martian), sometimes she will be influenced or determined by the memory of a foreign word in—English, Hungarian, German or Sanskrit—with a natural preference for the idiom which best suits the place of the scene.

This given, I try to apply more closely this hypothetical procedure to the phrase here below, for example. 1) "Je" [I] must be transformed. Can her memory provide an exotic alternative? Not one. So we randomly select *a* for "je." (Perhaps in fact, this *a* is inspired by the English *I*, pronounced aï, but this is not necessarily so.) 2) "vous bénis"; or "bénis vous," because if, for example, the word for "je" was suggested by English, it could follow that an English construction would be involuntarily followed in the words placed immediately after. One marks in consequence "bénis vous" by *tiê yâ*. The *yâ* could have been taken from the English *you* (modified in regard to the most dominant Sanskrit vowel). The *tiê*, "bénis," comes from nowhere, as in Martian. 3) "au nom de Ganapati," obviously the actual name Ganapati is not part of this process and should be taken as it is. Which leaves "au nom de," which I will express by *nâmâ*, could be by recollection of the German *Name*, or could be by the revival of a Sanskrit *nâmâ*, also appearing sometimes; finally the construction, which contradicts the order of French words, would be arrived at on the wings of the German *Name*, after the German expression *in Gottes Namen* [in God's name], *in Ganapati's Namen*. In sum, gibberish that takes its elements from where it can, and invents them the rest of the time with the only rule not to allow the French basis from which it flees to be revealed.

These ingenious conjectures of M. de Saussure should be seen for what they are worth: that is to say a simple representation, to which he didn't otherwise hold, in the linguistic procedures in the oeuvre of Mlle. Smith. In fact, he is probably quite correct in his view of the genesis of *ganapatinâmâ*; for if the Martian author did not know a word of German, as one has seen, this is not a reason for the transcriber of Sanskrit to share in the same ignorance, on the contrary. If one compares the characters and content of Hélène's two exotic cycles, it is evident that the Hindu cycle is less childish than the Martian, corresponding to an age and a degree of development of the whole personality that is notably more advanced than the Martian dream;[1] if then one admits, as I have shown (p. 307), that these somnambulistic stories constitute a sort of hypnoid vegetation of ancient strata belonging to the childhood or youth of Mlle. Smith, it would be very likely that the strata that engenders and feeds the Hindu cycle is at least contemporary with the time when she learned German (between the ages of twelve and fifteen), if not a little later, so that the memories of this language would not have been without influence on the construction of the Hindu.

As for *atiêyâ*, I doubt that one could make the reminiscences of English intervene here, since Mlle. Smith totally gave up studying it after two lessons. As no theory is in itself too trivial or too silly when it concerns the explanation of phenomena that are essentially of the order of the dream, and where the foolishness of an association of ideas would not be an objection to its probability, I would prefer to draw this exclamation, which seems to have the meaning of "I bless you" or "be blessed," from the popular onomatopoeic exclamation *"atiou!"* that children and their entourage use to express or simulate a sneeze, and which is indissolubly linked through secular usage to an invocation of divine benediction. Such childish connecting of ideas, combined with a tendency to conserve the original number of

French syllables in the neologism and joined to the choice of a final sanscritoid form, seems to me to explain in a plausible fashion, until better judgment, the supposed transformation of "bénis sois-tu" into *atiêyâ*.

However, despite the attraction of this method of exegesis, I shall not apply it to the other Hindu texts, not only because of the inevitable arbitrariness of its applications, but above all because its central principle seems to be subject to caution, in the case of Mlle. Smith's Sanskrit.

[1] Compare for example the sentiments of the only two couples who appear in these cycles. The creation of the married Hindu couple Simandini and Sivrouka suggests an adolescent or adult imagination, whereas the Martian couple Matémi and Siké seem to be described by a child who had attended the betrothal of an older sister or brother, and who had heard several fragments of conversation between the happy lovers. (See page 119 and texts 20 and 27).

P. 203

NOTE: A. Lang, *The Making of Religion* (London, 1898), p. 10, 12, 324, *et seq.*

P. 203

Here are some typical examples. In a seance where the Hindu cycle predominated, these words were obtained, among others: . . .*balava* (or *bahava*) *santas* . . . *émi bahu pressiva santas* . . . They are of interest firstly because there are traces of inflection, quite a rare phenomena in Hélène's Sanskrit: alongside *bahu* "beaucoup" [much, many], says M. de Saussure, is *behava* (the nominative plural of *bahu*, meaning *multi*), the fact that it is placed immediately before *santas*, "etant(s)" [being(s)], another plural, makes it all the more interesting; *bahavah santas* means "etant nombreux" [many beings] in good Sanskrit.

But here is the note of M. de Saussure that is most important for us here: "The Sanskrit word *bahu* 'beaucoup,' is one of the most common words, but it would be interesting to know if Mlle. Smith pronounced it *bahou* or even *bahü* in a French manner as in 'battu, tondu.' This last instance would be one of the most flagrant proofs that she mechanically repeated a written form."

As there is no doubt on the pronunciation *bahü* (and never *bahou*) by Hélène, this little fact speaks clearly in favor of the purely visual origins of her Sanskrit. One has already seen how she made the same mistake in pronouncing the word *sumanas* (p. 314). The same error occurs again in another form, which does not lack interest, in her graphomotor automatisms. One will soon see her pen occasionally slips in real Sanskrit characters without her knowledge while in the course of her French writings; it is curious to discover that those characters that should really be pronounced *ou*, for her have the value of the French *u*. For example, I have a letter of Hélène's where, in the description of a Hindu vision, the word *discutaient* is written with a Sanskrit *u* isolated in the middle of other letters of her ordinary writing. Likewise, the reader can see in the sample text, fig. 38, that the Sanskrit character that is pronounced *rou*, but which one represents in French letters by *ru*, plays the role of this last syllable in the subliminal consciousness or inner speech of Hélène, since she automatically employs it for writing the French word *rubis*. All this well denotes an acquisition solely through reading.

P. 204

In other cases, it is hardly as if the normal consciousness is troubled by the underlying dream, which surfaces just enough to substitute Sanskrit equivalents here and there for several French characters, without altering the flow of words or ideas, and Mlle. Smith remains stupefied by the unknown hieroglyphs that an inexplicable distraction of her pen has slipped in to the labels and invoices she has been writing. (fig. 38, p. 206)

P. 204

For example, in fig. 37, the words *instant* [moment] and *ils* [they] begin with a sign that, in Sanskrit, only represents the *i* in all other conditions (the Sanskrit *i*, isolated or initial, is completely different). Moreover this sign is often met in Sanskrit writing at the material beginning, I want to say at the extreme left, of certain words, but in pronunciation it only comes after the consonant situated to its right. This detail is a new indication of the visual origin of Hélène's knowledge of Hindu: of the two Sanskrit characters indicating *i* that can equally be found at the beginning of a word (graphically, to the left) the eye above all retained the most simple, which resembles the French capital I, even though it is this that is never found first by ear or in pronunciation. Hélène's Hindu Ego does not seem to have pushed the study of Sanskrit beyond detached characters, because it never transcribes whole words in this language. Even in the case of exotic terms such as *radyiva* (fig. 37), it prudently confines itself to a Sanskrit initial and completes the word in French, as if it does not dare risk plunging into the composition of the letters between them. Similarly with the word *plis* (fig. 38), the first three signs— which actually play a very artificial role here, denoting great ignorance of their ordinary meaning in Sanskrit—are drawn in isolation, instead of being joined together, which a graphic automatism better acquainted with current Sanskrit writing would not fail to do. On this very subject, M. Glardon remarks that whenever the Hindus wish to write, they always begin by drawing a horizontal bar along which the letters of each word are attached; so if Mlle. Smith ever had any notion of joined up Hindu writing, it is hard to understand why she remembered isolated characters yet forgot the bar that in practice always precedes and links them.

P. 204

Perhaps the amateurs of the supernormal prefer to believe that even if Mlle. Smith's Hindu (the graphic form of its Sanskrit characters, pronunciation, etc.) does not derive from memories of a previous existence, it should at least have been *telepathically* transmitted to her by some habitué of her seances possessing more or less extensive Oriental notions. As for MM. de Saussure and M. Glardon, whose names spring immediately to mind, they attended only four of Mlle. Smith's seances, and these were at a late stage when she had already produced most of her Hindu texts, in particular all the graphic examples in figs. 37 and 38. In that which concerns myself, I confess to have followed a course in Sanskrit given by Professor P. Deussen Keil, then a privat-docent at the University of Geneva, over a quarter of a century ago when I was a young and inquiring student, ready to try anything. I have so few conscious memories of the course that I did not even recognize the characters that appeared in Hélène's letter (fig. 37), and I have never seriously entertained the idea that she could have telepathically retrieved her notions of Hindu from my latent memory; mainly because if this were the case she should also have produced some Hebrew, which I studied for a year at the same period and which my subliminal strata would certainly have absorbed far more of than Sanskrit, even if scarely any more conscious memories of it remain. As for other persons connected with Mlle. Smith, I know of no one who has the slightest knowledge of Sanskrit or any other Indian language. It is true that there could have been occasional spectators performing these functions at the seances that she gave at a variety of locations from 1892 to 1894. In this case, it would be a good method, before invoking a telepathic link between them and Hélène, to be first of all absolutely sure that they had not shown her several books or notebooks of Sanskrit at the end or during a seance—this is precisely my hypothesis, which permits everything to be explained by a normal and ordinary manner when one takes into account the powers of conservation, imitation, and reconstruction belonging to the subliminal faculties.

P. 206

When the previous pages had already gone to press, M. de Saussure was struck by an idea, as likable as it is ingenious. To enable me to give a more living estimate, some sort of tangible impression, of the nature of Mlle. Smith's Hindu to readers who aren't Indianists, he wanted to write for them an ostensibly Latin text that bore the same relationship to the language of Tite-Live or of Cicero as the Sanskrit of Samandini bears that of the Brahmins. In other words, the following "Latinate" specimen has been constructed by a manner that all these remarks suggest applied to the "Sanskrit" productions of Hélène, simply changing the name.

The following words are supposed to have been pronounced in a "Roman" somnambulist scene, in place of a "Hindu" one: *Meâte domina mea soróre forinda inde deo inde síni godio deo primo nomine . . . obera mine . . . loca suave tibi ofisio et ogurio . . . et olo romano sua dinata perano die nono colo desimo . . . ridère pavére . . . nove . . .* Here are the kind of observations that this singular passage would probably give rise to, and that are identical to those which comprise Mlle. Smith's Hindu texts.

1) There is no general graspable meaning, if one searches for it in a phrase. From time to time, however, several words form a good enough sequence by themselves, a fragment of a phrase. 2) Taken each in isolation, like a collection of words one takes in a dictionary several words are irreproachable (such as *domina*); others are partially correct (*ogurio*, etc.); others, finally, have no evident identity with a Latin word (*dianta*, etc.). 3) The text is completely poor on the specific point of grammatical endings. Not only does one not see anything that resembles characteristic endings such as *-orum* or *-ibus*, but there are not even consonantal endings such as *-as*, *-os*, *-is*, *-us*, or even *-um*, at the end of a word. It is as if the writer found making proper grammatical endings too great a task. 4) The same sentiment seems to manifest itself outside of the endings in

that the text uses only very simple words in their consonant structures, such as *do-mi-na*, avoiding any form that might present complications, like *octo*, *somnus, semper, culmem*. Elsewhere two important constants are apparent: 1) The text is not a mixture of "two languages." However, unlike Latin, these words do not suggest the intervention of a third language such as Greek, Russian, or English; in this first negative sense, the text has precise value. 2) It equally offers a precise value by the fact that it *presents nothing that is contrary to Latin*, even in places where it does not correspond to anything due to the absence of the meaning of words. If we now leave the Latin and return to Mlle. Smith's Sanskrit: this Sanskrit *never contained the letter f*. This is a notable fact, although negative. The *f* is effectively a stranger to Sanskrit; but, in free invention, one would have a twenty to one chance against creating Sanskrit words including the *f*, for this consonant seems as legitimate as another if one did not know.

This last remark of M. de. Saussure's presents a further and hitherto unnoticed complication in the problem of Hélène's Sanskrit. For one thing, although it does not exist in Sanskrit, the *f* is one of the most common in Western tongues, especially French, and there is in effect something very remarkable in its complete absence from all the Hindu fragments of Hélène's that have been recorded. Elsewhere this intimate knowledge of the genius of the Sanskrit language that seems to be implicated by Mlle. Smith is contradicted by the previously mentioned fact (see p. 314) that many of her Hindu words end with the French sound *u*,[1] which, like the *f*, does not appear in Sanskrit where it is pronounced *ou*. So if the absence of the *f* resulted from a real possession of this idiom—as would be normal (due to the study of Sanskrit under the direction of teacher), or supernormal (due to the reminiscences of a past life, a telepathic transmission, etc.—it his hard to understand why she does not similarly avoid the *u*, particularly because in certain cases she does not make the mistake and correctly pronounces *ou* (for example, in the fairly frequent expression *mama soukha*).

In awaiting the enlightenment that the future can bring to us on this cruel enigma, I provisionally retain my hypothesis here, that Mlle. Smith absorbed what she knew of Sanskrit in an essentially visual manner, by leafing through a grammar or other written documents during her suggestible phases. For this hypothesis is not contradicted by the absence of the *f*. I do not think, in effect, that this would give too much honor to the subliminal faculties—after all that one knows of their speed, finesse, and their sometimes astonishingly exquisite and delicate flair—by admitting that the hypnoid imagination of Hélène's could easily have noticed the absence of the letter *f* in the Sanskrit alphabet given by the grammars, and respected this trait in its subsequent creations of an imaginary Hindu; even if she did not notice that the letter *u* in this alphabet has a different value to the French.

As for the words where she says *ou* as it should be, perhaps she encountered them with their pronunciation noted in parentheses, unless her visual initiation wasn't accompanied by some audible information, furnished by the people who showed her the printed documents.

I am not dissimulating that there is little satisfaction in conjectural explications circumscribed by *perhaps*, *probably*, etc. But in all types of causes, the same difficulties subsist, and a little reflection suffices to show that the occult hypotheses are stuck with exactly the same problem as my purely normal hypothesis. For, if this is really the language of an Arabo-Hindu princess that emanates from the lips of Mlle. Smith, or some telepathic infusion of an authentic idiom, or all that one would wish of the supernormal, how can the grammatical inaccuracy of the speech taken as a whole be explained when compared to the exactitude of certain rare words? The remarkable omission of the *f* joined to the faulty presence of the French sound *u*? The possession of isolated graphic signs and the ignorance of the bar that precedes and links together all cursive writing? The appearance of a Persian word such as *boulboul* (fig. 37), and the absence of Arabic words, particularly strange on the part of a daughter of a sheik that the Muslims didn't cease to introduce to the languages of India, etc.? The occultists would doubtless say that Simandini *could have* forgotten these things, whereas I say that Mlle. Smith could *have retained* them; that the princess of the past has *perhaps* confused the *ou* of Hindu with the French *u*, whereas I say that Hélène *probably* didn't know that the *ou* is usually transcribed as *u* in Franco-Sanskrit grammars, etc. As far as evidence and precision, one would agree that these explanations are of equal worth: they are white cap and cap white [bonnet blanc et blanc bonnet]. From which I conclude that, all things considered, if one prefers the occult hypothesis to the normal hypothesis, this is not because it gives a better account of the concrete details of the case, far from it, but simply because it is occult. It is a question of taste that I leave to the appraisal of the reader, more especially as I have already previously said what I think of it (pp. 188–190).

  [1] M. de Saussure seems to have lost sight of this point in the last of his remarks. Judging the Hindu fragments on their *written* compilation, he has forgotten that all the *u*s that figure there are not preceded by an *o* where pronounced by her as in French, contrary to what is usual by the Sanskritists for whom this letter is the transcription of the sound *ou*. M. Glardon informs me that the French sound *u* also does not exist in Hindustani, and that actually again the Hindu race does not use the letter *f* and cannot pronounce this letter; however, the Muslims introduced words containing *f* into Indian dialects, which the Hindus write *p* these with a ph, and pronounce the *p* by breathing in.

P. 207

NOTE: S. Freud, "Über Abwehr-neuro-Psychosen," *Neurologisches Central-blatt*, 1894, p. 362 and 402. Breuer and Freud, *Studien über Hysterie*, op. cit., passim. etc.

P. 208

NOTE: It seems to me that mediums would be particularly susceptible to this issue, which creates dangerous emotional conflict for the Ego of the subject, thanks to the habits of mental splitting, of psychic cleavage so to speak, that the seances and other spiritual exercises develop in them. The practice of spiritualism thus would constitute, on certain occasions, a safety valve, a channel for derivation, or a kind of insurance policy against the risk of possible difficulties—an advantage of the same order as the privilege of certain left handed people who escape aphasia in cases of right hemiplegia!

P. 208

NOTE: Mlle. Smith had several dreams concerning M. F. which she candidly related either to M. Lemaitre or to me, and which, under various symbolic images, betray a subliminal preoccupation analogous to that where thoughts flash across the brain of Elisabeth von R. like a flash of lightning (Breuer and Freud, loc. cit., p. 136). It is certainly an enormous advantage for Mlle. Smith, attributable to her mediumistic faculties and habits, that the *Abwehr* [defense] took the form of an somnambulistic romance, which avoided for her normal personality and her everyday life all the inconveniences of the *Conversion psychischer Erregung in's Körperliche*, to employ the terms of Freud.

P. 209

NOTE: See for example W. Brugelmann, "Suggestive Erfahrungen," *Zeitschrift für Hypnotismus* 5 (1897): 256.

P. 210

NOTE: Mlle. Smith avers, actually, that she never thought herself to be the reincarnation of Feliciani, but having no firm reasons to reject this hypothesis of Mme. B she maintained a doubtful silence on this point, which her entourage wrongly interpreted as an acquiescence.

P. 223

NOTE: To avoid wasting time and disappointment the reader should be warned that if he is looking for firm and final conclusions on the subject of the paranormal, he should go no further; for I have none to offer him, and at the end of this chapter he will find himself as ignorant as before, on telepathy, spiritism and other connected issues that contemporary curiosity is infatuated with.

P. 223

NOTE: F.C.S. Schiller (in his critique of *Studies in Psychical Research* by F. Podmore), *Mind N.S.* 8 (1899): 101.

P. 223

NOTE: See among others the word "supernormal," F.W.H. Myers, "Glossary of Terms used in Psychical Research," *PSPR* 8 (1982): 174.

P. 224

NOTE: See among others the charming page of Galileo in his letter to Kepler, August 19, 1610: *Opere di Galileo*, ed. de Florence, 1842–1856, 6: 118.

P. 225

NOTE: La Bruyère, "De Quelques usages" in *Les Caractères ou les moeurs de ce siècle*.

P. 225

NOTE: Laplace, *Essai philosophique sur les probabilites*, 2d ed. (Paris, 1814), p. 110.

P. 226

NOTE: "There are more things in heaven and earth, Horatio, than are idreamt of in your philosophy." (*Hamlet*, I, v).

P. 226

NOTE: It goes without saying that this principal does not claim an *objective* truth and does not signify that all things would in reality be possible in themselves. It simply expresses a *subjective* disposition, the mental attitude that is found only among weak beings, lost in a contingent universe from which the last resorts escape them, and too ignorant to deny a priori the possibility of that which could be.

P. 227

If you gave the same account of a supernormal phenomena to several illustrious savants, trained in experimental methods, you would see the differences between their reactions! They would be unanimous, assuredly, in criticizing the insufficiency of the evidence; but that aside, some would listen with an obliging ear to your stories, while the others would declare that you were mocking them, and would hardly wish to hear anything, with all the nuances in between. Even the most practical men are not pure machines of calculation and reasoning, functioning by following the rigid laws of mathematical logic; they, only a little less than the vulgar (and then not always), are a bundle of affections and preferences, not to speak of prejudices. Behind their official laboratories they cultivate in secret a small private garden, packed with a pile of droll metaphysical vegetation; they nourish *in petto* opinions on things, the world, life, in short a *Weltanschauung* that science, by its essence, cannot justify. And then, that which agrees with the inherited or acquired ideas behind their heads, that which fits in well with their flower beds, they facilely acquire and see only as very plausible, although still not demonstrated; whereas all that does not find a place already prepared there, they beat cold and oppose, embellished with an absolute conclusion of nonreception with grand airs of offended good sense. It is the same where there isn't any metaphysical problem at play. Even where it is only a question of indifferent philosophical matters, the extraordinary and still not classed phenomena nearly always provoke curious differences of mental attitudes with the savants, denoting that they are hardly of the same sentiment concerning the strangeness of facts and the value of favorable or unfavorable presumptions; nothing is more varied in intensity and in direction than the completely subjective current of vague impressions, of instinctive flair, of unreasoned intuition, which tends to carry and incline some to reject, and others to admit the supposed facts, so far as the debate hasn't been objectively settled by preemptory proofs.

Laplace truly believed to find in the employment of probabilities a means of introducing a little objectivity and scientific precision in these obscure and controversial regions: "It is here," he writes after the passage I have quoted, "that the calculation of probabilities becomes indispensable for determining up to what point one must multiply observations and experiences in order to obtain in favor of the agents (both normal and supernormal), where they indicate a superior probability to the reasons which one could have otherwise not admitted."

I do not know very well if, even when handled by a Laplace, the calculation of probability could tell us exactly how much is necessary from the Piper ladies and from the doctors Hodgson, or from the Eusapias and from the Professors Richet, to break open with the weight of proofs the doors of official science, which are barricaded against the difficulty of accepting telepathy or the movement of objects without contact; or to obtain at the least, in favor of the reality of these phenomena, "a probability superior to the reasons which one could have to not admit them." Without calculation, I imagine that if there had actually been in civilized countries fifty cases similar to those two there (Mrs. Piper and Eusapia), and studied with as much seriousness, savants would already be completely blasé about such common phenomena and no one would dream of seeing there anything that would be strange or of the supernormal, no more than in the cures performed at the tomb of deacon Pâris, or the lachrymal wound of the young Perier cured by the touch of Saint-Epine, and so many other miracles from the past attributed to autosuggestion or hypnosis. Perhaps only thirty such cases as these two would already amply suffice to convince everyone; perhaps twenty, or only ten. But, here, as for the just men of Sodom, ten cases have not been found; there are only two, one of each type; and while there are some observers who agree that the evidence furnished by these two cases is sufficient to balance the strangeness of the facts, the majority of savants find that this is insufficient.

It is not that I wish to speak ill of the calculation of probability, whose service to all kinds of investigations cannot be overestimated; but it should not be thought that it can put people in agreement on the chances of truth or error in supernormal hypotheses. There are already fecund applications of this calculation in this domain, notably in the famous Census of Hallucinations, where results have shown, figures in hand, that the relative frequency of cases of veridical apparitions of the dead to the distant living speaks strongly in favor of causal connection rather than a supernormal explanation.[1] And yet, one knows how many disputes have arisen over this result, and how little the savants are unanimous—in the presence of a statistic that was nevertheless conducted with as "scrupulous" attention as Laplace would have wished in such a matter—in deciding if the weight of the possible could finally be regarded as surpassing the strangeness of the facts. If then, on a terrain that lends itself better than others to the introduction of the calculation of the odds, it is very difficult to conclude that the supernormal is at play, there is all the more reason not to expect conclusive decisions, regardless of their meaning, in the majority of infinitely less favorable cases, where one is reduced to vacillating and always contestable estimations of "good sense" to console oneself on the inapplicability of calculation.[2]

[1] Professor Sidgwick's Committee, "Report on the Census of Hallucinations," *PSPR* 10 (1894).

[2] "The theory of probabilities is only at bottom good sense reduced into calculations," Laplace said (loc. cit., p. 190). Doubtless. Except in unfortunate cases of living concrete reality, where this reduction is impracticable and where good sense itself condemns it! What is the use in giving an illusion of mathematical precision by assigning arbitrary numerical values to things that have nothing to do with them? Certainly one can by way of an exercise or game estimate at 9/10 the veracity of a witness who inspires confidence, and at 7/10 that of another who inspires less; but who would be more convinced by the Bertillonesque result

of calculations established on such bases, rather than by the purely qualitative reasoning of good sense (which is after all something completely different from common sense)?

P. 229

NOTE: See the interesting essay on the classification of "parapsychic" facts by M. E. Boirac, *Annales des sciences psychiques* 3 (1893): 341.

P. 229

It is hardly necessary to add that all the curious facts already seen in this volume—Léopold's communications, the use of unknown languages, the personifications of Simandini or Marie-Antoinette, revelations of past lives,[1] etc.—were equally considered as mysterious and supernormal by Hélène and her entourage; but I think I have now shown enough of my way of thinking things false, or having reason both for and against, and my good or bad manner of interpreting them, to have no more need to return to them.

[1]The doctrine of *past lives* or previous incarnations seems to be a special legacy of Allan Kardec to the spiritism of the old continent and contradicts the spiritism of the New World, which greatly diminishes the dogmatic value of this doctrine and saves me the trouble of discussing it here. Its role in the mediumship of Mlle. Smith shows well the suggestive influence of her milieu.

P. 230

Among the witnesses of these events who I have been able to find, I have met with all manner of opinions, ranging from complete conviction of their authenticity to the most absolute skepticism, and including a prudent eclecticism which allows that some of these apports were genuine, but that others could have been produced from the pocket of this or that member of this large enough and mixed group. Mlle. Smith herself, and Léopold whom I have often questioned on this subject, seemed to have no final ideas, and I could do no better than to imitate them.

P. 231

NOTE: M. Thury, *Les Tables tournantes considérées au point de vue de la question de physique générale qui s'y rattache*, etc. (Geneva, 1855).

P. 231

NOTE: A. Lehmann (*Aberglaube und Zauberei*, pp. 270–273) has insisted on the glaring contradictions (or at the very least differences) between Crookes's two accounts, which cast a certain suspicion on the value of these experiences; but, on the other hand, the unfavorable light that Lehmann's remarks indirectly reflect upon Home accord badly with what seems to have been the latter's true character. This leads me to add a word on the famous case of Katie King. Even though I have not spoken of this in relation to Mlle. Smith, who never showed the least signs of "materialization," I wish to say, so as not to be completely misunderstood, that I am extremely skeptical on this point. I find the proofs published by Crookes weaker in this case than in that of Home, such that the fact to be proved is in my opinion colossally more difficult to admit; furthermore, that which one knows of the comparative characters of Home and Mlle. Cook seems to me to give advantage to the former, and does not contribute to augmenting my confidence in Crookes's experiences with the second.

P. 231

NOTE: See F. Podmore, *Studies in Psychical Research* (London, 1897), chap. 5, "Poltergeists," *PSPR* 7: 45; and the dialogue between Lang (*The Making of Religion* [London, 1898], app. B), Podmore (*PSPR* 14 [1898]: 133–136), Wallace (*JSPR*, February 1899), etc.; this dialogue continues in the *JSPR*, and throws instructive light not only on the question itself, but moreover upon the differences in psychological reactions among those who take part over against supernormal accounts.

P. 232

NOTE: Galileo, *Sydereus Nuncius, Oeuvres*, ed. de Florence, 3: 59, 76, etc.

P. 232

Only here, as previously, the principles of Hamlet and Laplace subsist: I make no denial of the possibility that the events in which I took part were at bottom nothing more than illusion or trickery, but then I would need, to keep this hypothesis in the air, several proofs proportionate to the strangeness of a trickery or of an illusion that escapes when one tries to fix it, and whose nature no one has managed to indicate. Because it does not suffice to vaguely invoke general causes— cunning swindlers, errors of the senses or memory, the autosuggestion of assistants, etc.—as all this vanishes as soon as one tries to make them precise, or fails in front of the given circumstances.[1] Although I cannot see a single explanation that adequately and specifically covers such phenomena as I have described, although on the contrary all the explanations that would be valuable on other occasions are here excluded due to the concrete conditions under which the observations took place, the strangeness of the phenomena being for me at least more than compensated by its empirical certitude, I remain, until proof to the contrary, convinced of its supernormal authenticity. To speak or think differently would be, from the actual position of my experience in this domain, to lose the privilege of counting myself among La Bruyère's "strong spirits," just as, on the contrary, I do not hesitate to place into the category of "credulous souls" the reader who will believe in the movement of objects without contact solely on the basis of what I have told him!

[1]The subterfuges that Eusapia unconsciously employs when one lets her do so (letting go of a hand, etc.), which have been unmasked a long time ago, had no place in the seances that I attended. The presence at two of them of M. Myers, then under the impression of the disastrous Cambridge experiences (1895), and the strong desire of Eusapia to finally convince him, made these seances particulary remarkable.

P. 235

NOTE: Compare, for example, the experiences of "unconscious fraud," in the waking state and in the trance state, observed with Eusapia Palladino: Ochorowicz, "La question de la fraude, etc," *Annales des sciences psychiques* 6 (1896): 99 *et seq.*

P. 236

At bottom, if one finds this quality within oneself, it is because one has already begun by treating it benevolently, by making of this imponderable link between organisms a purely spiritual communication, from soul to soul, independent of matter and space. I would very much like for such a metaphysical union to exist in itself, but this is to gratuitously commit oneself to a confusion of genres and fall into the sophism of the ignorance of the question and replaces this problem with high speculation, which abandons the properly scientific terrain, and refutes the principal of psychophysical parallelism. As for the empirical problem of telepathy, it can accommodate parallelism very well, and does not contradict the established sciences.

P. 236

NOTE: "One hundred bad proofs don't make a good one" is a frequent objection to claims of telepathy. But the very vagueness of this sonorous aphorism seems to undermine it. What is a bad proof, and what is a good one? In the sciences of empirical facts (and leaving aside the question of mathematics) we rarely— perhaps even never—deal with an absolutely good or bad proof, and, consequently, one of infinite weight or of none. All our proof is relative, of finite and variable weight, and each case must be studied individually, in itself and in its relationship to others. The same for refutations or proofs to the contrary. We do not leave probabilities. And a new truth of superior probability, of quasicertitude, can easily issue from the joining together of several isolated mediocre proofs—just as in other cases a reciprocal weakness, a contradiction, ruins them; this depends on their nature and relations, and one cannot say anything general here. It seems to me that the concrete and detailed examination of the evidence for and against telepathy actually produces a strong *for* it.

P. 239

I could not ask for more, and here I have far less objection in principal than I have to the powers of the crystal ball and all the other trappings of crystalloscopy that "externalize" telepathic or other impressions, which remain latent and unknown without them, and which have been brought to light by a group of observers.[1]

[1] See among others: Miss X, "On the Faculty of Crystal Gazing," *Essays in Psychical Research*, p. 103; "Recent Experiments in Crystal-vision," *PSPR* 5 (1889): 486; F. Myers, *PSPR* 7 (1891): 318–319; A. Lang, "Crystal-Visions Savage and Civilised," *Making of Religion*, p. 90. In a completely different line of thought, P. Janet, "Sur la divination par les miroirs," *Névroses et idées fixes*, 1: 407; with Lang's reponse, loc. cit., p. 367.

P. 240

Mlle. Smith had, it seems, many other telepathic intuitions concerning M. Balmès activities. He himself left the office after a few months, and finished by finding that this sort of occult surveillance exercised on his private life by a third person was uncomfortable and intrusive, and moreover that it exhausted him, and that he would be glad to be through with these mysterious encounters in a strange existence that interested him very little. This group of phenomena, combined with diverse analogous visions relating to other people of her acquaintance, seems to me to constitute a bias in favor of genuine telepathic influences undergone by Hélène, but I have never succeeded in finding an absolutely conclusive instance. Example 2 here below, which is the best to my mind, is hardly any more irreproachable. But one knows how rare it is in this domain, above all when one doesn't oneself play the role of the percipient or agent and when one is entirely reduced to the testimony of others, to find cases which satisfy all the demands of a demonstration.

P. 241

It is unfortunate, and I would be within my rights to draw the most skeptical conclusions. However I shall not do so, and I prefer to fall back on a less severe interpretation by recalling the great role of elective affinity and of the *rapport* in the psychological processes that unfold in the presence of our fellow men.

P. 241

But this is understandable enough, and it is to be believed that this antinomy between the state of the soul indispensable to the production of these phenomena and that which is for their verification will not be the thorn in the heel destined to hold back the progress of psychic researches.

P. 245

NOTE: "Hypermnesic Dreams," *PSPR* 8 (1892): 381–92. See also "Miss X," *Essays in Psychical Research*, p. 112 *et seq*.

P. 245

The latter, with his lantern and typtological indications, is in a sense the equivalent of the Assyrian who showed M. Hilprecht in a dream how he would discover the meaning of an inscription sought in vain the night before.[1] Here one finds again the evident identity of the processes of the mediumistic imagination and those of the dream. Perhaps there was no shortage of people who believed in the Assyrian just as with Léopold. Everything is possible. But it is truly regrettable that, if these beings who populate our oneiric or hypnoid states are something other than the purely subjective creations of our imagination, they would not be more far-seeing of means to convince us of their reality. Why has Léopold, for example, who has always given the case of the lost broach—found thanks to him— as the proof of his objectivity, never deigned to tell me the written word or the hidden object outside of his medium's field of vision that I pointed to during the countless seances when he claimed to be floating in the atmosphere, invisible yet seeing everything, separated from Mlle. Smith, while communicating through her?

[1] W. R. Newbold, "Cases of Dream Reasoning," *Psychological Review* 3 (1896): 132; and *PSPR* 12 (1896): 14–20.

P. 246

There are typtological mediums (I know some) whose unconscious and perfectly sincere art consists in drawing out via the pedestal table the subliminal secrets from people who come to consult them. It is the inquirer himself who dictates the responses and regulates the knocks on the table: when alone, he would not make it knock, but his imperceptible and involuntary variations of pressure are felt by the hands of the medium, who translates them into joltings of the furniture and thus plays without doubt the role of an amplifying apparatus.

P. 247

One could still imagine that, despite dictionaries and other existing documents, and without the intermediary of assistants, these historical facts had arrived in Hélène's brain by supernormal means. But I have already spoken (with regard to the completely similar case of the citation from Marlès, pp. 188–190) what I think of such a supposition from the methodological point of view, and I will not return to it here.

P. 248

NOTE: My mother and my aunt were the Claparède girls (sisters of the naturalist E. Claparède, who died in 1871). Their double wedding was on September 17, 1853. M. Dandiran, who had been a widower for several years, remarried and became a professor at Lausanne University where he is today venerated as the grand old man. We always maintained affectionate relations, and it's thanks to him, as one will soon see, that I have been able to clarify with certitude the origins of Mlle. Smith's retrocognitions.

P. 248

For why should such a faculty confine itself exclusively to the relation of facts that could be perfectly explained by a forgotten oral transmission, instead of also concerning itself with more intimate and personal facts, which are refractory to this mode of propagation, as is the case with other mediums.[1]

[1] It is known, for example that a good proportion of Mrs. Piper's revelations to her visitors concerned details that could have been known only to them personally and would not have been the subject of conversations with a third person. The difference between messages that have connotations of exterior information or rumor and those whose nature make this origin difficult to accept cannot be overemphasized and speaks, at least at first sight, in favor of telepathy or other unknown causes. See among others F. Podmore, "Discussion of the Trance-Phenomena of Mrs. Piper," *PSPR* 14 (1898): 50.

P. 248

In effect, if these memories of a past life that interest me derive either from a supernormal (a telepathic transmission of my own memories, conscious or latent, to Hélène; messages from discarnate souls, etc.), or a normal present cause (information gleaned by Hélène to reinforce her seances, etc.), I don't see why she should concentrate on such a limited region instead of one with a much more vast expanse; for without actually returning to the above-mentioned epoch, there are no less than six distinct areas from which telepathy, discarnates, or local gossipers could have supplied abundant material for Hélène's mediumship for the retrocognitions destined for me: my personal past, that of my wife (who was present at most of Mlle. Smith's seances), and those of our four paternal and maternal families. Yet, I repeat, all of the supposed revelations made by Hélène concerned solely my mother's family, and for a very limited time. This seems to me to clearly indicate firstly (and this is superfluous for me in the given case) the complete good faith of the medium, who would have had no trouble in finding in the six areas of which I spoke thousands of facts of the same order as those contained in the above vision to offer to me during seances; then the exclusive choice of this very limited group of old events, all known in their time by an extensive public, must have had for its very natural and normal cause several stories of traditions from the epoch which, once they reached the ears of Hélène, then left her conscious memory little by little.

P. 249

"You questioned me about the name (Smith). Is it because of these preoccupations that you visit me? The fact is I suddenly distinctly remembered that my mother and my aunt,[1] the latter in particular, were very much interested in a young woman of this name, whom they had already known and employed as a couturier or milliner before her marriage to a Hungarian. I can still picture the latter (his features were very distinctive), when he waited on his wife in conversation with my mother and my aunt. I believe, without being able to affirm it with certitude, that these ladies, for the young girl's interest, introduced her to the Claparèdes. But it is definitely in the courtyard of the Pension de P. that I place in my memories the figure of M. (Smith)."

[1] Mlle. Vignier, who will again be of concern later, was the mother of M. Dandiran.

P. 250

All sincere and lived convictions are absolutely respectable, even if one does not share them; I also wish in advance (and retrospectively) to make honorable amends to all my spiritist friends and acquaintances for the deflections of the pen that they could (or that they already have) made me make in the course of this volume, torn as I am, I repeat, between the respect I have for the personalities and the rather comic impression of the doctrine, with all its procession of consequences and supporting proofs.

P. 250

For if then, letting oneself be carried away from the terrain of rigorous observation onto that of moral and religious philosophy, one would have bad taste not to recognize the immense superiority of this doctrine above all others, they close your mouth in affirming, in contradistinction to its rivals, which are only errors or unverifiable hypotheses, theirs has the incomparable advantage of being scientifically established. And the circle starts again, to such good purpose that one is discouraged from discussing a system that in its scientific and religious liveries is always prompt, unlike Master Jacques, to endorse precisely that which one has only done for the time being.

P. 251
NOTE: The Gospel according to St. Luke 20:38.

P. 253
Some are in the habit of returning to the pedestal table each night before going to bed, to have a little chat with their dear departed; why, in heaven's name, should we rob them of this innocent pleasure by telling them that their dialogue is really a monologue, and that they are talking to themselves and their latent memories? They receive at all moments, by automatic writing, on the trifling experiences of everyday life, the confidences or opinions of everybody's deceased, and it would be a hard and useless disillusionment to show them that all this is a pure conduit for their own observations and subconscious inductions. Some, in all embarrassing circumstances, consult a dead parent who immediately indicates the line of conduct; what good would it be to destroy their confidence in this precious invisible pythoness, and leave them to their personal reflection, where they might find equally useful or often better advice, but whose authority would seem less to them, so that they certainly lose due to the change in the profit, the promptness, and the firmness of their decisions? And so on. For millions of people under a hundred diverse titles: religious belief, moral consolation, solemn and mysterious ritual, an old habit, a chosen distraction, etc., spiritism is today the pivot and sustenance of existence; wouldn't it do more harm than good to disturb this, and wouldn't it be better to leave things to take their course? Why stop a man from feeding himself with dreams if that is his pleasure? All the more so since definitively—who knows?!

P. 254
while we others, *incarnate* spirits, carry in addition a heavy casing of ponderable atoms, through which we (particularly the mediums) occasionally sense certain influences from these intangible neighbors, who are the source of diverse vibrations, of which our organisms let some pass and absorb the others, like all types of waves.

P. 255
Let it please the Spirits to soon give their irreproachable demonstration—in showing us the means of eliminating the combined action of the *subliminal imagination*—the malice of which one knows well, and of *telepathy*, of which we certainly don't know the limits! But for the time being one must not forget that the proceedings are still pending.

P. 255
They present themselves mired in a formidable mixture of confusion, errors, apparent illusions of all sorts, that truly—short of having the time and the patience of Dr. Hodgson, and a medium as remarkable as Mrs. Piper (which would be extraordinary)—it is foolish pretention to wish, in a given case, to declare that it truly results from the discarnates, and to discern with certitude from the milieu that which on the contrary ought to be attributed to the latent memories of the

medium, to her subconscious imagination, to involuntary suggestions and the corruptibility of assistants, to the telepathic influence of more or less distant living individuals, etc. When people understand that this whole range of factors are usually all beyond our control, they are perhaps disgusted by experiences where they have a ninety-nine to one chance of being duped either by themselves or others and where, even more vexing, if they have the luck of falling on the one in a hundred chance, they have no certain means of knowing it!

One rarely sees people searching for gold in the sands of the Arve, where there is perhaps some, because the game is not worth the candle and no one wants to sift through so much mud for a problematic grain of gold; and yet we have touchstones and reactions that permit us to instantly distinguish the precious metal from that which isn't it! Similarly, unless the spirits do not deign to bestow us with a suitable reagent, a magic touchstone to distinguish their real presence from all the admirable counterfeits that the subliminal faculties unceasingly present to the mediums and their entourage, it seems to me probable that spiritist practices would more and more lose their charms in the measure that science better brings to light the rarity of pure, authentic messages, and the quasi-impossibility of actually recognizing them. It is true that to children gilt and paste will always make the same effect as real jewels.

P. 259

3. Case of Mme. Flournoy

My mother (who died in 1875) was twice incarnated in Mlle. Smith. I will be content to disclose and discuss two episodes mentioned in M. Lemaître's article (loc. cit., p. 78) from among these somnambulist scenes, and I will show that they provide no positive proof of the alleged presence of my mother.

1. My mother was very rheumatic and unable to fully extend her ring finger nor her little finger. These fingers were always more or less bent; I was briefly struck by seeing Hélène's hands in this attitude, and I pointed it out to those present. I thus explained it to myself as some sort of involuntary mental suggestion on my part; this explanation is no longer necessary since I discovered that Hélène knew my grandparents. For how can it be proven that Hélène had never heard about this trait of my mother's hands, or that she did not perhaps witness it in her childhood? This would be sufficient to understand how she had naturally and automatically reproduced such a gesture while personifying my mother.

2. The second fact cited by M. Lemaître: according to Léopold, Hélène as the incarnation of my mother insisted upon entering a room adjoining my library, where she stopped in front of a small cupboard of dismal appearance that she eventually opened. In real terms, this can be explained as a movement of the mediums' own instinctive curiosity, rather than by the authenticity of the supposed incarnation. It is true that I was most surprised at this cupboard's appeal for Hélène, as it was the only piece of furniture in the room that my mother would have been familiar with. I was again inclined to see this as an example of a telepathic influence from my own memories. A more detailed analysis of the circumstances, however, has since shown the incident to me in a different light. In fact, there was another object in this room that would have been equally familiar to my mother, although I had not noticed it at the time. This object—a sword hanging

on the wall—used to belong to my father and formerly decorated my parents' bedroom. Between the cupboard and the sword, I am certain that the latter would have had a stronger emotive value in my mother's memory, and by consequence should have drawn her primarily to it. However, it was passed unnoticed, although it was in full view and necessarily would have been in Hélène's range of vision many times while she was standing in front of the cupboard and as she walked up and down the room. On the other hand, there is nothing remarkable about Hélène's curiosity being whetted by this closed cupboard, by its very ugliness perhaps—more so than any of the other objects or furniture.

Generally speaking, this incarnation is explained very easily from the medium's point of view, but not if one relates it to the deceased person. Had my mother really been present, surrounded by unfamiliar objects that meant nothing to her, searching in earnest for a single old cupboard, why did she not instead sift through the library? This is where the seance took place, and it is full of furniture, paintings, books, and associated objects, all of which form a mixture of old things known by and beloved to my mother, and subsequent acquisitions dated after her death. The only object that "she" saw there and touched was her portrait, easily recognizable to Mlle. Smith, who, on the other hand, knew nothing of the origins of the remaining objects.

All the same, the strong desire to go into the room adjoining the library, compared with a complete indifference to the former room, is not explicable if we are to assume the real presence of my mother. On the other hand, it is perfectly explained if we see it as an ordinary and natural impulse of the medium herself. Mlle. Smith was already familiar with my library, where she was currently holding her third seance, but this door, always kept shut, the counterpart to the front door, must have intrigued her and awoken a desire to find out where it led. This is not to say that Hélène would be so inquisitive in her waking state; on the contrary, she is extremely reserved and discreet. However, there is no need to be a learned psychologist to have observed one's inability to be received into a room more than once without thinking up ideas—with an already innate state of curiosity—about what is perhaps behind closed doors, or in the cupboards one notices. Moreover, superficial inhibitions created by education and the mores of polite society are among the first to be suppressed by hypnosis. It is also not surprising that in a state of autosuggestibility when one is imagining oneself to be the mother of the owner of the house, one is no longer held back by embarrassment from at last finding out what is in the neighboring room, and from opening a peculiar cupboard.

I would be taking superfluous lengths were I to discuss other incidents concerning the alleged incarnations of my mother, the analysis of which would lead to the same negative conclusions.

4. Diverse examples

It is always hard to judge the reappearance of a person not known, and whose identity is obvious to those related to them. M. Lemaître has cited two such cases; the incarnation of a "very lively" character, "who enjoyed cleaning up" (such a person could easily be identified by someone outside the immediate family), and that of Mme. Duboule, who came back to speak intimately with her husband (in fact she was asking his forgiveness, which surprised no one). There have even been more cases, all of which, I believe, have evinced the belief of those present.

These scenes of incarnation, which are often full of pathos, and at which times pink is tinged with grey, burlesque is mixed with tragedy, never take place without drawing from the unassuming spectators a spirited reaction; one imagines that it would touch only relatives or friends! However, such nervous effect and organic impressions—palpitations, constrictions of the throat, cold sweats along the nose and cheeks, small shivers along the spine, etc.—could well psychologically engender a certain *coefficient of reality*, giving one an immediate sense of the actual presence of the dead. This subjective conviction in no way constitutes an argument that could logically be taken seriously. It is therefore impossible for me to reach a conclusion.

For, if I declare that in each example of the phenomena I have been told of or witnessed myself, I could see nothing that transcended not hypothetical telepathy, but simply an artificial reconstitution of a supposed disembodied incarnation by the hypnoid imagination using the gifts of public knowledge and very normal inductions; if I say that, in the voice of the entranced Mlle. Smith, I have never noticed anything but alterations sufficiently explained by her own passing emotion (whereas those who knew the deceased believe it to be his or her tone of voice and intonation; deluded, in my opinion, by such a tremendously ordinary process); in a word if I made a critical work instead of abandoning myself to the immediate overall aesthetic impression, I am inevitably a frightful skeptic, a prejudiced man, a spoilsport, etc. I would also do better to keep quiet after the habitual refrain *anything is possible*, even the return of the dead through the cooperation of Mlle. Smith. However, even yet, the proofs are not weighty enough to support the enormity of such a fact.

P. 267

Just as teratology clarifies embryology, which in its turn explains teratology, both of which shed some light on anatomy, similarly one can hope that the study of mediumistic fact will one day contribute to a profitable and sound view of normal psychogenesis. This will then give us a better understanding of these curious phenomena and from it will come a better and more precise conception of the human personality.

P. 267

There remains only Mlle. Smith's final judgment on this work, which seems to both herself and me to be from neither a supernormal origin nor a supernormal authority. In effect, although it approximately expresses the opinion of her normal personality, it comes from an unknown external voice, and a different one from that of Léopold. This voice comes from the right (whereas Léopold normally talks to her on the left) and left this opinion ringing in her ears one morning before getting up. Most fortunately, she wrote it down immediately, for otherwise it would have been impossible for her to remember. Subsequently, the voice had even on several consecutive days repeated the sentence at her awakening. I set myself the task, at her request, of publishing verbatim this automatic dictation, which spares me the trouble of encapsulating Mlle. Smith's verdict on this work myself: "Searching for and grabbing anything which could be inconsistent in the spiritist cause, she alleges that I take pleasure in misrepresenting the most interesting instances of her mediumship and her most beautiful psychological phenomena, in a scholarly and requisite critique."

Before I submit to this condemnation, I ask to make a distinction between the instances, or phenomena, and their interpretation. I do not believe that I have "misrepresented" any of the former, and that on the contrary I applied myself to noting them with all the precision possible, by following the original documents, the verbal processes of the seances, notes taken down at the time, etc. As for their interpretation, not being a follower of the spiritist philosophy, I recognize the accusation as based on the fact that I had no reason to show a special, or extra-scientific, consideration for such a belief, nor did I experience any temptation to conceal its imperfections, nor to be unjust to its rivals by favoring it when I came to explain given facts. Moreover it is known that the spirits easily take what is not more than impartiality or prudent reserve for uncalled-for skepticism and injustice. They are all too willing to see something which is not straightaway *for* them as being *against* them. I am also not surprised that they regard me with an evil eye; moreover, while waiting for conclusive, irrefutable, and scientifically valuable proof of their interventions in our world, I hold to the methodological principle that I have recalled more than once, but which they do not seem to appreciate terribly: in an uncertain and obscure case, it is legitimate and reasonable to give preference (at least provisionally, until we find evidence to the contrary) to good old ordinary explanations, which have proved themselves, rather than to extraordinary and supernormal hypotheses, whose beauty assuredly charms our idle curiosity and innate taste for the marvelous, but which have the unfortunate habit of disappearing like a mirage when circumstances allow for the facts to be examined in greater detail.